The Cambridge Companion to *The Communist Manifesto*

The Cambridge Companion to The Communist Manifesto covers the historical and biographical contexts and major contemporary interpretations of this classic text for understanding Marx and Engels, and for grasping Marxist political theory. The editors and contributors offer innovative accounts of the history of the text in relation to German revolutionaries, European socialism and socialist political projects; rhetorical, dramaturgical, feminist and post-colonial readings of the text; and theoretical analyses in relation to political economy, political theory and major concepts of Marxism. The volume includes a fresh translation into English, by Terrell Carver, of the first edition (1848), and an exacting transcription of the earliest, and rare, English translation by Helen Macfarlane (1850).

Terrell Carver is a professor of political theory at the University of Bristol. He has published widely on Marx, Engels and Marxism since 1975, including texts, translations, commentaries, biographies and political theory. Most recently he published a two-volume study of Marx and Engels's German ideology manuscripts (2014), and he is also the author of *The Postmodern Marx* (1998).

James Farr is a professor of political science and directs a Chicago-based civic internship program at Northwestern University. He is the coeditor of *After Marx* (Cambridge University Press, 1984) and, most recently, *The General Will: The Evolution of a Concept* (Cambridge University Press, 2015). His studies place Marx and Engels in the context of historical debates about method and their reception in the history of political thought.

Cambridge Companions to Philosophy

The Cambridge Companion
to *The Communist Manifesto*

TERRELL CARVER
University of Bristol

JAMES FARR
Northwestern University

CAMBRIDGE
UNIVERSITY PRESS

CAMBRIDGE
UNIVERSITY PRESS

32 Avenue of the Americas, New York, NY 10013-2473, USA

Cambridge University Press is part of the University of Cambridge.

It furthers the University's mission by disseminating knowledge in the pursuit of education, learning, and research at the highest international levels of excellence.

www.cambridge.org
Information on this title: www.cambridge.org/9781107683075

© Cambridge University Press 2015

First published 2015

Printed in the United States of America

A catalog record for this publication is available from the British Library.

ISBN 978-1-107-03700-7 Hardback
ISBN 978-1-107-68307-5 Paperback

Contents

Figures

Notes on the Editors and Contributors

Elisabeth Anker is Associate Professor of American Studies and Political Science at George Washington University. She works at the intersection of modern political theory and contemporary cultural critique. She is the author of *Orgies of Feeling: Melodrama and the Politics of Freedom* (2014) as well as numerous articles in journals such as *Political Theory, Social Research, Contemporary Political Theory, Theory & Event* and *Politics & Gender*.

Terence Ball is Professor of Political Science and Philosophy at Arizona State University, to which he moved in 1998 after a long career at the University of Minnesota. He has held visiting appointments at the universities of Cambridge and Oxford and the University of California, San Diego. He is the coeditor (with Richard Bellamy) of *The Cambridge History of Twentieth-Century Political Thought*, and for the Cambridge Texts in the History of Political Thought series he has edited *James Mill: Political Writings* (1992), *The Federalist* (2003), *Abraham Lincoln: Political Writings and Speeches* (2013) and (with Joyce Appleby) *Thomas Jefferson: Political Writings* (1999).

Terrell Carver is Professor of Political Theory at the University of Bristol, UK. He has published extensively on Marx, Engels and Marxism, including texts, translations, biographies and commentaries, for more than forty years. His most recent publications include a two-volume definitive study (with Daniel Blank) of the "German ideology" manuscripts and its "Feuerbach chapter" by Marx and Engels entitled *A Political History of the Editions of Marx and Engels's "German ideology Manuscripts"* and *Marx and Engels's "German ideology" Manuscripts: Presentation and Analysis of the "Feuerbach chapter"* (2014).

James Farr is Professor of Political Science and Director of the Chicago Field Studies at Northwestern University. He coedited (with Terence Ball) *After Marx* (Cambridge University Press, 1984) and has contributed essays to the *Cambridge Companion to Marx* (Cambridge University Press, 1991), *Engels*

After Marx (1999) and to scholarly journals on Marx, method and political theory.

Jürgen Herres is a historian working for the Berlin-Brandenburg Academy of Sciences (BBAW). In 2012 he published a history of Cologne in the nineteenth century, *Das preußische Köln 1815–1870/71*, and in 2009 he wrote an edition of the writings of Marx and Engels in the era of the first international (*Karl Marx / Friedrich Engels, Gesamtausgabe* (MEGA), Abt. 1, Bd. 21: *Werke, Artikel, Entwürfe. September 1867 bis März 1871*). In 2015 he will publish (with François Melis) an edition of the writings of Marx and Engels from February to October 1848 (MEGA, Abt. 1, Bd. 7).

David Leopold is Associate Professor of Political Theory at the University of Oxford, and John Milton Fellow of Mansfield College. He is interested in Karl Marx and Friedrich Engels, "utopian socialism" and the relationship of the former to the latter. His publications include a study of Marx's political philosophy *The Young Karl Marx. German Philosophy, Modern Politics, and Human Flourishing* (Cambridge University Press, 2007), and an edition of the utopian novel by William Morris, *News From Nowhere* (2003).

James Martin is Professor of Politics at Goldsmiths, University of London. His work explores Continental political theory and theorists, and interpretive approaches to political discourse and rhetoric. He has published monographs and edited collections on various figures, such as Gramsci and Poulantzas. His most recent volume is *Politics and Rhetoric: A Critical Introduction* (2014).

Leo Panitch is the Canada Research Chair in Comparative Political Economy and Distinguished Research Professor of Political Science at York University, Toronto. For the past three decades he has been the coeditor of the annual *Socialist Register*. His recent book (with Sam Gindin), *The Making of Global Capitalism: The Political Economy of American Empire* (2012), was awarded the Deutscher Prize in the United Kingdom and the Davidson Prize in Canada. Among his other books are *In and Out of Crisis: The Global Financial Meltdown and Left Alternatives* (2010) and *Renewing Socialism: Transforming Democracy, Strategy and Imagination* (2008).

Emanuele Saccarelli is Associate Professor of Political Science at San Diego State University. His publications include articles on Plato, Rousseau, Gramsci, Silone, Hardt and Negri, as well as the book *Gramsci and Trotsky in the Shadow of Stalinism* (2008). His new book, *Imperialism Past and Present* (coauthored with Latha Varadarajan) is forthcoming.

Robbie Shilliam is Reader in International Relations at Queen Mary University of London. He is the author of *The Black Pacific: Anticolonial Struggles and Oceanic Connections* (2015) and *German Thought and International Relations* (2009). He is inaugurator and co-convener of the British International Studies Association's Colonial/Postcolonial/Decolonial working group, inaugurator and coeditor of the book series "Kilombo: Colonial Questions and International Relations" and a correspondent for the Transnational Decolonial Institute.

Manfred B. Steger is Professor of Political Science at the University of Hawai'i-Manoa and Professor of Global Studies at RMIT University in Melbourne, Australia. He has served as an academic consultant on globalization for the US State Department and is the author or editor of more than twenty books on globalization, global history and the history of political ideas, including *The Rise of the Global Imaginary: Political Ideologies from the French Revolution to the Global War on Terror* (2008) and *Justice Globalism: Ideology, Crises, Policy* (2013).

Jules Townshend is Emeritus Professor of Political Theory at Manchester Metropolitan University. He has written books, articles and chapters in edited collections on Marx, Marxism, post-Marxism and liberalism, including *Politics of Marxism: The Critical Debates* (1996), *C.B. Macpherson and the Problem of Liberal Democracy* (2000) and (with Simon Tormey) *Key Thinkers from Critical Theory to Post-Marxism* (2006).

Joan C. Tronto is Professor of Political Science at the University of Minnesota and has published extensively on gender and feminist political theory. She is the coeditor (with Cathy Cohen and Kathy Jones) of *Women Transforming American Politics* (1997), and the author of *Moral Boundaries: A Political Argument for an Ethics of Care* (1994) and *Caring Democracy: Markets, Equality and Justice* (2013).

Acknowledgments

We are grateful to Robert Dreesen and the editors and staff of Cambridge University Press, New York, for their patient assistance with this volume.

Chapter 12, "The Manifesto in a Late Capitalist Era: Melancholy and Melodrama," by Elisabeth Anker, draws extensively on her previously published article "Left Melodrama," *Contemporary Political Theory* (2012), 11: 130–152, reproduced by permission.

Karl Marx and Friedrich Engels, *Manifesto of the Communist Party*, ed. and trans. Terrell Carver, is reproduced verbatim from *Karl Marx: Later Political Writings* ("Cambridge Texts in the History of Political Thought"), ed. and trans. Terrell Carver (Cambridge University Press, 1998), pp. 1–30.

Abbreviations

CM   Karl Marx and Friedrich Engels, *Manifesto of the Communist Party*, in Terrell Carver (ed. and trans.), *Marx: Later Political Writings* (Cambridge: Cambridge University Press, 1996), 1–30. Page references are to Part IV of the present volume.

CW   Karl Marx and Frederick Engels, *Collected Works* in fifty volumes (London: Lawrence & Wishart, 1975–2004).

MEGA² Karl Marx and Friedrich Engels, *Gesamtausgabe*: (Berlin: Akademie Verlag, 1972–ongoing).

Editors' Introduction

Terrell Carver and James Farr

Even among the world's classics – in any field and of any genre – there are few texts that have been reprinted so many times in so many editions, and translated into so many languages (repeatedly), as the *Communist Manifesto* of 1848 by Karl Marx and Friedrich Engels. It is both revered and reviled, which has something to do with its phenomenal circulation. A text that inspires such disparate reactions is certainly intriguing. Whether the ideas are loved or hated, the *Manifesto* is a standard work both in popular political circulation and on academic reading lists. The hagiographical and debunking literatures on Marx (and his self-styled "second fiddle," Engels) are enormous, as are the rather more considered academic commentaries and – since the global financial crises of 2008 – respectable journalistic notices. Marx is back! And so is the *Manifesto*. There is an audio book, an illustrated comic and various animations on YouTube, including the incomparable "Communist Manifestoon."[1]

But while there are more readers than ever for the thirty-or-so pages that this short text usually occupies, there is surprisingly little commentary focused specifically on it, other than introductory essays, biographical run-throughs and bibliographical histories. The purpose of this collection, therefore, is to remedy this state of affairs, and to put the most famous and widely read work of the two iconic authors front-and-center throughout in a critical *Companion*.

As with many, indeed most other manifestos, this one could easily have disappeared into the archive (and in this case, the police archive) and have had little influence or readership beyond its initial publication in the revolutionary years of 1848–1849. Its main public notice in that period was in the counter-revolutionary trials and tribulations of the 1850s. While it took a concerted political effort in the mid-1860s and finally in 1872 to make this document speak to mass audiences, the overwhelming truth is that the *Manifesto* communicates astoundingly well to this day, despite its obvious roots in a German-speaking political world long gone. This is because it asserts general propositions about politics, society, humanity, technology, labor, production, economics, trade, morality, family, women, ideas, action, class, war, peace, government, nationhood and much else. Its language is colorful, even fantastic and Gothic, famously invoking specters and sorcerers. The diction is direct, hortatory, provocative, scornful and inspiring, and it has generated familiar apothegms and catchphrases in its "authorized" English rendition: "A spectre is haunting Europe" (CW 6: 481)[2]; "The history of all hitherto existing society is the history of class struggles" (CW 6: 482)[3]; "every class struggle is a political struggle" (CW 6: 483); "The executive of the modern State is but a committee for managing the common affairs of the whole bourgeoisie" (CW 6: 486)[4]; "no other nexus between man and man ... than callous 'cash payment'" (CW 6: 487); "the idiocy of rural life" (CW 6: 488); "All that is solid melts into air" (CW 6: 487)[5]; "What the bourgeoisie ... produces ... is its own grave-diggers" (CW 6: 496); "The working men have no country" (CW 6: 502); "The ruling ideas of each age have ever been the ideas of its ruling class" (CW 6: 503); "to win the battle of democracy" (CW 6: 504)[6]; "Political power ... is merely the organised power of one class for oppressing another" (CW 6: 505); "the free development of each is the condition for the free development of all" (CW 6: 506); "The proletarians have nothing to lose but their chains" (CW 6: 519); "WORKING MEN OF ALL COUNTRIES, UNITE!" (CW 6: 519).

However, bold assertions and memorable catchphrases do not in themselves explain the extraordinary power and interest of this work, appropriate as these gems are to manifestos, where the object is to arouse emotion and get people onside. As Engels said at the time, "some history would need to be narrated" (CW 38: 149) in order to back up the "principles of communism" (CW 6: 341–357) which he had been drafting. The authors were aiming to get their message across, or rather the message to which they wanted the League of Communists to adhere, and with which they as international colleagues could then agitate for more support. The large-scale political struggle at the time – which the *Manifesto* makes clear – was for representative and responsible (rather than monarchical and authoritarian) governments, and indeed it took a number of generations, and many, many lives, before this was realized – as much as it has been – in democracies of the twentieth century. We should certainly ponder the entrenched and often violent resistance of ruling elites in even constitutional regimes throughout the nineteenth and early twentieth centuries to any extension of the franchise – and granting of civil rights generally – to majorities of women and working class people, and to minorities excluded from full citizenship on racial, religious or other grounds. Unlike other manifestos, the *Communist Manifesto* by Marx and Engels contextualizes this democratizing struggle within a history of human civilization as such, conceived on a global scale.

What keeps the *Manifesto* fresh and relevant is its opening gambit: societies have long been divided between ruler and ruled, rich and poor, but then, we learn, oppressor and oppressed. This politicizing turn to what is otherwise a familiar and uninspiring litany disarms resignation, complacency and – crucially for the new model atheists Marx and Engels – any next-worldly get-outs. But rather more importantly from our perspective – and also from that of the newly industrializing societies of the 1840s – the focus on technology, power-driven production and mass consumption economies is spot on. For Marx and Engels, and for the committed and could-be communists of their intended audiences, human history has turned on the industrial revolution. Whether or not this upheaval has reached anyone in particular, it is – as the text states with horrifying imagery – on an unstoppable march across the globe.

It is quite possible to read the opening sections I and II of the *Manifesto* as a "hymn to the bourgeoisie," where "bourgeoisie" is simply a reference to the commercial, property-owning and capital-accumulating classes of society that anyone – then and now – can recognize on the street and read about in the news media. That is because there is paragraph after paragraph recounting their achievements in revolutionizing technologies and constantly improving the means of production and communication, erecting architectural wonders and conjuring "whole populations ... up from the ground" (CM 238–241). All of that is clear on the page, and one need not buy the political conclusion at all – that the "downfall" of the bourgeoisie is "unavoidable"[7] – in order to be gripped by the narrative (CM 246). Rather the reverse – the narrative is what makes the text vivid today, and intellectually interesting. While referencing the history of the last few hundred years, the picture painted by this highly visual text is far from quaintly historical – it is instantly recognizable to us since we live in a globalized world of manufactures and markets, producers and consumers, rich and poor, even if the shoppers seldom see the workers in their (often "developing world") factories and sweatshops.

Moreover, the text works hard to explain the political reactions that we have – one way or another – to the social circumstances that it outlines. It sweepingly identifies both the commonplace and the academic wisdoms of an age with the interests of the ruling classes – the bankocracy, oligarchs and their political counterparts. It dismisses claims to timeless truths of moral resignation, or to assurances that elites act in the best interests of the oppressed. It then points the finger directly at such hypocrisies, and challenges us to consider our own positioning carefully, given the "more or less hidden civil war" in society (CM 245) that it urges us to acknowledge.

This argumentative tactic is an unsettling, troubling experience for the reader of whatever social class, since it challenges the peace/war, order/disorder and even rural/urban and national/international binaries through which – so we are educated to believe – the world is made intelligible, and through which morally justified actions (or inactions) must be viewed. It is a bold step indeed to bin history as previously understood – dynasties, wars, "clashes of civilizations" – and substitute for that mesmerizing array the quotidian business of getting a living and making a society that everyone engages in. But it is even bolder to exclaim that order is really disorder – breaking out "here and there" – and that it is "class struggles" which are "political struggles," not the usual flimflam and flummery put on by rulers, whether dictators or democrats (CM 243). "Workers have no nation of their own" (CM 250) is not an empirical, descriptive statement that is either true or false, and it is certainly not meaningless: it is a wake-up call to think about things afresh, and way out of the box.

The chapters in this volume approach the text from a variety of different but complementary perspectives, drawing out diverse but overlapping insights, and enriching our appreciation of the authors' achievements in writing such a remarkable work. The contributors approach the work contextually, in terms of local politics, intellectual history, biographical chronology, rhetorical analysis, reception studies, a variety of critical political engagements and current theoretical ones. In looking at the *Manifesto* in so many different ways, and finding so many different things within it – and so much to say about it – this volume is unique.

POLITICAL AND BIOGRAPHICAL CONTEXT

Chapter 1, by Jürgen Herres, contextualizes Marx and Engels as Rhineland radicals, energized by the French revolutionary ideals of the 1790s and the July Revolution of 1830. These events were current within their own living memories, or at least those of their near-elders. In the Prussian (and Prussianizing) context in which they lived, such ideas were borderline treasonous, and certainly scandalous views to hold. The chances to express them – even in coded form – were strictly controlled. Socialist or communist ideas were the cutting edge of social criticism, but were barely known in the region. These visions were truly outrageous, since they proposed – one way or another – a wholesale remaking of society, including personal and family relationships, morals and religion and law and government, if indeed government even survived at all in their thinking. Herres presents the contextual and textual details through which these radicals – in later years the "'48ers" – operated at the time, negotiating the barriers of nation and class as they thought, wrote and (clandestinely) speechified. Marx and Engels were not unique, and they were not alone. They had their distinctive qualities, individually and as a duo. But Rhenish radicalism was a milieu, and while many of its denizens may not seem important to us now, they were important to Marx and Engels at the time, given their active political – and not simply intellectual – engagements.

David Leopold's Chapter 2 explores the intellectual context through which Marx and Engels conceived the *ad hominem* section III of the pamphlet, probably the least read and most neglected part of the work. Yet this section was uniquely chosen by Marx himself for excerpting during the closing days of the revolutionary events (Draper 1994, 26–27). The thinkers subjected to critical scrutiny there were all being read and were considered inspiring – to various degrees – at the time, for example, Saint-Simon, Fourier, Owen and Proudhon. Leopold explains in detail what works and ideas were under consideration by Marx and Engels, and thus clears up obscurities that trouble readers today. He outlines the chronological and textual distinctions through which Marx and Engels understood contemporary socialisms and communisms, and dispels the myth that the two were wholly dismissive of utopians. Indeed, Leopold explains why the two acknowledged the distinct achievements of the utopian genre, and records that they offered similarly generous views of other ideas and visions. Marx and Engels emerge as knowledgeable rather than merely hostile critics. Of course, any critique by the two is not merely one of ideas but rather of politics, and of strategies for (or displacements of) the kind of world-changing activity that they aspired to. Section IV of the *Manifesto*, brief as it is, thus follows on from section III, so that communists – having confronted class struggle *and* thinkers who have missed the point – can move on to local engagements.

The rhetoric of the *Manifesto* is often referred to in passing, but has never before been analyzed in detail. James Martin's Chapter 3 explores the argumentative strategies deployed in the text, and shows how they work together to generate action, rather than mere assent. Rhetoric is thus presented as an art of persuasion, rather than crafted – and crafty – deception, as it is often taken to be today. Martin contextualizes Marx and Engels within the still-lively traditions of classical rhetoric of their educations, and deploys the classical canons to show us exactly why their text has the power to persuade. This reading of the text thus departs from usual strategies of rationalist reductionism such that emotion and values count for nothing. Martin shows instead how *ethos* and *logos*, character and reason, norms and facts, are marshalled throughout to make a political case, even noting the rhythmic character of the paragraphing and the dramatic form of the narrative. In this way the images and imagery of the text come to life. Many readers have skipped over such "ornaments" and exaggerations, and instead parsed the text into testable propositions. These propositions might be interesting enough in some contexts, but are in fact violent excisions from a powerful experience. Through Martin's analysis the *Manifesto* comes into its own as not just another polemic, but a work of insurgency.

Terrell Carver's Chapter 4 considers the *Manifesto* in Marx's and Engels's lifetimes, looking critically at how and whether it was important to them, and, crucially, to others, especially those in the self-styled "Marx party" within the German socialist movement of the mid- to late 1860s. Marx, as ever, was looking for publicity and influence, and Wilhelm Liebknecht and others were looking for a "founding father." Politics in Germany was turning to mass activity and partisan elections, and a readable and rousing pamphlet, together with an aged and geographically removed icon, proved a good project. The re-publication and circulation of 1872, eventually incorporating the signed, if somewhat ambivalent prefatory thoughts of the authors, made Marx into Marx and the *Manifesto* one of "Marxism." This was key to the biographical reception of Marx, and to the bibliographical reception of his works, which developed over the next twenty years or so. Carver shows that even critical, rather than overtly hagiographical, accounts of the lives and works of Marx and Engels take the importance of the *Manifesto* throughout their careers too much for granted, given that its premier position – reflected in its often out-of-chronology positioning in many twentieth-century editions of selected works – has made it the "intro" to Marx. In conclusion Carver conducts a thought-experiment, asking what the *Manifesto* would mean today if the reception of its authors had developed counterfactually without Marx becoming iconic and his "thought" becoming an "ism."

POLITICAL RECEPTION

While Engels set up the reception of Marx's "thought" as an eponymous "ism," he fought shy of the term "Marxism," and, after all, in an authoritative sense, he simply *was* "Marxism." After his death, the situation was different. Chapter 5 by Jules Townshend takes us into an era of "footnotes" to Marx, some literal (and by Engels), and others much more metaphorical. These amendments and addenda, though, were united in claiming a posthumous *imprimatur.* Townshend tracks the relationship between the *Manifesto* and Marxist ideology as it developed, a process through which the "general principles," said by the authors in 1872 to reside in the text, were filled in, interpreted and re-interpreted, and then adapted as political "unknown unknowns" came over the horizon. The *Manifesto* was understood to present a dialectical analysis of historical contradictions through which a class politics of revolutionary change has taken – and is currently taking – place. He concludes that the *Manifesto* – as a political document infused with theoretical rigor – was written to avoid elitism and authoritarianism through a combination of radicalism and realism, given the condition-dependency frame through which human activity is presented. On this view, the dialectical pulse that Townshend finds in the *Manifesto* may beat weakly at present – even in an era of global capitalist crisis – but that merely restates the need for action. And action, after all, was the performative project of the text.

Chapter 6, by Emanuele Saccarelli, takes us directly to the world of action. Reviewing the fifty years of global politics from 1848, Saccarelli argues that the *Manifesto* was right in broad outline – predicting rapid economic development and class-driven democratization – but that the substantive political agenda was proceeding only in an uneven and contradictory manner: propertied classes (the bourgeoisie of the text) were prone to compromise with authoritarian, imperialist and even absolutist regimes, and working classes (the proletariat of the text) sometimes preferred compromising reform to revolution. In Russia and Germany in the early years of the twentieth century, the *Manifesto* was a flashpoint in theory-and-practice debates over the "permanent revolution" involving Kautsky, Bernstein, Trotsky, Luxemburg and others, including scholars such as Mehring and Ryazanov. This posed the question as to whether a socialist (and eventual communist) revolution would have to proceed in stages, typically involving a bourgeois-democratic regime, or could – in some cases – transform an economically and politically underdeveloped country or region into a socialist and democratic workers' state. Rather than functioning as a point of orthodox doctrinal deduction, the *Manifesto* – as Saccarelli shows – posed a highly political and deadly practical dilemma in its very structure: how does a synoptic yet analytical view of human historical development lead readers to a program of practical proposals? Moreover, the "Communist Party" of the title was equally problematic: was it descriptive or hortatory? And was the geographical progression of revolution quite as smooth and universal as the text seemed to say?

Some of the answers to these questions emerge in Chapter 7 by Leo Panitch. The central thesis of the *Manifesto* is that of "class struggle," and indeed in modern and modernizing times as an ever-simplifying struggle between two classes only: bourgeoisie and proletariat. Panitch shows how crucial states have been and are in this complex process and "more or less hidden civil war." In his reading of the text, nation-states – of whatever class character – are in no way epiphenomenal to the politics of revolutionary transformation and counter-revolutionary resistance. In the post-Second World War decades since 1950 Panitch charts an increasing commitment within democratic/capitalist states to integrate technological innovation with capital accumulation, and to "globalize" this to their advantage at the expense of the "developing" world. Siding with Schumpeter against Piketty, Panitch cites the *Manifesto* on the truly revolutionary role of the bourgeoisie and of state power (*Staatsgewalt*) as their "device." Rather similarly he finds the *Manifesto* both revolutionary and prescient in its treatment of the proletariat, pointing out that the text argues both ways dialectically: workers are increasingly thrown together in close proximity and also able to use technologies of mass transport and communication, yet specifically organized mass socialist/communist parties – to which the text looks forward – can be crucial to the success of this process. Even Marx's own work later in the International Working Men's Association from 1864– and the international work of further generations of committed socialists – is prefigured as a structural feature of politically committed social change. The *Manifesto* argues that the bourgeoisie produces its own gravediggers, but proletarians must do the digging in solidarity.

Joan C. Tronto's Chapter 8 shows us exactly how women make cameo appearances in the *Manifesto*, but are haunting it throughout. After contextualizing and reviewing Marx's and Engels's writing on women, Tronto acknowledges the varied inspirations that a wide variety of feminists have taken from their work. She then leads us back to the text of the *Manifesto* in order to examine its imagery in relation to feminist concerns. These concerns – far from resolved in present-day societies – relate to sex, gender and sexuality in the workplace, and this in turn reveals much the same picture in the "family," namely, that of male dominance and masculine privilege. Spectral women – intimidated in factories and abused as prostitutes – lurk in the recesses of the text. Yet interestingly, some of the most rhetorically and sarcastically effective sections of the *Manifesto* are the ones where the two authors raise "women" and "family" as major concerns, and are clearly working hard to engage their readers. In the end, however, Marx and Engels are steamed up to attack bourgeois masculinity, yet rather cool on engaging with any very specific ideas of proletarian – hence *human* – transformations, particularly in the "family" context. Moreover, among the specters haunting the *Manifesto* Tronto detects a fear that proletarians need to "man up" lest they be subjected to, and even content with, feminization and passivity. Idioms of revolutionary rhetoric, familiar to Marx and Engels as well as to their intended (male) audience, reproduce gendered hierarchies in among the critical comments on the contemporary – for them and us – gender order.

INTELLECTUAL LEGACY

The *Manifesto* is a canonical work in political theory over and above its familiar introductory value in relation to Marx and Marxism. James Farr and Terence Ball, in Chapter 9, show how its reception developed through engagements involving liberal philosophers and philosophically minded liberals. They consider the contributions of Bertrand Russell, John Dewey, Sidney Hook, Isaiah Berlin, Karl Popper and John Rawls. Employing a version of ideology-critique, these writers responded to the assertions and arguments in the text relating to the issues they regarded as classic ones: individual freedom, governmental legitimacy, the nature and scope of human rights, the status of moral truths, the circumstances through which justice might be realized, the proper justification for political violence, the very nature of – and reason for – human society and in particular, of course, what would constitute a good one. Political theorists do their theorizing well aware of current political contexts and personal political commitments, and Farr and Ball contextualize their key philosophers within contemporary events and engagements, thus revealing many varieties of liberalism and variations in political orientation. The *Manifesto* has thus gained a second life in the twentieth century as a textbook item, ideal for seminar discussion and debate. The work was emphatically not written for intellectuals in particular, or for university students in general, but well-educated intellectuals around the world – liberal philosophers first and foremost – are all presumed to have read it.

In Chapter 10, Manfred B. Steger develops a genealogy of globalization as a social science term and as a political discourse, mapping our factual relations to – and ongoing concerns with – the rapidly industrializing world so remarkably delineated by Marx and Engels. Steger thus provides a frame through which to view the more recent manifestos issued by two scholars of the left – Jacques Derrida and David Harvey – both of whom draw considerable inspiration from the concepts and analysis rhetorically expressed by Marx and Engels in 1848. These contemporary efforts have fought back against neo-liberals – ideologues of "market globalism" – who have declared the death of Marxism and irrelevance of Marx. Derrida and Harvey work from the *Manifesto* to construct a discourse of globalization that challenges current economic orthodoxies decisively, and impacts productively in a publicly political way. Steger credits Derrida with having launched a revitalized *Manifesto* into the worldwide debate on the nature and future of capitalism, and having used it to prefigure a New International arising from anti-globalization movements and protests. Harvey credits Marx and Engels's *Manifesto* with an innovatory grasp of spatial thinking in relation to economic activity, and thus to global history. Steger concludes that the *Manifesto* was stalking neo-liberalism and neo-liberals and that now – as then – it openly proclaims that there is an alternative and a new world to be made.

While the *Manifesto* has lately been criticized for its Eurocentricity – as indeed how many "standard" works have not? – Robbie Shilliam's Chapter 11 takes a more productive and interesting tack within the post-colonial framework. Arguing that the slave, and in particular the plantation slave, occupies a spectral and recessive place in the narrative, Shilliam shows us how the "slave analogy" animates the figure of the proletarian "wage-slave" in the text. In that way the world market, and colonial imperialisms and conquests, appear in the *Manifesto*, but swiftly recede as the European working class comes to the fore. The European proletarian is thus the active agent of world-historical change. Shilliam pursues the pre-history of the text by investigating Engels's earlier works, which narrate the slave analogy – itself derived from Tory radicals and Chartists – in order to make the misery of the European proletariat intelligible and affecting. Shilliam's point is that this discursive practice denotes a non-engagement with the histories and realities of enslaved peoples. Moreover, the economic struggle between bourgeoisie and proletariat – as the two great classes of industrial society – displaces the historical and contemporary integration of capitalism with imperialism. Both sides of the dialectical class duo are thus imbued with a presumption of white supremacy. Shilliam concludes that it was the practice of black Marxists that attempted, at least, to transcend the merely analogical engagement of the *Manifesto* – and subsequent other Marxisms – with slave labor and racial oppression.

The closing critical engagement of the volume is Elisabeth Anker's Chapter 12, which takes up Walter Benjamin's theme of "left melancholy." This is a condition which disables contemporary critique precisely through an emotional attachment to an object, namely the *Manifesto*. The object is dis-avowed – because its promises have failed and its goals are unreachable – but leftists nonetheless hold fast to it, in particular to its methods of critique and style of narration. In a novel turn, Anker argues that this melancholia mimics the melodramatic content of the *Manifesto* itself, where melodrama enacts "moral self-righteousness, galvanizing sentiment and binary diagnostics of oppression." Taking Giorgio Agamben and joint authors Michael Hardt and Antonio Negri into her sights, Anker shows how their texts recapitulate the melodrama of the *Manifesto*, and how this occludes their ability to engage with the politics of the present. Their works focus on a past ideal – as embodied in the promise of emancipation and the virtue of the proletarian class subject. Melodrama in the *Manifesto* itself – by sharp contrast – focuses forward and is not motivated by loss and regret. Moreover, melodrama also works performatively to construct agency in individuals and collectivities – the grave*diggers* of the bourgeoisie. In Anker's view the *Manifesto* is not itself a melancholic text, lost in mournful disavowal and intellectual righteousness. It was written to inspire responsible collective action in the face of shameless oppression. It celebrates whatever it takes to break with the "history of all society up to now" (CM 237).

MANIFESTO OF THE COMMUNIST PARTY

The English translation by Terrell Carver appended to this volume was freshly done from the first, 1848 edition of the *Manifesto of the Communist Party* (the original title of the anonymous pamphlet). It is thus somewhat different from the "authorized" (by Engels) translation of 1888, reproduced innumerable times as an English-language "standard" text, which (as with the catchphrases quoted above) it obviously is. The purpose in doing a translation in that way was to frame the work as a political intervention, rather than one of theoretical "doctrine" that had somehow wandered in to the wrong genre. It was also possible to correct a number of errors and oddities, and to challenge readers with some unfamiliar turns of phrase. These renditions are rather more literally attuned to the German original than are the freedoms taken by Samuel Moore and Engels, the English-speaking surviving author. The chapters below are referenced to this version, and the citations and quotations from the other works of Marx and Engels are to the fifty-volume *Collected Works* (1975–2004), or, where not included, to the *Marx-Engels-Gesamtausgabe* (in progress since 1972).

MANIFESTO OF THE GERMAN COMMUNIST PARTY (1850)

Also based on the first edition (1848) of the *Manifesto*, Helen Macfarlane's English translation was the first to be published, albeit rendering the German text in a somewhat shortened form. In the Chartist periodical *The Red Republican* her work – which appeared in successive installments in November 1850 – was prefaced with a short note by G. Julian Harney, a radical Chartist campaigner and sometime political associate of Engels and Marx and their communist *confrères*. While odd-sounding in some places (the "frightful hobgoblin" of the opening sentence, for instance) her version is also more accurate at other points than the translation by Samuel Moore (assisted by Engels) dating from 1888, and never out of print since then. Marx and Engels seem variously to have been both approving and disapproving of her work on the few occasions when it crossed their paths. Macfarlane's version had a readership in its own time (including a reprint in *Woodhull & Claflin's Weekly* in New York in 1871) and is presented here, as it is not widely read today. Like Marx and Engels's original it was presented as an inspiration rather than a work of "theory," and – as with Carver's version – Macfarlane's also displays the "hot-off-the-press" character of a directly authored text and – in its time – political intervention.

TIME PAST/TIME FUTURE

As Marx and Engels wrote in their preface of 1872, the *Manifesto* is a historical document, of its time and therefore somewhat out of time in the present. But as they also commented, its principles – or perhaps, putting this more generally, the vision and views expressed there – are remarkably current. What they modestly missed in their own assessment – and what is key to its continued circulation and popularity – is its readability. Any number of publications, studies, reports and indeed manifestos speak to the issues it raises: economic inequality, class politics, globalizing capitalism. But for sheer drama the *Manifesto* has no rival, and it's just the right length. The alternative title of 1872 also helped: from being the manifesto of a particular "party," and by context "German party," the re-published version made it more generically "communist," and its subsequent, numerous translations – and lately "pop" versions – have made it more global than simply European. Of course it has been claimed, re-claimed and disputed in any number of partisan circumstances – all of which testifies even more to the quality of the writing, and the punchiness of the thinking. The *Manifesto* has acquired a life that surprised its authors and stimulates its readers, linking the future with the past – not quite two centuries yet, but getting there – and telling our present how it came to be and what to do about it.

REFERENCES

Berman, Marshall. 1988 [1982]. *All That Is Solid Melts into Air: The Experience of Modernity*. New York: Viking Penguin.
Derrida, Jacques. 2006 [1994]. *Specters of Marx: The State of the Debt, the Work of Mourning, and the New International*. Translated by Peggy Kamuf. New York: Routledge.
Draper, Hal. 2004. *The Adventures of the Communist Manifesto*. Alameda, CA: Center for Socialist History.
Sperber, Jonathan. 2013. *Karl Marx: A Nineteenth-Century Life*. New York and London: Liveright.

PART I

POLITICAL AND BIOGRAPHICAL CONTEXT

I

Rhineland Radicals and the '48ers

Jürgen Herres

Karl Marx and Friedrich Engels could hardly have chosen a more provocative title for the political manifesto they composed in 1847–1848, which was intended to express the founding principles of the Communist League, a secret organization of German laborers and intellectuals living abroad. By presenting this political credo as a manifesto, Marx and Engels invoked François (Gracchus) Babeuf's "Manifesto of Equals" of 1796, thus linking their text to the Jacobin tradition of the French Revolution.[1] With their public commitment to communism, Marx and Engels also consciously distanced themselves from German contemporaries who – so they believed – had misconstrued French and English social theories in order to define communism negatively in relation to socialism.[2] And, not least, by pronouncing themselves to be a party, they proclaimed a proper political movement, an illocutionary act that signified something far more than individuals who were merely announcing common political convictions (Andréas 1963; Jones 2002; Stammen and Classen 2009).

HISTORICAL AND POLITICAL CONTEXT

The *Manifesto* emerged from two decades of political turbulence. The July Revolution of 1830 in France had reverberated throughout Europe, reasserting the political impulse of Western liberalism. This doctrine advocated constitutions that conferred legislative and budgetary powers on the upper middle classes, thus enabling property owners, educated professionals and the business class of finance and industry to represent their interests in state legislatures and ministries. These constitutions ensured such basic rights as press freedom, judicial independence and the freedom of thought and faith.

But moderate liberals opposed any further extension of political participation, above all the universal male suffrage proclaimed in the French constitution of 1792, which they thought could only result in radicals coming to power. Such liberal moderation was manifest in the rise of Louis Philippe, the "citizen king," a scion of the Orléanist branch of the French Bourbons and one of the richest landowners in the country, who embodied middle-class ideals of capitalism and constitutional rule. No less of a bellwether was Belgium, which wrested its independence from the Kingdom of the Netherlands in 1830. Its constitution of 1831, hailed in the Prussian Rhineland as a model for others to follow, detailed a comprehensive list of basic rights and subjected the government to the will of parliament. Yet it restricted the franchise to the wealthiest.

Similarly, in France, the revolutionary cradle of modern Europe, barely 2 percent of adult men had access to the ballot box, while the 1832 Reform Act in Great Britain, despite increasing the number of adult men entitled to vote from 11 percent to 18 percent, had done nothing to enfranchise the lower social classes (Mares 2002, 38 ff.; Hippel and Stier 2012, 126, 143). In the Palatinate in western Germany, upwards of 30,000 people assembled at the ruins of Hambach Castle and demonstrated for freedom through constitutional rule and the dignity of national unity. Elsewhere in the German confederation, middle-class elements rioted in Saxony, Hanover, Brunswick and Hesse-Kassel, which led to the promulgation of constitutions. But Austria and Prussia, the two great powers of central Europe, remained authoritarian, neo-absolutist states without constitutions, and quickly uprooted these tender shoots of democracy.

In these years, democrats and republicans reasserted their principles and flourished as an oppositional force. Radical factions protested against curtailed voting rights and, more generally, against the political privileges accorded to property holders. Throughout Europe, liberals and radicals alike looked upon Chartism, often described as the world's first independent labor movement, with great regard. In its mass meetings and spectacular petition drives to the British Parliament, Chartists assembled 1.3 million signatures in 1839 and 3.3 million in 1842 calling for the extension of the franchise to all adult men. In spite of Chartism's immediate failure to sway Parliament, European radicals averred that a democratic male franchise would reinvigorate all aspects of politics. Similarly, they believed that social reform would recast constitutions and political relations with the ruling classes.

In December 1842, the twenty-two-year-old Friedrich Engels expressed this confident spirit in the *Rheinische Zeitung (Rhenish News)*, whose editor-in-chief, Karl Marx, was only two years older and a recent acquaintance of Engels: "The working class is daily becoming more and more imbued with the radical-democratic principles of Chartism and is increasingly coming to recognise them as the expression of its collective consciousness" (CW 2: 375–376). This article was one of the first contributions sent by Engels from Manchester, known as the "workshop of the world," where his father, a textile manufacturer from what is now Wuppertal in Germany, had sent him to learn the business of trade.

The Industrial Revolution, which began first in Britain and then spread through Western Europe in the early nineteenth century, brought in its wake great social upheavals. Although many perceived large-scale mechanized production as the collapse of society, others realized that this dawning epoch demanded a new interpretation of freedom that moved beyond the limits of democratic republicanism (Marti 2007; Roth 2010). Embracing the proposed but unrealized French revolutionary ideals of *liberté, égalité, fraternité*, radicals and early socialists demanded that freedom should not merely be limited to equality before the law. Reform of society and the collectivization of property, they argued, were also necessary prerequisites for society in order for citizens to live as one united public body. During the French Revolution, Babeuf had accused the Jacobins of half-heartedness and was the first to advocate radical democracy and social equality. In 1796 he organized the Conspiracy of Equals and was condemned to death on account of it. In 1828 his disciple Philippe Buonarroti wrote a history of the conspiracy, which radical secret societies throughout Europe hailed as a paradigm of doctrine and political organization.

Socialism and communism gradually emerged as omnibus terms for radical social reform. In the 1830s, English followers of Robert Owen replaced the original term Owenism with the broader appellation "socialism." In France, contemporaries grouped the theories of Owen, Fourier and Saint-Simon all under the same rubric. By 1842 the concept of communism had become common coinage in French political vocabulary, a term that referred to all programs that espoused egalitarianism through the abolition of private property (Schieder 1982, 473). In Germany, translations of English and French works on social literature dominated discussions into the 1840s. As a consequence, the German public viewed supporters of English and French social theories as socialists.

But socialism was always more than a signifier of collective radical reform. The concept also acted as a synonym for sociology, understood as "the science of society." Not until after the revolutions of 1848 did contemporaries distinguish more sharply between socialism and social science. In these early discussions, commentators also freighted the term communism with negative connotations, characterizing it as a flawed alternative to socialism (Schieder 1984). For example, in 1847, in a series of lectures on socialism and the questions that it raised, Karl Biedermann argued that while socialism strove for "balance or justice," communism espoused a "commonality of interests and property" which in no way reflected human nature (Biedermann 1847, 176).

Before communist ideas reached Germany in the 1840s, German workers and refugees living abroad debated the doctrine in their – often illegal – associations and clubs. Before 1848, around 10,000 German workers resided in Switzerland and London; in Paris, there were twice that number. In 1834, members of the *Deutscher Volksverein* (to which Ludwig Börne and Heinrich Heine also belonged) founded the *Bund der Geächteten* (League of Outlaws). In 1836–1837 other members formed the splinter group, the *Bund der Gerechten* (League of the Just), which was the forerunner of the *Bund der Kommunisten* (Communist League). By 1839, punitive measures taken by the French government forced many of "the Just" to flee to London. The number of workers and intellectuals who organized politically, however, was small. At the end of 1842, the figure in Switzerland was probably between 800 and 900;

in Paris in 1835–1836 around 120, and in 1840 perhaps more than 200; and in London never more than 100 between 1836 and 1842 (Schieder 1963, 96 ff., 14 ff., 118 ff.). Yet this small collectivity radically redefined the concept of private property.

These associations, founded by émigré Germans, aimed to reform both political systems and the organization of society. They increasingly regarded social equality as an indispensable condition of political freedom, even to the extent of insisting on collective ownership of property. Karl Schapper, a former forestry student who led the League of the Just, demonstrated the level of theoretical thinking in a paper found by French authorities at Schapper's home. Social reform, it maintained, had become a necessary prerequisite of the revolutionary program to establish political democracy. "Collective property," Schapper argued, "is the first and most essential requirement of a free democratic republic, and, without it, this is neither thinkable nor possible. With an unequal division of property we remain completely and absolutely dependent on the wealthy" (German text quoted in Schieder 1963, 320–321).

In order to lend weight to the new demand for revolutionary socialism, the tailor apprentice Wilhelm Weitling (1808–1871) penned an essay which cast light on the "possibility and the necessity of collective property." Published anonymously in 1839 as "Mankind as It Is and as It Ought to Be," it constituted the first communist manifesto written in German which resonated in radical circles. In his "Communism for Young Craftsmen," a peculiar fusion of religious ideas with French thought, Weitling sought to align the perfect society with a flawless economy – all achieved with centralized planning for supply and demand. Equality and individual freedom would be realized with a change of work every two hours, whereby everyone would have the possibility of pursuing several careers at once.

During the 1840s, socialist and communist ideas and theories eventually seeped into German political discourse (Dowe 1970; Sperber 1991; Brophy 2007). Taking advantage of a brief period of relaxation of state censorship in Prussia in 1842–1843, a group of young businessmen ventured to start up a liberal daily in Cologne, the *Rheinische Zeitung*, which played a particularly important role in these developments. When in 1814–1815 the Congress of Vienna allocated Westphalia and most of the Rhineland to Prussia, the Hohenzollern kingdom extended from the River Memel in East Prussia, which bordered Russia, to Saarbrücken on the French frontier. The western bank of the Rhineland had been ruled by the French state for almost twenty years and had adopted its legal system and constitution. In matters of law, economy and social policy, the Rhineland enjoyed more favorable conditions than those of Prussia's older provinces east of the Elbe. In the Prussian Rhineland, where both Marx and Engels were born, a liberal economy with free movement of goods and workers was well established. The church was furthermore secularized, and noble privilege largely abolished. For these reasons, Rhinelanders resisted integration into the Prussian state's authoritarian culture and held fast to their French inheritance of a modern economy and the Napoleonic Code. Rhenish political identity clearly diverged from Prussia's neo-absolutism, a circumstance which nettled Berlin elites. In his memoirs, Otto von Bismarck remembered how "repugnant" he had found the emergence of the "liberalism of the French Rhineland." All he could gain from it was "the impression of imported stereotypes" (Bismarck 1932, vol. 15, 16).

MARX AND ENGELS AND COMMUNISM

After studying law and philosophy in Bonn and Berlin, Marx assumed editorship of the *Rheinische Zeitung* in October 1842. At first he rejected socialist and communist ideas. He did, however, garner attention as a political critic with articles that attacked the "secret body politic" in Prussia. Addressing a repressive censorship that hindered an open discussion of public affairs, he claimed that "the German knows his state only from hearsay." He demanded that the "mysterious priest-like body of the state" be turned into the "flesh and blood of its citizens, into a bright secular body belonging and accessible to all" (MEGA² I/1: 333). He found fault with Prussia's policies for the Rhineland and defended the legal system, especially the public jury system, instituted by the French. But to his writers and fellow editors he declared himself opposed to smuggling in "communist and socialist doctrines," favoring instead a "quite different and more thorough discussion of communism" which he himself only began after the proscription of the *Rheinische Zeitung* in the course of 1843. To accommodate the censorship and the increasingly ruthless redactions of officials, Marx also rejected all articles "pregnant with revolutionising the world and empty of ideas." He demanded "less vague reasoning, magniloquent phrases and self-satisfied adoration," and, in their place, "more definiteness, more attention to the actual state of affairs, more expert knowledge" (CW 1: 394). Even as late as September 1843 he could still see in communism only "a dogmatic abstraction," as he noted to Arnold Ruge, the left Hegelian author and radical editor (MEGA² III/1: 55).

It was, in fact, Moses Hess (1812–1875) who first used the *Rheinische Zeitung* to raise the question regarding the "imbalance between rich and poor" and the "contrast between pauperism and [the] extreme wealth of the bourgeoisie" (in Mönke 1980, 184). Hess was the son of a Cologne sugar merchant and a member of the group that had founded the *Rheinische Zeitung*. Even before the appearance of Lorenz von Stein's pathbreaking book in 1842, *Socialism and Communism in France Today*, Hess introduced readers to the ideas of French communism. Based on his travels through the Netherlands and France, his later writings *The Sacred History of Mankind* (1837) and *The European Triarchy* (1841) reflected his egalitarian humanism, influenced by French socialism. He hoped for a "new Jerusalem" that would arise in "the heart of Europe" under the leadership of France and Germany, one in which the original historical condition of collective ownership would be reinstated (Hess 1837, 344–345; 1959, 79 ff.; Silberner 1966, 91 ff.).

Writing in the *Rheinische Zeitung* in April 1842, Hess contrasted the "communist manifesto" of the social philosopher Jean Baron de Colins and his supporters with "verbose liberalism." This manifesto called for a "rational people's community (a commune as understood by committed communists)." Since no form of government was in a position to remedy the current social evil and to abolish firmly established contradictions, Hess maintained that only through "a complete overthrow of the present social order could the future of nations be assured" (Hess 1842). Six months later Hess emphasized that the French Revolutions of 1789 and 1830 had simply passed power to the people, yet it is "up to the present generation to emancipate the people." From his point of view "certain ideas hung in the air . . . ideas that no one could gainsay." Until recently, he continued, no one had thought that even "in republican institutions of our time freedom miscarries because of poverty." The "impoverishment of the people," he continued, "has forced their struggles toward new and original direction." "One feels," he concluded, that "the struggles towards liberalism have been up to now insufficient to raise the majority of people out of a condition which is tantamount to slavery" (in Mönke 1980, 191–192.)

Through Hess, Marx and Engels first encountered the subject of French socialism with any accuracy. While Marx still kept his distance, Engels was converted as early as 1842. Reporting on a conversation Hess had had with Engels in Cologne, he wrote, "we talked about the questions of the day and he parted . . . from me as an ardent communist" (Hess 1959, 103; Dowe: 1970, 54). This account can no longer be otherwise confirmed, but, regardless, Hess first presented communism to Engels as the next necessary step in the development of radicalism. Engels certainly adopted these tenets. It is true for democracy, as it is for every other form of government, he wrote in 1843, that "political liberty is sham-liberty, the worst possible slavery." "England, France and Germany, the three great and civilized countries of Europe," he suggested, would have recognized "that a thorough revolution of the social arrangements, based on property held in common, has now become an urgent and unavoidable necessity" (CW 3: 392).

Unlike Marx's critique of capitalism, Engels's derived from direct observation of industrialization. His book *The Condition of the Working Class in England* (1845), which made his name in the German-speaking world, drew on his observations in Manchester where he had lived between November 1842 and August 1844 (CW 4: 295–583). Famously disregarding social connections to the business world, Engels sought contact with Chartists such as James Leach and George Harney, and also immersed himself in the actual workers' way of life. He enabled Marx to consider the economy for the very first time in an essay of 1844, "Outlines for a Critique of Political Economy" (CW 3: 418–443). Moreover, in 1845 he brought Marx with him to London and Manchester for his first research into economic history (for Marx's notebooks, see MEGA² IV/4: 7–358).

COMMUNISM, WORKERS AND CORRESPONDENCE COMMITTEES

Marx began his study of socialist and communist literature in 1843 in the Rhenish spa town of Bad Kreuznach, where he married his long-term fiancée, Jenny von Westphalen. After his move to Paris in October 1843, where he published the *Deutsch-französische Jahrbücher* (*German-French Annals*) in association with Arnold Ruge, he made great strides "towards 'crass socialism'." In March 1844 he parted ways with Ruge. As the latter noted, "he [Marx] could no longer work in partnership with me since I am merely a political man and he is a communist" (Ruge 1846, 139–140). Marx attended meetings of French workers, and, much impressed, he wrote in August 1844 to Ludwig Feuerbach, the materialist philosopher of religion, "you would have to attend one of the meetings of the French workers to appreciate the freshness, the nobility which burst forth from these toil-worn men." The experience further inspired him to consider broader political meanings. Even if "the German artisan" – despite his "theoretical merits" – was, wrote Marx, "still too much of an artisan," he was confident that "history," along with French, English and German workers, would provide "the practical element for the emancipation of mankind" (CW 3: 355).

It was not until he arrived in Brussels with his family in February 1845, following his expulsion from France, that Marx took the final step into active politics. Working together with Engels, who had also settled in Brussels in the summer of 1845, he set about building an international network of so-called correspondence committees. Because few committees other than those in London and Cologne were formed, Marx and Engels finally decided in 1847 to become members of the *Bund der Gerechten* (League of the Just) and work for its reorganization (Schieder 1991, 35 ff.).

During this period, discussion of the socialist/communist program had intensified in German secret societies and expatriate unions. In Switzerland, German workers' unions were only allowed to operate as promoters of education and apprenticeship. After Weitling's agitation, they turned political. Consequently, Weitling was arrested in Zürich in June 1843, interned for over a year and then deported. Radical circles celebrated his arrival in London in 1844, but the views of leading members of the League of the Just had already deviated widely from those of Weitling himself. Their participation in revolutionary movements in Paris and, after 1840, in London, set them in a different direction.

Members of the German Workers' Educational Society, founded in London in 1840, soon fell out with one another (Grandjonc et al. 1979, 23, 27–39; Lattek 2006). Extracts from minutes that have survived from 1845 reveal the conflicting views expressed in the heated discussions on the nature of communism, its propagation and its execution. From the perspective of the Londoners, the time for conceptualizing communist systems was past. "There was a time for systems," Schapper declared, "but for me that time is over." The ideal society as envisaged by Owen, Cabet and Weitling was for him too "soldier-like," allowing "only a barracks existence." Weitling defended his program and argued for using "everything" in order to reach the goal of communism speedily. For him, "through feelings" it was possible to attain "what was impossible with reason." As a temporary measure, he was willing to accept a dictatorship. "If we bring about communism by revolutionary means then we must have a dictator in supreme command." The Londoners opposed this proposal, objecting to "leaping at one go from A to Z." They stressed instead the need for "education" and "enlightenment." Schapper put forward the view that "only through knowledge" could one approach communism. It was of no help "for the community to get carried away by passionate speeches; such over-excited masses must of necessity suffer all the worse downfall. Nationalist and religious passions would soon reinstate the old confusion" (Nettlau 1922, 384, 382, 367, 380, 372, 368).

Weitling's religious socialism, which had indeed been the League's standard doctrine since 1839, was rejected as insufficient, and he returned to Brussels, where he quarreled with Marx. At a sitting of the communist correspondence committee on 30 March 1846 Marx inveighed against the "awakening of fanciful hopes." "In a civilised country like Germany no success is possible without rigorous scientific principles and objective teaching" (Hess 1959, 151; Dowe 1970, 104–105). Hess, who did not participate in the meeting, was likewise convinced that the movement must be based on "premises of history and economy" (MEGA² III/2: 270). Some months later Weitling emigrated to New York, only to return when the Revolution of 1848 erupted. In the autumn of 1849 he once again returned to the USA and took part in the creation of a communist settlement.

THE COMMUNIST LEAGUE

With the assistance of Marx and Engels, the Communist League was founded in 1847. The founding congress, about which little is known, took place in London on 2–9 June (Andréas 1969). The primary aim of the new secret organization, which arose out of the League of the Just, was "the emancipation of man through the dissemination of the theory of collective property." In the version adopted in December, its aims read as "the overthrow of the bourgeoisie, the rule of the proletariat, the abolition of the old bourgeois society based on class distinction and the establishment of a new society without class and without private property" (Förder et al. 1970, vol. 1, 466, 626 and 475 ff.).

In subsequent meetings of the newly formed League (only fragments of the minutes are extant), the outline of a proposed communist "confession of faith" came under discussion, presumably drawn up by Schapper and Engels. (A surviving copy, found 1968 in Hamburg, was written in Engels's hand (Andréas 1969, 20–23 and 53–58).) Its adoption was to be decided upon at a second congress, which took place in the same year between 29 November and 8 December, once again in London. Members were declared to believe that "the primary condition for the transition from contemporary society to the collective was the political liberation of the proletariat through a democratic national body." "A reduction in private property" by means of "progressive taxes, a reduction in inheritance rights, etc." should pave the way for a "gradual change into community ownership." "All children should be brought up and taught in state institutions." They did not, however, plan for a "community of women": "We will not interfere in the private relationship between man and wife and at all in the family except insofar as the new social order is adversely affected by it" (Nettlau 1919, 393).

In Paris, Hess and Engels again modified the proposal in October–November (CW 38: 133–140; Hundt 1993, 367). In a series of articles which appeared in this same period, Hess deemed a bourgeois revolution against the feudal state impossible, thus portraying the proletariat as the sole instigator of the political revolution that must follow (Hess 1847; Mönke 1980, 427–444). After several weeks of passionate debate in which this time both Marx and Engels participated, the congress delegated to them the task of drawing up a definitive program (CW 17: 78–80; Förder et al. 1970, vol. 1, 624). After resuming and expanding the discussions, which were at times both far-reaching and extremely controversial, they duly delivered the reworked program to London at end of January 1848, along with the new wording of the manifesto (Hundt 1993, 371 ff.). Because the February revolution broke out in France directly after its appearance, it was never possible to submit it for discussion to the communities of the Communist League.

Over the last century, the Communist League has all too often been evaluated within the context of party historiography, especially by Marxist-Leninists. But it was less a party (not even in its loose contemporary understanding) than a network of communist workers and intellectuals. The secret association had branches in Brussels, London, Paris and Cologne; for Switzerland, perhaps Berne, La Chaux-des-Fonds and Lausanne. Including London, where the League is said to have numbered almost 90 members, the association totaled scarcely more than 300 men (Schieder 1966, 900–909; Förder et al. 1970, vol. 1, 539, 645 f.; Hundt 1993, 321, 324). In London, the men associated with Schapper from 1840 on developed a differentiated infrastructure which included public associations, educational institutes, lectures, assemblies and festive occasions. In 1847, Marx introduced similar measures in the Belgian capital. A public German workers' organization formed in the autumn quickly enlisted more than 100 members. Marx was furthermore active in the *Association Démocratique*, an international association with bourgeois-radical tendencies, which strove for a democratic European federation (*une Fédération de l'Europe*). When the society was formed at the beginning of November, it elected Marx as vice-president, along with the Polish historian Joachim Lelewel, who had been a member of the Polish national government during the rebellion of 1830–1831 (Andréas et al. 2004, 359). It further planned an international congress of democrats and workers in Brussels in September 1848.

In Prussia's western provinces during the mid-1840s, the *Rheinische Zeitung* led an intensified public discussion on the "social question." While the paper was still in circulation in 1842, a group of young lawyers, entrepreneurs, writers and doctors, including Karl D'Ester and Andreas Gottschalk, had assembled themselves and subsequently remained in contact with Marx, Engels and Hess. After the Silesian weavers' revolt in the spring of 1844, when lace-makers and entrepreneurs in Berlin founded a Central Association of the Working Classes, these Cologne intellectuals constituted a local branch of this association in order to propose more comprehensive and radical reforms. In the winter of 1844–1845 they initiated several public meetings in Cologne, first with 400 and eventually with 1,200 participants, where they argued for a new understanding of freedom. Along with greater political participation, a demand put forward by Rhenish liberals, this association further advocated economic and tax reforms as well as social and pedagogical improvements that encompassed the greater majority of the populace. They devised a cooperative program of self-help (see Boch 1991, 209, 211). Alongside "halls of industry, where the goods such as foodstuffs produced by their labour were to be sold," they envisaged the establishment of credit and advice centers, shopping cooperatives and a collective society with goods produced collaboratively. In this way, workers could hold their own in "competition with the power of capitalism" (Hansen 1942, 689 ff.).

The local branch never received the sanction of the Prussian Ministry of the Interior. In the local elections of 1846, the first ever held under the Prussians, a "democratic or people's party" split from Rhenish liberalism, which Karl D'Ester described as still merely a "party of plutocrats." In an exhaustive report, the *Kölnische Zeitung* (*Cologne News*) attributed the separation of the "young" from the "old" liberalism to a new social understanding of freedom. Equality before Rhenish law, it stated, would remain an "empty abstraction and an illusion" as long as the "inequality in the distribution of wealth" was overlooked. "No one can enjoy his political rights or fulfil his political duties" if he has not "already got himself the necessary education and the means to earn his bread." In any case, D'Ester's demand for a "reorganisation" of working conditions and social relationships found no majority; people feared that "reorganisation" meant "revolution," which they vigorously rejected (*Kölnische Zeitung* 1846).

In Bielefeld between 1845 and 1848, the doctor and author Otto Lüning published the monthly journal, *Das Westphälische Dampfboot* (*The Westphalian Steam-Packet*), an early socialist organ. In the *Trier'schen Zeitung* (*Trier News*), one of the dailies in Marx's home town, the author Karl Grün promulgated a self-styled "true" socialism. At the center of his political program he placed education and the state's "organisation of work," as envisioned by the French socialist Louis Blanc. In April 1844 Grün lectured on "true" education, which is regarded as the first public talk in Prussia's western provinces to expound socialist thinking (Dowe 1970, 66; Grün 2005, 89 ff., 395 ff.). In February 1845 Hess and Engels developed ideas on communism in public lectures with audiences of at least 200 listeners in Elberfeld, which was, like Engels's neighboring hometown of Barmen, an early industrial center.

"Communism is not a theory like any old philosophical system taught to us," proclaimed Hess; "communism is the end of the evolutionary history of society." Engels, speaking more as a practical man, addressed the "economic necessity" and the "economic advantages of communism" (Dowe 1970, 82ff.; Mönke 1980, 348–359; CW4: 243–264).

In the autumn of 1847 a branch of the Communist League was formed in Cologne. Gottschalk in particular and two former officers, Friedrich Anneke and August Willich, both of whom later fought for the Union in the American Civil War of 1861–1865, led the proceedings. In Prussia, the Revolution of 1848–1849 started in the Rhineland on 3 March 1848 with great ceremonial events in several towns. But the most spectacular event on that day was a demonstration by manual laborers and other workers in Cologne organized by Gottschalk, Annecke and Willich at City Hall. The participants, which grew from a few hundred to somewhere between 2,000 and 5,000, wore their Sunday best, in accordance with the gravity of the occasion. Their demands, known as the "people's demands," went beyond the usual desiderata in the programs of March 1848. They unequivocally demanded "legislation and administration by the people." They further demanded "the right to work and guaranteed welfare for all." They demanded "full education for all children at public expense." During the demonstration at City Hall, further flyers asked for "peace with all the nations" to be included as another demand (Herres 2012, 237 ff.).

COMPOSITION AND RECEPTION OF THE COMMUNIST MANIFESTO

In all probability Marx wrote down the *Communist Manifesto* in Brussels in January 1848 in one sitting. The single extant page in Marx's handwriting suggests that. Moreover, Engels was in Paris at that time. Yet Marx wrote on the basis of earlier outlines which Engels had drafted. Furthermore, Marx formulated shared political thoughts and aims, both the theoretical and the practical, which they had discussed and collaborated on prior to the January 1848 draft. In October/November 1847 Engels had put together a text which he called the "Basic Principles of Communism." In this text, he envisioned the proletarian revolution as the intention "to create a democratic state constitution and thereby, directly or indirectly, to produce the political supremacy of the proletariat." But "democracy" will be of "no use to the proletariat," he continued, "if it is not used as a means of pushing through further comprehensive measures designed to attack private property and to defend the existence of the proletariat" (Förder et al. 1970, vol. 1, 589–607). It was also Engels who proposed not to draft a communist confession of faith, but rather to present a manifesto in book form (CW 38: 146–150). Marx always insisted emphatically that Engels was entitled to co-authorship. Not until 1872 did the title page of the *Manifesto* name them as co-authors; this was not the case in the earlier editions.

In the *Manifesto* Marx presents the stages of development towards global capitalism in a time-lapse photography mode (Sieferle 1979, 77). He anticipates developments as having fully occurred, even though their first signs were barely visible. Instead of a carefully weighed analysis, revolutionary passion shouts from every sentence. But there is also the hope of a better society. The incendiary slogan "workers of the world unite!" had already cropped up some months before in papers belonging to the Communist League. It first adorned the sole issue of a *Kommunistische Zeitung* (*Communist News*) which had appeared in London in the summer of 1847, and it superseded the older motto "all men are brothers"; the more strident call to proletarian class solidarity replaced the general recognition of brotherhood. According to claims made by Friedrich Lessner in 1905 to Max Nettlau, the Bakunin scholar, Engels, having come from Marx in Brussels, was the one who introduced the new motto (Nettlau 1922, 387; Hundt 1993, 372). When the Communist League used it for the first time, Schapper deemed it necessary to explain to their supporters in a lengthy article the "origin and meaning" of the French-derived term "proletarian" (Grünberg 1921, 249–341).

Marx intrinsically linked social emancipation and all of its potential consequences to the ultimate fulfillment of the private property system. From a political standpoint, he was unwilling to go beyond this process. He posited a dialectic of progress to shape his argument.[3] The capitalist system of production will, like a sorcerer, summon its own grave-digger, and this grave-digger was the proletariat. In pronouncing this, he was not worried that, even in England, the Industrial Revolution had still not stamped any country as an industrial society. He could see a social revolution only as an accelerated effort to complete an already achieved socioeconomic transformation (Welskopp 2000, 677 ff.). Thus on 30 March 1846, at the sitting of the Communist Correspondence Committee previously mentioned, and in opposition to Weitling, he declared "we cannot yet speak of bringing communism into being; the bourgeoisie must first be in control" (Hess 1959, 151).

In view of the enormous impact that the *Manifesto* made in subsequent decades, it is critical to acknowledge the unimpressive effect of its first appearance.[4] Even though the revolutions of 1848–1849 were far more than constitutional and national movements, the text's insignificance is indubitable. Yet the potential for a positive reception existed. Indeed, contemporary observers interpreted the causes of the revolution more as social than political. In his famous speech of 31 July 1848 to the Parisian National Assembly, Pierre-Joseph Proudhon, the widely read socialist theorist and activist, replied to its deputies: "Socialism generated the February revolution; your parliamentary squabbling would not have moved the masses to action" (quoted in Stein 1848, 180). Even for unprejudiced contemporaries in 1848, the social aspect played a decisive role. The aristocrat Alexis de Tocqueville, vice-president of the French National Assembly, who could in no way be accused of revolutionary leanings, noted: "Socialism will remain the essential distinctive character of the February revolution. Seen from a distance the [Second French] Republic will appear only as a means and not as an end" (Geiss 1972, 253). Not least, even in Germany the revolution was primarily perceived as social. The Congress of German Manual Laborers' and Workers' Unions, which sat in Berlin between 23 August and 3 September 1848, expressed – in a petition presented to the German National Assembly in Frankfurt – the "conviction that the revolutionary movement was at heart a social one and, only stemming from that, had it become a political one" (Wigard 1849, vol. 7, 5100). Even Bismarck was convinced, as he explained in the Prussian State Parliament in September 1849, that not the national, but rather the "social element had been decisive for the revolution" (quoted in Gall 1980, 115). This confirmed his belief that the suppression of national liberal demands was unavoidable if a social *coup d'état* was to be prevented.

Although two thousand copies of the *Manifesto* had probably been distributed throughout Europe by the end of March 1848, it did not affect the revolution (Kuczynski 1995; Meiser 1996, 66–107). Even its authors, writing in the *Neue Rheinische Zeitung* (*New Rhenish News*), which they published in Cologne from June 1848 until May 1849 as a radical "organ of democracy," avoided any mention of their communist text. In February 1848, when the revolution began and within a few weeks threatened European monarchs, Marx was certain that this was "only a superficial beginning of the European movement." In March, at a meeting of Germans living in Paris, he announced that "the open struggle in France between the proletariat and the bourgeoisie" would soon erupt and that the success or failure of the European revolution turned on this struggle (Seiler 1850, 21). In April, when he came to Cologne as head of the Communist League – equipped with "discretionary plenary powers" – he soon admitted that his radical notions surpassed German reality (Förder et al. 1970, vol. 1, 714). To be sure, manual workers, who united in 1848 in radical-democratic associations, saw economic competition as a major evil of the day and sought relief in rights to social welfare and in the consolidation of cooperatives for production and consumption. But their central concepts were not "expropriation of the means of production," but rather "association," "organisation of work" and "the right to work" (Kocka 2012, 3–32).

In this fashion, Stefan Born strove to restructure the economy through producer- and consumer-cooperatives. Born was a governing member of the *Arbeiter-Verbrüderung* (Workers' Brotherhood), whose 18,000-strong membership of 1850 probably made it Germany's largest workers' organization during the Revolution of 1848. In October 1848, he wrote that "free associational work" should replace "the mode of production conditioned by capital and waged work" (Born 1898, 147; Rogger 1986, 132).

Marx directed all his energy to the publication of the *Neue Rheinische Zeitung*, which he turned into the most important mouthpiece of the democratic movement. The time for a proletarian revolution in Germany, he believed, was a long way off. He consequently turned against the workers' efforts to become politically independent, as Gottschalk had advocated in Cologne, and pushed instead for collective action that united proletarian and bourgeois democrats. His political aim was the establishment of a republic unified on the basis of a broad popular movement that encompassed the middle and working classes. The dictatorship of a single class, which Weitling had advocated a short time before in a public meeting of the Cologne democrats, Marx deemed "impractical and quite unfeasible." Indeed, he publicly declared in August 1848 that it was necessary to define sharply the present social contradictions and to emphasize the interests of the individual classes. But a government arising from a revolution would have to "comprise the most heterogeneous elements, which then through an exchange of ideas would then agree on the most pragmatic form of government."[5]

CONCLUSION

Of the many contemporary political discussions that emerged from the German workers' clubs abroad and in the Prussian Rhineland during the early industrial revolution, Marx and Engels fashioned a new social interpretation of political freedom. Rhenish radicals justified this new interpretation as the fitting legacy of French legal equality, but radicals of the German international associations also viewed it as the logical outgrowth of French and English forms of socialism and communism. In these discussions that defined the relationship between democracy and capitalism, social reforms and even social equality stood out as the necessary outcomes of a hard-fought democracy.

When in October 1852 members of the Communist League were tried for treason in Cologne, Marx and his *Manifesto* stood once again in Germany's public spotlight. In this jury trial the prosecution read aloud the *Manifesto* and even King Friedrich Wilhelm IV of Prussia, who had initiated the trial and secretly orchestrated its proceedings, read it with a confidant in his Berlin palace. The Cologne Communist Trial thus fulfilled its function of presenting a juridical interpretation of the revolutionary events in the Rhineland, for which the Communists were held solely responsible.

Marx and Engels later rejected subsequent attempts to update and revise the meaning of the *Manifesto*, characterizing it instead as a "historical document" (CW 23: 175). This certainly applies to sections III and IV of the text, which in particular display the pressures and exigencies of the moment. But the document also anticipates a forward-looking fascination with the economic-political developments of industrialization and their revolutionary potential, which only began to unfold in the late nineteenth century. This partially explains why Marx and Engels's theory was not about envisioning an organized socialist society, but rather how capitalism would look in the future. For them, socialism could only arise out of a highly developed capitalism, and not simply replace it. And perhaps herein lies the secret of why this historical text from two young passionate men still fascinates readers.

ACKNOWLEDGMENTS

Many thanks to Alison McConnell for translating my text and to James M. Brophy for revisions.

REFERENCES

Andréas, Bert. 1963. *Le Manifeste Communiste de Marx et Engels. Histoire et bibliographie 1848–1918*. Paris: Mailand.

Andréas Bert. Ed. 1969. *Gründungsdokumente des Bundes der Kommunisten*. Hamburg: Feltrinelli Editore.

Andréas, Bert, Jacques Granjonc, and Hans Pelger. 2004. *Association Démocratique, ayant pour but l'union et la fraternité de tous les peuples. Eine frühe internationale demokratische Vereinigung in Brüssel 1847–1848*. Trier: Eigenverlag Karl-Marx-Haus.

Biedermann, Karl. 1847. *Vorlesungen über Sozialismus und soziale Fragen*. Leipzig: Biedermann.

Bismarck, Otto von. 1932. *Erinnerung und Gedanke. Kritische Neuausgabe auf Grund des gesamten schriftlichen Nachlasses*. In *Die gesammelten Werke*, eds. Gerhard Ritter and Rudolf Stadelmann, vol. 15. Berlin: Deutsche Verlags-Gesellschaft.

Boch, Rudolf. 1991. *Grenzenloses Wachstum? Das rheinische Wirtschaftsbürgertum und seine Industrialisierungsdebatte 1814–1857*. Göttingen: Vandenhoek und Ruprecht.

Born, Stephan. 1898. *Erinnerungen eines Achtundvierzigers*. Leipzig: G.H. Meyer.

Brophy, James M. 2007. *Popular Culture and the Public Sphere in the Rhineland, 1800–1850*. Cambridge: Cambridge University Press.

Dowe, Dieter. 1970. *Aktion und Organisation. Arbeiterbewegung, sozialistische und kommunistische Bewegung in der preußischen Rheinprovinz 1820–1852*. Hannover: Verlag für Literatur und Zeitgeschehen.

Förder, Herwig, Martin Hundt, Jefim Kandel, and Sofia Lewiowa. Eds. 1970. *Der Bund der Kommunisten. Dokumente und Materialien, vol. 1: 1836–1849*. Berlin: Dietz Verlag.

Gall, Lothar. 1980. *Bismarck. Der weiße Revolutionär*. Frankfurt am Main/Berlin: Ullstein.

Geiss, Imanuel. Ed. 1972. *Tocqueville und das Zeitalter der Revolution*. München: Nymphenburger Verlags-Handlung.

Grandjonc, Jacques, Karl-Ludwig König, and Marie-Ange Roy-Jacquemart. Eds. 1979. *Statuten des Communistischen Arbeiter-Bildungs-Vereins. London 1840–1914*. Trier: Eigenverlag Karl-Marx-Haus.

Grün, Karl. 2005. *Ausgewählte Schriften in zwei Bänden*, ed. Manuela Köppe, vol. 1. Berlin: Akademie-Verlag.

Grünberg, Carl. 1921. "Die Londoner Kommunistische Zeitschrift und andere Urkunden aus den Jahren 1847–1848." *Archiv für die Geschichte des Sozialismus und der Arbeiterbewegung, Jg. 9: 249–341*.

Hansen, Joseph. Ed. 1942. *Rheinische Jahrbücher zur gesellschaftlichen Reform, vol. 1, Darmstadt: Rheinische Briefe und Akten zur Geschichte der politischen Bewegung 1830–1850*, vol. 1. Bonn.

Herres, Jürgen. 2012. *Köln in preußischer Zeit 1815–1871*. Köln.

Hess, Moses. 1837. *Die heilige Geschichte der Menschheit*. Stuttgart.

Hess, Moses. anon. 1842. "Die Communisten in Frankreich." In *Rheinische Zeitung, Köln*, Nr. 109, 19 April 1842. Beiblatt.

Hess, Moses. 1847. "Die Folgen einer Revolution des Proletariats." In *Deutsche-Brüsseler Zeitung*, Nr. 82, 87, 89 and 90, 14 October–11 November.

Hess, Moses. 1959. *Briefwechsel*, ed. Edmund Silberner. 'S-Gravenhage.

Hippel, Wolfgang von, and Bernhard Stier. 2012. *Europa zwischen Reform und Revolution 1800–1850*. Stuttgart: UTB.

Hundt, Martin. 1993. *Geschichte des Bundes der Kommunisten 1836–1852*. Frankfurt am Main.

Kocka, Jürgen. 2012. *Arbeit und Freiheit. Die Revolutionen von 1848*. Göttingen: Vanderhoeck & Ruprecht.

Kölnische, Zeitung. 1846. "Die Versammlungen zur Vorbereitung der bevorstehenden Gemeindewahlen zu Köln." Nr. 242, 30 August, 1. Beilage.

Kuczynski, Thomas. 1995. *Das Kommunistische Manifest (Manifest der Kommunistischen Partei) von Karl Marx und Friedrich Engels. Von der Erstausgabe zur Leseausgabe. Mit einem Editionsbericht*. Trier: Eigenverlag Karl-Marx-Haus.

Lattek, Christine. 2006. *Revolutionary Refugees. German Socialism in Britain, 1840–1860*. London, New York: Routledge.

Mares, Detlev. 2002. *Auf der Suche nach dem 'wahren' Liberalismus. Demokratische Bewegung und liberale Politik im viktorianischen England*. Berlin and Vienna: Philo Verlag.

Marti, Urs. 2007. "Tocqueville und Marx – Nach dem Kalten Krieg." *Internationale Zeitschrift für Philosophie, Heft* 1: 92–106.

Meiser, Wolfgang. 1996. "Das Manifest der Kommunistischen Partei vom Februar 1848. Zur Entstehung und Überlieferung der ersten Ausgabe." In *MEGA-Studien, Heft* 1: 66–107.

Mönke, Wolfgang. 1980. *Moses Hess, Philosophische und sozialistische Schriften 1837–1850. Eine Auswahl*, 2nd edn. Berlin: Akademie-Verlag.

Nettlau, Max. 1919. "Marxanalecten." *Archiv für die Geschichte des Sozialismus und der Arbeiterbewegung, Jg.* 8: 392–394.

Nettlau, Max. 1922. "Londoner deutsche kommunistische Diskussionen, 1845. Nach dem Protokollbuch des C.A.B.V." In *Archiv für die Geschichte des Sozialismus und der Arbeiterbewegung*, ed. Carl Grünberg, vol. 10. Leipzig, 362–391.

Rogger, Franziska. 1986. "Wir helfen uns selbst!" *Die kollektive Selbsthilfe der Arbeiterverbrüderung 1848/49 und die individuelle Selbsthilfe Stephan Borns*. Erlangen: Palm und Enke.

Roth, Klaus. 2010. "Kommunismus und revolutionäre Selbstveränderung." In Karl Marx and Friedrich Engels, *Die deutsche Ideologie*, ed. Harald Bluhm, 70–77. Berlin: Akademie-Verlag.

Ruge, Arnold.1846. *Zwei Jahre in Paris. Studien und Erinnerungen*, vol. 1. Leipzig: Jurany.

Schieder, Wolfgang. 1963. *Anfänge der deutschen Arbeiterbewegung. Die Auslandsvereine im Jahrzehnt nach der Julirevolution von 1830*. Stuttgart: Ernst Klett Verlag.

Schieder, Wolfgang. 1966. "Der Bund der Kommunisten." In *Sowjetsystem und Demokratische Gesellschaft*, ed. R. Piper, vol. 1. Freiburg.

Schieder, Wolfgang. 1982. "Kommunismus." In *Geschichtliche Grundbegriffe*, vol. 3. Stuttgart: Ernst Klett Verlag, 455–529.

Schieder, Wolfgang. 1984. "Sozialismus." In *Geschichtliche Grundbegriffe*, vol. 5. Stuttgart: Ernst Klett Verlag, 976–989.

Schieder, Wolfgang. 1991. *Karl Marx als Politiker*. München, Zürich: Piper.

Seiler, Sebastian. 1850. *Das Complot vom 13. Juni 1849, oder der letzte Sieg der Bourgeoisie in Frankreich. Ein Beitrag zur Geschichte der Gegenwart*. Hamburg: Hoffmann und Campe.

Sieferle, Rolf Peter. 1979. *Die Revolution in der Theorie von Karl Marx*. Frankfurt am Main: Ullstein.

Silberner, Edmund. 1966. *Moses Hess. Geschichte seines Lebens*. Leiden: Mouton.

Sperber, Jonathan. 1991. *Rhineland Radicals: The Democratic Movement and the Revolution of 1848–1849*. Princeton, NJ: Princeton University Press.

Stammen, Theo, and Alexander Classen. Eds. 2009. *Karl Marx. Das Manifest der kommunistischen Partei*. Paderborn: Schönigh.

Stedman Jones, Gareth. Ed. 2002. *Karl Marx and Friedrich Engels: The Communist Manifesto*. London: Penguin.

Stein, Lorenz von. anon. 1848. *Die socialistischen und communistischen Bewegungen seit der dritten französischen Revolution*. Leipzig and Vienna: Wigand.

Welskopp, Thomas. 2000. *Das Banner der Brüderlichkeit. Die deutsche Sozialdemokratie vom Vormärz bis zum Sozialistengesetz*. Bonn: J.H.W. Dietz Nachf.

Wigard, Franz. Ed. 1849. *Reden für die deutsche Nation 1848/49. Stenographischer Bericht über die Verhandlungen der Deutschen Constituirenden Nationalversammlung zu Frankfurt am Main*, vol. 7. Frankfurt am Main: Sauerländer.

2

Marx, Engels and Other Socialisms

David Leopold

This chapter is concerned with the most neglected part of the *Communist Manifesto*, and is written with the conviction that this neglect is to be regretted. Section III of the *Manifesto* is entitled "Socialist and Communist Literature," and it provides a typology of, and some brief critical engagement with, certain other – that is, non-Marxian – socialisms. (Note that I use the term "Marx*ian*" here to refer to the views of Marx and Engels, and not to those of later "Marx*ist*" writers and activists.) The significance of the *Manifesto* is, of course, widely acknowledged, but this discussion of other socialisms is often said to be outdated, opaque and uninteresting. There have even been editions of the text which chose to omit part or all of this particular section. That editorial excision began in Marx's own lifetime; for example, section III was missing from the abridged version of the *Manifesto* which appeared in *The Social Economist* (in August and September 1869), published by Cowell Stepney (1820–1872); and a large part of it was excluded from the Spanish edition, translated by José Mesa (1840–1904) and published in six installments in *La Emancipación* (in November and December 1872). And the process continues into the present; for example, the discussion of other socialisms was omitted from a recent graphic version of the *Manifesto* on grounds that it is something of a "dated relic" (Rigakos 2010, 2).

The suggestion that section III is peculiarly outdated seems misplaced. Its discussion of other socialisms obviously only covers the period before 1847, and consequently includes nothing, for example, about the state socialism of Ferdinand Lassalle (1825–1864), the anarchist socialism of Mikhail Bakunin (1814–1876) or the agrarian socialism of the Russian populists. Yet the *Manifesto* as a whole should be understood not as some timeless summary of Marxian views, but rather as an intervention into a particular political context at a particular point in time. Section III is not a uniquely antiquated part of the text. Interestingly, it was the only section of the *Manifesto* which Marx and Engels ever published separately; a revised version of it subsequently appeared in the *Neue Rheinische Zeitung, Politische-ökonomische Revue*, edited by Marx, in November 1850. (Marx's textual revisions were minor and mainly concerned the structure of paragraphs.) Moreover, in the preface to the 1872 German edition, Marx and Engels portrayed the *Manifesto,* as a whole, as "a historical document which we have no longer any right to alter," and gave examples from throughout the text where they no longer held quite the same views (CW 23: 175). In addition, although some of the critical targets of section III have largely disappeared from view – one would be hard-pressed, for example, to find anyone who considered that the German "true socialist" Karl Grün (1817–1887) has much to teach us – others are still thought to have more than "merely" historical relevance. For example, there are modern commentators who insist that the social vision of Pierre-Joseph Proudhon (1809–1865) is of "obvious relevance today" (McKay 2011, 51). Finally, the purported irrelevance of these other socialisms is much less apparent once the critical targets of section III are construed less narrowly. There might, for instance, be few modern readers of J. C. L. Simonde de Sismondi (1773–1842) – maybe there should be more (see Stedman Jones 2004, 145–157) – but the idea of a backward-looking socialism that romanticizes pre-modern community certainly does have resonance for some of our contemporaries. So understood, the *Manifesto* discussion of non-Marxian socialisms is less outdated than it might initially appear.

Section III is also often said to be opaque, and it is certainly true that the socialists whom Marx and Engels discuss are not always easy to identify from the *Manifesto* alone. Moreover, even once these critical targets are accurately identified, their actual views remain unclear to many readers. The authors' apparent assumption that most of their intended audience would have some familiarity with these critical targets does not hold for most modern readers. However, this provides a rationale, not for neglecting section III, but rather for precisely the kind of exegetical under-laboring that the present chapter engages in. In what follows, I alleviate some of this opacity by identifying these other socialisms, and by explaining what Marx and Engels say about them. Note that the issue of whether, and to what extent, this Marxian assessment of other socialisms is accurate or fair is largely left for another occasion. An adequate evaluation of their critical engagement with other socialisms would not only require more room than is available here, but also risk taking the focus away from the *Manifesto* itself.

Finally, this discussion of other socialisms is also sometimes portrayed as uninteresting. This is typically a conclusion drawn from the two assumptions that I have just rejected: that is, this section of the *Manifesto* is said to be uninteresting *because* it is outdated and opaque. However, insofar as this claim – that section III is uninteresting – has independent weight, the remainder of the present chapter should be construed as a rejection of it. The tendency of commentators to downplay or ignore this section of the text is understandable but regrettable. It is understandable because section III is somewhat inaccessible; not least, its critical targets require some identification and elucidation. It is regrettable because, once it is suitably clarified, the Marxian discussion of other socialisms is of considerable interest. Section III variously illuminates: the variety of nineteenth-century socialisms; the authors' (especially Marx's) characteristic way of working; the authors' (not wholly dismissive) view of other socialisms; the authors' own positive Marxian views; and the immediate political ambitions embodied in this particular text. Anyone concerned with those subjects should be interested in the account of, and engagement with, other socialisms contained in this part of the *Manifesto*.

SOCIALISMS AND COMMUNISMS

It is important to realize that the title of section III would have had a modish air in 1848. "Socialism" [*Socialismus*] and "communism" [*Kommunismus*], together with their various cognates, were relatively recent words, whose meanings were evolving rapidly and which had not yet triumphed over their terminological competitors such as "associationism" and "communalism." Relevant German usage of both terms lagged behind, as well as reflected, English and French usages. The term socialism had appeared earlier in English, where it was used in the 1820s to refer to the Owenite movement, and French, where it was used in the early 1830s to refer to the doctrine of the Saint-Simonians. (Earlier German examples drawing on Latin and Italian usages – had used the term to connote something more like sociability.) Similarly, the German use of communism to mean the common ownership of goods postdated English and French usage, not really taking off until after the social upheavals of 1840 (Grandjonc 1989). (Again, earlier German examples connote an adjacent sense at most, referring to certain rural property rights in the *ancien régime*.) It is consequently no surprise to discover that Marxian usage of these terms in this period has a certain fluidity. Socialism and communism were both new-fangled words whose meaning and popularity were still in a process of consolidation. The *Manifesto* discussion reflects, and contributes to, that process.

Socialism and communism are portrayed in the *Manifesto* as having overlapping but not identical meanings. Socialism and communism both share (positively) an approval of community, association or cooperation, and (negatively) a disapproval of the individualism and competition that increasingly characterized modern bourgeois society. However, they differ in both the demandingness of their proposed social reforms, and the class associations of their (actual and potential) support. In his preface to the 1888 English edition of the *Manifesto*, Engels observed that he and Marx would not have been minded to call their work a "socialist" manifesto, because socialism was already linked not only with "the most multifarious quacks," whose various solutions to contemporary social ills offered no fundamental threat to "capital and profit," but also with a largely middle class movement (CW 26: 516). In turn, communism had already come to indicate not only a scheme of social reform more ambitious than socialism (as just described) – in that its institutional aims included some public control of productive resources (and consequently the transformation of private, or "bourgeois," property) – but also a political orientation towards the working class. In the same 1888 preface, Engels recalled that the term communism had already gained an association with a "working-class movement," and that – given their own insistence that "the emancipation of the working class must be the act of the working class itself" – there had been no doubt about which of the two labels he and Marx should identify with in the *Manifesto* (CW 26: 517).

Note that Marx and Engels treat the movement for socialism and communism as a modern phenomenon. Commentators are sometimes tempted to treat socialism and communism in a historically expansive fashion – dating back, for instance, to the institution of the jubilee in pre-exilic Israel, or to the social arrangements of primitive Christianity. However, Marx and Engels maintain that socialist and communist systems "proper" [*eigentlich*] emerged only with the first stirrings of the struggle between bourgeoisie and proletariat, a struggle which they describe earlier in the *Manifesto* (CM 257). Pre-modern expressions of socialism and communism might, of course, be of interest, but they necessarily foundered on the "undeveloped condition" of the proletariat and the lack of "material conditions for its emancipation" – two conditions which are only met with the development of the bourgeois epoch (CM 257). Until the theoretical and practical connection is made between the movement for communism and the interests of the proletariat, Marx and Engels insist that communism will remain nothing more than an aspiration.

In the *Manifesto*, Marx and Engels present a typology which identifies three main types of non-Marxian socialism, which they call "reactionary socialism," "conservative" or "bourgeois socialism" and "critical utopian socialism." The first of these is subdivided into three sub-categories which they call "feudal socialism," "petty-bourgeois socialism" and "German" or "true socialism." In short, Marx and Engels discuss five individual non-Marxian socialisms, which they see as exemplifying three basic types of such socialism. As well as the obvious chronological limit (existing before 1848), all of these other socialisms are deemed to be of some contemporary relevance. On the grounds of lack of contemporary relevance, for example, they omit sustained discussion of the primitive communism of Gracchus Babeuf (1760–1797). So-called Babouvism had embodied a "general asceticism" and "crude egalitarianism," and is associated, by Marx and Engels, with the earliest efforts of the proletariat to articulate its interests during the upheaval accompanying the overthrow of feudalism (CM 257). In short, section III offers a snapshot of certain non-Marxian socialisms deemed sufficiently relevant to their German audience at this particular time.

It seems likely that Marx and Engels were not unalterably wedded to this particular way of dividing up other socialisms. The account in section III certainly differs in detail from the alternative typologies found in Engels's "Principles of Communism" [*Grundsätze des Kommunismus*] (1847) (CW 6: 341–357) and in Marx's "Draft Plan for Section III" (1847) (CW 6: 576). We should probably think of this part of the *Manifesto* as one of a series of attempts in the late 1840s to categorize other socialisms.

Note that this particular typology is organized primarily, not, as often suggested, on the class basis of their support, but rather on where these contemporary non-Marxian socialisms locate the good society. Socialist accounts of the good society are typically based on a commitment to certain values (such as equality and community) and a conviction that certain institutions (for instance, producers' cooperatives) would best embody those values. However, socialists disagree amongst themselves not only about which values and institutions are the right ones, but also about the historical association of their good society. Simply put, backward-looking socialisms (such as the three varieties of reactionary socialism) identify the good society with some part of the past; sideways-looking socialisms (such as conservative socialism) identify the good society with some, suitably reformed, aspects of the present; and forward-looking socialisms (such as critical utopian socialism) identify the good society with the future. In what follows, I address each of these three types of socialism in turn, explaining whom they refer to, and outlining the assessment of them contained in the *Manifesto*.

REACTIONARY SOCIALISM

Reactionary socialism [*reaktionaire Socialismus*] is backward-looking; it associates the good society with some part of the past. Those identified with it are reactionary in the literal sense that they want, at least in part, to return to a pre-bourgeois society, "to turn back the tide of history" (CM 244). In the "Principles of Communism," Engels describes this otherwise diverse group as adherents of the "feudal and patriarchal society" which had been, and continued to be, destroyed by the large-scale industry which characterized bourgeois society. These reactionary socialists are said to recognize some of the "ills of present-day society," but from the existence of those ills they erroneously drew the conclusion that "feudal and Patriarchal society should be restored because it was free from these ills" (CW 6: 355). Marx and Engels not only think that such a restoration is impossible; they also share little of this pre-modern nostalgia. Indeed, a constant thread in the *Manifesto* is their celebration of the revolutionary role of bourgeois society and, in particular, its destruction of the parochial, static and patriarchal world of feudalism. Marx and Engels subdivide reactionary socialism into three different contemporary strands which they discuss separately: "feudal socialism," "petty-bourgeois socialism" and "German" or "true socialism."

The first form of reactionary socialism, feudal socialism [*feudale Socialismus*], refers to the critique of modern bourgeois society offered by certain elements of the French and English aristocracy. It is linked with the July Revolution (1830) in France, and the Reform movement in England; more precisely, a section of "the French legitimists" and "the Young England movement" are identified as representatives of feudal socialism (CM 252). This particular socialism can also have a whiff of "Christian asceticism," perhaps unsurprisingly, given not only the flexibility of Christian declamations against private property and the state, but also the Marxian judgment that the feudal parson was always "hand in glove" with the feudal lord (CM 253).

The French "legitimists" here are those who sought the restoration of the Bourbon monarchy (overthrown in the July Revolution). The feudal socialists among them – those who championed some reform of the conditions of workers and the poor – perhaps included the vicômte Frédéric Alfred Pierre de Falloux (1811–1886), who stressed the social duties of the nobility and argued against the right to work. (The Christian variants of feudal socialism might be thought to include French "social Catholics" such as Paul Alban Villeneuve-Bargemont (1784–1850) and cômte Charles Forbes de Montalembert (1810–1870).) In turn, "Young England" was the name of a conservative political and literary group which included Lord John Manners (1818–1906) and the young Benjamin Disraeli (1804–1881). Thomas Carlyle (1795–1881), the author of *Past and Present* (1843), is also often associated with it. Carlyle's writings, especially before 1848, embodied the relevant combination of an admiring account of the hierarchies of the feudal past, together with some fierce criticism of the bourgeois present – including trenchant observations concerning crises of overproduction in which "in the midst of plethoric plenty, the people perish," and the poverty of social relations in which "cash payment" increasingly forms "the one nexus of man to man" (Carlyle 1960, 6, 163).

Marx and Engels offer a complex assessment of feudal socialism. They recognize that the social criticism of this movement is not without effectiveness; the feudal socialists are said to provide a "bitter, witty, biting" verdict on the bourgeoisie which strikes the latter at their "very core" (CM 252). Indeed, some of Carlyle's criticisms of bourgeois society are directly echoed in the *Manifesto* itself; for example, in the Marxian characterization of contemporary bourgeois society as fostering no social bond which is not based on "unfeeling 'hard cash'" [*gefühllose "baare Zahlung"*] (CM 235). However, these feudal socialists are also criticized for their limited grasp of the "course of modern history," for hoping to restore a world which in their romanticized form (overflowing with feudal "love and honour") had never existed, and which in its unromanticized form had actually given birth to the new world against which they now raged (CM 253). Furthermore, the political appeal of the movement is judged to be incoherent; feudal socialists have to appeal to the exploited against the bourgeoisie, but the modern working class would have no place in the aristocratic idyll which these socialists sought. Marx and Engels suggest that modern workers recognize this political incoherence and the concealed aristocratic standpoint which generates it. The astute social criticism might draw "the people" close to feudal socialism, but, once they can see the old feudal coat of arms on the "hind quarters" of feudal socialism, they soon desert "with loud and irreverent laughter" (CM 252). Marx's imagery is drawn from Heinrich Heine (1797–1856), who in *Deutschland. Ein Wintermärchen* (1844) [*Germany. A Winter's Tale*] had written mockingly of "Knights errant and lords superior, Who bore true faith upon their breast, Coats of arms upon their posterior" (Heine 1982, 487). Marx was a huge admirer and good friend of the great German poet, and this text was one that Marx had first published for Heine in *Vorwärts!* [*Forward!*]. Feudal socialism is seen less as a serious political movement to restore the old world, than as a literary response to the threat to aristocratic "conditions of life" presented by modern bourgeois society (CM 253). Lastly, Marx and Engels note that, in practice, and for all their complaints about the bourgeoisie's treatment of the exploited, the members of this movement always end up supporting "repressive legislation" against the working class (CM 253). In short, the social criticism of feudal socialism had some undoubted merit, but its historical understanding is limited, its political appeal lacks coherence, and its practical ambitions are ultimately reactionary. The result is a socialist-tinged lament for the past which never entirely manages to avoid a slightly "comic" air (CM 252).

The second form of reactionary socialism, namely petty-bourgeois socialism [*kleinbürgerliche Socialismus*], embodies the response of sections of the petty bourgeoisie (like sections of the aristocracy in the case of feudal socialism) to the threat to its "conditions of life" presented by modern bourgeois society (CM 253). The petty bourgeoisie typically earn their living by their own labor, together with some ownership of means of production (such as tools or premises). (It is presumably this association with premises which led Helen Macfarlane to replace *kleinbürgerliche Socialismus* with the imaginative, if not entirely successful, neologism "shopocrat socialism" in her 1850 English translation of the *Manifesto*.) Marx and Engels identify two different types of petty bourgeoisie, reflecting different levels of industrial and commercial development. In less-developed countries, such as France, the petty bourgeoisie consist primarily of peasants. In countries where "modern civilisation has developed" more fully, such as England, a new petty bourgeoisie had emerged, a class of small independent producers (including self-employed artisans) whose existence remains precarious and whose members are increasingly forced into the proletariat as a result of competition (CM 253).

The best-known exponent of petty-bourgeois socialism is said to be Sismondi. (No other examples are named in the *Manifesto*, but Eugène Buret (1811–1892) is often thought to be an additional candidate.) Sismondi is now usually thought of as a political economist – the author of *Nouveaux principes d'économie politique* [*New Principles of Political Economy*] (1819, 1827) – but he was also a distinguished historian of medieval Italian city states. Sismondi's critique of modern industrial society – which drew on his visits to Britain – emphasized its inevitable crises of overproduction, the associated misery and suffering of the workforce and its increasingly global impact on rival producers. Sismondi's historical enthusiasm for civic virtue over the steam engine suggested, to his own mind at least, the need to create a modern analogue of the guild system which had once enabled peasants and artisans to lead lives of self-reliance and virtuous citizenship.

Marx and Engels are enthusiastic about the *critical* dimension of petty-bourgeois socialism, and especially its negative diagnosis of the ills of contemporary society. Petty-bourgeois socialism is said to have "dissected with great perspicacity the conflicts inherent in modern relations of production," and in doing so to have exposed the "hypocritical apologetics" of contemporary economists (CM 253). More precisely, petty-bourgeois socialism had demonstrated "incontrovertibly" the ways in which modern relations of production – through their use of machinery, concentration of capital and overproduction – have generated destructive social consequences. Alongside the dissolution of traditional morality, family relations and national identities, Marx and Engels mention the ruin of the small trader and peasant, the poverty of the proletariat and the "flagrant disparities in the distribution of wealth" that have resulted (CM 254).

Marx and Engels are less sympathetic to the *constructive* dimension of petty-bourgeois socialism, that is, its positive proposals for social change. These socialists are said to seek either to restore wholly the property relations and society that belong to an earlier epoch, or somehow to contain modern means of production within the confines of previous property relations. In practice, Marx and Engels remark that "guild socialism for artisans and patriarchal relations in agriculture are the last word here" (CM 254). These constructive proposals are judged "reactionary" [*reaktionär*] and "utopian" [*utopistisch*] in equal measure; they are "reactionary" in the literal sense that they attempt to reverse the historical process (to restore aspects of pre-bourgeois society), and they are "utopian" in the popular sense that this goal is impossible to realize (CM 254).

The third form of reactionary socialism, namely German or true socialism [*deutsche oder ... wahre Socialismus*], is a result of what might be called combined and uneven historical development across Europe. More particularly, it reflects the distinctive German circumstances which Marx had earlier diagnosed as combining philosophical precocity with economic and political backwardness (Leopold 2007, 22–26). Its origins are said to lie with a group of Teutonic literati who took French socialist literature – including the work of Charles Fourier (1772–1837), Henri de Saint-Simon (1760–1825) and their various followers – and adapted it to the very different social conditions that obtained in the German confederation.

In the *Manifesto*, these various "philosophers, semi-philosophers, and word-smiths" are not named, but we can confidently identify them from the group of texts usually known as *Die deutsche Ideologie* [*The German Ideology*] (1846–1847) (CM 254). The best-known true socialists are perhaps Karl Grün and Hermann Kriege (1820–1850), but the group also included Hermann Semmig

(1820–1897), Ernst Dronke (1822–1891) and others. In *The German Ideology*, Marx and Engels emphasized that the true socialists' knowledge of their French sources looked to be weak and derivative, having been gained secondhand from the superficial accounts found in the works of Lorenz von Stein (1815–1890), Theodor Oelckers (1816–1869) and others. Indeed, Marx and Engels entertain themselves – at some length – by identifying striking examples of true socialist plagiarism from this limited range of barely adequate and second-hand accounts of socialism in France.

In the *Manifesto*, the true socialists are said to combine much seemingly "idle speculation concerning the true society or the realization of the human essence" together with a critique of a bourgeois society which does not yet exist in Germany (CM 254). (Interestingly, and for reasons which are unclear, this last sentence is omitted from the 1888 English translation by Samuel Moore and revised by Engels.) This combination captures the changes to both the theoretical form, and the political meaning, of these French ideas, which resulted from their relocation to German soil.

This relocation of French ideas to German circumstances transformed their theoretical form, as abstract philosophical speculation was substituted for practical and concrete social criticism. Marx and Engels elaborate this substitution using a satirical and slightly strained contrast between, on the one hand, the historical progress embodied in the practice of medieval Christian monks who wrote their lives of saints over the pagan manuscripts that they had discovered, and, on the other, the historical regression embodied in the process whereby these German literati wrote "their philosophical nonsense under the original French" (CM 255). (This palimpsest image may also have been drawn from Heine, although it is not unknown elsewhere (Prawer 1976, 139, n. 3).) The process of translating this "secular French literature" back into their own traditional philosophical idiom is seen as a distinctive and reactionary one (CM 255). Thus, under the French critique of monetary relations, the true socialists "wrote 'externalisation of the human essence'," and under the French critique of the bourgeois state "they wrote 'transformation of the reign of abstract generality'" (CM 255). Given that Marx's own early writings were not entirely unmarked by this distinctive Teutonic idiom, it is tempting to see some implicit self-criticism here. (In his "Draft Plan for Section III," Marx uses the label "German philosophical socialism" for this movement (CW 6: 576).) In this context, we might note that the intellectual forebears of true socialism include several figures with whom Marx and Engels had recently been intellectually and personally close; most obviously the writer and activist Moses Hess (1812–1875) and the left-Hegelian philosopher Ludwig Feuerbach (1804–1872).

The relocation of French ideas to German circumstances also transformed their political meaning. Simply put, they were "punctiliously emasculated" by this move (CM 255). It is this political transformation which helps explain both the classification of true socialism as a form of reactionary socialism, and the fierceness of Marxian efforts to minimize its influence in the nascent German workers' movement. That original socialist literature presupposed the existence of the economic and political conditions characteristic of "modern bourgeois society," and its political meaning was transformed by this relocation to a country in which the bourgeoisie were only just beginning to struggle against "feudal absolutism" (CM 254). Simply put, what was in France an attack on the bourgeois present functioned in Germany as a defense of the pre-bourgeois present. Marx and Engels insist that to struggle "against the representative state, against bourgeois competition, bourgeois freedom of the press, bourgeois justice, bourgeois freedom and equality" before any of those things exist, is to lend support to the efforts of pre-modern German absolutism to maintain its power (CM 255). In this way, true socialism is seen as encouraging resistance to the very economic and political developments which would – on the Marxian account – make communism possible. Whatever their intentions, the true socialists provide practical succor to "the absolutist regimes in Germany," offering them a "welcome scarecrow" to help frighten off "the rising bourgeoisie" which threatened them (CM 255).

CONSERVATIVE OR BOURGEOIS SOCIALISM

Conservative or bourgeois socialism [*konservative oder Bourgeois-Socialismus*] is sideways-looking. Unlike reactionary socialism, it does not resist or regret the arrival of bourgeois society, but rather attempts to ensure its preservation (to conserve it) by seeking to moderate the "struggles and dangers" that, according to the Marxian account, are a necessary companion to "the living conditions of modern society" (CM 256). Of course, this particular socialism does not always understand itself in these terms, but essentially it would be happy with existing bourgeois society if only certain regrettable "*social grievances*" could be redressed (CM 256; emphasis in original).

This conservative socialism can take a more systematic or a less systematic form. In the more systematic category, we find the French radical Proudhon. In the less systematic category, we find "economists, philanthropists, humanitarians, do-gooders for the working classes, charity organisers, animal welfare enthusiasts, temperance union workers, two-a-penny reformers of multifarious kinds" (CM 256).

Proudhon is now usually thought of as an anarchist, but the idea of anarchism as a systematic competitor to Marxian views had not yet emerged. Marx had very recently attacked the views of Proudhon, whom he knew personally, in his *Misère de la philosophie* [*The Poverty of Philosophy*] (1847). (Marx's title satirically reverses the subtitle of the object of his criticism – namely, Proudhon's *Système des Contradictions Économiques ou Philosophie de la Misère* [*System of Economic Contradictions, or the Philosophy of Poverty*] (1846).) Very roughly, Marx had criticized three threads in Proudhon's work: Proudhon's economic views, especially his ambition to establish a system of free and equal exchange which would somehow avoid the unearned income and inequality of contemporary economic arrangements; his hostility to certain political struggles, not least his rejection of both militant trade union activity and the revolutionary strivings of the proletariat; and his misguided enthusiasm for, and misunderstandings of, German philosophy, in particular his unfortunate predilection for a Hegelian dialectic involving the hypostatization of concepts. The *Manifesto* picks up on the first of those threads and portrays Proudhon as a conservative socialist who seeks to reform rather than overthrow existing society.

In its less systematic and more practical form, conservative socialism also sees bourgeois society, suitably reformed, as in the interests of the working class. It typically seeks to persuade the proletariat that the political changes sought by revolutionary movements will make little difference to them, and that they should seek material changes to their circumstances instead (CM 256). However, the material changes that conservative socialists propose fail to threaten the "bourgeois relations of production," and consist of "administrative reforms" which do little more than reduce the costs to the bourgeoisie of their "political rule" (CM 256). The basic "relationship of capital and wage-labour" is left unchanged by the reforming ambitions of these various advocates of charity and philanthropy (CM 256).

The central Marxian complaint about conservative socialism concerns its inability to grasp that certain failings are the necessary accompaniment to modern bourgeois society. In the "Principles of Communism," Engels describes these socialists as "adherents of present society" who fear that the "evils inseparable from it" threaten its survival (CW 6: 355). As a result, they "endeavor to preserve present society but to remove the evils bound up with it" (CW 6: 355). Some of them propose "measures of mere charity," whilst others offer "grandiose systems of reform," which purport to reorganize present society but end up retaining its "foundations" (CW 6: 355). In either form, the endeavor is futile given the inseparability, on which the Marxian argument insists, of bourgeois society and its attendant miseries.

CRITICAL-UTOPIAN SOCIALISM AND COMMUNISM

Finally, we reach forward-looking (but still non-Marxian) socialisms. In this category we find what the *Manifesto* calls critical-utopian [*kritisch-utopistische*] socialism and communism. These critical utopians are portrayed as the authors of the first "proper" [*eigentlich*] socialist and communist systems, which emerged in the period when the struggle between proletariat and bourgeoisie was only just developing (CM 257). This group includes the famous original triumvirate of utopian socialists: Fourier, Robert Owen (1771–1858) and Saint-Simon. These three form an age cohort, and the mature form of their work appeared at around the same time; namely, on the cusp of the eighteenth and nineteenth centuries. (No utopian communists are identified in the *Manifesto* itself, but in the preface to the 1888 English edition,

Engels named Étienne Cabet (1788–1856) and Wilhelm Weitling (1808–1871) as examples.)

Accounts of the Marxian attitude towards other socialisms often make two erroneous claims: they suggest that Marx and Engels divide socialism into two exhaustive categories, scientific and utopian, as if all socialists had to be one or the other; and they suggest that Marx and Engels are unremittingly hostile to the utopian alternative. The erroneous character of the first of these claims should already be obvious (given the diversity of other socialisms discussed above), but the second claim is also unfounded. Marx and Engels have positive things to say about utopian socialism and communism, as indeed they do about feudal and petty-bourgeois socialisms (see above).

I have argued elsewhere (Leopold 2005) that, in order to make sense of the considered Marxian view of utopian socialism, it is necessary to notice two distinctions at work in the writings of Marx and Engels. The first is a chronological distinction between the original generation of utopians (including Fourier, Owen and Saint-Simon) and the subsequent generations (including assorted followers of that original triumvirate). The second is a textual distinction between the critical dimension of utopian writings, which attacks contemporary bourgeois society, and the constructive dimension of those works, which portrays the ideal society of the future. These two distinctions are important, not least in making sense of the balance of Marxian approval and disapproval of utopian socialism. Simply put, Marx and Engels are more enthusiastic about the first generation of utopians than they are about the subsequent generations, and they are more enthusiastic about the critical than they are about the constructive dimension of utopian writings. This structure can already be discerned in the *Manifesto*'s discussion of utopian socialism.

The chronological distinction, and its associated levels of approval and disapproval, is apparent in the claim that there is an "inverse relationship" between historical development and the significance of utopian socialism (CM 258). We are told that the first generation were "revolutionary in many senses," whereas their disciples – the subsequent generations – have "in every case formed reactionary sects" (CM 258). Note that these subsequent generations are thought to hold broadly the same theoretical and practical views as the first generation (including the mistaken views about the transition to socialism discussed below). However, because they were working in circumstances in which both the proletariat and the material conditions for its emancipation were as yet underdeveloped, this first generation had some historical excuse for those (mistaken) views; that is, they could not in all fairness be blamed for holding them. That historical excuse is not available to their later followers, who operate in very different circumstances, and utopian socialism subsequently "loses all practical worth, all theoretical justification" (CM 258). Indeed, these later generations of utopians can easily degenerate into reactionary or conservative forms of socialism, distinguished only by their "systematic pedantry" and faith in the miraculous effects of their own "social science" [*socialen Wissenschaft*] (CM 257). In this context, Marx and Engels note the opposition of some contemporary utopians to the independent political activity of workers, observing that the "Owenites in England oppose the Chartists" (that is, the movement for democratic political reform organized around the People's Charter of 1838), and that "the Fourierists in France oppose the *réformistes*" (that is, the political tendency organised around the radical-liberal daily *La Réform* (1843–1850)) (CM 259).

The textual distinction, and its associated levels of approval and disapproval, is apparent in the Marxian enthusiasm for the attacks on "the fundamental principles of existing society" to be found in utopian writings, and the contrasting hostility to the "fantastic images of future society" which those works also contain (CM 258). The "critical elements" in utopian writings, although they are not discussed further in the *Manifesto*, are judged to be "very valuable for the enlightenment of the workers" (CM 258). In contrast, their "positive proposals concerning future society" are said to "have a purely utopian import" in that they transcend existing society but only in the imagination; that is, they are utopian in the popular sense that they have no impact on reality (CM 258).

In the *Manifesto*, Marx and Engels do not criticize the *content* of utopian ambitions, which, they note, include: overcoming the divide between "town and country"; transforming the existing "family" and "wage labour"; converting the state into "a mere agency for administering production"; and proclaiming "social harmony" (CM 258). Indeed, it will be apparent that Marx and Engels share not only the utopians' chronological location of socialism in the future, but also many of these social and political objectives, broadly construed. However, Marx and Engels do criticize the utopian socialists for failing to understand the character of historical change, and failing to grasp how these socialist objectives might come about. In particular, the utopians are said to fail to see that historical development is providing the conditions for socialism, and instead seek to substitute for such solutions – that is, those being delivered by the historical process – their own "personally invented forms of action" (CM 257).

On the Marxian account, this is no trivial misunderstanding, and it has serious consequences for the utopians' misguided attitude towards the proletariat and class struggle. The utopian socialists acknowledge the existence of class conflict, but they "discern on the side of the proletariat no historical autonomy, no political movement of its own" (CM 257). That is, the utopians see in the proletariat only "the class that suffers most," and fail to recognize its potential as a collective agent which can change the world (CM 257). In turn, the utopians imagine themselves to stand above "the conflicting classes," and would ideally prefer to appeal to the "whole of society without distinction" (CM 257–258). However, since their communal experiments (see below) require considerable financial support, they usually find themselves having to appeal to "the philanthropy of the bourgeois heart and purse" (CM 258).

The utopian misunderstanding of historical change is also reflected in a misguided attitude towards political action. They are said to reject all political action, especially revolutionary action, in favor of the "power of example," imagining that "small scale experiments" provide a peaceful and effective method of social change (CM 258). The utopians are associated here with what might more accurately be called "communitarian socialism," which identifies intentional communities – that is, small, voluntary settlements of individuals living and working together for some common (religious, moral or political) purpose – as both the means of transition to, and the final institutional form of, socialist society (Leopold 2012). (The links here are more complicated than the *Manifesto* account suggests, since not all utopians are communitarians, and not all communitarians are socialists.) Marx and Engels insist that these "pocket editions of the new Jerusalem" – "individual phalansteries" (Fourier), "home colonies" (Owen) or "a little Icaria" (Cabet) – are all doomed to failure (CM 258). (Marx and Engels are not alone in their linguistic conflation of Fourier's proposed community, properly called a "phalanx," with its central building, the "phalanstery.") In section III Marx and Engels do not elaborate on this tendency for these communitarian experiments to "naturally fail," but elsewhere they suggest that these little islands of socialism are liable, in some way, to be undermined and corrupted by their surrounding non-socialist environment (CM 258). There are few remaining signs in the *Manifesto* of the young Engels's earlier, and short-lived, enthusiasm for communitarian socialism (Leopold 2012).

CONCLUSION

At the beginning of this chapter, the neglect of section III of the *Manifesto* was described as understandable but regrettable. I maintained that the Marxian account of other socialisms was not a uniquely outdated part of the text, and promised to mitigate its opacity by identifying the various non-Marxian socialisms and communisms that are discussed, and by outlining the objections to them contained in the *Manifesto*. Those subsequent exegetical efforts were also intended to lend support to the suggestion that section III is an interesting and integral part of the text. These concluding remarks do not provide a complete account of what is interesting about this discussion of other socialisms, but simply make explicit a few reasons for regretting the neglect that it has often received.

First, section III can be said to confirm and illustrate the striking variety of socialisms in the first half of the nineteenth century. These five particular examples obviously do not exhaust the range critiqued in the *Manifesto*, but they do give some sense of the diversity of non-Marxian socialisms. More generally, the discussion here might be thought to put pressure on a clichéd and inaccurate historical narrative that has proved surprisingly resilient. That implausible narrative portrays a historical development in which a single non-Marxian – usually utopian – socialism prepares the way for, and then more or less gracefully concedes the ground to, its Marxian successor. That narrative has many sources (Marxian, Marxist and other), but it finds little support from this section of the *Manifesto*, in which Marxian socialism exists alongside a variety of contemporary alternatives. Some modern scholars have recently shown interest in these other socialisms, and sought to recover them from the neglect into which they have fallen (Beecher 1986; Pilbeam 2000). More work remains to be done here, but it is already apparent that these other socialisms contain much that is of historical and theoretical interest.

Second, this section of the *Manifesto* challenges a familiar but inaccurate account of the unremitting hostility that Marx and Engels are said to have exhibited towards non-Marxian socialisms. Marx, in particular, is often portrayed as an irascible and ungenerous critic. Yet he was not wholly dismissive of the writings of other socialists, and recognized the value of continuing to read, and engage with, their work (Leopold 2014). In the present case, I have already drawn attention to some positive threads in the Marxian account of other socialisms: feudal socialism is said to provide a "bitter, witty, biting verdict on the bourgeoisie" which strikes them at their "very core" (CM 252); petty-bourgeois socialism is portrayed as having "dissected with great perspicacity" the social problems resulting from modern relations of production (CM 253); and the social criticism of the utopian socialists is described as "very valuable for the enlightenment of the workers" (CM 253). Marx and Engels obviously, and rightly, thought of themselves as opponents of non-Marxian socialism, but their enmity was typically colored by an appreciation of the latter's achievements, as well as its failings. The result is a more even-handed, and more interesting, assessment of alternative socialisms than is often appreciated.

Third, section III illustrates something of its authors' working practices. Marx, in particular, nearly always developed his thoughts through critical engagement with the work of others. It is a striking feature of his own major works that, almost without exception, they originated as critiques of other writers and activists (usually better-known at the time than Marx himself). Consider, for example, his best-known writings before the *Manifesto*: much of *The German Ideology* is an attack on Max Stirner (1806–1856); *Die heilige Familie* [*The Holy Family*] (1845), where some chapters are written by Engels, is largely a polemic against Bruno Bauer (1809–1882); *The Poverty of Philosophy* is a polemical response to Proudhon; and so on. The discussion of other socialisms in the *Manifesto* is part of the same biographical pattern. In short, section III is reflective of, and contributes to, the process of critical engagement with others which was so central to Marx's – and, to a lesser extent, Engels's – intellectual evolution.

Fourth, this section of the *Manifesto* reveals much about the content of Marxian communism. Positively, there are many affinities between these other socialisms and the views of Marx and Engels. Some of these affinities are explicitly acknowledged. For example, Marx and Engels clearly share some of the critique of contemporary society offered by "petty-bourgeois socialism," not least the latter's account of the ways in which contemporary use of machinery, concentration of capital and overproduction have generated disastrous social consequences, including the poverty of the proletariat and "flagrant disparities in the distribution of wealth" (CM 252–254). Other positive affinities are not explicitly acknowledged but seem obvious enough. For example, the Marxian characterization of contemporary bourgeois society as fostering no social bond which is not based on "unfeeling 'hard cash'" (CM 239) clearly echoes the "feudal socialist" complaint that "cash payment" increasingly forms "the one nexus of man to man" (Carlyle 1960, 163). (Marx and Engels were both familiar with Carlyle's *Past and Present*.) Nor are these positive affinities limited to the *criticism* of contemporary bourgeois society. For example, it seems certain that Marx and Engels share many of the *constructive* social and political ambitions of utopian socialism; for instance, overcoming the divide between town and country, reducing the state to a more administrative role and so on. Indeed, one distinguished commentator has claimed that "very nearly everything that Marx and Engels said about the concrete shape of communist society is based on earlier utopian writings" (Hobsbawm 1982, 9). However, it is not only these positive affinities (both critical and constructive) which illuminate the content of Marxian views. Negative complaints about other socialisms can also confirm corresponding but antithetical elements of the Marxian view. For instance, Marx and Engels find fault with other socialisms for their misunderstanding of the historical process (feudal socialism), their rejection of political action (conservative socialism), their understanding of the proletariat (utopian socialism) and so on. From these complaints we can confirm that the communism of Marx and Engels rests on an account of the proletariat as a collective agent which is able, through political and revolutionary action, to bring about the socialist future that historical development is preparing.

Finally, section III confirms and clarifies the strategic ambitions of Marx and Engels in 1848. There is a political dimension to their celebration of the role of the bourgeoisie in destroying the parochial, patriarchal and static world of feudalism. In the German context, Marx and Engels supported the bourgeoisie when, and insofar as, it acted against the interests of absolute monarchy and the feudal landowning class (indeed, they did not merely support the bourgeoisie in these circumstances, but also spurred them on to more radical action). That political strategy helps to explain the hostility directed at true socialism in particular. By opposing "bourgeois competition" and "bourgeois freedom and equality" before any of those things existed in Germany, the true socialists are seen both as helping a pre-modern absolutism to maintain its power, and as resisting the very economic and political developments which would make communism possible (CM 255). Given this assessment, it is scarcely surprising that Marx and Engels should classify true socialism as reactionary, and strive to limit its influence on the nascent German workers' movement. In this way, section III constitutes an important reminder that the *Manifesto* is best understood not as a timeless summary of Marxian arguments, but rather as a political intervention into a particular historical context.

Section III of the *Manifesto* may present certain difficulties for those unfamiliar with the non-Marxian socialisms that Marx and Engels discuss, but these hurdles are not so hard to overcome. Tracing the details of their discussion mitigates many of the difficulties facing modern readers, and helps to elucidate why those efforts might be worth making. Not least, the account of other socialisms that Marx and Engels provide can be seen to illuminate: the intriguing variety of nineteenth-century socialism and communism; the authors' own characteristic way of working through critical engagement with others; the authors' not ungenerous critical engagement with certain non-Marxian socialisms; some constituent threads in the authors' own Marxian views; and aspects of their immediate political strategy in 1848. The conclusion seems irresistible: section III is an integral and interesting part of the *Manifesto*, which deserves much greater attention than it has typically received.

REFERENCES

Beecher, Jonathan. 1986. *Charles Fourier. The Visionary and His World*. Berkeley, CA: University of California Press.
Carlyle, Thomas. 1960 [1843]. *Past and Present*. Introduced by Douglas Jerrold. London: J.M. Dent.
Grandjonc, Jacques. 1989. *Communisme/Kommunismus/Communism. Origine et développement international de la terminologie communautaire pré-marxiste des utopistes aux néo-babouvistes 1785–1842, vol. 1: Historique, vol. 2: Pièces justificatives*. Trier: Karl Marx Haus.
Heine, Heinrich. 1982 [1844]. *The Complete Poems of Heinrich Heine. A Modern English Version by Hal Draper*. Boston: Suhrkamp/Insel.
Hobsbawm, Eric J. 1982. "Marx, Engels and Pre-Marxian Socialism." In *The History of Socialism, vol. 1: Marxism in Marx's Day*, ed. Eric J. Hobsbawm. Bloomington, IN: Indiana University Press, 1–28.
Leopold, David. 2005. "The Structure of Marx and Engels' Considered Account of Utopian Socialism." *History of Political Thought*. 26(3): 443–466.
Leopold, David. 2007. *The Young Karl Marx: German Philosophy, Modern Politics, and Human Flourishing*. Cambridge: Cambridge University Press.
Leopold, David. 2012. "'Socialist Turnips': The Young Friedrich Engels and the Feasibility of Communism." *Political Theory*. 40(3): 347–378.
Leopold, David. 2014. "Marx and British Socialism." In *The Oxford Handbook of Nineteenth Century British Philosophy*, ed. William Mander. Oxford: Oxford University Press, 402–422.
McKay, Iain. 2011. "Introduction." In *Property Is Theft! A Pierre-Joseph Proudhon Anthology*, ed. Iain McKay. Oakland, CA: AK Press, 1–82.
Pilbeam, Pamela. 2000. *French Socialists before Marx: Workers, Women and the Social Question in France*. Teddington: Acumen.
Prawer, S. S. 1976. *Karl Marx and World Literature*. Oxford: Clarendon Press.

Rigakos, George S. Ed. 2010. Karl Marx and Friedrich Engels, *The Communist Manifesto Illustrated*, ch 1: *Historical Materialism*. Introduced and re-imagined by George S. Rigakos, illustrated by Red Viktor. Ottowa: Red Quill Books.

Jones, Gareth Stedman. 2004. *An End to Poverty? A Historical Debate*. London: Profile Books.

WORKS CONSULTED

Andréas, Bert. 1963. *Le Manifeste Communiste de Marx et Engels. Histoire et Bibliographie 1848–1918*. Milan: Feltrinelli.

Cole, G. D. H. 1955. *A History of Socialist Thought, vol. 1: The Forerunners 1789–1850*. London: Macmillan.

Draper, Hal. 1998. *The Adventures of the Communist Manifesto*. Berkeley, CA: Center for Socialist History.

Kuczynski, Thomas. Ed. 1995. Karl Marx and Friedrich Engels, *Das kommunistische Manifest (Manifest der kommunistischen Partei) von Karl Marx und Friedrich Engels: Von der Erstausgabe zur Leseausgabe*. Trier: Schriften aus den Karl-Marx-Haus.

3

The Rhetoric of the *Manifesto*

James Martin

The *Communist Manifesto*, by definition, is a polemical treatise. The word polemic stems from the Greek *polemikos*, meaning "war," and the *Manifesto* presents itself, accordingly, as the exposé of a "more or less hidden civil war" between social classes, and exhorts its readers to take sides with the participant whose interests it promotes (CM 245). These features of the text are sufficient to remind us that Marx and Engels are engaged in a distinctively rhetorical exercise. Their task in the *Manifesto* is to supply arguments that define the prevailing situation and, thereby, to persuade their audience to adopt and uphold a position in relation to it. The text achieves this by a combination of arguments that narrate a story, populate that story with characters, identify and explain its central dramatic conflict, ridicule opponents, deliberate over alternative strategies and, finally, exhort a rallying call to arms. The *Manifesto* is not just a treatise *on* politics; its arguments *are* its politics.

In this chapter, I examine the rhetorical dimensions of the *Manifesto*. That involves thinking about the text as an assemblage of argumentative strategies designed to capture its audience's attention, reason with them about the current circumstances and orient their allegiance to a specific cause. Here rhetoric is understood not merely as the formal or literary aspects of discourse, but, more expansively, as an effort to intervene in a situation in order to shift people's perceptions and adjust their actions (see Martin 2015). In the *Manifesto*, Marx and Engels accomplish this through a variety of rhetorical strategies; in particular, by appeals to reason (*logos*) and to character (*ethos*). Together these appeals fashion a combative, ironic style that privileges the text's distinctive stance and casts its reasoning in an unabashed, partisan light. Here the *Communist Manifesto* follows many of the generic conventions of the manifesto format that emerged from the French revolution: articulating an impatient rage by refusing conciliation with the present order. Its distinctive rhetoric supplies the text with an intellectual depth and creative verve that, although occasioned by a particular set of circumstances, have allowed it to speak beyond its original setting. Indeed, the *Manifesto* has become itself a "rhetoric," in the sense of a sourcebook of repeatable argumentative *topoi* and aphorisms available for application elsewhere. If that is a sign of its historical success as a text, it is nonetheless also a weakness. The rhetoric of the *Manifesto* exhibits a highly motivated sense of its own authority and a singular clarity of purpose that, for Marxists, has been difficult to square with other theoretical and organizational commitments.

RHETORIC AS POLITICAL ACTION

Let us begin by asking what it means to talk of rhetoric as a type of political action. As the name for the ancient art of speech and persuasion, in recent centuries rhetoric has been dismissed as the practice of deceit and manipulation, that is, as language fashioned simply to lure people into believing something their reason would caution them against. Indeed, the dismissal of rhetoric has a long history in political thought (see Garsten 2006), but ancient scholars did not understand rhetoric that way. For them, it was the central skill in civic life. Certainly it could involve manipulation and often deceit, but only because that is a feature of all human association. In fact, most respected rhetoricians (such as Aristotle or Cicero) recommended telling the truth and using words to illuminate rather than obscure matters. What they also accepted, however, was that the truth was never easy to find in all cases, especially in politics or law. Most political and legal disputes do not admit to a single, absolutely final resolution. There are usually different sides to a debate and other ways of explaining apparent wrongdoing or law breaking. At such moments, it may be necessary to deliberate over the advantages and disadvantages of a policy or allow opposed parties to set out their cases. Civic life in ancient Greece and Rome was uniquely organized around public platforms that offered opportunities for disagreements to unfold, where citizens could debate the common good and permit others to shape their judgments through rousing oratory and artful dispute (on key features of ancient rhetoric, see Habinek 2005).

To be a citizen in classical Greece and Rome was to be prepared not only to fight for one's community but also to participate in public debates, citizen juries or political assemblies by listening and arguing. That required access to a rhetorical education, or at very least handy instruction, comprised of the various techniques of argument. Citizens were taught how to select the right kind of appeal for the issue and for the occasion, how to arrange speech in a coherent way, elements of style including figures and tropes, advice for the best delivery and techniques to memorize their case. Rhetoricians taught how to argue from both sides (*in umtramque partem*) so as to be prepared to refute an opponent's case, how to utilize "commonplaces" (that is, commonly agreed values and sayings) to make an argument seem reasonable, how to adapt to the audience's expectation (*decorum*) and so on (on the classical techniques and categories of rhetorical instruction, see Martin 2014, esp. chs 4–5).

From a contemporary perspective, rhetoric can be understood as a form of "situated speech." That is, it is a means to present an argument by deliberately crafting it for a specific issue, audience and occasion. The techniques and devices of ancient rhetorical instruction describe different maneuvers to help shape an audience's judgment. To bring the audience to a preferred conclusion speakers adopt strategies (i.e. they calculate in advance which steps to follow) that, at least in part, adjust the argument to prevailing expectations and values. That way the audience hears something it recognizes, something that speaks to its preconceptions about the situation it faces. But the argument usually has to transform the audience's judgments, not simply affirm their prejudices, by demonstrating through its own reasoning that the situation should be conceived one way rather than another. In this respect, the speaker (or *rhetor*) has to find a creative way to re-situate the issue such that it conforms to her preferred conclusions. That typically involves a creative but also selective redescription of events so as to enhance certain aspects over others, foregrounding some qualities of the issue or ascribing motivations to behavior, in order to constrain the kind of judgment that audiences will make. The numerous techniques of rhetoric are therefore designed for the purposes of appropriating a situation such that an audience will judge it from the stance offered by the speaker.

I mention these aspects of rhetoric partly because I will use them to discuss the content of the *Manifesto* but also because this way of fashioning arguments for the purposes of making political interventions was familiar to Marx and Engels. Brought up in conservative and authoritarian Prussia, neither was a stranger to controversy or the potential danger of speaking out of turn. Indeed, they rather thrived on courting public criticism. Both were heirs to a classical understanding of politics that informed educated elites in Europe, if only as a throwback to a bygone era. Each had received a classical education from the *Gymnasium*, which involved learning Greek and Latin (Sperber 2013, 25–26; Carver 1989, 6). As a doctoral student, Marx, in particular, was very familiar with the philosophers and writers of ancient Greece. Writing to his father on 10 November 1837 the young Marx even claimed to have "translated in part Aristotle's *Rhetoric*" (CW 1: 19). In the 1840s he and Engels spent much of their time writing essays, debating and giving speeches to radical groups and workingmen's associations. Marx, however, is reported to have been a poor public orator, difficult to understand because of his Rhenish accent and lisp (Sperber 2013, 105; on Marx's and Engels's speech-giving, see Carver 1983, 61–62). More importantly, the two were heirs to a distinct variety of rhetorical practice based around journalism, the circulation of subversive philosophical arguments, correspondence networks and the printing of declamatory pamphlets and manifestos. These had been central to the literature of the French revolution of 1789 and were a recognized part of radical politics by the 1840s. Unlike classical oratory, with its orientation towards sustaining civic order, the press enabled swift and widespread dissemination of controversial ideas and arguments, often anonymously and explicitly at odds with communal authorities. As Janet Lyon argues, manifestos in particular comprise a distinctly *modern* rhetorical genre, oriented to imagining an improved future by announcing the incompleteness of the present (Lyon 1999, 9–45). Unlike the petition, which appeals for recognition by an accepted order, the manifesto proclaims the intrinsic unacceptability of that order. Opposing the assumed universality of dominant values, manifestos adopt a self-consciously provocative attitude to the present, acknowledging the modern view that society can be remade. But they announce this sense of incompletion with a view, ultimately, to fulfilling the unachieved promise of universal inclusion. As such, manifestos – political or artistic – mark out a distinct argumentative position for an excluded group or perspective to present *itself* as the prefiguration of a more complete society to come.

As radical intellectuals and journalists, typical heirs to French revolutionary ideals, Marx and Engels by 1848 were already masters of the neat turn of phrase, summary argument and detailed technical narration, as well as the biting, critical epithet and the philosophical insult. Engels's capacity for detailed reportage was demonstrated in his *The Condition of the Working Class in England*, and Marx's notorious *ad hominem* attacks, merciless sarcasm and relentless philosophical criticism were regularly exercised in, for example, his essays on the young Hegelians and in his lengthy attack of 1847 on Proudhon entitled *The Poverty of Philosophy* (on Marx's sarcasm, see Carver 2010, 102–118). The latter texts were crafted for a rather restricted audience of radical philosophers, and their style is often convoluted and abstract, reflecting in part the difficulty of doing political dissent in public. Yet their underlying practical orientation to radical social and political reform was never far from the surface. Marx's experience in the early 1840s as editor of the *Rheinische Zeitung* prepared him for a wider, less specialized public. By the time they were invited in 1847, as members of the Communist League, to write the *Manifesto*, Marx and Engels were leading radical intellectuals and experienced in writing for audiences, fashioning arguments to get around (and often to challenge) the censor, and mobilizing evidence to fit the cases they made.

Marx and Engels were rhetorically gifted but they had something of a rhetorical agenda of their own, too. That is to say, by 1848 they already had a particular argument to make and a desire to make it in a distinctive way. Their agenda had philosophical and practical dimensions – though both were closely interlinked – and their combination supplies the basic thrust to the *Manifesto*. Their philosophical stance was a self-proclaimed "new" materialism and entailed a set of arguments that, they believed, distinguished them sharply from other philosophical radicals, professed socialists and political reformers, and laid the basis for a revolutionary politics based on the distinct interests of the working classes. The contents of these arguments are well known and were set out, but not published, in the manuscripts that later came to be posthumously known as *The German Ideology*. The essential claim there was that the social structure of property relations supplies the vital preconditions shaping all other social institutions and forms of consciousness: "what individuals are depends on the material conditions of their production" (CW 5: 32). Depending on how one sees it, that claim might be regarded as a causal account of how societies necessarily evolve in history, or, less rigidly, as identifying the broad social mechanisms that have shaped the emergence of capitalist societies. What is clear, however, is that the claim has a rhetorical function that Marx and Engels continued to promote as a point of principle. Marx and Engels's outlook was never simply a statement of revealed fact but an argumentative strategy that purposefully foregrounded the substitution of one way of thinking with another. Although there was more to it, the argument was elegantly expressed in the summary form of *antimetabole* (the reversal of word order in successive phrases): "It is not consciousness that determines life, but life that determines consciousness" (CW 5: 37). The assertion of the primacy of property relations in social organization overturned the self-conception of bourgeois radicals as the organizing conscience of reform, whether as prophets, poets or self-organizing architects of human emancipation. In one fell swoop, Marx and Engels dismissed philosophical idealists, sentimental reformers and utopian experimenters as ludicrous self-indulgent dreamers who preferred above all to reason from fanciful concepts and feelings – what Sperber calls "lifestyle-based radicalism" (Sperber 2013, 162).[1] With epistemological privilege given to the class structure of property relations, Marx and Engels asserted that it simply makes no sense to speak from any other position. A genuinely radical argument had to reflect the underlying logic of a rigorously examined social structure. To do otherwise was to accommodate the iniquitous conditions that gave rise to demands for reform in the first place. This was certainly an appeal to *wissenschaftlich* reason (with its disdain for logical inconsistency and contradiction), but it was also an audacious assertion about what it meant to reason properly. Rational comprehension, claimed Marx and Engels, must begin with the real circumstances and relationships of everyday life, not the purity of concepts isolated from social struggles for power. Any kind of reasoning that launched its mission from abstract notions of human essence betrayed its origins in a deliberation over "the material conditions of life" (CW 5: 31).[2] It resulted simply in "combating *phrases*" and not "the actually existing world" (CW 5: 30). Such a claim may now seem banal, at least to some, but at the time it required a substantial shift of emphasis. For thought to remain true to its origins, as philosophers often argued, now meant transferring the debate from the comforting region of lofty ideals and abstract concepts to the historically contingent and concrete categories of property relations. In short, Marx and Engels thought they had found new argumentative grounds for revolutionary critique, grounds that addressed directly an urgent political problem.

In practical terms, Marx and Engels wanted their socialism to guide the political movements for reform emerging in the mid-1840s around the working classes in Europe. For them, a communist movement, one that reasoned from an analysis of property relations and not sentiments, was different from all existing

types of socialism in identifying the proletariat as the agent of historical transformation. The working classes were not mere supplements to change, a mere
ragbag of the poor, laborers and artisans who may or may not take part in
major social transformation; as the linchpin of the whole system of capitalist
property relations they were the only constituency in whose collective name –
the proletariat – revolution could seriously be undertaken. This explicit identification of an agent with revolutionary interests had important implications for
how to do socialist politics. Marx and Engels rejected the clandestine model of
agitation they had hitherto accommodated: communism was to be an out-in-
the-open movement calling for the abolition of private property relations, not a
secret society servicing primarily its members. Communists were to make their
revolutionary intentions clear to the world. Moreover, theirs was a long-term
project to unify different groups and organizations across national barriers.
That meant embracing a degree of diversity and building coalitions with different types of radicals and different struggles. The point was to promote their
arguments by joining with others, not withdraw into doctrinaire isolation. At
the same time, both were eager to ensure that their own movement (the
Communist League) remained clear in its objectives and distinct from other
kinds of socialist organizations. That, of course, was controversial for those
members who continued to be attached to the sentimental socialism that Marx
and Engels dismissed. Equally, other individuals and groups were competing to
lead the struggle for radical reform and to shape the broad movement of
opposition to autocracy and reaction that had been simmering for years.
Marx and Engels were eager to privilege the voice of their movement as the
herald of a crisis that many already felt was about to explode.

These rhetorical preoccupations, then, were brought to the writing of the
Manifesto and are central to its strategy of argumentation. They indicate what
Marx and Engels had come to believe radicals should be arguing about and
how. Despite having dismissed abstract ideas and pure consciousness as the
philosophical starting point for reasoning about historical change, they
clearly recognized the vital importance of argument as a tool of political
action. The *Manifesto* thus sets out to define the situation from the stance of
a critical socialism that Marx and Engels felt was uniquely their own and uses
this as a platform to define "the party of communists" as a genuine movement
for promoting revolutionary politics. Let us now examine the techniques used
to accomplish this.

RHETORIC IN THE MANIFESTO

The *Manifesto* is replete with rhetorical devices, some of which had already
been employed either by Marx or Engels in earlier texts. The famous closing
exhortation, for example – "*Proletarians of all countries unite!*" (CM 260;
emphasis in original) – was the motto Engels gave to the newly formed
Communist League in 1847 (Nicolaievsky and Maenchen-Helfen, 1976, 133).

As is well known, much of its historical account of the bourgeoisie was taken from Engels's earlier journalism.[3] This recycling of phrases and narratives is common in political rhetoric and reflects the way many texts are assembled quickly and with a content that is deemed already fit for purpose. Indeed, far from being fundamentally unique, the *Manifesto* follows many of the rhetorical conventions noted by Lyon: above all, a hortatory, insistent technique that proclaims its view of the world with a sense of urgency and transparency. The arguments of the text are in part fashioned to match this format, which connects it to a longer tradition of manifesto-like interventions in the modern era, and also to give it a distinctive twist.

How should we examine rhetoric in the text of the *Manifesto*? As I suggested above, the classical structure of classifications and categories in rhetorical instruction provides a useful guide for drawing out distinctive elements of an argumentative strategy. That involves noting the first three of the five canons of rhetoric, often known by their Latin names: its choices of argumentative appeal (*inventio*); the arrangement of the parts of the discourse (*dispositio*); and the stylistic qualities of its language (*elocutio*). Let us look at each aspect in turn.

What is the argument of the *Manifesto*? Of what is it trying to persuade its audience? As a political manifesto, the overt purpose of the text, as it says itself, is to "lay before the world" the "perspectives," "goals" and "principles" of communists (CM 237). In that respect, it is also a document designed to clarify and affirm the identity of the League. Instead of producing a customary list of claims and demands, Marx and Engels opted for a discursive style that set the scene and elaborated the case for their new outlook, permitting the text to adopt an ironic voice that scorns at the same time as it informs. There are, then, a number of argumentative appeals interwoven in the *Manifesto*. According to classical rhetoric, political speech concerns the best course of action for the future. That is what the *Manifesto* aims at in promoting revolution; communists, it claims explicitly towards the end, "represent the future" (CM 259). In this, it is *logos*, or rational argument, that is the primary mode of appeal. The *Manifesto* famously offers up reasons why revolution is unavoidable and why the proletariat constitutes a distinct class whose interests ultimately lie in disposing of bourgeois society and abolishing private property. But the text is not merely a dry account of social theory or abstract political principle. Rational argument is bound up with a constant and combative assertion of the text's superiority as a perspective on ideas and events. "Communism," it asserts on its first page, "is already recognised as a force by all the European powers" (CM 237). Rather than fear us, it implies, look at things from our point of view. This notion of communism as an "already recognised ... force" (CM 237), an advance guard that sees what others fear, initiates a simultaneous appeal to character, or *ethos*, that, as we shall see, returns throughout the text.

It might be helpful to look at these combined appeals in terms of their *topoi*, or "topics." The topics were common formulae for argumentation that classical rhetoricians often listed thematically so that an appropriate argument could be selected for the occasion. An appropriate argument, for example, in a legal controversy may concern whether something happened that contravened the law (topic of evidence), what precisely it was that happened (topic of definition) or how the event is to be accounted for (topic of motive) (Corbett and Connors 1999, 124–126). Stemming from the Greek word *topos*, meaning place, the argument lets its object be seen as a particular type of issue and this choice serves as a privileged place from which an audience can perceive the situation. The argumentative topic therefore re-situates the events and issues in question and, depending on how they are disclosed, constrains the audience's perception of and orientation towards them.

The appeal in the *Manifesto* to reason begins by interweaving topics of definition (what something is) with topics of cause and effect (how something comes about) so as to situate the present circumstances in a specific way. Thus the text locates communism in the space of history defined by perpetual forms of class struggle, culminating in "modern bourgeois society." The latter society is defined by the causal agency of the bourgeoisie, itself "the product of a long process of development," which constantly acts to make things happen: gaining political control over the state, severing "the motley bonds of feudalism," resolving "personal worth into exchange-value," "continually revolutionising the instruments of production" and so on (CM 238–241). Social classes clashing and transforming conditions in order to sustain and expand their material interests, then, define history's trajectory – an account that is Eurocentric and also privileges one reading of the French revolution. By analogy, the process continues with a further causal effect: the workers, "produced" by the bourgeoisie, whom the *Manifesto* anticipates will, in turn, develop their own common interests and transform bourgeois society (CM 241). In this they are assisted by the degradation of wage-labor – its material decline, not its advance, as with the bourgeoisie – that compels it to adopt a polarized position against the bourgeoisie and upturn the entire, exploitative order (CM 245–246).

Thus the reasoning of the first section of the *Manifesto* defines the present situation as one phase in a wider, unfolding historical drama between classes. This sketch of a dynamic historical movement, with its apparent chains of cause and effect, antecedent and consequence, describes the situation as one of inexorable but ultimately intelligible conflict, rather than as a series of mere accidents or unaccountable disruptions to an otherwise harmonious world. Moreover, conflict is treated as an offshoot of fundamental material interests, bringing about collective agents with their own purposes and, in a sense, personalities. This is where the appeal to *ethos* becomes evident. The account given of the development of the bourgeoisie is not just descriptive; it is normative, too. It identifies an opponent worthy of emulation. Although they avoid moralizing, Marx and Engels present the bourgeoisie as a relentless, rapacious agent of change, cynically divesting the world of all residues of sentiment and custom in its quest to expand markets and secure its profits. This is surely the unsentimental and merciless pursuit of class interest they implicitly recommend for advocates of proletarian revolution. By clarifying the character of bourgeois ascendency, the *Manifesto* offers up a template for how powerfully destructive a social class can be.

That is precisely the thrust of section II, in which Marx and Engels shift their focus to the relationship of proletarians to communists. The topic remains one of definition, but, having established the premise of history as class struggle, the text indicates how communism amplifies the revolutionary interests of the proletariat. It begins negatively by saying what communism is not, its alignment being with "the common interests of the whole proletariat" and not any specific wing, and it goes on to link that interest with "the overthrow of bourgeois rule," an echo of the bourgeoisie's development. The distinctive demand of the communists, it points out, is "the transformation of private property" (CM 247–248) which it then explains as a social structure of wage-labor and capital. Here Marx and Engels give a reasoned account of the exploitative nature of capitalism. But having already declared its allegiance to the proletariat, the narrative takes on a partisan character, not unlike a legal defense in court. Notably, for example, the text turns and provocatively addresses its readers as if *they* were the bourgeoisie. Invoking questions and imagining both accusations and responses, the text deliberates with its imagined readers by mimicry and irony:

It horrifies you that we wish to transform private property. But in your existing society private property has been transformed for nine-tenths of its members; it exists precisely in that it does not exist for nine-tenths. You reproach us for wanting to transform a type of property which presupposes the propertyless of the vast majority of society as a necessary condition. (CM 247–248)

Section II continues by repudiating bourgeois conceits and the wholesome notions – freedom, the family, marriage, nationhood – that serve as objections to communist aims. The strategy here is to undermine potential criticisms of communism by demonstrating the invalidity of their objections, partly by virtue of their limited extension to all cases (hence not universal) and partly by dismissing all purportedly "eternal truths" that fail to reason from the premise of class conflict (CM 250). All such "forms of consciousness," it announces confidently, will "finally vanish only with the total disappearance of class conflict" (CM 251). Again, the focus is on exposing commonplace ideas and arguments that might soften socialist politics. "Bourgeois phrases" are thus ridiculed and dismissed from the elevated position of a communist outlook that nonetheless stoops to enumerate and disavow them: "The communist revolution is the most radical break with traditional property relations, so it is no wonder that in its process of development there occurs the most radical break with traditional ideas" (CM 251).

For a text that asserts the self-evidence of its outlook, it is noticeable that the majority of its pages are given over not to demonstrating theoretical claims but to distinguishing its position from others. Having dismantled the phrases of the bourgeoisie, the final sections go on to clarify further where it departs from other "socialist and communist literature" (section III) and other "opposition parties" (section IV). This tallies with the political function of the text – which has a practical aim to define and separate off the communist position from others – rather than a work of political philosophy aimed at conciliating different points of view. It underscores my claim that *ethos*, as well as *logos*, is a driving appeal in its argument – the topics of cause and effect serve to enhance the authority of the text's voice, its intransigent stance in opposition to the present situation. But it also means that rational argumentation is inextricably linked to a normative orientation in its rhetoric in order to foreground and amplify the position of communists as the privileged voice of a historical process. That can make the view of history in the *Manifesto* seem crudely teleological, especially if we try to read it exclusively as a rational argument. But if we view the argument as a strategy appealing to both reason and character, then its science functions not simply as a description of facts but also as a rhetorical platform erected to sustain an enduring struggle against bourgeois property relations. As Lyon argues, in the manifesto genre, history "functions more like myth than like empirical historiography" (Lyon 1999, 15). The force of a historical narrative lies principally in underscoring the rupture it seeks with the present. This requires a combative approach that can take various forms and make alliances with numerous different groups, but, because communism is rooted in none of these alliances as such, it is conceivably prepared to abandon them when they "dull the class struggle" and "ameliorate conflict" (CM 258).

The arrangement of the argument in the *Manifesto* also mirrors the underlying appeal to *ethos* that gives it its thrust. Arrangement concerns the assemblage of successive segments of a discourse in a particular order and according to a conception of what needs to be said (or not) and when. In classical oratory, speech was divided into various parts, such as the introduction (*exordium*), the narration of facts (*narratio*), the division (*divisio*), the setting out of proofs (*confirmatio*), rejection of counterarguments (*refutio*) and, finally, the conclusion (*peroratio*). Which of these needed to be included or amplified depended on the occasion and the prevailing genre conventions.

As a printed document, the *Manifesto* differs from live speech in that it has to win the attention of its audience in its first pages and sustain its momentum throughout. Moreover, as a distinctly modern genre, its structure enacts the type of intervention in space and time that it wants its audience to undertake. It narrates the present as a crisis moment that portends a fundamental breach with history and a refashioning of the future (Lyon 1999). That requires readers to know, in broad outline, what the situation is and how they are implicated in it. Thus the brief introduction reaches for its audience's attention by presenting communism as an object of irrational fear (pursued in a "witchhunt") whose identity demands explanation (CM 237). Section I then narrates the facts, as the authors see them, that bring communism into being. This is a narration that also presents its proofs in the form of aphoristic assertions concerning the historical emergence of modern society. As we have seen, section II then functions as a series of refutations of counterarguments that defines the communists by their hostility to bourgeois society, culminating in a ten-point list of practical demands. Section III continues this distinction-by-refutation in relation to other forms of socialism and communism. Finally, section IV concludes by widening its perspective and indicating the presence of different communist struggles throughout Europe, ending its peroration with a rallying cry to unify proletarians. This overall structure offers a disciplined order of exposition that differs markedly from Marx's often complex and unwieldy philosophical essays. At each step, readers are given something useful: a positive starting point, a simple key to interpret events, definitions of political terms, principles and practical measures, conceptual discriminations from other movements and affirmative phrases to repeat. Rather than relentless nitpicking criticism of theories and individuals, the *Manifesto* arrangement addresses simple issues such as "who are we," "what do we believe" and "what do we want"?

Finally, we turn to the style of the language Marx and Engels use, which is notable for its accessibility and economy. As Lyon reminds us, the manifesto genre typically eschews ornament in favor of clarity and transparency. In the manifestos and pamphlets of the French Revolution, for example, rhetorical complexity was associated with secrecy and intellectual language with the codes of exclusive groups at odds with the aims of the revolution. The manifesto genre, on the other hand, puts a value on speech that incites action, not deep reflection or deliberation (Lyon 1999, 13–14). In the *Manifesto*, that objective coincides with its general purpose to present and clarify communist principles but also its refusal to get caught up in terminological debates and questions of nuance. The hortatory style goes straight to the point: it means what it says; it "fosters antagonism and scorns conciliation. It is univocal, unilateral, single-minded. It conveys resolute oppositionality and indulges no tolerance for the fainthearted" (Lyon 1999, 9). The text therefore lacks the misty abstraction of other texts by the authors. But it is no less stylistically impressive for this. Indeed, it is filled to the brim with rhetorical schemes and tropes that dramatize its message, as well as make it memorable. Where schemes work on the phrasing of sentences, tropes (or figures) deploy words and concepts in distinctive ways. Let us a look at a number of these.

The *Manifesto* exhibits much of the "paratactical" style of syntax common to many texts in the genre. *Parataxis* describes the placing of sentences or phrases side by side with no conjunctions; an abrupt, unmediated language where claim follows claim with few subordinate clauses or qualifying digressions (Lyon 1999, 15). Throughout the *Manifesto* we see this scheme employed variously: in sentence-length paragraphs describing the situation (see CM 237); in defining the distinctive features of communists (see CM 246–251); and in listing their demands (see CM 251). In the first part of the *Manifesto* in particular, the scheme is combined with a sweeping narration that recounts the repetition of property divisions and their transformation through class struggles. The swift movement of history up to the present thus follows the uncomplicated flow of language itself, permitting not only a magisterial gaze across the panorama of class struggles (with all its stops and starts) but also a simplified story of one class evolving its interests against other classes. That use of *antithesis* – oppositional categories – represents, of course, the central antagonism to which Marx and Engels wish to draw attention. It is also the key binary that drives their account of the inexorable character of revolution, which cannot therefore be resolved within the framework of the bourgeois order. Thus *antithesis* is presented, not simply as an assertion of class against class but, more instructively, in the citation of numerous contradictions and inversions that demonstrate the impossibility of reconciliation. For example, in comparing wage-labor in bourgeois and communist society, they argue:

In bourgeois society living labour is merely a means to increase accumulated labour. In communist society accumulated labour is but a means to broaden, to enrich, to promote the whole way of life of the worker.

Therefore in bourgeois society the past rules over the present, and in communist society the present over the past. In capitalist society it is capital that is independent and personalised, while the living individual is dependent and depersonalised. (CM 247)

These elaborate examples of *chiasmus* (or *antimetabole*) reverse the terms of the first phrase, making what is a solution for the first into a problem in the second (e.g. in the first paragraph "increased labor" is a solution/goal made into problem/means). This logic of inversion not only demonstrates a balanced opposition (between bourgeois and communist societies) but also unleashes an internal dynamic that seeks to exhaust the terms of conflict between one thing and another, permitting no middle ground (Lanham 1991, 33). Marx and Engels repeatedly deploy this technique in order to undercut the bourgeoisie's apparent advances and solutions, to expose their contradictions and invite the demand for further resolution. This ties in with Lyon's view that the manifesto genre functions primarily to expose the inadequate universalism of one outlook and to invite its future fulfillment by other means.

Similar techniques are at work in the figures deployed in the *Manifesto*, which frequently offers up images of transient objects and qualities. From specters and witchhunts (CM 237) to sorcerers (CM 241) and workers "enslaved by the machine" (CM 242) who then become capitalism's gravediggers (CM 246), the *Manifesto* displays an array of Gothic images and spectral figures in order to amplify its dramatization of the tantalizingly "hidden civil war" between the classes (CM 245).[4] Often things are not quite, or are more than, they seem. Moreover, some things magically change into other things: in the transition to capitalism, feudal society "goes up in smoke" (CM 239), expansive "universal commerce" substitutes for narrow "national self-sufficiency" (CM 240), means of production transform into "fetters"; in capitalism proper, bourgeois property relations become "too narrow" for the forces they unleash (CM 241), and workers metamorphose from commodities in a market to enemies of older classes, and then into a coalition against the bourgeoisie, a class and, finally, a party (CM 242–244). In their explosiveness and destructiveness, these transformations are more unpredictably alchemical than intelligible sequences in a predetermined causal chain. In the figurative depiction presented by the *Manifesto*, the evolution through capitalism does not follow a foreseeable order but is the consequence of unstable compounds in an experiment whose elements expand and react against each other and then burst out of all control.

These figurations of class and societal change underscore the story in the *Manifesto* of breathless change and perpetual upheaval. They serve to produce a sense of the present as a moment of transition, the culmination of a series of explosions set to erupt once more. In this, the *Manifesto* veers towards what classical rhetoricians viewed as the purpose of "epideictic" discourse – the ceremonial orientation to common feelings in the present that joins the community together. But rather than a commemoration (such as a speech after a major battle), this modern form of the genre looks to the future as the locus of communal fulfillment. The present is defined by its excessive instability, the incapacity of property relations to contain the powerful forces its combines. Thus the *Manifesto* configures a new source of a public unity in the form of the proletariat. This class is a complex metaphor for the variety of workers, their families and supporters, rather than a strict sociological category. It is a class born from bourgeois society but not reducible to it. Here the *Manifesto* follows the genre by invoking what Lyon calls a "transitional identity," a projected subject of unfulfilled universal demands rather than an empirical subject, with which its readers can identify (Lyon 1999, 34–39).

A survey of the main rhetorical features of the *Manifesto* demonstrates the view, noted at the start, that its arguments are its politics. Of course, we can still read it as a (partial) summation of Marx and Engels's theoretical views, a moment in the evolution of their ideas about capitalism. But to do so would be to lose sense of the strategies it mobilizes as a distinctive iteration of the manifesto genre in relation to a particular situation. To read it as a form of rhetorical intervention highlights the ways the text seeks to appropriate the circumstances into which it intervenes by enacting argumentatively its own take on events. Undoubtedly that involves reasoned argument in order to describe the circumstances, clarify their underlying logics and propose and defend a revolutionary response to them. But rational explanation (the appeal to *logos*) is here closely interwoven with – at times subordinate to – a polemical intent to performatively stake out an authoritative, critical attitude (the appeal to *ethos*). In revolutionary conditions, perhaps this is about all one can really expect when numerous groups are struggling to define and guide events. From the perspective of its rhetoric, the *Manifesto* is less a report on events and more an argumentative foothold that its readers occupy simply by reading it in order to turn events in a particular direction. It offers them vivid phrases and strikingly posed aphorisms, dramatic contrasts and (apparently) reasoned arguments and narratives to apply again and again, all enveloped in a sneering, oppositional attitude that implies its own superior stance.

THE MANIFESTO AS A RHETORIC

Like all manifestos, the *Communist Manifesto* was written to supply its readers and supporters with arguments, definitions and a general understanding that could be taken into new contexts. In this respect, it serves not simply as an instance of a rhetorical genre but, moreover, as a unique rhetorical resource in itself. A handbook for popular digestion rather than theoretical analysis, the *Manifesto* is itself a rhetoric with a content iterable for the purposes of political education and struggle. Though it may have been written with a particular situation in mind, its format nonetheless permits it to extend a politics that lies outside the immediate purview of its authors. Such, of course, is the way with many popular treatises in the history of political thought. Yet, as the numerous disputes over the meanings of, and methods to understand, historical texts demonstrate, this is not an uncontroversial activity.

The *Manifesto* is of particular interest since it has since become not merely a popular statement of Marx's politics (which Marx and Engels updated with new prefaces from time to time as a testament to a past political engagement) but also connected to a wider body of theory – Marxism – that lays claim to a theoretical and ideological project for which the text was not originally designed. That project, which builds upon Marx's work after the 1850s, has become the benchmark by which earlier texts have come to be judged. From that later perspective, which dwells upon the 1859 preface to *A Contribution to a Critique of Political Economy* and the volumes of *Capital*, Marx is deemed to be largely concerned with theoretical issues of political economy, the formal anatomy of capitalism and the laws of its movement. But the rhetorical politics in the *Manifesto* is not easy to fit with the theoretical commitments that Marx's (and Engels's) later works inspire. Like other texts, such as the *Eighteenth Brumaire of Louis Bonaparte* (1852) or *The Class Struggles in France* (1850), it is overtly concerned with political matters. But unlike them it is not a commentary but an intervention that addresses its readers as potentially partisan and foregrounds its own apparatus of principles and concepts as themselves symbols of allegiance: it offers a digestible but noticeably conflictual account of the so-called materialist conception of history ("the history of all society up to now ..." (CM 237)); a readable, potted account of the emergence of the bourgeoisie and capitalism ("the bourgeoisie cannot exist without continually revolutionising the instruments of production" (CM 239)); highly quotable conceptions of the state ("merely a device for administering the common affairs of the whole bourgeois class" (CM 239)), ideology ("the ruling ideas of an age were always but the ideas of the ruling class" (CM 250)) and other features of capitalism; a sense of capitalism's inexorable drive towards conflict and division ("society as a whole is tending to split into two great hostile encampments" (CM 238)); principles to distinguish communism from other socialisms ("the communist revolution is the most radical break with traditional property relations" (CM 251)); and a pleasingly egalitarian hint at what communist society might be ("an association in which the free development of each is the condition for the free development of all" (CM 252)). The aphoristic form by which many of these concepts and claims are made invites them to be read as revolutionary commonplaces, established certainties not hypotheses. They come in the form of chiliastic common sense to be repeated, not tested or elaborately justified in the way Marx's later work addresses its readers.

Outside the moments of revolutionary advance, the rhetorical posturing in the *Manifesto* can seem dogmatic and, frankly, simplistic. In part this is because Marx's later work brought greater focus and complexity to many of the topics he brushed against in the *Manifesto*, but also because the numerous objects and relations described in that text – capitalism, the bourgeoisie, the proletariat, modes of political struggle and so on – have changed in countless ways since its publication. By the late nineteenth century, the *Manifesto* was an early text among others in the library of Marxism; one that was evidently spirited but peculiar to a particular moment. Outside of that moment, we might say, it seemed all "revved up" but with no place to go, a ticket to a fight that had long since been fought. By the 1890s Marxism had been proclaimed a theory of history, a total social theory that traced the laws of capitalist development in the manner of natural science. In comparison, as the Italian Marxist philosopher Antonio Labriola claimed in a commemorative essay in 1895: the *Manifesto* "contains more substantial declarations than demonstrations" (Labriola 1966, 26). The text may give us, in synthesis, a whole new conception of history, one driven towards a revolution effected by class struggles, but it does so largely by communicating in the imperative, not as a rational explanation. According to Labriola, it gives "only the scheme and the rhythm of the general march of the proletarian movement," but that scheme has become more complex and the rhythm more varied than Marx and Engels could ever have predicted (Labriola 1966, 58). As such, the *Manifesto* was an inspiration, a revelation, a guide, but nothing more, for those who oppose capitalism. Likewise, the French syndicalist Georges Sorel claimed in his 1902 essays on Marxism that the *Manifesto* "seems totally impregnated with idealism, full as it is of symbols and images. Marx could not have treated otherwise a work addressed to men of action" (Sorel 1976, 112). It was, he claimed, a "bizarre and obscure" text, ill-suited to the deterministic science to which figures such as Karl Kautsky reduced Marx's teaching (Sorel 1976, 111).[5]

Both Labriola and Sorel were opponents, in different ways, of the deterministic creed that Marxism had become. They marveled at the motivational force of the *Manifesto* and the images that it employed to inspire workers' struggles. Indeed, it was precisely this sense of moral inspiration that, for them and other thinkers like them, Second International Marxism lacked, with its appeal to iron laws of capitalism and inevitable revolutionary collapse. Such reasoned hypotheses, they reckoned, only pacified the proletariat. Their criticisms register a sense of the rhetorical dimension of any political theory worth its salt. For all Marxism's critique of ideology and the superstructural forms of consciousness that distract and obscure capitalism's inner workings, it still has to speak to those ordinary people ready to be swayed and recruited to the cause. Political action needs to have its stimulus, its rhetorical forms of engagement and provocation that can generate a degree of certainty in order to persuade, if only momentarily, its audiences to make their commitment. Marxism's record throughout the twentieth century suggests it never found an enduring means to translate its theory into a consistently provocative and motivational political rhetoric, though it has had its moments.

The *Manifesto* is one form that such rhetoric might take, but it is by no means the only one. Its combined techniques perhaps work better to announce a new movement, a self-declared dissenting minority that claims to speak for the majority, than to support established political groups and movements. Its clarity and intransigence raise a flag for an as yet unrecognized group and inscribe it within the genre's longer, modern history of radical opposition. But, once in place, it cannot repeat itself with the same force. Thus the manifesto form has since become the favored device of insurgent art movements and minoritarian political causes.[6] Heavily reliant on making an impact, its force is more aesthetic than intellectual, provocative and punchy rather than deliberative. In many respects it can only promise more than it can deliver, directed as it is permanently towards the future it wants to shape. Marxism, on the other hand, soon became weighed down by its invocation of tradition, canonical texts and defense of the past strategic choices. From a rhetorical perspective the *Manifesto* looks like a troublesome text for such a tradition: too confident of its own story, too succinct and irreverent for a work of theory, too intransigent for the sacrifices required to build coalitions and make compromises.

CONCLUSION

All political action is premised on judgments and commitments that are held by human subjects with some degree of certainty. But certainty is a quality that must be rhetorically crafted. That is, it is held in place by arguments and principles constructed so as to make us complicit with their logic and affectively bound to their direction of force. The Marxian tradition is no less rhetorical in this respect than any other ideological and political movement. But Marx and Engels employed a variety of rhetorical strategies that addressed their readers in different ways, not all of which necessarily cohere. Marxists have made much of the appeal to reason in their theories and philosophical studies – and for good reason. But the *Manifesto* adopted and extended an argumentative style designed to force itself onto the agenda at a moment of crisis. To be persuaded by such a document meant not simply to be reasoned with as an intellectual but also to be recruited to an authoritative and insistent stance from which a distinct political project could be envisaged, even if in reality compromises had to be made and other positions tolerated. Indeed, precisely *because* such compromises were likely, it made sense to insist so firmly. The *Manifesto* makes a claim for its readers' allegiance not by the veracity of its arguments about capitalism and the accuracy of its reading of class struggles, but on the extent to which it positions its audiences, by means of the variety of rhetorical techniques that we have examined, so that they can interpret the prevailing situation from its point of view.

REFERENCES

Carver, Terrell. 1983. *Marx and Engels: The Intellectual Relationship*. Brighton: Harvester-Wheatsheaf.
Carver, Terrell. 1989. *Friedrich Engels: His Life and Thought*. Basingstoke: Macmillan.
Carver, Terrell. 2010. "Marx and the Politics of Sarcasm." *Socialism and Democracy*. 24(3): 102–118.
Corbett, Edward P. J., and Robert J. Connors. 1999. *Classical Rhetoric for the Modern Student*, 4th edn. New York: Oxford University Press.
Garsten, Bryan. 2006. *Saving Persuasion: A Defense of Rhetoric and Judgement*. Cambridge, MA: Harvard University Press.
Habinek, Tomas. 2005. *Ancient Rhetoric and Oratory*. Oxford: Blackwell.
Labriola, Antonio. 1966. "In Memory of the Communist Manifesto." In *Essays on the Materialist Conception of History*, trans. Charles H. Kerr. New York: Monthly Review Press, 9–92.
Lanham, Richard A. 1991. *A Handlist of Rhetorical Terms*, 2nd edn. London: University of California Press.
Lyon, Janet. 1999. *Manifestoes: Provocations of the Modern*. London: Cornell University Press.
Marinetti, F. T. 2006. *F.T. Marinetti: Critical Writings*, ed. Günter Berghaus. Trans. Doug Thompson. New York: Farrar, Strauss & Giroux.
Martin, James. 2015. "Situating Speech: A Rhetorical Approach to Political Strategy." *Political Studies*. 63(1): 25–42.
Martin, James. 2014. *Politics and Rhetoric: A Critical Introduction*. Milton Park: Routledge.
Nicolaievsky, Boris, and Otto Maenchen-Helfen. 1976. *Karl Marx: Man and Fighter*. Trans. Gwenda David and Eric Mosbacher. London: Penguin.
Policante, Amedeo. 2012. "Vampires of Capital: Gothic Reflections between Horror and Hope." *Cultural Logic: An Electronic Journal of Marxist Theory and Practice*. clogic.eserver.org/2010/Policante.pdf. (Accessed January 2013).
Sorel, Georges. 1976. *From Georges Sorel: Essays in Socialism and Philosophy*, ed. John Stanley. New York: Oxford University Press.
Sperber, Jonathan. 2013. *Karl Marx: A Nineteenth-Century Life*. New York: Liveright Publishing.
Wilkie, Richard W. 1976. "Karl Marx on Rhetoric." *Philosophy and Rhetoric*. 9(4): 233.

4

The *Manifesto* in Marx's and Engels's Lifetimes

Terrell Carver

The story of the writing of the *Manifesto* is very well known, warranting a chapter section in Franz Mehring's biography of 1918 – the first full-length and scholarly re-telling of Marx's life with due attention to constructing a canon of what were to count as his major works (and which were to be merely minor ones, for various reasons) (Mehring 1951, 147–151). Marx and Engels had started off this process in separate texts of 1859, the former with the now well-known and very briefly autobibliographical preface to *A Contribution to a Critique of Political Economy* (1859) and the latter with his press review of Marx's slim volume the same year.[1] While there is little disagreement about the relevant facts and reliable sources for this particular episode of composition and publication in 1847–1848, that of the *Manifesto*, there is rather too much agreement on what the story is about. The story is *not* about how a major work by an important author (and his sidekick) came to be written.

The *Manifesto* was constructed that way – twenty-four years later, in 1872 – in order to make one man a major author (with a sidekick) and to make the *Manifesto* a major work in *his* canon. Had this construction not taken place in this way, the *Manifesto* could have remained a biographical curio in a short list of works of different sorts, and with different degrees of readership-reach. In the autobiographical context of the 1859 preface, Marx is actually much keener on getting readers to his *Poverty of Philosophy* (1847), which was directed towards a very well-known figure in European socialism (and even further afield) – Pierre-Joseph Proudhon. That book was in French (as was the *Discourse on Free Trade*, also mentioned). That international language enabled Marx to reach a far wider readership than he could with German, and indeed via respected publishing houses in Paris and Brussels. Moreover, he singles out *Poverty of Philosophy* over the *Manifesto* – about which he says nothing – for its "academic" account of "our conception" (although *Poverty of Philosophy* was sole-authored), but with apologies for its "polemical" content (CW 29: 264). Presumably he would have had to apologize for the entire content of the *Manifesto* on those terms. The terms that Marx is setting out in the 1859 preface are of course not personal terms, but political ones, concerned with getting his content out to an audience – which was not exactly the one targeted by his previous (and subsequent) polemics. But there is no evidence that for any purposes a republished or even revisited *Manifesto* would have fitted some kind of bill. During the 1850s and 1860s it was a rare item, and very, very few people were looking for it (Draper 1994, 3–32).[2]

MAKING MARX MARX

By 1872 the *Manifesto* was a nearly forgotten little work that unexpectedly became central to a consciously political process of construction. That process was intended to create Marx as an iconic founding father of socialism, and in particular of a major tendency in the German socialist movement, namely the otherwise informal associates of the "Marx party" – a loose association of German revolutionaries of 1848–1849 who had returned from exile after the amnesty of 1862. After that the grouping developed around Marx's sometime-friend and near-contemporary Wilhelm Liebknecht, and a bit later around the younger August Bebel. (Not that they didn't have their political differences; see Draper 1994, 36–38.) There was nothing inevitable about the decision to publish a little-known text, and those decisions were the ones which created the *Manifesto* as we know it. The mass recirculation of the text in 1872, and the "feature" edition with the new authorial preface, sparked over the years an enormous number of reprints and translations – and that process created Marx as a world-historical figure (Draper 1994, 48–52; Kuczynski 1995, 195–201). Until that point he was very little known (and then hardly ever favorably) outside the limited circles of German socialism.

The "Marx party" of the late 1860s was not, however, headed by Marx himself, who had long before settled into a correspondent role in relation to German politics (and even lesser roles elsewhere, including Britain, his country of residence since 1849). While Marx was also known in the wider circles of the International Workingmen's Association, where there was plenty of influential competition and rivalry, it had foundational documents of its own (Musto 2014). In all his international work, Marx's point of reference is the present and future, conceived with a sharp analytical take on strategy and tactics in his public texts (and a mean sense of how personal political action really is in his private correspondence). The *Manifesto* might well have represented failure and heartache, hopes dashed and alliances never formed. In any case, from his perspective it got more obviously out of date with every passing year, and it seems to have offered nothing very much worth quoting, even by allusion.

The story of the *Manifesto* as a major work by Marx and Engels is thus a fiction in the sense that in 1847 Marx and Engels were not writing a "major work." While they were certainly taking a very serious interest in what they were doing at the time – as a political intervention into various national and international contexts – the idea that it was anything very much beyond that did not strike them at all.[3] Indeed, a review of their correspondence, and of what they and others were producing, that is genuinely contextual to the time, shows us a fast-moving and uncontrollable situation with numerous twists and turns, where politics and personalities were very much the same thing (Sperber 2013, 153–203). Hardly anyone outside these inner circles had any idea that anything was going on with the League of Communists (or just communists or socialists) at all. Even the police spies had not yet swung into action, as they did in the post-revolutionary 1850s.

In reality the *Manifesto* was quite a short pamphlet of twenty-three quite crudely printed pages (Kuczynski 1995), and the intended audience – the Communist League – swiftly faded out in the glare of much more significant political developments on the Continent. Several thousand copies of the *Manifesto* were shipped in stages to Germany, meeting a demand from groups and readers and generating press notices and serializations, but – looking at the wider picture and turmoil of ephemera – we can safely stick with the general judgment that it had little effect on events, and had little lingering influence. The post-revolutionary show trials of the early 1850s in Cologne revived the work briefly when – ironically – the King of Prussia and other members of a conservative and frightened readership put the document into the public domain (Draper 1994, 20–32). It is true that the document was addressed rhetorically to "proletarians of all countries" (in a literal translation), and that the *Manifesto* itself promises numerous translations and worldwide circulation. However, hardly any translations were produced at the time,[4] all were soon forgotten and some that were variously mentioned have fallen into the doubtful zone as to whether or not they ever actually existed (Draper 1994, 23–25). It is clear that the *Manifesto* was a curio, noted very occasionally, and not a point of reference – and certainly not a "theoretical" point of reference – for anyone.

In the period from its publication in February 1848 until 1872, the *Manifesto* in Marx's and Engels's lives receded, and the two – having moved swiftly on to other things, notably mass-media revolutionary journalism – did not look back very much. After the turmoil of the revolutions, Marx continued as a political agitator, writing two works (among a plethora of shorter articles) that are now very little read, and indeed hardly anyone read them at the time. These were *The Great Men of the Exile* (only posthumously published) and the anonymously published *Revelations Concerning the Communist Trial at Cologne* (1853). The latter was a typically polemical pamphlet and strident intervention into an ongoing issue, namely the public trials of the 1848 "conspirators" and "traitors" for their rebellion against what were now restored, reactionary regimes. Almost the whole edition (printed in Switzerland) was seized before it reached the German states, though it circulated to some extent in North America (see CW 11: 656–657 n. 155, CW 672–673 n. 263).[5] In the notably "academic" (and of course censored) setting of the 1859 preface, Marx of course does not mention this work at all. That kind of activity – polemical intervention into ongoing political situations – was really where Marx's heart was, even if it is not at all what he is remembered for now, except in a contextual and often speedily biographical way, before getting on with the "good" (i.e. intellectual) "stuff." Such brief notoriety as Marx had at the time during the 1850s and 1860s was due to his guilt by association with the convicted revolutionaries, but among the exiles, of course, it was a red badge of courage. But famous, or a "theorist," he was not.

Episodes when Marx labors over polemical interventions are almost always treated by biographers and commentators as hiatuses in his intellectual development and career (and indeed those two are usually made into the same thing). But experientially there is huge testimony that this was not the way that Marx lived his life. His times of withdrawing into the study and the library, as he relates them in correspondence and (brief) autobiographical pieces, sound rather more like hiatuses in his pamphleteering journalism and political engagements with *confrères*, even if he enraged them, and they him. After the trials had died down he declared himself done with party men and called them jackasses to Engels in correspondence (CW 38: 285–286). This is all a great relief to us – Marx could then get on with writing great works, or at least undertake respectable journalism for international broadsheets such as the *New-York Tribune*, *Die Presse* of Vienna and numerous others. But it doesn't seem to have been his plan all along to spend so much of his time engaged in a rather remote way – exciting as it is for us – instead of pushing forward with the drive to democratize industrializing societies that would carry the communist agenda along. Even Frau Marx was concerned that Marx was putting so much time and energy into the super-polemical *Herr Vogt* of 1860 – probably the least read of all his works of any length (CW 17: 21–329; CW 41: 568). For Marx the exposure of a police spy – who responded by libeling him – was of the utmost importance, and it fits with his previous form as a pamphleteer. He moved from cause to issue to personalities to critique (and, in the Vogt case, his own libel action), and had been doing so since the very early 1840s, when he took on the brothers Bauer, Max Stirner, Karl Grün and his "True Socialists" and ultimately Proudhon. That was Marx's *métier*.

In the special preface to the "feature" edition of the *Manifesto* in 1872 – which Marx and Engels were pressed into writing – they sound really rather bemused about the re-publication of the somewhat scrappy little work (CW 23: 174–175). After all, they had written quite a few things that had had their day in the struggle, and, given that the struggle for them was still very much ongoing, what exactly was the point of looking back? Hadn't the *Manifesto* really manifested not very much at all, and wasn't the real point to write a new one anyway? Of all the pieces to pick to advertise Marx, and to set people straight about contemporary politics, this long-forgotten flash-off-the-press was for Marx and Engels hardly the obvious choice.

ENGELS'S MARX

Engels had begun the job of introducing Marx to the world-at-large in 1859 with his review of Marx's first published installment of the *magnum opus*, "academic" study *Capital*, conceived as a comprehensive critique of political economy and "bourgeois" society in numerous volumes. Given that in his review Engels presents Marx to the (German-speaking) world as the new Hegel, and thus worthy of the greatest respect and interest, if not veneration, the *Manifesto* would certainly be off-message in relation to Engels's enterprise. In the *Manifesto* Hegel is not even mentioned. And neither are most of the other building blocks of what would later become Marxism, e.g. contradiction, dialectic, materialism/idealism, base/superstructure, even science and law (in other than commonplace senses). Perhaps oddly, Marx's 1844 conceptualization of alienation, summarizing his critical approach to classical political economy at the time, did not make it into the text either (though of course that concept didn't make it into any form of Marxism – and then only very controversially – until the early 1960s).

Marx was hardly ever inclined to look backward to his own past rather than to the political present, and thus forward to making the communist future. He was good at discarding books and drafts, and starting things over again afresh. When he finally got his 1859 *Contribution* to the press, he remarks in his preface that he had an old "general introduction" (posthumously recovered and dated to 1857), but that he had set it aside (Carver 1975; Chambers 2014); rather similarly he remarks in *Capital* that his former slim volume of 1859 had been reworked into the new one of 1867, or in other words: don't bother going there (CW 29: 261; CW 35: 7). There were thus a number of ways for the "Marx party" to make good Marx's insertion into the wider political publics that had evolved in the German states since the 1840s and 1850s. Engels's branding of Marx as the new Hegel in 1859 was hardly read by anybody, and an appropriate public persona had not followed. That is what the editors of *Der Volkstaat*, recently founded in 1869 as the central organ of the Social Democratic Workers' Party, were looking for (CW 23: 677–678, n. 131).

Wilhelm Liebknecht, August Bebel and their colleagues were rather better at doing this than Engels, and the "hook" was indeed looking backward, but not to Marx as a person and what he did in the revolution, since the goal of the exercise was different. It was to get him (and the party organization, as well as the "Marx party" tendency, internally conflicted as it was) much better known and mutually identified in the present. By 1872 the events and personalities of 1848 had faded enough into history to make a resurrection of the "glory days" of the revolutions an option. Looked at that way, the little committee needed something colorful to head up their project that wasn't a heroic tale about a person yet would identify someone living with the "glory days" and socialist truths. Only a very few had any knowledge of the *Manifesto* at all, and it was almost impossible to find and read. But it was a good choice. And fortunately yet another treason trial had lately put the text into the public record (Draper 1994, 48–49).

The *Manifesto* was certainly colorfully written, very much "of the period" to be evoked, and full of the "Yes, we can!" spirit that the "Marx party" wanted to encourage.[6] Even if anyone had had access to the unremarkable, possibly rather insignificant-looking little pamphlet, they wouldn't have known from the cover who had written it – after all, it had been published anonymously. Marx and Engels (the latter particularly) had achieved some local and (fortunately for him) brief notoriety for the stripped-down, flysheet version, which put their names to the *Manifesto*'s demands at least, though not to the whole text (CW 7: 1–7, 601–602, n. 1; Draper 1994, 22). But then that document was not resurrected until the collected works editions of the twentieth century, and there it was framed in a scholarly way as a synecdoche of the real thing. For a while, at least, the signed flysheet was dynamite, printed in mass-circulation periodicals, reprinted as a pamphlet, and archived by numerous police forces – something the *Manifesto* never achieved at the time of publication. However, in 1872 the *Manifesto* suddenly became central to making Marx Marx in a way that *Capital* had failed to do in 1867 (and still fails to do). It made him go with a swing.

THE VIEW FROM 1872

In their 1872 preface Marx and Engels are overtly critical of the whole enterprise of publishing the document from bygone days again, fearful that the obvious anachronisms would show them in a bad light. They caution readers to remember that the political and economic situation relevant to the development of socialism had changed radically over nearly twenty-five years, and that overall the *Manifesto* was in fact merely historical – not really a manifesto anymore at all. Even the review of communist literature in section III was written off, since it terminated in 1847 and could not therefore provide up-to-date ideas. The "general principles" in the text, while broadly endorsed (but not enumerated in the new preface), were referenced only in relation to the recent events of the Paris Commune, and then the reader was directed to a document that was in fact up to date, namely *The Civil War in France* (CW 23: 174–175).[7] This had just been published in 1871 by the General Council of the International Working Men's Association, and was written by Marx (in English) on their behalf (CW 22: 665–667, n. 163). While in the preface of 1872 the two authors proudly summarize the circulation of the *Manifesto* in various languages after 1848, they knew – as the present-day reader finds out from twentieth-century and later research – that these were specialist and generally small-audience media, making political points by interesting their local readers in a historical curio, and from a somewhat exotic locale.

Even by the 1870s hardly any of Marx's works were available, except in very limited editions of short print-runs for German-speakers, though doubtless some had a life in second-hand shops and hand-around usage, even if we do not really know what for. Marx and his writings were a long way from becoming an object of study (beyond the very, very occasional respectful review), and his "thought" was – as the contemporary reference in the preface of 1872 itself demonstrates – addressed to and evaluated within ongoing political circumstances. This applied to even the most "academic" productions of (apparently) non-polemical critique. Given that the man was actually alive and politically engaged – in correspondence and organizational affairs – he could not be a cult figure, and refused this by repute. Engels repeats the "I am not a Marxist" overheard remark somewhat differently in two items of correspondence after Marx's death (CW 46: 356; CW 49: 7), and this comment fits with the rest of what we know about the (not yet even then) "great man." If Engels had thought the "general principles" of particular import in the wording of the *Manifesto* specifically he would have quoted them – something he does not do when summarizing Marx's contributions to science and politics in numerous texts written before, or even after, Marx's death, other than in his own introductions to two further editions of the *Manifesto* and two translations (into Russian and English).

From 1845 onwards Engels constantly urged Marx to get on with his major work, the critique of political economy. It was indeed Engels's own "Outlines" of that approach, published alongside two of Marx's early works in 1844, that inspired Marx to make that his lifetime project, and similarly inspired Engels to make him try to complete it (CW 3: 418–443; for discussion, see Carver 1983, 32–44). Even in republishing the 1872 German edition of the *Manifesto* in 1883 after Marx's demise and introducing the two translations, Engels clearly sees the text as suspect, both in relation to dialectical methodology and scientific content, which for him meant a critical excursus on contemporary political economy. All of that interest for him was elsewhere, notably in the 1859 preface to the *Contribution* which Marx had written, where Marx offered a "guiding principle" for his research, which Engels had glossed in relation to Hegelian method and scientific validity in his 1859 review. Eventually Marx's substantial critical work on political economy appeared in the published first volume of *Capital* (1867) and subsequent French edition, approximately contemporary with the 1872 republication of the *Manifesto* in the German political context. At that point socialist agitation was legal – at least to a degree – in the newly unified Germany, and electoral politics was just getting underway on a vastly increased scale under a new, but not very democratic, constitution. Obviously the "Marx party" in the recently united imperial Germany thought that the potboiler of 1848 would gain it some ground, anachronisms and misapprehensions notwithstanding.

Choosing something untimely (i.e. "out of time") usefully displaces intra-tendency debate on contemporary questions by highlighting a supposed common heritage that is just far enough in the past to be past generating controversy in the present. The intervention was to be performative – the *Manifesto* became a communicative object and something of an empty signifier, a focus for a variety of projections and interpretations united and uniting in a desire to unify. The focus on the man identified as lead author did much the same job as their republication of the text, despite Marx's status as a (voluntary) exile, his "academic" inaccessibility as author of *Capital* and his scary reputation as a political operator. Engels, who had had by far the more brilliant career and public persona up to 1845, had by 1872 somewhat slipped from view in his self-adopted role as "second fiddle." The republication of the *Manifesto* did not create Marx "the great man"; but then Marx the "great man" did not exist before the republication of this rather *outré* pamphlet. The highly readable text did its work in making the man "great," though not at all for the reasons he – so far as we can tell – really wanted, nor Engels either. But then simple pictures travel best – the man became great because he wrote the people's manifesto, and the people's manifesto cast greatness upon its author. The two became iconic together.

In 1872 Engels and Marx – at some remove from the scene, and on a rather different intellectual wavelength from "the locals" – obviously differed from the returned '48ers in their evaluation of the "Marx party" project, which was to invest time and energy in a retro-production. But German politics of the 1870s was not really Marx and Engels's scene, or their *métier* any more either; the visits the two made to Germany (not together) were non-political. In the preface of 1872 they apologize for not updating the work, refraining from "bridging the gap from 1847 to the present day." But then their view that the *Manifesto* has "become an historical document which we no longer have any right to alter" suggests no real enthusiasm for anyone doing just that (CW 23: 175).

In 1872 Engels was, as usual, intent on getting Marx back to his study to complete the vast critique of political economy in the further planned volumes (and indeed Marx was working on manuscripts posthumously edited as volume two of *Capital*). Yet Engels was also supporting Marx in his constant political engagement with an array of correspondents and organizations of different sorts within socialism worldwide. Marx's passion was certainly for democratic control over both political and economic institutions for the benefit of the many, rather than the few. But that old *Manifesto* – or even a new one – played hardly any role at all in that enterprise as he saw it. He let the little work go – for what it was worth to others – and occupied himself with cutting-edge ideas in his critique and cut-throat politics within the International.

POSTMORTEM AND IN MEMORIAM

It was only after Marx's death in 1883 that the *Manifesto* began to acquire its status as an iconic – and living – text, because in that decade and subsequent ones Marx became a set of texts, rather than a political actor. Engels fuelled this posthumous enterprise, introducing nearly two dozen of Marx's works (and his own) as texts for study, helpfully guiding readers over the bumpy terrain of anachronism, long-forgotten polemical encounters and genre-induced obscurities and *longueurs*. The republished "great works" of an emerging canon did not elevate Marx to the status of *savant* or guru; rather, his status as a secular saint of socialism elevated those works to a status they clearly did not have when they were produced, and certainly did not have in his later life, Engels's and "Marx party" efforts notwithstanding. But thanks to its mass and "feature" republication in 1872 (and thanks much more to numerous subsequent German and other editions) the *Manifesto* became the "intro" work to Marx (as supposedly complementary to Engels's widely read versions of "our conception" which appeared from 1877 onwards) (Carver 1983, 96–158).

Engels himself praised his own work as more readable than Marx's, in a sort of false modesty of substitution (see, e.g., Engels to Joseph Bloch, September 21–22, 1890, CW 49: 36). But then this created a void for the readable work(s) of the man himself, pre-eminently the re-published *Manifesto*. Handing over sole authorship of the *Manifesto* to Marx was thus a notably political act in a clever – and doubtless quite sincere – publicity strategy. This activity of reception took place, then as now, in a world of engagement that was both scholarly and political. And of course the reception of Marx and Engels biographically and bibliographically has been a major political activity on a global scale ever since. But reception is fundamentally different from the first-order activities of Marx and Engels when they did what they did, and wrote what they wrote, at the time of writing – and doing – both in 1847–1848 and in 1872.

It is of course difficult, if not impossible, to read any work now as if history had not intervened and burdened us with knowledge that we cannot unlearn. Nonetheless it is an illuminating exercise to undertake a contextualization in relation to the *Manifesto* that at least tries to dispel the framing of the work as foundational to a doctrine, and the authors as therefore undertaking it in this way, or at least doing so inadvertently. It would have been difficult convincing the two authors even in 1872 that the "general principles" in the *Manifesto* – roughly expressed as they were in often overheated and sarcastic language – were really worth serious study, compared to the much better works that they had written since 1848. Indeed the disjunction between their later works post-1848 and the obviously rambling and somewhat disorganized assertions and cheerleading predictions of the *Manifesto* is hard to escape.

Having set up the *Manifesto* and its author as icons of German socialism, both required appropriate histories, and Engels obliged, contributing two texts. One of these acquired international notice in socialist circles – his "graveside" tribute to Marx (1883) (which does not mention the *Manifesto*), and the other– his *History of the Communist League* (1885) – provided a memoir (which certainly does) (CW 24: 463–471; CW 26: 312–330). This latter work was widely read in German circles (and was followed by other works in the genre, as eyewitness participants were confronting the inevitable). Mehring then provided the reference points for standard accounts of life and "thought," which have not changed much over the years, even with the publication of new documentary sources as they have become available.

In his preface to an 1883 memorial edition of the *Manifesto* (CW 26: 118–119), Engels made Marx the leading author, and certainly the important one. That gesture – whether of generosity or displacement – combined with the scholarly rule of "the last hand" as authoritative, has generally replicated that attribution, whether through a focus on the "great man" and his relation to the "great ideas" of Marxism, or through an incurious attitude to Engels (scholarly notice of his highly significant prior draft works notwithstanding) and a rather lazy emphasis on a bibliographical rule. Marx remitted the manuscript fair copy to the printer himself, and was hence, according to the rule, the last authorial hand (CW 6: 96–103; CW 6: 341–357; Carver 1983, 85–95). While commentary has generally focused on squaring the *Manifesto* with what – since the late 1870s – has figured as Marxism, this strategy has been a rather odd exercise in trying to futurize it.

See, for instance, Sperber's attempts to do this (2013, 204–214), and Stedman Jones's work (2002, 70–184). Sperber spends no time at all on Engels, and Stedman Jones makes his comments in just ten pages, compared with ten times as much on Marx. These two works are largely ideas-related commentary, rather than text-related analysis in terms of close comparison. For text-related analysis, Stedman Jones (2002, 52 n. 4) refers the reader to a mere four pages in Bert Andreas's edition of the work. The resolution to this dilemma – how to make the *Manifesto* fit nicely with a Marxism of the later Marx – has thus been to make the later Engels into Marx by validating Engels's views through sleight of Marx's "last hand," or Engels magically into Marx because much later on Engels wanted it that way in his prefaces and introductions – for political reasons at the time.

Those commentators who have focused on the forebears of the *Manifesto*, by contrast, have made efforts to locate its ideas, language and tropes in *Marx's* earlier works, but this is in fact not all that easy, again, for reasons mentioned above. A more satisfactory strategy is to look into the relationship of *Engels's* drafts (particularly the more impressive "Principles of Communism," which was anyway a revision of the "Communist Confession of Faith") to the 1848 text of the *Manifesto* as we have it, and also to open up the question of the prehistory of Engels's prior drafts themselves in terms of his earlier works. This is not to say that Marx had no influence on the final draft, or indeed that he had none on Engels as drafter along the way. In the absence of manuscript materials, of course, there is an element of speculation.

Moreover, it is clear that the *Manifesto* draws on the jointly composed "German ideology" manuscripts of 1845–1846 (see Carver 2010b), in particular historical sections still in rough draft. The two authors had discarded those discontinuous manuscript sheets at the time as evidently unsuitable for the sustained polemics which they were actually writing. Those manuscript sheets, though, are almost entirely in Engels's handwriting, which raises similar questions of authorship all over again, rather than resolving any, as some commentators have assumed or argued.[8]

The pre-history of Engels's prior drafts (and therefore of much of the final text) lies in his articles "Outlines of a Critique of Political Economy" (CW 3: 418–443) and "The Condition of England" (CW 3: 444–468), his book *The Condition of the Working Class in England* (1845) (CW 4: 295–583) and his "Speeches in Elberfeld" (CW 4: 243–264). In most ways the genre, diction and actual content of the first two sections of the final *Manifesto* are far more similar to Engels's interests in history, technology and generally getting intelligent readers on board with communism than to Marx's much more recondite, convoluted and philosophical critiques for the *literati*. Marx generally told readers in no uncertain terms whom and what *not* to believe, cited by name, chapter and verse, which is not at all the way that sections I and II are written. For the *Manifesto* Marx seems to have provided quite a lot of German political specificity, turning Engels's Anglo-French focus on "developed" markets, industries and political institutions into a revolutionary locus in the German states – up to that point a rather surprising idea in communist circles. Marx was also adept at turning economy of expression into a surplus of sarcasm (Carver 2010a), a rhetorical style at which Engels was not quite so highly skilled.

Marx was really at his most Marxian in sections III and IV; Engels at his most Engelsian in sections I and II. This is not to suggest a formal division of labor or any particular potential for disagreement of divergence of views. But it is rather to argue that commentators have generally striven to find the "great ideas," later attributed solely to Marx (not least by "second fiddle" Engels) as the important ones in sections I and II, and the important ideas in sections I and II selected out as such according to this criterion. However, it might be refreshing to take the joint authors at their word in the 1872 preface and try to list the "general principles" that they said were there in the text itself, independent of this kind of scholarly but rather over-determined quest. And we might also want to note that if the *Manifesto* is evidently very thin on the ground with the "right" concepts (familiar from the Marxism of the later 1870s), that might possibly be a virtue. Or at least it might be a clue to a more contextual reading, even if copies were few at the time in 1848, and readers possibly even fewer in later years until the republication in 1872 and during the rest of the decade.

RE-READING THE MANIFESTO

In 1872 the authors evidently thought that the *Manifesto* could be abstracted to "general principles" and, apparently, a residuum, which was presumably different. The speculation that Marx was heavily involved in drafting up the "critique" sections (taking rival forms of socialism and communism to task) in section III, and also the political strategy and immediate tactics listings in section IV, points us toward the idea that the burden of the document was at least 50/50 at the time of writing: 50 percent "general principles" backed up with historical narration (as Engels mentioned) (CW 38: 149), and 50 percent "what not think," and "what to do and how." In that way the two had produced quite a balanced document for a newly minted confederation of disparate groups at a specific moment of foundation and direction-setting. Later on, in 1872, more than a little embarrassed by having this pamphlet published out of its time, they had to suggest an unbalanced view, giving far more weight to the "general principles" that had survived and were worth repeating, and not giving readers any guidance on what exactly to do with the rest.

This view of course set the reading strategy that has since then been the one most commonly adopted, but in 1872 there was as yet no clear framing from the authors in widely circulated form through which readers could judge which passages were really the relevant "general principles" and how to arrange them in an order of significance. Marx's preface to his *Contribution* of 1859, and Engels's review of the same year, were possibly accessible to a few, and Engels had written a very short Marx biography of sorts, published in 1869. It gives the *Manifesto* the barest mention and says that it was "substantially" Marx's work (CW 21: 61). But that again was not a mass-market product, nor one that is known to have circulated in a way that would establish an influential frame for his work. Marx's *Eighteenth Brumaire of Louis Bonaparte* (CW 11: 99–197) was coincidentally republished in 1869, but this was as a political rather than a doctrinal intervention, given its highly unflattering view of Bonaparte, who had by then become the bellicose and unpopular emperor Napoleon III. As a frame through which to view Marx and thus to lend clarity to his "general principles," the *Brumaire* would have been an even worse choice than the *Manifesto* (not that anyone is known to have suggested this). The *Brumaire* is a micro-study of French politics, and – for all its staggering virtues – it has none of the historical sweep and rhetorical force of the *Manifesto*, sections I and II.

Oddly though, section II declares that communists do not have sectarian principles. Instead communists point out proletarians' common interests, represent the interests of the "movement as a whole," and understand "the line of march," "general conditions" and "ultimate general results" – "theoretically." Communist propositions, says the text, are "theoretical" yet *not* based on "ideas or principles." "Principles," says the text in a snide remark, are "invented" or "discovered" by "this or that reformist crank." Marx and Engels do not engage with this referential paradox in their rather bland comments in the preface of 1872, though of course in 1847–1848 the notion of unauthored "principles" (coinciding with proletarian class interests) fortified the illocutionary identification of a class with a text that was itself an anonymous one rather than authored. Given the claimed coincidence of interests between Communist Party and proletarian class, and the Party's articulation of its position in the otherwise unauthored text, readers are evidently not then in the grip of "this or that reformist crank." Moreover, the Party eschewed anything like sectarianism by describing itself as a "section" of other proletarian parties, just the "most resolute and thrusting" among them (CM 246).

This position is worked out through a set of substantive claims in sections I and II about the actual relations of an existing class struggle, where an asserted actuality is backed up by referring to past history. Thus the communists' definitional aim of abolishing the relations of private property is backed up by noting previous historical circumstances in which property systems, for example, the feudal one, had been abolished by the French revolutionaries. This cues a descriptive and evaluative discussion of the current "bourgeois" property system in relation to "actual" proletarian interests, once the universalizing hypocrisies of the bourgeoisie have been exposed. Readers are then warned about these in considerable detail (in relation to wages, capital, money, rent, the family, education, women and the nation) (CM 237–251). Interestingly, what might otherwise be described as a principle or indeed a theory appears here as a heuristic, and indeed one that readers will know *already*: "Does it require a profound insight to grasp that man's presumptions, views and conceptions alter according to their economic circumstances, their social relations, their social existence?" (CM 250)

Communism thus emerges as, on the one hand, the immediate and authentic representation of proletarian class interests, and on the other hand, the sole abolitionist movement that will really end enthrallment to the "eternal truths" of "freedom, justice, etc.," as well as "religion and morality," ideological constructions which merely disguise bourgeois class interests. It is not clear whether the 1872 reference to authored "general principles" is reinscribing these claims or contradicting them, since Marx and Engels at that point are not endorsing the "section" strategy in relation to other political parties. The "Marx party" enterprise undertaken by Liebknecht and Bebel was essentially sectarian in relation to other socialist tendencies, and through the re-publication of the *Manifesto* it was aligning itself – by unintended implication – with "this or that reformist crank," at least in terms of creating iconic (if honorary) founders, and referencing a foundational text, albeit not one the "outed" authors chose themselves.

After 1872 the "Marx party" enterprise evolved swiftly into the German Social Democratic Workers' Party, itself one of the principals in the "unity" congress held at Gotha in 1875, when it merged with the Lassalleans. Marx's comments on that party program were not flattering, and did not reproduce the novel relationship posed by the *Manifesto* between principles and class interests (which rejected individual/joint authorship by "cranks" of "principles," and favored collective expression of "propositions," or at least the appearance of this). Nor did Marx's comments on "the Gotha program" reproduce the novel "party" strategy expressed in the *Manifesto*, which eschewed sectarianism in favor of what was probably something like later strategies of "entryism" into mass movements and political organisations (CW 24: 75–99).

READERS AND READINGS

Thus far this chapter has outlined two reading strategies commonly taken in considering the *Manifesto*. The first is to read subsequent Marxism(s) back into it in order to produce a "match" of ideas. There are indeed distinct overlaps between the *Manifesto* and the very brief, soberly written yet enigmatic preface to Marx's *Contribution* of 1859 (which became canonical in "Marx studies" only at the turn of the twentieth century, and has spent some time since then in a premier position). But this is a way of incorporating the *Manifesto* into the posthumous canonical hierarchy, where Marx's "thought" is seriously and more or less critically explored. But that is not what the "Marx party" was doing in their "feature" edition of 1872, nor what Marx and even Engels were worried about when they reluctantly went along with the scheme. While Marx and Engels were certainly keen to promote "our conception" within the communist and socialist concatenations of 1847–1848, their way of doing it was textually and rhetorically quite different from the later "academic" renderings of this by Marx (in his preface of 1859) and by Engels (in his review of that year and works of 1877–1878 onwards). Re-processing the *Manifesto* to fit that discursive model removes the politically stimulating (and putatively performative) qualities that have made the work world famous.

The other strategy is to read the prior works of Marx (and sometimes Engels, but usually in a very subordinate way) into the text of the *Manifesto* in order to apportion authorship, or to identify the "important author" (i.e. Marx) with its composition *tout court* (Engels's prior texts and drafts notwithstanding). This would certainly have struck Marx and Engels post-1848 as entirely weird in intellectual terms and politically way off the point. And it is certainly nothing like what the "Marx party" of 1872 wanted to do in developing a public and appropriately politicized persona for Marx by recirculating a text that made sense – or at least some sense – on its own terms in their current political situation (and anyway made a rousing read). Moreover, it is often not the published works of Marx and Engels that are read into the *Manifesto* in order to establish its *bona fides* as a "great work" of Marxist (or more usually Marxian) thought, but rather their unpublished (and therefore unpolished) works, whether earlier ones, such as the "Economic and Philosophical Manuscripts of 1844" or later ones, such as the "Grundrisse" and "Critique of the Gotha Program." This again is a questionable move, but oftentimes the fetishism of the archive suffices by way of justification (see Stedman Jones 2002, 99–184).

So why not take a cue from the "feature" edition of 1872 and promote the *Manifesto* to premier status within the canon? To do this we could conduct a thought experiment that will enable us to fill out the "general principles" that were said to be there, but not listed or explored in 1872 (and not projected onto the text from later or earlier works as in the reading strategies described above). Suppose counterfactually that Engels had dropped dead in 1875 before writing *Anti-Dühring* (CW 25: 5–309), which – more than any other work – set the Marxist terms through which the "great man" was understood as not merely iconic, but intellectually distinctive in his "thought" and *sans pareil* as a communist "revolutionary." While Engels's framing of Marx as a philosopher and scientist, and of his thought as dialectical and materialist, dates from much earlier (namely 1859 in his review of Marx's *Contribution*), the mass circulation of these ideas came only with his work of 1877–1878, which caught the attention of a socialist public. If that work – *Anti-Dühring* – had not existed, we would not have had the first reading strategy delineated above (making Marx into the later Engels), and the second one (finding the early Marx in the *Manifesto*) would not have emerged with all the interest that it derived from Marx's elevation to an "ism." *Marx before Marxism* is quite a telling though paradoxical title (McLellan 1980).

If we were in that way left with the *Manifesto* as a premier socialist text, jointly authored by two communist '48ers who were briefly honored in 1872, the relative importance of the two authors – and the significance of the content in and between its four sections – would look very different. The "class struggle" view of history would stand out, but not the puzzle of how and in what way this "conception" is "materialist." The focus on the revolutions in production and politics that marked the change from European feudalism to bourgeois economies and regimes would come to the fore, but without posing issues of "historical staging" across other modes of production, and the question as to exactly how those modes of production are constituted. The critique of political economy rehearsed in the *Manifesto* – which is *sans* scholarly citation and referential apparatus – would be easily and perhaps importantly identified as a popular rewrite of Engels's rather more serious diction in his "Outlines of a Critique of Political Economy," which might indeed get a revival. The sociology of the proletariat in the *Manifesto* would also look quite sketchy in relation to Engels's *The Condition of the Working Class in England*, and almost nothing like any of Marx's published work at all, other than the "Primitive Accumulation" chapters at the very end of *Capital*. The exhumation of the "German ideology" manuscripts (which were quite unloved until the early 1920s), and of Marx's earlier philosophical musings of 1844 on a subject – political economy – which he hardly knew as yet, would not look a particularly interesting enterprise, nor would an investigation into the voluminous "economic" materials in draft from 1857 onwards.

Further aspects of the *Manifesto* would leap out, in particular the argumentative thesis that "products of the intellect" – including supposed universal truths of religion, morality, philosophy and law – are "refashioned along with material ones" (CM 250). The snappy sentence, "the ruling ideas of an age were always but the ideas of the ruling class" (CM 250), would count as the corollary in intellectual life of the "class struggles" thesis in political life. The assault on bourgeois hypocrisies and "phrases" about marriage and the family, and the various proposals for thoroughgoing reform of a system relentlessly identified as exploitative, oppressive and brutal on a global scale, would appear as the sort of rhetorically rousing speechification one would want in a manifesto (CM 248–251). Indeed, raising "the advancement of the proletariat to ruling class, victory for democracy" (CM 251) might – as a slogan – have done considerable good work in the socialist movement, as opposed to invocations of science, dialectics, materialism, base/superstructure, Hegel and even the theory of surplus value. The *Manifesto* is overwhelmingly vigorous in its evocation of proletarians-in-action, the "gravediggers" of the bourgeoisie (CM 246). This hardly counts as an invitation to go looking in cast-off notebooks for a "theory of alienation."

CONCLUSION

The *Manifesto* is seldom framed as "theory" but rather viewed as consistent with the "theory" expounded elsewhere, whatever its variants and sources. Perhaps it was a lucky – but sometimes narrow – escape. No one would claim that the *Manifesto* was or is an atheoretical work. But it is revealing to consider what the text might say to us if it were – hypothetically – made the premier work of Marx and Engels (as the 1872 political framing effectively stated) and allowed to speak for itself in their lifetimes (as it briefly did).

The *Manifesto* was made central to the project of centering Marx in the socialist hierarchy of "greats," and his works in the socialist canon of venerated texts, albeit in varying and changing hierarchies. The little pamphlet of 1848 achieved a premier status, acknowledged from the 1930s when collections of "selected works" of Marx and Engels began to appear. It kicked off these collections, appearing as the first item, uniquely out of the otherwise chronological ordering.

The *Manifesto* was thus made to function as the "intro" text and way to higher things and further study. The rhetorical force and circumstantial engagement of the work were somewhat downgraded – these were presumed to be simple and simplistic, "of the time" and insufficiently transferrable to other situations. Other works by Marx and Engels were selected and positioned as more "theoretical" in character, and thus more interesting and useful to the initiated (once they had read the *Manifesto*).

On the one hand it is certainly true that other works by Marx and Engels were written to have wider and more general reference and application; on the other hand, the contemporary positioning of those works as political interventions by Marx and/or Engels has been devalued through this "theoretical" framing. In that light, the *Manifesto* represents something of a useful balance: the political engagement and specificity are obvious and electrifying, and the "theory" – if we must call it that – is clear, succinct and economical. This short pamphlet is still hailing readers into a political engagement with situations and issues that other perspectives dismiss as normal or merely ordinary. As long as this disjunction animates our politics, the *Manifesto* will find a readership.

REFERENCES

Andréas, Bert. 1963. *Le Manifeste communiste de Marx et Engels: Histoire et bibliographie 1848–1918*. Milan: Instituto Feltrinelli.
Carver, Terrell. 1975. *Karl Marx: Texts on Method*. Oxford: Blackwell.

Carver, Terrell. 1983. *Marx and Engels: The Intellectual Relationship*. Brighton: Wheatsheaf.

Carver, Terrell. 2010a. "Marx and the Politics of Sarcasm." *Socialism and Democracy*. 24(3): 102–118.

Carver, Terrell. 2010b. "The German Ideology Never Took Place." *History of Political Thought*. 31(1): 107–127.

Chambers, Samuel A. 2014. *Bearing Society in Mind*. Lanham, MD and London: Rowman & Littlefield International.

Draper, Hal. 1994. *The Adventures of the Communist Manifesto*. Berkeley: Center for Socialist History.

Kuczynski, Thomas. 1995. *Das Kommunistische Manifest (Manifest der Kommnistischen Partei) von Karl Marx und Friedrich Engels: Von der Erstausgabe zur Leseausgabe*. Trier: Schriften aus dem Karl-Marx-Haus, 49.

McLellan, David. 1980. *Marx before Marxism*, 2nd edn. London: Macmillan.

Mehring, Franz. 1951 [1936]. *Karl Marx: The Story of His Life*. Trans. Edward Fitzgerald. London: George Allen & Unwin.

Musto, Marcello. Ed. 2014. *Workers Unite! The International 150 Years Later*. London and New York: Bloomsbury.

Sperber, Jonathan. 2013. *Karl Marx: A Nineteenth-Century Life*. New York and London: Liveright.

Stedman Jones, Gareth. 2002. "Introduction." In Karl Marx and Frederick Engels, *The Communist Manifesto*. Harmondsworth: Penguin, 3–187.

Thomas, Paul. 1991. "Critical Reception: Marx Then and Now." In *The Cambridge Companion to Marx*, ed. Terrell Carver. Cambridge: Cambridge University Press, 23–54.

PART II

POLITICAL RECEPTION

5

Marxism and the *Manifesto* after Engels

Jules Townshend

The history of Marxism as a self-consciously action-oriented political ideology could be described as in effect a series of footnotes to the *Communist Manifesto*, begun by Marx and Engels themselves and continued by their disciples. They were footnotes generated principally by the experience of class struggles occurring in different social, political and economic contexts that the authors of the *Manifesto* could not have wholly foreseen. Such a history also demonstrates, however, that Marxist theory and practice, by and large, increasingly departed from what Marx and Engels termed the "general principles" of the *Manifesto*, claiming in 1872 in a new preface that they were "as correct today as ever." Yet they acknowledged that their "practical application" depended "everywhere and at all times, on the obtaining historical conditions" (CW 35: 174). In other words, they thought that these theoretical principles could accommodate contingent "known unknowns." Yet we can see retrospectively that circumstances have not been kind to the wholesale enactment of these principles. There were also "unknown unknowns." Thus these footnotes to the *Manifesto*, which started as supplements and amendments, in effect ended up as radical revisions.

This chapter tracks some of these historical footnotes in order to trace the relationship between the *Manifesto* and subsequent Marxist ideology, showing how leading Marxist thinkers attempted to remain faithful to these general principles in differing contexts and how the experience of historical conditions meant that a comprehensive application had become deeply problematic, leading in many cases to their practical as well as theoretical abandonment. The general principles of the *Manifesto*, as they travelled through geographical space and historical time, were in for an uncomfortable ride.

THE "GENERAL PRINCIPLES" OF THE MANIFESTO

While Marx and Engels did not specify the form and content of these general principles,[1] they can be identified in the text of the *Manifesto* itself, as well as in antecedent and subsequent works and by what Marx's followers thought them to be. Fundamental to understanding these general principles is Marx's attempt to educate the radical imagination. He rejected the "will" principle of politics, which he argued had led to the Jacobin Reign of Terror in France (1793–1794) and to the divisive and inconsequential, conspiracy-style politics of some of his contemporaries, such as Wilhelm Weitling, Auguste Blanqui and Mikhail Bakunin (CW 3: 199). Equally, he dismissed the non-violent, utopian model of socialism: it failed to appreciate the role of class agency in effecting social change, as well as the societal and historic context in which the proposed experiments were to be conducted.[2] In any case, he deemed both brands of socialism as elitist. His intellectual strategy to avoid any taint of egalitarian authoritarianism was grounded on a belief expressed before the *Manifesto* that "reality" had to "strive towards thought" (CW 3: 183). What Marx sought to demonstrate in the *Manifesto* was that capitalist reality was indeed creating conditions favorable to actualizing the "thought" of the French Revolution – freedom, equality and community for all – in short, communism. In other words, Marx was espousing what may be termed a "condition-dependency" principle: social, economic and indeed cultural conditions create the limits and possibilities for political action and thus for fundamental societal transformation.

In Marx's view, the most important condition for social and political transformation was the economic and class structure of a particular society. The famous narrative spine of the *Manifesto* concerning class struggle is undergirded by a dialectical ontology, that is, a notion that reality itself has dialectical properties. In particular, Marx presented a dialectical analysis of capitalism (structure) and the proletariat (agency). Although the term "dialectic" is absent from this text, which after all was written for popular consumption, the dialectical principle lies at the theoretical heart of the *Manifesto*. Marx held that there were two basic contradictions immanent in capitalist reality. The first was between the cooperative production of wealth by workers, and its private appropriation by capitalists (CM 245). The second contradiction was between the phenomenal growth in the production of wealth by workers and their growing immiserization (CM 245). Their chronically low pay meant that they could not consume this output, causing a crisis of overproduction and thereby fettering economic expansion (CM 241). These two contradictions provided the underlying dynamics of the class struggle between capitalists and proletarians, and could only be resolved through the common ownership of society's productive assets. All the instruments of production would be centralized in the "hands of the state," enabling the "total productive forces" to be developed "as rapidly as possible" (CM 251). This process required a proletarian revolution on a global scale, because capitalism was in the process of becoming global, creating a world proletariat. In dialectical terms, such a revolution constituted the *Aufhebung* or "sublation" of capitalism – its highly productive and cooperative features preserved, and its dysfunctional and exploitative elements, associated with private property, transcended.

To achieve this, Marx assumed that another kind of dialectical pulse was immanent in reality, involving the development of working-class consciousness and the organizational capacities which would ultimately equip it to become a new ruling class. The bourgeoisie were unwittingly creating their own "grave-diggers" (CM 246), enlisting the proletariat in struggles against the feudal class and also against the bourgeoisie of other nations, dragging the proletariat into the political arena and thereby supplying it with "materials for self-development" (CM 244). Thus the bourgeoisie used the proletariat as a weapon in order to gain "supremacy" for itself as a class, but this weapon would later turn against them (CM 244, 252, 259). Further, workers would be aided by renegade "bourgeois ideologists," such as Marx himself, who understood theoretically the "whole historical development" (CM 244) However, Marx was clear that the proletariat was developing its own political efficacy through a struggle that assumed a dialectical trajectory, starting with conflict between workers and employers, leading to the creation of trade unions and rendering the proletariat "into a class, and hence into a political party" (CM 243). To use Gramsci's terminology, the workers' movement would go through three phases: an initial one, when it would be dominated by "economic-corporate" consciousness; then it would seek "politico-juridical equality" with the ruling class; and finally it would attain a "universal" consciousness that would prompt it to organize its own political "hegemony" (Gramsci 1971, 181–182).

The idea of workers creating their own party, based on the principle of self-emancipation, was a crucial aspect of Marx's endeavor to avoid radical authoritarianism. Communists, he stated, did not "form a separate party as opposed to other workers' parties," nor did they establish special principles "for shaping the proletarian movement," a strategy which we could describe as "hard" and potentially autocratic vanguardism (CM 246). The role of intellectuals and communists was merely to make explicit – to make *manifest* and draw out – the logic of a "historical movement that is proceeding under our own eyes" (CM 246). Communists had "theoretical insight" (CM 246). In effect, Marx was proposing a "soft" and democratic vanguardism. Communists knew the truth of history, or, as Marx had stated earlier, they could solve the "riddle of history" (CW 3: 296–297). Yet they had to relate this truth to workers' own experience of capitalism, as well as uniting, rather than dividing them, enabling them to become a new and cohesive ruling class.

In strategic terms, the self-emancipatory principle also meant "victory for democracy" (CM 251), culminating in proletarian political "supremacy as a class" (CM 252), later termed the "revolutionary dictatorship of the proletariat" (CW 24: 95). Force in some shape or form would have to be used to dispossess the capitalist class. Such a victory was "unavoidable" (CM 246) owing to capitalism's dysfunctionality, and to the development of the proletariat's hegemonic capacities as it became the overwhelming majority of the population. Overall we can therefore see a distinct historical teleological principle at work, with capitalism necessarily creating the conditions for, and becoming the revolutionary agent of, its own downfall. The *Manifesto* is thus intended to make the proletariat fully aware of its own potential political strength and to imbue it with a sense of historical mission as humankind's liberators. In other words, the *Manifesto* aimed to create a revolutionary proletarian identity.

POST MANIFESTO: THE PROBLEMS OF PRACTICAL APPLICATION

Marx, as a result of his analysis of capitalism's contradictions, was convinced that reality was striving towards thought. He admitted that he could not predict precisely how the future would unfold. Yet the future could be anticipated in a way that was consistent with the general principles of the *Manifesto*. In other words, there were "known unknowns," enabling Marx and Engels and their followers to remain optimistic about the future. Thus getting from the present emergence and consolidation of bourgeois revolutions, as suggested in section IV of the *Manifesto*, to the model of proletarian revolution in the future as depicted in section I was only a question of time. Their dialectical analysis meant that as capitalism matured the class struggle would intensify (CM 243). Although Marx was forever an optimist, he acknowledged after the failure of the 1848 "bourgeois" revolutions that he would have to be patient. Workers would possibly have to "undergo twenty or fifty years of civil war" if they wanted to "change conditions" and make themselves "capable of government" (Marx 1973, 341). A crucial "known unknown" was precisely what form the "victory for democracy" would take. After the Paris Commune in 1871 Marx maintained – in his and Engels's 1872 preface to the *Manifesto* – that this involved a democratic transformation of the state, just as the "ready-made State machinery" was not suitable for working class purposes (CW 23: 175). Yet a year later he claimed that, in the light of suitable "institutions, customs and traditions," and in the absence of large bureaucracies and standing armies, a non-violent, parliamentary road was possible. He had in mind the United States, England and possibly Holland (CW 23: 255). Thus, we have two contrasting dialectics of democratic transformation as a result of different contexts for political action. This strategic openness was consistent with Marx's condition-dependency principle, and also that of self-emancipation, i.e. not directly telling the workers how to emancipate themselves.

Nevertheless, there were the "unknown unknowns" that were perhaps decisive in determining the fate of Marxism as a political ideology in the long run, and its relation to the *Manifesto*. These too were the outcome of processes going on before Marxists' "own eyes" (CM 246) that had not been anticipated, undermining the belief that they were riding the tide of history. If there was anything that haunted Marxists in the West it was the possibility of class compromise and collaboration, and the persistence of a deeply entrenched reformism. Marx assumed in the *Manifesto* that the proposed legislation to reduce working hours in England in 1847 was merely evidence of the growing power of the working class (CM 243–244), and yet would not give them a stake in capitalism. Again, the immiserization thesis was undermined by the growth in workers' living standards, which suggested that maybe the proletariat could live with capitalism. Moreover, even if workers did not have a significant stake in capitalism, they still seemed to have one in the nation. What if national identity trumped that of class, binding workers to the nation-state? And what if the process of binary class simplification within capitalist society – into a sharp division between capitalists and workers – was more complex, given the rise of an urban middle class, as Marx acknowledged towards the end of his life? (Marx 1972, 62–63) Furthermore, what if the peasantry proved to be a source of anti-capitalist radicalism? And equally important, could a regime claiming to represent the proletariat and proclaiming its Marxist credentials on coming to power maintain the general principles of the *Manifesto* and avoid the left-wing authoritarianism of the Jacobins? In essence, there proved to be two major unanticipated outcomes of class struggle itself: class compromise in the West, and authoritarian egalitarianism in the East.

EUROPEAN MARXISM

Unsurprisingly, the Marxism of the Second International (1889–1914) was closest to the general principles of the *Manifesto*. Karl Kautsky, the chief Marxist ideologist of the time, was – after Engels's death in 1895 – Marx's acknowledged theoretical successor. Kautsky saw himself as applying the principles of the *Manifesto* to German conditions. For him the *Manifesto* "laid the scientific foundation of modern socialism" (Kautsky 1971, 199). Its principles, method and characterization of capitalism were "more valid today than ever before" (Kautsky 1988, 127).

The view presented here contrasts with that of Gareth Stedman Jones, who suggests that the significance of the *Manifesto* for Western and Central European labor and socialist parties between 1870 and 1914 was "largely emblematic" (Stedman Jones 2002, 18). Stuart Wilks-Heeg (1998, 121) also offers a view contrary to Jones's, arguing that in Germany the SPD's ideology was powerfully shaped by the *Manifesto*, and that other European socialist parties modelled themselves on the SPD, the most successful socialist party at the time.

For Kautsky, the rapid industrialization of Germany, the growth of trade unions and the creation of the German Socialist Party (SPD) in 1875 and its electoral success after the lifting of the Anti-Socialist Laws in 1890 confirmed for him that reality was indeed striving towards thought – very much in keeping with the spirit of the Engels's introductions to the English (1888) and German (1890) editions of the *Manifesto* (CW 26: 512–518; CW 27: 53–60). (These were the editions in which the *Manifesto* acquired literal footnotes, also by Engels.) The working class was emancipating itself by achieving the "victory for democracy" within a parliamentary framework, as Engels had argued (Marx and Engels, 1962: 135; Kautsky 1971, 184–189). As in the *Manifesto*, Kautsky envisaged the growing demographic preponderance of the proletariat translating into strong economic and political organization as its struggles against the capitalist class intensified.

Kautsky held that the parliamentary route to socialism was essential in enhancing the capacity of the working class to become a ruling class, making use of weapons created by the bourgeoisie itself. It needed the organizational cohesiveness and skills required for a proletarian dictatorship (Kautsky 1909a, 40). Not only would parliamentary activity do this, but also participation in trade union organisations and local government, an expression of how the working class became organised as a "class" (CW 23: 175). Crucial to the proletariat's hegemonic capacities was its unity, especially party unity. Following the soft vanguardist spirit of the *Manifesto*, Kautsky assumed that the SPD had to represent the *whole* of the working class, which at the time meant both revolutionary and reformist elements (Kautsky 1971, 189). This notion of representation formed the basis of Kautsky's so-called centrism.

Yet Kautsky had few parliamentary illusions. For him extra-parliamentary struggles involving trade unions, demonstrations, extensive propaganda activity and even the judicious use of mass strikes were also crucial (Kautsky 1909a, 44–45; 2007, 104). Furthermore, he called for the full democratization of the German state, albeit within a parliamentary form. In *The Social Revolution* he referred to the "decay of parliamentarism," as the bourgeoisie became more reactionary, meaning that parliament itself was losing its legitimacy, requiring a revolution to make it "more efficient" (Kautsky 1909a, 38–39). Moreover, like Engels he was fully aware of the possibilities of a counterrevolution if the proletarian majority used its legitimate power to socialize property relations (Salvadori 1979, 66). Kautsky also acknowledged that he was up against the powerful German state which had outlawed the SPD between 1878 and 1890, and which was defended by a large and well-organized army. The only hope was that the democratic process would render it "faithless to its rulers" (Kautsky 1913, 88).[3] His emphasis on the role of democratic legitimacy in societal transformation was adopted for another reason: he wanted to minimize the effects of a revolutionary rupture on the productive capacity needed by the proletariat after the revolution.

Kautsky's application of the principles of the *Manifesto* did not go unchallenged. Bernstein, who co-authored the SPD's Erfurt Programme (1891), along with Kautsky and August Bebel, explicitly questioned the Marxist fundamentals (Bernstein 1993, 1). Influenced by his years of exile in England (1888–1901) during and after the Anti-Socialist Laws (1878–1890), Bernstein had been looking at what was going on under his "own eyes" (CM 246). The future did not belong exclusively to the proletariat, but rather to a harmonious multi-class society of citizens (Bernstein 1993, 147), especially because a new, urban middle class had arisen and was unlikely to disappear as large-scale business organizations developed (Bernstein 1993, 78). For him, the outcome of trade union struggles and the growth of democracy was not social revolution. The potential revolutionary zeal of the workers was being undermined as they acquired a growing stake in a capitalism that showed few signs of collapsing, especially as a result of the expansion of the system of credit. Moreover, the working class was too fragmented to become a ruling class. Reality, then, was not striving to meet the thought of revolution. Bernstein's revisionism challenged root and branch the general principles of the *Manifesto* – a dialectical understanding of capitalism and an attendant historical teleology resulting in communism and proletarian self-emancipation.

More than a ten-year period, in a number of works defending the revolutionary identity of the proletariat, Kautsky reiterated objections to Bernstein's assault that were broadly similar to the principles of the *Manifesto*. The class struggle was intensifying rather than abating, and capitalism was constantly destabilized by chronic under-consumption, just as the *Manifesto* had posited (Salvadori 1979, 65). Further, although workers were not immiserated in the absolute sense, as suggested in the *Manifesto*, they had become so in relative terms (Kautsky 1909a, 20–22). Moreover, the class struggle was becoming increasingly politicized as employers' organizations were formed in order to combat trade union action. Strikes were now beginning to assume a political character (Kautsky 2007, 80), and the question of the further democratization of the German state was put squarely on the agenda, especially because the political class was in the thrall to the financiers, who had no interest in democracy (Kautsky 1909a, 40; 2007, 85, 101). With the "moral decline" of the ruling class, workers and their representatives were the true tribunes of democracy. Thus for Kautsky the "victory for democracy" also entailed a democratization of political institutions (Kautsky 2007, 102–104), so that workers could enact a social revolution involving the socialization of property relations (Kautsky 1909b, 3–8). All this was "unavoidable," as the *Manifesto* had announced, explicitly assuming proletarian volition (Kautsky 2007, 36).

Rosa Luxemburg's *Social Reform or Revolution* (1899), perhaps not as influential as Kautsky's works at the time, became an anti-revisionist classic. It focused on what she saw as Bernstein's theoretical deficiencies. More than Kautsky, she reaffirmed the validity of the dialectical account of capitalism in the *Manifesto* as well as the centrality of social class in understanding the nature of political institutions. This provided the basis for her defense of a historical *telos*, that is, historical necessity. She doubted whether capitalism could overcome its contradictions, especially through the expansion of credit, which ultimately exacerbated them through "reckless speculation" (Luxemburg 1971, 61). She held that there were objective limits to capitalist expansion, especially of markets, because capitalists were compelled to reduce workers' aggregate wages. This under-consumptionist explanation of capitalism's ultimate failure was in keeping with the analysis in the *Manifesto*. Luxemburg's dialectical approach also underlay her arguments, which indicated the limitations of reformism. In particular she questioned the extent to which the state could be democratized sufficiently so as to meet the needs of the working class, and whether trade unions could overcome capitalist exploitation. Nevertheless, she held that the workers' struggles for reforms were vital to the process of their self-emancipation in developing their organizational capacities, sense of their own class interests and historical destiny (Luxemburg 1971, 52, 119).

In retrospect we can see that Bernstein, even if he was too optimistic about capitalism's economic stability, was closer to the mark in questioning the proletariat's desire to become a new ruling class consequent on its integration into capitalism. In doing so, he postulated a fundamental "unknown unknown" that the *Manifesto* did not anticipate. Nevertheless, at the time, Kautsky and Luxemburg could at least show to their own satisfaction that in the particular economic, social and political conditions of late nineteenth– and early twentieth-century Germany, as in other advanced capitalist countries, the class struggle and capitalism's contradictions were not disappearing. So faith in the possibility of proletarian hegemony required no deep interrogation. They still had reasons to be cheerful, so to speak. For them the large "known unknown" remained: *when* would the working class become the hegemonic class?

THE GREAT SCHISM: LENIN AND THE RUSSIAN REVOLUTION

The Lenin-inspired Russian Revolution of October 1917 seemed to answer this question. Yet the justification of the Revolution and the Bolshevik practices that followed required a radical departure from Kautsky's application of the principles of the *Manifesto* to Germany and to other advanced capitalist countries. This development gave rise to Marxism-Leninism. Until Lenin's arrival at the Finland station in Petrograd in April 1917, all leading Marxists in Russia, except Leon Trotsky, anticipated in their different ways the need for a Kautskyan revolutionary strategy at some point in the future, given Russia's relative political and economic backwardness. The immediate task was to bring about the full democratization of the Russian state, which would then enable capitalism to develop rapidly, thereby facilitating at some point in the future the political ascendency of the proletariat, when it had become a majority of the working population. In calling for "all power to the soviets" and for Russian workers to initiate a global proletarian revolution, Lenin broke the Kautskyan mold, yet saw himself firmly within the letter and spirit of Marx and Engels' *Manifesto*. His two major texts before the Revolution sought to demonstrate that reality was striving towards thought. We should note that in 1914 Lenin became fully aware of the significance of Hegel's dialectic, especially *The Science of Logic*, for understanding Marxism; this revelation informed his analysis of imperialism and proletarian dictatorship (Dunayevskaya 1958, 167–193).

Imperialism: The Highest Stage of Capitalism (1916) and *The State and Revolution* (1917) provided the theoretical basis of Lenin's revolutionary strategy. *Imperialism* shared the optimistic teleological spirit of the *Manifesto*, as its subtitle "the highest stage of capitalism" suggests. *Imperialism* also used underconsumption to explain the capitalists' need for territorial expansion (Lenin

1969, 213). For Lenin, the First World War represented *the* crisis of global capitalism. The leading imperialist powers were compelled by finance capital to "re-divide" the world (Lenin 1969, 239). The "universal ruin" caused by war had led to a "world-wide revolutionary crisis ... which cannot end otherwise than in a proletarian revolution and its victory" (Lenin 1969, 173). Thus action by the Russian proletariat, together with the help of the peasantry, could start a chain reaction. Russia's social and economic backwardness would soon be overcome as a result of the assistance provided by workers who had made revolutions in the advanced capitalist countries. This international transformative dynamic was evident both in the *Manifesto* itself in relation to 1840s Germany as the catalyst, as well as in the 1882 preface to the second Russian edition in which Marx suggested that Russia might be in effect be the new Germany (CW 24: 426).

Although *The Civil War in France*, Marx's celebration of the Paris Commune of 1871 and of proletarian self-emancipation, formed the basis of Lenin's ideas about the soviet state in *The State and Revolution*, he quoted Marx's own "footnote" to the *Manifesto*, that is, the preface of 1872. The working class, in constituting itself as a ruling class, could not simply "lay hold of the ready-made State machinery, and wield it for its own purposes" (CW 23: 175). Lenin regarded this statement as an "important correction" to the *Manifesto* (Lenin 1969, 289), which had treated the state in an "abstract manner" (Lenin 1969, 282). The Paris Commune had demonstrated concretely how workers could emancipate themselves through the "victory for democracy" (Lenin 1969, 291), which involved the "smashing" of existing state power. Kautsky, Lenin maintained, had not seen the revolutionary significance of the Commune, which had replaced "bourgeois democracy by proletarian democracy" (Lenin 1969, 341). For Lenin, the soviets – which were revolutionary assemblies of workers and soldiers – in taking power would be a latter-day embodiment of the Commune; that is, of proletarian dictatorship. He therefore rejected Kautsky's proposition that "the victory for democracy" would assume a parliamentary, "bourgeois" form.

These two works by Lenin represented a massive break with Kautsky's Marxism. First, in defining and thereby essentializing the current epoch as imperialism, especially as a decaying one, he was asserting the moment of global revolution. Kautsky, although he referred to "ultra-imperialism" and the possibility of inter-imperialist cooperation in exploiting backward countries, nevertheless saw revolutions in the West occurring gradually within each state. Second, Lenin, in making the distinction between "bourgeois" (parliamentary) and proletarian (soviet) democracy, was suggesting that Kautsky's parliamentary strategy was historically redundant, because the Bolshevik strategy could be generalized in this new imperialist era (Lenin 1969, 516).

In the historic duel between Lenin and Kautsky, which marked a paradigm shift from social democratic Marxism to Marxism-Leninism, the question of fidelity to Marx and Engels and to the general principles of the *Manifesto* was critical, if only because Lenin's revolutionary project sought its legitimacy in Marxist methods and ideals. Much could be said, and has been said (e.g. Draper 1987), about who was the true "son" – to use Jacques Derrida's formulation (Derrida 1999, 213–269) – of Marx, or the better interpreter of Marxism or of the *Manifesto*. Nevertheless, both Kautsky and Lenin in their different ways reflected Marx's strategic flexibility during and after the revolutions of 1848 as a result of not knowing how long conditions favorable to proletarian revolution would take to ripen. Equally, both could appeal to the different transformational models offered by Marx in 1871–1872, either a commune or a parliamentary state.

These choices in part reflected the different dispositions and roles of the two within their respective parties: Kautsky, the risk-averse theoretician; Lenin, the theoretician *and* bold party leader, concerned with revolutionary actualities. More than this, they were located in different operational contexts. Kautsky was situated in a dynamic, industrial capitalist society with a strong army, well-developed bureaucracy, a maturing trade union movement and a developing democratic superstructure with strong working class representation. In all this he saw a realistic possibility of the "victory for democracy," of turning the political conditions created by the bourgeoisie against them, as part of the process by which the bourgeoisie had created their own gravediggers by giving the proletariat "weapons." He proposed, as did Luxemburg (albeit in a different way), to work both *within* and *against* "bourgeois" democracy, thereby transforming its class content (Luxemburg 1971, 180–181; Miliband 1977, 161–162). Kautsky saw this strategy as crucial for his ultimate goal of enabling the proletariat to become a new ruling class by developing its political efficacy. Indeed, this was the question that Kautsky stubbornly put to Lenin in his post-revolutionary polemics (e.g. Kautsky 1964, 23).

Lenin, on the other hand, was organizing and writing in a situation of economic and political backwardness, as well as profound social, economic and political dislocation in the midst of war. The Tsarist state had collapsed, and the question of what sort of state would fill the power vacuum was paramount. There were no well-established parliamentary institutions, and the soviets could make some claim to represent if not all the people, at least the workers, peasants, soldiers and sailors. His identification of proletarian dictatorship with a democratization of the executive/military arm certainly replicated closely Marx's account of the Paris Commune of 1871. Thus in a formal sense Lenin dealt with the question of *how* the working class should rule, but he was relatively untroubled by the question – at least in 1917 – of whether it had the *capacity* to rule. Nevertheless, the key question remained: was Lenin's call for revolution fully consistent with the condition-dependency principle? Was reality moving towards thought, and could Lenin and the Bolsheviks remain faithful to the general principles of the *Manifesto*?

THE SPLINTERING SYNTHESIS

Whether through circumstance (continuing economic dislocation, civil war and foreign invasion), design or both, Lenin's theory and practice after the October Revolution saw a rapid jettisoning of the general principles of the *Manifesto*, which in synthesis sought to avoid authoritarian radicalism. The principle of proletarian self-emancipation was the first casualty. Just before the Revolution, at a declaratory level Lenin was a soft vanguardist. He rejected accusations of Blanquist adventurism by not calling for another revolution after the February Revolution of 1917 which had toppled the Tsar. Lenin recognized that a majority had to be won over in the soviets. Thus it was a question of "*struggle for influence within*" them (Lenin 1917). Yet by 1919 Lenin had in effect given up on the idea that the soviets were centers of active working-class rule. As a result of the "low cultural level" of the working class, the soviets were "in fact organs of government *for the working people* by the advanced section of the proletariat [i.e., the Communist Party]" (quoted in Draper 1987, 136). And by 1921 Lenin had completely substituted the idea, implicit in the *Manifesto*, of *class* dictatorship through soviets with *party* dictatorship: "the dictatorship of the proletariat is impossible except through the Communist Party" (quoted in Miliband 1970, 312).

Nevertheless, these ad hoc responses of making a virtue out of necessity in a situation of intense economic, social and political upheaval were not rendered doctrinal (i.e. into an "ism") until after Lenin's death in 1924. Joseph Stalin, seeking to position himself in his rivalry with Trotsky as the theoretical and political heir to Lenin, wrote *Foundations of Leninism* (1924) (Sandle 2007, 61). This became the basis of Marxism-Leninism (Stalin 1940). For Stalin, Leninism was "Marxism of the era of imperialism and of the proletarian revolution" (Stalin 1940, 10). Although proletarian revolution was a central feature of his work, he stressed the importance of the national "bourgeois-democratic" revolutions in combating imperialism as part of the wider struggle against capitalism. Successful national struggles deprived capitalist imperialist powers of their super-profits. Equally, in the imperialist epoch of a moribund capitalism such revolutions would soon become proletarian revolutions, unlike the two-stage theory of revolutionary development envisaged by Kautsky and others of the Second International (Stalin 1940, 34). This process was facilitated by the fact that, given the political weaknesses of the bourgeoisie itself, the task of even a bourgeois revolution fell to the proletariat, supported by the poorer peasantry. Thus a proletarian dictatorship was but a small step, especially as Stalin thought that national movements should not be judged by formal democracy, but by whether or not they were effective against imperialism (Stalin 1940, 34).

Stalin followed the post-revolutionary Lenin in eliding soviet with party dictatorship. Stalin identified soviet power with the "state organization of the proletariat as the *vanguard* of the oppressed and exploited mass and as the ruling class" (Stalin 1940, 51–52, emphasis added). Yet he also claimed that the party was the vanguard of the working class, its general staff or its organized detachment (Stalin 1940, 96, 99), and the "highest form of class organization of the proletariat" (Stalin 1940, 102). Thus the party had a monopoly of power and political initiative, an unequivocally hard vanguard that through proletarian dictatorship would, quoting Lenin, have "to re-educate ... the proletarians themselves, who do not abandon their petty-bourgeois prejudices" (Stalin 1940, 46). Equally, to maintain its unity and dynamism the party was required to purge itself of "opportunists and reformists, social-imperialists and social-chauvinists, social-patriots and social-pacifists" (Stalin 1940, 108–109).

Stalin differentiated himself more obviously from Trotsky in seeing the peasantry as vital to the success of the revolution (Stalin 1940, 38–40, 65–66). This revolution "can and must," with the peasants' help, "build up a Socialist society," even if this did not mean the "complete and final victory for Socialism," for which an international revolution was needed (Stalin 1940, 41). In other words, Stalin was contrasting his vision of socialism in one country with the "permanentist" Trotsky, who stressed the necessity of international revolution in guaranteeing Russia's path to socialism.[4] Such a revolution for Stalin thus became an optional extra in building socialism. His understanding of socialism rested on the demand in the *Manifesto* for all "instruments of production" to be centralized "in the hands of the State" (CM 251). Yet, unlike the *Manifesto*, Stalin's hard vanguardism meant that socialism was effectively disconnected from proletarian *self*-emancipation, resulting from the "victory for democracy." Thus, Stalin was committed to the idea of state socialism in one country.

Whilst the *Foundations of Leninism* provided the theoretical justification for Marxist-Leninist practice, Stalin's *Dialectical and Historical Materialism* (1938) offered a totalizing world view, seeking to reaffirm the scientific truth of the Marxist account of nature and society. Stalin grounded the dialectical element of the text on a significantly revised account of Engels's interpretation of dialectical thought, with the law of the negation of negation absent, because it might have given legitimacy to Marxist critics of the Soviet state (Sandle 2007, 64–65). As for the historical component, this was a rehash of Marx's *Preface to a Contribution to a Critique of Political Economy* (1859), which echoed the teleological thrust of the *Manifesto*.

MAO'S MARXISM

In world-historic terms Stalin's Marxism-Leninism was far more successful in the East than in the West. It provided the ideological basis of the Chinese Revolution of 1949, led by Mao Tse-tung. Thus the significance of the Chinese national revolution was framed within Lenin's theory of imperialism; the peasantry were acknowledged as a force for this revolution, albeit under the leadership of the proletariat, that is, the Chinese Communist Party (CCP). Given the proletarian leadership of this bourgeois-democratic revolution, the construction of socialism, that is, an economically dynamic society based on the state ownership of productive assets, was possible (Mao 2007, 82, 97). Hence, Mao embraced Stalin's idea of socialism in one country, that is, independent, state-led and organized economic development (e.g. Mao 2007, 130).

Mao, too, portrayed dialectical materialism in hard vanguardist terms, proclaiming it in *On Practice* to be universally true (Mao 2007, 62). The responsibility for correctly knowing and changing the world had been "placed by history upon the shoulders of the proletariat and its party" (Mao 2007, 65). And those who opposed change "must go through a stage of compulsion before they enter the stage of voluntary, conscious change" (Mao 2007, 65). Consistent with the "truth" of dialectical materialism, he analyzed all the basic class conflicts and changes within Chinese society and the role of the CCP within them in terms of different kinds of contradiction, as expressed in *On Contradiction*. He adumbrated a typology: "universal and particular" contradictions, "principal contradiction and principal aspect of a contradiction" and "antagonistic and non-antagonistic contradiction." Apart from the universal contradiction between capitalists and the proletariat, the content of these contradictions was subject to change. Thus, as he said in his later work *On the Correct Handling of Contradictions among the People* (Mao 2007), the capitalist/proletarian contradiction was "antagonistic" in a capitalist system, whereas under socialism it could be "non-antagonistic."

Like Stalin, Mao held that ideological differences within the CCP represented contradictions between different class forces (Mao 2007, 100). The Cultural Revolution initiated by Mao in 1966 was an attempt to purge the state and party apparatuses of "capitalist roaders." Thus even a non-antagonistic contradiction could become an antagonistic one. Although Mao was strongly critical of Stalin's unwillingness to foster popular enthusiasm for his theoretical-political stance, nevertheless he worked within Stalin's and Lenin's notion of a proletarian dictatorship leading to socialism (Mao 2007, 117). Hence the Cultural Revolution was not intended in any way to reduce the CCP's control over the state's most important institution, the army (see Point Fifteen of the Sixteen Points, most probably written by Mao himself, which were published at the beginning of the Cultural Revolution in August 1966 (Badiou 2010, 126)).

In sum, Mao's "Marxism-Leninism" in certain ways was faithful to the general principles of the *Manifesto*. The possibilities for political action were analyzed in terms of a dialectical understanding of economic, social and political conditions. Mao enlarged the dialectical lexicon in order to analyze specific circumstances relevant to China, taking into account its unique class formation and political situation, which included a large peasantry under quasi-feudal conditions, and existing within the context of Japanese imperialism. Interestingly, Marx in the *Manifesto*, when referring to Poland, insisted upon an "agrarian revolution as a precondition for national emancipation" (CM 259). Mao also followed the *Manifesto* in aiming to resolve the forces/relations of production contradiction through state ownership of those productive assets. Nevertheless, he acknowledged that communal land ownership was for the time being more appropriate for the peasantry (Mao 2007, 125–127). Finally, he embraced the historical teleology of the *Manifesto*, arguing that history in effect gave the CCP the mandate to rule. Unsurprisingly, he shared with Lenin and Stalin a hard vanguardism that brooked no institutionalized opposition, and like Stalin had little faith in the proletariat as a genuinely self-emancipatory force in history.

Yet in retrospect such confidence in history has been misplaced. Mao might have had some satisfaction in today's "socialist" China out-performing the capitalist West in terms of economic growth, though he would need to realize that this success was due in no small part to Deng Xiaoping, the "capitalist roader" whom he had purged during the Cultural Revolution, and who had become "paramount" leader between 1978 and 1992. Deng recognized the great unanticipated "unknown unknown" of the *Manifesto*, namely, the fact that capitalism was far more resilient than it had appeared to be in 1848. Ironically, despite the constitution's description of China as "a socialist state under the people's democratic dictatorship," a more fitting appellation might rather be "state capitalist," with a state bank, state-owned industries and massive state support for private industry. Thus, there was a serious disconnect between an attachment to the general principles of the *Manifesto* and politico-economic practice.

WESTERN MARXISM

In the West the evolution of Marxist ideology and the application of the general principles of the *Manifesto* after the Russian Revolution was somewhat different. With the exception of various Trotskyist groupings, the main communist parties in Western Europe by the 1990s had explicitly abandoned the general principles animating the *Manifesto*. Initially there was unbounded optimism about the prospects for revolution in Europe, despite the failures in Germany (1918), Hungary (1919) and Italy (1919–1920). Thus Georg Lukács, in *History and Class Consciousness*, conceded that the politics of a revolutionary party may not "accord with the empirical reality of the moment," but the "ineluctable course of history will give it its due" (Lukács 1971, 42). This comforting thought also framed the Stalin-dominated Communist International's (1919–1943) view of fascism after the Great Crash of 1929. "Objectively," the world economic situation was ripe for revolution. The social democrats, especially in Germany, were effectively propping up the fascists, deeming them "objectively" social fascists. Anyway, fascists did not have to be taken too seriously as popular support for them would melt away as the economic crisis deepened (Townshend 1996, 111–112).

The Italian Antonio Gramsci, however, did not share this optimism. In his *Prison Notebooks*, written while incarcerated in a fascist jail between 1929 and 1935, he rejected any idea of historical inevitability, the product of an unfolding dialectic. "Immanentist conceptions," he said, were like religion or drugs in their stupefying effect, whose purpose was to provide solace in times of proletarian defeat (Gramsci 1971, 168, 336). His analysis of European, especially Italian, conditions suggested that, unlike Russia, revolutions in advanced capitalist countries would be long, drawn-out affairs, entailing a "war of position" through winning the battle of ideas in civil society, composed of such private institutions and associations as the church, trade unions, schools, political parties and cultural associations. In the West the strength of the capitalist class resided in its "soft" power, with "hard" power an ultimate resort.

Stalin, too, after the Second World War also recognized that proletarian revolutions in the West would be a lengthy process because of the strength of traditional institutions. In effect, he abandoned Lenin's soviet notion of the "victory of democracy," and embraced the strategy of transforming the bourgeois-created state, as found in Kautsky's writings and in the *Manifesto*. He approved of the *The British Road to Socialism* (1951), which scorned the idea that communists wanted "to introduce Soviet Power in Britain and abolish parliament" (Stalin 1951). Communists would "transform capitalist democracy into a real People's Democracy, transforming Parliament, the product of Britain's historic struggle for democracy, into the democratic instrument of the will of the vast majority of her people" (Communist Party of Great Britain 1951). Yet, unlike the *Manifesto*, the *British Road to Socialism* did not refer to the *telos* of historical inevitability.

Marxist-Leninist orthodoxies, insofar as they rested on the general principles of the *Manifesto*, were further abandoned in the early 1970s, with the rise of Eurocommunism in Italy, Spain, France and Britain. The orthodoxy's central tenet – the dictatorship of the proletariat – was jettisoned in order win over voters who associated the term with the totalitarian regimes of the Eastern Bloc. Eurocommunists assumed that – unlike the *Manifesto* (and Kautsky) – under modern, post-Fordist conditions the traditional, manual working class did not constitute a natural majority, and, with class dealignment, there was a need for electoral alliances. In Italy's case this meant an alliance with the right-wing Christian Democrats. Eurocommunists had given up on the distinctly proletarian narrative of the *Manifesto*. The extent of the change in what it meant to be a Marxist was illustrated in the *Manifesto for New Times* (1990), published by the British Communist Party, which abandoned the "anti-monopoly alliance" strategy led by the working class in favor of a "broad democratic alliance" (Communist Party of Great Britain 1990, 58). This was grounded in new social movements concerned with gender, ethnicity, the environment, sexuality and peace, as well as in the trade unions. All this was a world away from the focus in the *Manifesto* on class and production relations, although not from the *principle* of coalition-building in economically underdeveloped countries, as advocated in section IV. Nevertheless, as with the Continental communist parties, some of which became deeply divided and changed their names in the 1990s, there still remained the spirit of anti-capitalism.

CONCLUSION

Apart from inciting workers to revolution, the *Manifesto* aimed to educate the radical imagination through an understanding of capitalist reality and of the potentially hegemonic capacities of the proletariat. It sought to combine radicalism and realism. As Marx wisely said elsewhere, men can make history only in circumstances "directly encountered, given and transmitted from the past" (CW 11: 103). The circumstances faced by Marx's followers demonstrated that the general principles of the *Manifesto*, which had been designed to avoid elitism and authoritarianism, were indeed demanding ones. The conditions within which they operated created a massive dilemma: how to avoid the conflicting formulas for change offered by Robespierre or Bernstein? In remaining loyal to the condition-dependency principle, they found themselves in situations not necessarily anticipated by Marx – facing realities that were not benignly striving towards thought, a fateful combination of "known unknowns" and "unknown unknowns." These realities generated a variety of Marxisms – social-democratic, Marxism-Leninism, Trotskyism, Maoism and Eurocommunism – all of which could be described in some way as revisionist if benchmarked against the general principles of the *Manifesto*.

The self-emancipatory principle associated with "victory for democracy" was the greatest casualty. The Second International Marxism of Kautsky had optimistically assumed that in the West the growing proportion of the proletariat as part of the working population, combined with the democratization of the capitalist state, would create a revolutionary ascendancy for the working class. However, over time it seemed that Bernstein's doubts about the hegemonic capacity or disposition of the proletariat became increasingly valid in the West when Marxism there developed reformist strategies in order to "live with" capitalism. Eurocommunism of the 1970s was in reality a full acknowledgement that Bernstein might have been correct, with any notion of a transcending, proletarian interest or identity written out of the Marxist political script. The Russian Revolution had appeared for a brief moment to refute Bernstein's prognosis. But whether through inclination or as a result of circumstance, or both, Lenin and the Bolsheviks laid the basis of a one-party state, consolidated by Stalin, and emulated by Mao in China, who led a peasant rather than a proletarian revolution. Such dictatorships, justified by the ideology of Marxism-Leninism, ruled merely in the name of the proletariat.

The abandoning of the self-emancipatory principle was also reflected in the jettisoning, or drastic amending, of two other *Manifesto* principles. The Russian Revolution seemed for a moment to confirm the teleological principle of historical inevitability (but not without the help of proletarian agency). In *History and Class Consciousness* Lukács celebrated this view of historical directionality and momentum, but he also reasserted the dialectical principle from the *Manifesto*, which underpinned the notion of a historical goal. Indeed, some kind of correlation existed between the loss of faith in a historical *telos* and the meaning of dialectic. Thus in Stalin's account the "negation of the negation" was omitted from dialectical laws, in effect putting less emphasis on the idea of a forward, transcending movement of history. The negation of the negation was also absent in Mao's notion of contradiction, as was the Hegelian notion of *Aufhebung* in the work of Althusser (Althusser 1971), who along with Gramsci was the main intellectual influence on Eurocommunism.

For Marxists in the twentieth century the realities of class struggle and capitalist development tested the general principles of the *Manifesto* to breaking point because the central protagonist – the proletariat – for whatever reason, refused to play its revolutionary part. The Hegelian, dialectical imprint of the *Manifesto* on Marxist ideology has faded. Yet as Marxist activism has receded, and thus also Marxism as an action-oriented ideology, we should not conclude that Marxism as a worldview, first outlined in the *Manifesto*, is from a bygone era. The capitalism that Marx wrote about in 1848 may look different from today's, but in terms of its ethics, its deeply rooted social and economic conflicts and its boom-bust dynamics, has its essence really changed? If not, it may still generate a transformative dialectic, but not quite the one anticipated by Marx.

REFERENCES

Althusser, Louis. 1971. *For Marx*. Trans. Ben Brewster. London: Allen Lane.
Badiou, Alain. 2010. *The Communist Hypothesis*. Trans. David Macey and Steve Corcoran. London and New York: Verso.
Bernstein, Eduard. 1993 [1899]. *The Preconditions of Socialism*. Cambridge: Cambridge University Press.
Communist Party of Great Britain. 1951. *The British Road to Socialism*. www.marxists.org/history/international/comintern/ /britain/ ... /1951/51. (Accessed September 9, 2013).
Communist Party of Great Britain. 1990. *Manifesto for New Times*. London: Lawrence & Wishart.
Derrida, Jacques. 1999. "Marx & Sons." In *Ghostly Demarcations*, ed. M. Sprinker. London and New York: Verso, 213–269.
Dunayevskaya, Raya. 1958. *Marxism and Freedom*. New York: Twaine Publishers.
Draper, Hal. 1977. *The "Dictatorship of the Proletariat" from Marx to Lenin*. New York: Monthly Review Press.
Gramsci, Antonio. 1971. *Selections from the Prison Notebooks*, eds. and trans. Quintin Hoare and Geoffrey Nowell Smith. London: Lawrence & Wishart.
Gramsci, Antonio. 1978. *Selections from Political Writings (1921–1926)*. Trans. Quintin Hoare. London: Lawrence & Wishart.
Kautsky, Karl. 2007 [1909]. *The Road to Power*, ed. John H. Kautsky. n.p.: Center for Socialist History.
Kautsky, Karl. 1909a [1902]. *The Social Revolution*. London: Twentieth Century Press.
Kautsky, Karl. 1909b [1902]. *On the Morrow of the Social Revolution*. London: Twentieth Century Press.
Kautsky, Karl. 1913 [1902]. *The Social Revolution*. Chicago: Kerr.
Kautsky, Karl. 1964. *The Dictatorship of the Proletariat*, ed. John H. Kautsky. Ann Arbor, MI: University of Michigan Press.

Kautsky, Karl. 1971 [1892]. *The Class Struggle*. Trans. W. E. Bohn. New York: Norton.

Kautsky, Karl. 1988. "The Communist Manifesto after Six Decades." In Marx, *The Communist Manifesto*, ed. Frederick L. Bender. New York and London: Norton, 127–131.

Laclau, Ernesto, and Chantal Mouffe. 1985. *Hegemony and Socialist Strategy: Towards a Radical Democratic Politics*. London: Verso.

Lenin, V. I. 1917. Letters on Tactics. www.marxists.org/archive/lenin/works/1917/apr/x01.htm. (Accessed September 9, 2013).

Lenin, V. I. 1969. *Selected Works*. London: Lawrence & Wishart.

Lukács, Georg. 1971 [1923]. *History and Class Consciousness*. Trans. Rodney Livingstone. London: Merlin Press.

Luxemburg, Rosa. 1971. *Selected Political Writings*, ed. Dick Howard. New York: Monthly Review Press.

Mao, Tse-tung. 2007. *On Practice and Contradiction*. London and New York: Verso.

Marx, Karl. 1972. *Theories of Surplus Value, Part 3*. Trans. J. Cohen. London: Lawrence & Wishart.

Marx, Karl. 1973. *The Revolutions of 1848*, ed. David Fernbach. Harmondsworth: Penguin.

Marx, Karl. 1988. *The Communist Manifesto*, ed. Frederick L. Bender. New York and London: Norton.

Marx, Karl, and Frederick Engels. 1962. *Selected Works*, vol. 1. Moscow: Foreign Languages Publishing House.

Marx, Karl, and Frederick Engels. 1965. *Selected Correspondence*. Moscow: Progress Publishers.

Miliband, Ralph. 1970. "Lenin's *The State and Revolution.*" In *The Socialist Register 1970*, eds. Ralph Miliband and John Saville. London: Merlin Press, 309–319.

Miliband, Ralph. 1977. *Marxism and Politics*. Oxford: Oxford University Press.

Salvadori, Massimo. 1979. *Karl Kautsky and the Socialist Revolution, 1880–1938*. Trans. John Rothschild. London: New Left Books.

Sandle, Mark. 2007. "Soviet and Eastern bloc Marxism." In *Twentieth Century Marxism*, eds. Daryl Glaser and David M. Walker. London and New York: Routledge, 59–77.

Stalin, Joseph. 1940. *Foundations of Leninism*. London: Lawrence & Wishart.

Stalin. 1951. *On the Communist Manifesto*. www.marxists.org/history/erol/uk.postww2/stalin-pollitt. (Accessed September 9, 2013).

Stedman Jones, Gareth. 2002. "Introduction." In Karl Marx and Frederick Engels, *The Communist Manifesto*. Harmondsworth: Penguin Books.

Townshend, Jules. 1996. *The Politics of Marxism, The Critical Debates*. London and New York.

Trotsky, Leon. 1988. "On the Ninetieth Anniversary of *The Communist Manifesto*." In Marx, *The Communist Manifesto*, ed. Frederick L. Bender. New York and London: Norton, 139–145.

Wilks-Heeg, Stuart. 1998. "The Communist Manifesto and Working-Class Parties in Western Europe." In *The Communist Manifesto: New Interpretations*, ed. Mark Cowling. Edinburgh: Edinburgh University Press, 119–131.

6

The Permanent Revolution in and around the *Manifesto*

Emanuele Saccarelli

On the eve of the revolutionary events of 1848–1849, the *Communist Manifesto* issued a series of staggering and broad-ranging pronouncements. By the turn of the next century, fifty years of tumultuous historical development appeared to have powerfully vindicated the document. With every teetering step in domestic and foreign policy, the old absolutist governments demonstrated their historical exhaustion. Capitalism had penetrated and was proceeding to transform every corner of the globe. The bourgeoisie continued to oversee upheavals in the instruments of production and the organization of labor, which in turn led to manifold and uncontrollable political consequences. Most importantly, the modern working class, which earlier must have appeared (when it registered at all), as inconspicuous and inconsequential, particularly outside of England, had indeed become a large, conscious, organized and menacing force.

But if the *Manifesto* proved to be remarkably correct, half a century of history had not passed in vain. While the bourgeoisie continued its revolutionary transformation of economic and social relations, this process was taking place in a sharply uneven and contradictory manner. The political behavior of the bourgeoisie had taken a troubling turn, to the point that it routinely deferred to and openly supported archaic and viciously undemocratic regimes, particularly at the periphery of capitalist development. Meanwhile, the explosive growth of the socialist mass parties in Europe was also a contradictory phenomenon that introduced new challenges, including a creeping conservatism blunting the revolutionary edge of Marxist theory on the part of a layer of intellectuals and trade union bureaucrats affiliated with the movement.

These developments prompted a series of heated and connected debates in Germany and Russia on the orientation and reorientation of the socialist movement. Would capitalism eventually reproduce its original English template in those countries, or would it continue to enforce and reinforce political outcomes such as the Tsarist autocracy and the highly distorted parliamentary regime overseen by the Kaiser? Should socialists merely perform auxiliary services as the left wing of the hitherto unattained or incomplete bourgeois revolution, or should they fight for the political independence of the working class and for the immediate development of the revolutionary process in a socialist direction?

These questions found their most historically compelling expression in the actual upheavals of 1917 Russia. Rather than two distinct stages separated by decades, if not centuries – first, bourgeois democracy as the "normal" form of capitalist rule, then the socialist revolution – the revolutionary process in a peripheral country could only take a single, compressed form, which moreover could only find its successful completion in the international arena. The revolution, in this sense, would have to be "permanent." In the decades that followed 1917, the permanent revolution became the center of a massive Stalinist campaign of falsification and repression directed against its most prominent theoretician – Leon Trotsky – and the political legacy of the October revolution. This campaign began in 1923 in a series of lectures on the Bolshevik Party by Zinoviev (Zinoviev 1973). It assumed various forms in the twentieth century, also finding echoes in "Western Marxism," beginning with Gramsci's *Prison Notebooks* (Saccarelli 2008). The controversies over the permanent revolution, however, had begun before these better-known episodes.

Early in their political life, Marx and Engels employed various versions of the expression "permanent revolution" to describe the more radical phase of the French Revolution. Marx's "On the Jewish Question" characterized the Jacobin terror as "declaring the revolution to be permanent." *The Holy Family* counterpoised the "permanent war" of Napoleon to the "permanent revolution" of the Jacobins. Finally, Engels's article "The Magyar Struggle" included a comparison of contemporary events to the "revolution in permanence" of 1793 (quoted in Day and Gaido 2011, 3–4). The failure of the 1848–1849 Revolutions, and in particular the political cowardice and treachery of the bourgeoisie, became the occasion for the development of what had been essentially a mere historical reference into a theoretical and political concept of great significance. Most notably, Marx and Engels's "Address of the Central Committee to the Communist League" of March 1850, in drawing up the essential lessons of the revolutionary experiences in Europe for the working class, moved the permanent revolution decisively into the field of contemporary politics. In order to accomplish their "final victory," Marx and Engels urged the proletariat to "take up their position as an independent party as soon as possible," rather than accept the political leadership of the bourgeoisie. "Their battle cry must be: The Revolution in Permanence" (CW 10: 287; for a recent discussion of Marx and Engels's use of the term and a reappraisal of its political significance, see van Ree 2013).

From the turn of the century to the fallout of the 1905 revolution in Russia, some of the most outstanding figures of European socialism became involved in an international discussion of the permanent revolution (in texts made available only recently by Day and Gaido 2011). While these debates had a broader and complex political logic of their own, they often took the form of arguments over the lessons of 1848–1849, and, more specifically, the proper understanding of the *Manifesto*. Marx and Engels's historic document emerged as a recurring flashpoint in the discussion of the permanent revolution involving significant figures such as Georgy Plekhanov, David Ryazanov, Leon Trotsky, Karl Kautsky and Rosa Luxemburg. This chapter will examine this important and largely unheeded aspect of the legacy of the *Manifesto*. It will do so by discussing the general relation between the *Manifesto* and Marxism as it pertained to the later debates on the permanent revolution. It will then turn directly to those debates, examining the contested legacy of the *Manifesto*, first in understanding the pattern of capitalist development in countries such as Germany and Russia, and then in establishing a suitable political strategy and orientation for the working class.

MARXISM AND THE MANIFESTO: TEXT, METHOD, ORTHODOXY

Before examining the substance of these debates, it is necessary to deal with a few preliminary considerations. Insofar as the discussions of the permanent revolution took the form of arguments over the nature and continuing relevance of the *Manifesto*, a series of issues concerning not just the nature of the document, but more fundamentally that of Marxism as method and doctrine, immediately came to the fore. Experiences with and hearsay about later orthodoxies are likely to condition the contemporary reader to regard Marxism not as a scientific method to understand and act in the world, but as a fixed catechism, consisting of immutable truths, codified in canonical texts and learned by rote. The debates that will be examined here are instructive from this standpoint. Some measure of respect for the early tradition of texts and authors was undoubtedly present in all the exponents of classical Marxism. And this could hardly be regarded as unreasonable, given both the stature of Marx and Engels as intellectuals, and the special political and theoretical challenges involved in creating a method and doctrine aimed at systematically elevating the consciousness and providing political direction for the most oppressed layers of society. Writing half a century after the *Manifesto*, however, many of the Marxists involved in these discussions did not approach it in the manner of a once-and-for-all fixed catechism, and were quite aware of the dangers of an unthinking orthodoxy, rather than intelligently formed and developed one.

Kautsky, for example, instructively titled his 1903 introductory essay to the Polish edition of the text, "To What Extent Is the Communist Manifesto Obsolete?" (in Day and Gaido 2011, 169–185).[1] Before going on to make a number of remarks related to the permanent revolution, Kautsky noted that "sixty years could not pass without leaving their mark on the . . . *Manifesto*. The more correctly it comprehended and corresponded to its time, the more it must necessarily grow obsolete and become an historical document that bears witness to its own time but can no longer be definitive for the present" (171–172).

Similarly, in a 1907 speech on the prospects for a bourgeois revolution in Russia, Rosa Luxemburg attacked Plekhanov's attempt to settle the question merely by repeating certain quotations from the *Manifesto*: "the dialectical thinking that characterizes historical materialism requires that one assess phenomena not in a frozen state but in their movement. A reference to the way Marx and Engels characterized the role of the bourgeoisie fifty-eight years ago, when applied to present-day reality, is a startling example of metaphysical thinking and amounts to converting the living, historical views of the creators of the *Manifesto* into frozen dogma" (550). The burning political questions of the day – in particular, the nature of capitalist development and the necessary political strategy for the working class in the peripheral countries – could not be addressed by means of a mechanical repetition of old formulas.

To be sure, certain foundational propositions – the nature of the state, the central role of class struggle in the historical process and so on – were not to be subjected to constant reassessment and renegotiation. But as the revisionist controversy in Germany had demonstrated, this resolve was not a religious taboo or the product of *a priori* assumptions, but the hard-won theoretical essence of Marxism, to be defended politically against manifold class pressures that were coming to bear on the socialist movement. Nonetheless, a concrete and multi-sided analysis of social relations as they actually existed was an indispensable, constitutive component of Marxism. As Kautsky explained, this was the real living legacy of the *Manifesto*: "Nothing would be more erroneous than to stamp the whole of the *Communist Manifesto* as simply an historical document. On the contrary, the *principles* developed by it, the *method* to which it leads us, and the *characterisation* it gives in a few strokes of the capitalist mode of production, are today more valid than ever" (172, emphasis in original).

Kautsky argued along similar lines in another text titled "The American Worker," which also had an important role in the elaboration of the permanent revolution. The fact that the proletariat of Russia, "the most backward" of the capitalist countries, would serve as a model for Europe might be regarded as a peculiar one insofar as it "seems to contradict the materialist conception of history, according to which economic development constitutes the basis of politics." In reality, Kautsky noted, "it only contradicts that kind of historical materialism of which our opponents and critics accuse us, by which they understand a *ready-made model* and not a *method of inquiry*" (621, emphasis in original).

Kautsky's approach to the *Manifesto* echoed Marx and Engels's own. Reflecting on the significance of the *Manifesto* in their 1872 preface, Marx and Engels also remarked that its "general principles" remained "on the whole" correct, despite the antiquated demands at the end of the second section and the criticism of long-defunct political tendencies in the third. In this sense, they noted, the *Manifesto* had "become an historical document which we have no longer any right to alter." However, they also insisted that the "practical application of the principles will depend ... on the obtaining historical conditions" (CW 23: 174–175). That is, a proper understanding of the *Manifesto* had to be mindful of its inherent historical limitations.

Outside of certain basic parameters, which the *Manifesto* expressed brilliantly, Marxism would simply turn into something of a very different political character. Yet this text (any text), written at a specific moment in time, however powerful its intuitions and predictions, could not possibly fulfill the constant task of analysis and verification, of orientation and reorientation, demanded by the Marxist method. The *Manifesto*, thus, did not appear in the debates on the permanent revolution in a ritualistic manner. The fact that it emerged as a textual battleground for an important theoretical and political reorientation was not simply a function of its celebrated standing. While broadly expressing the essential tenets of Marxism, it also inevitably contained certain limitations. More specifically, the debates on the permanent revolution took place in the space opened by two definite gaps that were inherent in the nature of the document. The first was between historical analysis and political program, while the second was between the evocation of the political organization of the proletariat and its actual development in the form of a mass political party.

One of the most remarkable features of the *Manifesto* is that it simultaneously contains a broad, cogent theory of historical development, as well as a series of concrete and programmatic indications for contemporary political action. The two complement each other. Because of the former, the latter emerges not arbitrarily, or as a result of purely pragmatic considerations, but itself constitutes a definite and necessary moment of a larger historical process. Because of the latter, the former does not remain an impossibly distant historical abstraction but acquires an active, rather than contemplative character. However, this duality also constituted a potential pitfall from the standpoint of one of the crucial issues involved in the permanent revolution: the political role of the bourgeoisie.

On the historical plane, the *Manifesto* famously insists that the bourgeoisie played a "highly revolutionary role" (CM 239). This assessment is not entirely divorced from the political register of the *Manifesto* since the point also worked to undercut the position of various backward-looking forms of socialism. The broad historical assessment of the bourgeoisie was essentially carried over to the field of politics. Wherever the bourgeoisie had not yet triumphed – which is to say, in nearly every country of the world – the working class would be compelled to fight side by side with it against various pre-capitalist residues: "At this stage the proletariat does not struggle against its enemies, but rather against the enemies of its enemies" (CM 243). When Marx and Engels expressed the same idea in the more properly political section of the *Manifesto*, however, they introduced an important qualification: "In Germany, [the Communists] fight with the bourgeoisie *whenever it acts in a revolutionary way*" (CW 6: 519, emphasis added to the "authorized" English translation of 1888). Though in 1847 Marx and Engels could fairly be said to expect the revolutionary role of the bourgeoisie to continue, they also understood that the question had to be gauged on the basis of the actual unfolding of events. The 1848–1849 Revolutions provided a powerful answer in this regard, as the bourgeoisie first reluctantly went along, then in the face of working class militancy decisively cast its lot with reaction. Marx and Engels registered this epochal shift in a series of interventions during and in the aftermath of the events, especially in *The Class Struggles in France, 1848 to 1850* (1850) and *The Eighteenth Brumaire of Louis Bonaparte* (1852). But as the socialist movement began to grow, it could hardly be said to have completely assimilated the political and theoretical lessons of these struggles. Between the general historical praise in the *Manifesto* for the bourgeoisie, and the incomplete and conditional assessment of its political orientation, the iconic text could confuse as much as enlighten on this critical question. The arguments over the permanent revolution in part took place in the gap between the historical and the political registers of the *Manifesto*, representing a later attempt to settle these accounts.

In the *Eighteenth Brumaire*, Marx famously observed that that while bourgeois revolutions lived in the past, draped themselves in old clothes, and borrowed the vocabulary and imagery of previous epochs, the new proletarian revolutions, on the agenda after 1848, had to strip off "all superstition about the past" (CW 11: 106). But this was something to strive for, not an accomplished fact. As shown in the *Manifesto*, the past – in particular the revolutionary past of the bourgeoisie – continued to haunt the imagination of even the most advanced modern revolutionaries. As Engels later admitted,

When the February Revolution broke out, all of us, as far as our conceptions of the conditions and the course of revolutionary movements were concerned, were under the spell of previous historical experience … It was, therefore, natural and unavoidable that our conceptions of the nature and the course of the "social" revolution proclaimed in Paris in February 1848, of the revolution of the proletariat, should be strongly coloured by memories of the prototypes of 1789 (CW 27: 509).

The *Manifesto* also contained another gap that turned out to be salient in the debates over the permanent revolution. On the one hand, it boldly announced the advent of a Communist Party – that is, the political maturity of the proletariat – not as a specter, but as an actual organization. The fact that the *Manifesto* was commissioned by the Communist League, which at one point chastised "citizen Marx" for his delays in producing such a document, demonstrates that this announcement was no mere literary or prophetic gesture. On the other hand, the rise of mass, modern socialist parties was to come decades later, and what existed in 1847 essentially constituted an important, though embryonic experiment.

The political reorientation of the bourgeoisie discussed above was intimately connected to this issue. In 1906, Kautsky noted that since in Russia the workers had come into political being not as the appendage of a broad democratic party, but directly in the form of social democracy, the Russian bourgeoisie was "intimidated by the slightest stirring on the part of the proletariat" (602).

Similarly, when Ryazanov in 1903 identified the peculiarities of Russian development from the standpoint of revolutionary politics, his first point was that capitalism existed there *"under 'open surveillance' of socialism"* (85, emphasis in original). As its stirring opening lines indicated, the *Manifesto* deliberately sought to inaugurate this period of open surveillance. But the more the Communist Party invoked by the *Manifesto* turned into a menacing and well-organized reality, the more the prospective class alliance with the bourgeoisie became an unrealistic and indeed dangerous expectation. Here, too, arguments for the permanent revolution arose within a gap inherent in the nature of the *Manifesto* and of the method it exemplified.

THE NATURE OF CAPITALIST DEVELOPMENT

In addition to the relations between the bourgeoisie and the proletariat (to be discussed in the next section) the debates on the permanent revolution turned on a different, though related problem: the geographic pattern of development of capitalism. Again, the *Manifesto* left a contradictory legacy. Its account of the inevitable expansion of capitalism across the planet not only proved to be correct in a broad historical sense, but also arguably remains to this day the most brilliant exposition of the ongoing processes of "globalization." However, particularly in the light of later theoretical refinements, the *Manifesto* was also characterized by a certain one-sidedness on this question. The upshot of the analysis in the *Manifesto* was that the bourgeoisie was in the process of creating "a world in its own image" (CM 240). Insofar as this pithy characterization captured the inevitable, *combined* character of capitalist expansion beyond all national peculiarities and resistance – the battering down of "all Chinese walls" – it affirmed what history would prove to be an indisputable general tendency. But the development of capitalism was also, and simultaneously, of a sharply *uneven* character. Rather than simply smooth over the surface of the globe by reproducing the original English pattern of development everywhere else, the international penetration of capitalism, particularly in the later form of imperialist control, paradoxically reinvigorated or reinvented those archaic social relations and institutions the *Manifesto* had famously portrayed (in the 1888 translation) as melting into air. Indeed, Marx and Engels later corrected the one-sidedness of the *Manifesto* once they paid closer attention to capitalist development at the periphery, especially the effects of British imperialism in India and the fate of the agrarian communal system in Russia (Nimtz 2002).

This question of uneven and combined development was taken up in a little known polemic between Ryazanov and Plekhanov in preparation for the historic second congress of the Russian Social Democratic Labor Party. The immediate point of contention was the political program. But, as had been the case from its inception, before Russian socialism could grapple with questions of strategy and program, it had to deal with the problem of capitalist development as a necessary theoretical premise. Accordingly, Ryazanov's political criticism of the congress's draft program espoused by Plekhanov began by rejecting its underlying assumption of a general pattern of capitalist development that would be reproduced in Russia: "these prejudices result from the fact that in our appraisals of Russian conditions, we were guided by the 'pattern' of Western Europe." Russian Marxism had emerged in a struggle against populist conceptions, according to which a capitalist stage in Russia could be bypassed altogether. Thus it had understandably insisted that Russia could not avoid a traumatic and transformative encounter with capitalism. But in doing so, Russian Marxism, and Plekhanov in particular as its founder, had also adopted an overly schematic conception of exactly what this encounter would produce: "in the debates with our proponents of 'exceptionalism' we over-emphasized developmental similarities between Russia and the West-European countries while setting aside or overlooking Russia's peculiarities. The fact is, however, that Russia is developing in a very unique way." The sensible application of Marxism thus did not consist of superimposing a ready-made pattern onto Russian reality, but rather analyzing the specific ways in which capitalism was transforming the country: "the activity of our party can only be effective ... if, while following the general principles of scientific socialism, we also begin with an accurate analysis of all the peculiarities in Russia's historical development" (84–85).

Concerned as it was with the thoughtful development and application of Marxist orthodoxy, the discussion not coincidentally pivoted on the problem of the *Manifesto* and its legacy. Having expressed his criticism of the draft program's schematic conceptions of capitalist development, Ryazanov asked, "but doesn't this contradict The *Manifesto* ... by Marx and Engels?" (91). The question was not a rhetorical one, since it was followed by a critical re-examination of Marx and Engels's political orientation during the 1848–1849 Revolution, to be reviewed later. On this question, too, as we have seen, the *Manifesto* could not be approached as a fixed catechism. Its account of the pattern of capitalist development was only correct at a certain level of abstraction, and a mechanical application of it to Russia would be a mistake: "The programme's authors are victims of 'the pattern' ... What makes sense in Western Europe is simply nonsense in our country" (119).

The question of the pattern of capitalist development had an important corollary that was taken up in the polemic. If, as Plekhanov believed, Russia was on its way to "normal" capitalist development and had to pass through a classic bourgeois revolution, all the existing pre-capitalist forms had to be regarded as "remnants," and the task of Russian social democracy was to eradicate them in collaboration with the bourgeoisie. From Ryazanov's standpoint, however, these pre-capitalist forms appeared in a different light: "there is an even greater question as to whether all those phenomena that are cited in the *Iskra* programme ... should really be attributed to 'remnants' rather than to the 'rudiments' of capitalism" (150). Tsarism in particular, according to Ryazanov, was not some unfortunate residue, but had in fact been reinvigorated and reinvented by capitalist penetration of Russia:

Our autocracy ... is not a *holdover* or some accidentally preserved fragment of the past. Alas, it is very much part of the *present*. And if the authors of our draft did not divide the whole of history into two periods – one being pre-capitalist and the other capitalist – they would see how much the character of our autocracy has changed since the time of Ivan III ... we will be much closer to the truth if we say that in its contemporary form our autocracy is a product of the rudiments of capitalism. (156–157, emphasis in original)

Ryazanov thus insightfully called attention to the fact that the appraisal of Tsarism as a "remnant" emerged from an overly schematic conception not just of the geographic patterns of capitalist development, but also of the Marxist conception of historical stages and temporalities.

On this question, too, the legacy of 1848 and of the *Manifesto* loomed large, playing an important role in Plekhanov's defense of the concept of pre-capitalist remnants. He asked pointedly, "Is it true, as Ryazanov supposes, that Marx saw no need to help in overcoming these relics of the past? And if Marx did see such a need, then how does it happen that we are guilty of betraying Marxism when we aim to abolish the countless fragments of the precapitalist order that still survive in Russia?" (144–145). In defending his position, Plekhanov appealed repeatedly to the authority of the *Manifesto* (145, 146, 147, 160). For example, he presented Ryazanov's ideas as an echo of the same pre-Marxist attitudes that were denounced in the *Manifesto* for their ultimately reactionary character, since they refused to acknowledge the revolutionary character of the bourgeoisie and opposed the necessary alliance with it in order to mop up pre-capitalist remnants: "If we thought otherwise, then we would resemble those 'true' German socialists of the forties, who were so sarcastically mocked by the *Manifesto* ... and with whom you have so much in common" (145).

These arguments had a certain force, particularly since they were being advanced by the most prominent and founding figure of Russian socialism. But Ryazanov's positions expressed much more accurately the nature of capitalist development in Russia, and a more profound and less scholastic understanding of Marxism. They constituted a significant step in the development of the permanent revolution, which was, not coincidentally, invoked toward the end of the text (131). Though Ryazanov's political tendency was in fact shut out of the historic second congress, his arguments contributed to a serious reassessment of the prospects for two distinct and separate revolutionary stages, and of the habit of gauging the ripeness of socialism on a country-by-country basis – a reassessment that found its most important expression in October 1917.

Rather than simply defer to the allegedly fixed orthodoxy contained in the *Manifesto*, Ryazanov posed the question of the genuine legacy of the document and the historical experience it reflected in a sensible manner: "What we do need is an intelligent and critical attitude towards the experience of Western Europe"

(98–99). His specific answer was insightful, at least in highlighting the concrete peculiarities of Russian development and their political significance. On the more general theoretical problem, however, Ryazanov's bold formulations left the possibility open for a certain confusion since he at times emphasized these peculiarities in a way that lost sight of the combined and international character of all capitalist development. He stated, for example, "the only thing that is repeated is the sequence of the main phases of social development, but they occur each time in a *completely new historical* context depending on the unique course of the *historical* development of any given social 'organism'" (99, emphasis in original). This tendency to overstate national peculiarities while detaching them from an integrated, international conception of capitalist development was a recurring one in many of the authors who contributed to the elaboration of the permanent revolution in this period. Kautsky, for example, while also rejecting the idea of a simple pattern inherited from the *Manifesto*, stated, "in every country many of these conditions are completely unique. Nowhere do they correspond perfectly to the conditions that influenced the writing of the *Communist Manifesto*" (184). This was not merely a question of choosing the correct adjectives and inflection, since later on a one-sided emphasis on the national peculiarities of Russia gave rise to catastrophic political degenerations in the name of a rejection of the permanent revolution.

The most farsighted and precise early formulations of the question of capitalist development, its corollaries and political implications were offered by Leon Trotsky. In an extraordinary text written in the thick of the 1905 revolution, for example, Trotsky developed a historical comparison with the events of 1848 that returned to and refined the terms of the earlier polemic between Ryazanov and Plekhanov. Trotsky reviewed the lessons of the expansion of capitalism around the globe since the writing of the *Manifesto*: "more than fifty years have passed since 1848. It has been half a century of capitalism's uninterrupted conquests throughout the entire world" (444). More so than all other Marxists in this period, Trotsky insisted on the combined and integrated character of capitalist development. In the parlance of social science, the fundamental unit of analysis for all political and economic phenomena could only be the world system, not the nation-state: "imposing its own type of economy and its own relations on all countries, capitalism has transformed the entire world into a single economic and political organism" (444). In this sense there was indeed a pattern of capitalist development, and there could be no question of exceptions and totally unique national conditions, as some of the other early theoreticians of permanent revolution had at times intimated. However, far from resulting in the reproduction of the original English template in every country, the global expansion of capitalism had in fact renewed and regenerated archaic institutions into its political and social fabric. Most importantly, it had transformed the bourgeoisie itself into a reactionary class that was at every turn compelled to betray its own revolutionary legacy:

[It has been] a half a century of the "organic" process of mutual adaptation between the forces of bourgeois reaction and those of feudal reaction ... Internalising all the pathological processes ... the bourgeoisie has ... avidly clung to every reactionary force without questioning its origins. Its friends range from pope to sultan and beyond. The only reason it has not extended its bonds of "friendship" to the Chinese Emperor is that he is not a force: it was more profitable for the bourgeoisie to plunder his possessions than to support him through the work of a worldwide gendarme ... In this way, the world bourgeoisie has made the stability of its state system deeply dependent upon the stability of pre-bourgeois bulwarks of reaction. (444–445)

By the beginning of the twentieth century, if it could still be said, in the words of the *Manifesto*, that the bourgeoisie had created "a world in its own image," it had to be acknowledged that the image had changed drastically. The bourgeoisie looked like a grotesque and disfigured version of what it had been in the period of its revolutionary youth, and the proletariat would need to revise its political orientation accordingly.

THE PERMANENT REVOLUTION AS A POLITICAL STRATEGY

The permanent revolution represented a fundamental reorientation of the proletariat away from a strategic alliance with the bourgeoisie and toward its own political independence. As we have seen in the previous section, this reorientation flowed in part out of a more sophisticated understanding of the geographical and historical patterns of capitalist development. It also flowed from a definitive reassessment of the political behavior that could be expected from the bourgeoisie. From this standpoint, the political actions carried out by Marx and Engels as participants in the 1848–1849 Revolutions, including the initial directives elaborated in the *Manifesto*, had a definite significance. A reappraisal of this record became one of the important fronts in the early debates on the permanent revolution. This was particularly true of Germany, since that country had been Marx's and Engels's primary theater of operations during this period.

As we have seen, the *Manifesto* alone, without a more complete assessment of the revolutionary experience it anticipated, could not serve as a reliable guide. But even when the full record was taken into account, the lessons of that struggle were by no means transparently clear to all. Part of the revisionist controversy involving Eduard Bernstein, for instance, dealt with the legacy of the *Manifesto* and the events of 1848–1849 in a way that ultimately stimulated important contributions to the development of the permanent revolution.

Bernstein took on the legacy of the *Manifesto* directly, focusing on the class character of the revolutionary process: "In 1847, *The Communist Manifesto* declared that, given the stage of development reached by the proletariat and the advanced conditions of European civilization, the bourgeois revolution, on which Germany was embarking, 'will be but the prelude to an immediately following proletarian revolution.'" According to Bernstein, this was an obvious blunder – a form of "historical self-deception" that would have been more fitting of a "run-of-the-mill political visionary" (16–17). Although the *Manifesto* formally upheld the two separate historical stages, it nonetheless effectively collapsed them by forecasting an immediate transition between the two. And this was not simply a matter of an incorrect prediction. The *Manifesto* not only underestimated the revolutionary commitments of the bourgeoisie, but it actively frightened it by putting it on notice of its impending demise at the hands of its erstwhile political ally.

Those who opposed revisionism also addressed this question. They too believed that the *Manifesto* included a significant error on this score. But the problem for them was quite the opposite of what Bernstein had diagnosed. According to Kautsky, the *Manifesto* failed to fully register the significance of the fact that "every demonstration of force on the part of the proletariat pushes the bourgeoisie to the camp of reaction." As explained above, these demonstrations of force very much included the publication of the *Manifesto* itself. In any case, the actual unfolding of events in 1848–49 powerfully demonstrated both sides of the political equation laid out by Kautsky. The proletariat had initiated and was at the forefront of the uprisings, while in response the bourgeoisie rapidly cowered behind the absolutist "remnants." According to Kautsky, then, Marx and Engels's "mistake was not to exaggerate the value of the proletariat, but that of the bourgeoisie" (19).

Kautsky's "To What Extent is the Communist Manifesto Obsolete?" included a particularly sharp and direct reassessment of the 1848–1849 events from the standpoint of the permanent revolution. Kautsky argued that the expectations expressed in the *Manifesto* for the political conduct of bourgeoisie, for the strategy to be adopted by the working class, and for the overall class character of the revolutionary process, proved to be incorrect. As a result of the bold revolutionary initiative taken by the working class, "the bourgeoisie was immediately forced to begin a life-and-death struggle against the proletariat itself" (178). For this reason, the general character of the 1848 Revolutions turned out to be very different from what was laid out in the *Manifesto*.

Marx and Engels had predicted two distinct stages, separated, to Bernstein's dismay, by a very short period. In fact, Kautsky noted, "since June 1848 a bourgeois revolution that could become the prelude to a proletarian revolution is no longer possible ... The next revolution can only be a proletarian one." The prospect of two distinct and separate revolutionary stages could no longer be regarded as realistic. Although the beginning of the process would in some respects retain the contours of a classic bourgeois democratic revolution, the old conception of two stages had to be abandoned: "the strengthening of the working class, and its elevation to a position that would enable it to conquer and retain political power, can no longer be expected from a bourgeois revolution that, in becoming permanent, grows beyond its own limits and develops out of itself a proletarian revolution" (178–179). And if the events of

1848–1849 had already decisively revealed this epochal shift, the continued deepening of the same processes – the numerical growth and political maturation of the working class, the political decay of the bourgeoisie – made the permanent revolution an ever more urgent theoretical and political necessity. Kautsky's conclusion was lapidary: "The *Communist Manifesto* could still declare: 'In Germany the Communist Party fights with the bourgeoisie whenever it acts in a revolutionary way. … Today we can nowhere speak of a revolutionary bourgeoisie" (176).[2]

However, at the same time Kautsky also insisted that Marx and Engels, using the same general method and principles elaborated in the *Manifesto*, were able to rapidly diagnose the new situation and adjust their political course accordingly. He wrote, "Thus some things have reached a different outcome from what the authors of the *Communist Manifesto* expected at the time of writing. But they were the first to recognise the new situation, and they did so because of the principles and methods they had developed in their *Manifesto*" (180). In short, the seeds of the permanent revolution had already been sown by Marx and Engels in 1848–1849 on the basis of a correct application of the general theoretical framework to the specific, and in many ways surprising events on the ground. It was in this sense that the *Manifesto* retained its central place in Marxist orthodoxy, and had to be defended against latter-day critics. In a not-so-veiled attack against Bernstein and the revisionists, Kautsky explained, "many a short-sighted mole, diligently digging for earth-worms, thinks himself far superior in range and clarity of vision to the masters of the *Communist Manifesto* and even looks down with pity upon their intellectual errors. But the fact is that … no socialists … comprehended the new situation sooner than Marx and Engels" (179). While fancying themselves theoretical mavericks, the revisionists in fact clung on to exactly those aspects of the *Manifesto* that had been superseded by the historical process. Kautsky noted that the *Manifesto*'s canonical formula justifying the political alliance with the bourgeoisie – "the Communist party fights together with the bourgeoisie" – had been incessantly invoked to justify every step toward a political rapprochement – ministerialism, reformism and so on. Here, Kautsky concluded, "we have a Marxist 'dogma' defended with truly dogmatic fanaticism precisely by the champions of 'critical' socialism" (180–181).[3]

Another outstanding figure of German Social Democracy also responded to Bernstein on this question. Franz Mehring, who, not coincidentally, was the party's foremost scholarly authority on Marx and Engels, also began from the standpoint that the initial perspective codified in the *Manifesto* was mistaken. With Kautsky, Mehring criticized the text's assessment of the bourgeoisie and the nature of the revolutionary process. The *Manifesto*, reflecting Marx and Engels' initial attitude on these questions, essentially invoked the coming of a classic bourgeois revolution for which the proletariat would have to serve as the left wing, fighting for a definite time "the enemies of its enemies." This orientation was expressed not just in the text, but also in Marx and Engels's initial political actions. For example, they had initially conceived their newspaper *Neue Rheinische Zeitung*, the headquarters of their revolutionary efforts, as the "organ of the democracy" – a designation that was more consistent with the broad class alliance initially envisioned in the *Manifesto* than with a struggle for the political independence of the working class.

Mehring was able to show convincingly that, once confronted with the actual course of revolutionary events, Marx and Engels had changed their political orientation. Their initial expectations concerning the bourgeoisie had been invalidated by its passivity and treachery – best illustrated by the June 1848 massacre in Paris, but reproduced in different form throughout Europe. As Mehring explained, "very quickly it became evident that ... out of fear of the incomparably more highly developed working class of the nineteenth century, [the bourgeoisie] was ready to accept the 'closure of the revolution' at any moment, even at the price of the most ignominious concessions to absolutism and feudalism." Mehring then spelled out more concretely the steps taken by Marx and Engels in their political reorientation:

Already in April 1849 Marx and his close followers retired from the democratic district committees in Köln because they saw the necessity for a close union of the workers' associations against the weaknesses and treacheries of the bourgeoisie. At the same time they decided to attend the workers' congress planned for June 1849, which had been convoked in Leipzig by the workers' movement east of the Elbe, to whom the *Neue Rheinische Zeitung* had not paid much attention until then. (458)

It was this episode in Marx and Engels's political biography that remained obscured by the shadow of the monumental legacy of the *Manifesto*, and constituted an important precedent in the formulation of the permanent revolution.

Similar and related debates also took place in Russia. There, the propulsive growth of capitalism, side by side with the reinforcement of Tsarism, endowed those same discussions with special sharpness and urgency. As explained in the previous section, Ryazanov had offered a criticism of the draft program of Russian Social Democratic Labor Party that was predicated on a different conception of capitalist development. In doing so, he was compelled to pose the question of whether his ideas contradicted the *Manifesto*. Ryazanov answered with a series of arguments that were very much in line with the ideas Kautsky and Mehring were developing in Germany. Like them, Ryazanov explained that the *Manifesto* began from a mistaken political premise, and that Marx and Engels were able to correct it in the course of the revolution.

For Ryazanov too, the essential problem was that "Marx and Engels overestimated the progressive character of the German bourgeoisie," expecting the repetition of a classic bourgeois revolution. As he explained poignantly,

they wanted to go along with the bourgeoisie, and they quite deliberately took a position on the extreme left wing of bourgeois democracy, differentiating themselves only by their more extreme political demands. During all of 1848 and the beginning of 1849, they helped the bourgeoisie to wage *its* political struggle, dictated its programme of action at each step of the way, energetically "pushed" it in the direction of determined opposition. (91)

But Marx and Engels were compelled to recognize that these efforts were in vain. "The fact is that the workers and the most radical strata of the petty bourgeoisie *made* the revolution. The bourgeoisie, as Engels said, only *endured* the revolution, and he and Marx soon understood that they had excessively idealised the bourgeoisie, which turned out to be completely incapable of fulfilling *its own* historical mission" (91, emphasis in original).

The notion of two separate revolutionary stages had led to an incongruous and ultimately untenable political line. Ryazanov then, in line with Mehring, provided a specific account of Marx and Engels's change of course in 1849 (92, 106–107, 124–125; and Ryazanov 1974). (The fact that Ryazanov was one of the first Marxist victims of Stalinist repression and was ultimately executed is no coincidence in the light of his enormous historical knowledge of the Marxist movement, and the less well-known fact that he had played a role in the early development of the permanent revolution.) In his account, Ryazanov was able to put in particularly sharp focus the issue of the political independence of the working class. The *Manifesto* had carefully explained that even in the course of cementing a political alliance with the bourgeoisie, the communists "never cease for a moment to instill in the workers as clear a consciousness as possible concerning the mortal conflict between bourgeoisie and proletariat" (CM 259). This principle had to be stated categorically precisely because Marx and Engels understood that political collaboration with the bourgeoisie would bring to bear definite pressures on the socialist movement. No matter how forceful its original formulation, however, this crucial political principle proved to be impossible to reconcile with the facts on the ground. As Ryazanov explained, "while 'inciting' the bourgeoisie, they were unable as devoted communists ... to function merely as the extreme left wing of bourgeois democracy or to hide the fact that by 'pushing' the bourgeoisie they only ended up all the sooner 'at loggerheads'. As a result, they ended up 'pushing away' the bourgeoisie, who had no interest in continuing a revolution that had been foisted upon them ... It became obvious that the working class could not wait for a bourgeois victory as a precondition for taking up its *own* task" (92).

As was true of Kautsky, the spirit of Ryazanov's intervention was not to cast aspersions on Marx and Engels's record as revolutionaries. They had made a mistake. But they had been able to correct it, developing Marxism theoretically and politically in the process. The more pressing issue was whether the movement, particularly in Russia, would be able to absorb and apply the lessons of this important historical episode: "there are different kinds of mistakes ... [Marx and Engels's] was a mistake ... rooted in objective conditions. But if we want to avoid repeating that mistake, if we want to avoid making our own strictly 'subjective' mistake, then we must not close our eyes to ... the fact that our bourgeoisie has shown itself to be emphatically incapable of taking any revolutionary initiative whatever" (92). Ryazanov's insight can be fully appreciated when one considers the terms of Plekhanov's response to him on this point.

Plekhanov comforted himself with the thought that, "if our relation to the liberal bourgeoisie is mistaken, then it turns out that we are in pretty good company, namely, *with the authors of the Communist Manifesto*" (147, emphasis in original). Though this remark was obviously a polemical gesture, it nonetheless revealed something about the tendency for a mechanical attachment to the *Manifesto* to produce unthinking and unhelpful orthodoxy. More importantly, even if Ryazanov's criticism was actually correct, that is, even if Russian Marxism overestimated the progressive role of the bourgeoisie, this error, said Plekhanov, "could not possibly be of any practical significance." He explained, "Do we cease, as a result, to develop in the minds of workers a consciousness of the opposition between their interests and those of the bourgeoisie? Do we strive even in the least to curtail the class struggle that is occurring in our country? ... *Our supposedly exaggerated expectations of the bourgeoisie do not cause us to diverge even by a hair's breadth from the line that we would follow if we had no such expectations at all*" (147–148, emphasis in original). This was a formal and politically naïve account of the danger. Plekhanov ascribed to the statement in the *Manifesto* powers it did not possess. His own political biography, particularly its inglorious end as a supporter of Russia's war effort during World War I, testifies to the fact that a formal commitment to the political independence of the working class, however forcefully proclaimed, could not act as a talisman to successfully ward off powerful class pressures. Here, too, a mistaken conception of the Marxist orthodoxy expressed in the *Manifesto* proved to have dire political consequences.

CONCLUSION

The debates on the permanent revolution in Germany and Russia at the turn of the century that have been reviewed here have a definite and generally unappreciated significance. They represent a crucial historical link between Marx and Engels's own initial reassessment of the political strategy necessary for the working class in the coming upheavals, and the better known experiences of the Russian revolution and its degeneration. They involved some of the most remarkable exponents of classical Marxism, in some cases in ways that complicate and enrich our understanding of their political life and legacy. Most importantly, they help to clarify not just a series of important theoretical and political problems in the development of Marxism, but the nature of the tradition in the most fundamental sense. In all these debates, the *Manifesto* played an important, if contradictory, role.

REFERENCES

Day, Richard B., and Daniel Gaido. 2011. *Witnesses to Permanent Revolution: The Documentary Record.* Chicago: Haymarket Books.

Marx, Karl. 1996. *Later Political Writings*, ed. and trans. Terrell Carver. Cambridge: Cambridge University Press.

Nimtz, August. 2002. "The Eurocentric Marx and Engels and Other Related Myths." In *Marxism, Modernity and Postcolonial Studies*, eds. Crystal Bartolovich and Neil Lazarus. Cambridge: Cambridge University Press, 65–80.

Ryazanov, David. 1974. *Karl Marx and Friedrich Engels.* New York: Monthly Review Press.

Saccarelli, Emanuele. 2008. *Gramsci and Trotsky in the Shadow of Stalinism.* New York: Routledge.

van Ree, Erik. 2013. "Marxism as Permanent Revolution." *History of Political Thought.* 34(3): 540–563.

Zinoviev, Grigorii. 1973. *History of the Bolshevik Party.* London: New Park Publications.

7

The Two Revolutionary Classes of the *Manifesto*

Leo Panitch

The uniqueness of the *Manifesto* is above all due to two things. One is its brilliant portrayal of the bourgeoisie as a revolutionary class. The other is its vision that the proletariat would become a revolutionary class.

In the *Manifesto* the identification of the revolutionary nature of the bourgeoisie – indeed its understanding that "the bourgeoisie cannot exist without continually revolutionizing the instruments of production, hence the relations of production, and therefore the whole relations of society" (CM 239) – has seemed ever more relevant through the recent decades of capitalist globalization. And the notion of states "administering the common affairs" (CM 239) of the bourgeoisie could be even more deeply appreciated as an incisive way of denoting that, far from capital having bypassed states, states have played a leading role in authoring, orchestrating and managing the process of capitalist globalization.

It is of course important that we should not understand what the *Manifesto* appropriately called the bourgeoisie's continuing "revolutionary role in history" (CM 239) in terms of unmitigated "progress," as Marx certainly did not either. This is obvious when one considers the severe ecological problems and often appalling social conditions even in the countries of advanced capitalism, let alone in the developing capitalist countries of the global south, where the conditions of newly proletarianized workers often look very similar to the conditions of life Engels described in Manchester in the 1840s (see his book, published in 1845, *The Condition of the Working Class in England* (CW 4: 295–583)). Moreover, the global financial volatility of recent decades repeatedly brought to the top of the quotable quote charts the depiction in the *Manifesto* of the bourgeoisie as resembling "the sorcerer who could no longer control the unearthly powers he had summoned forth" (CM 241).

ECONOMISTS AND CRISES

Keynesian economists and social democratic politicians, who had once imagined that states had developed the policy devices to prevent capitalist crises, had already been brought up short by the crisis of the 1970s. The neoliberal decades that followed made it, even superficially, look like the bourgeoisie had indeed "finally gained exclusive political control through the modern representative state" (CM 239). This need not be taken to mean that the internally competing capitalist classes had somehow come together to figure out their common interests, and to tell states what to do in face of the complex problems of managing a global capitalism. Rather it speaks to how states themselves had become more and more committed to promoting and facilitating capital accumulation, and had developed more and more bureaucratic and legal capacities and devices for coordinating it internationally, because of their ever-greater dependence on it for their revenues and their legitimacy. Having effectively abandoned their earlier limited practices of "failure prevention," capitalist states have increasingly adopted instead – as if discerning the inevitability of capitalist crises – the practice of "failure containment," most evidently in the first great global capitalist crisis of the twenty-first century (Panitch and Gindin 2012, chs 10 and 12).

The seminal contribution of the *Manifesto* in capturing the bourgeoisie's "revolutionary role" was once the subject of a famous article by Joseph Schumpeter, who, writing with all the pedigree of his recent presidency of the American Economic Association, averred:

> After having blocked out the historical background of capitalist development in a few strong strokes that are substantially correct, Marx launched out on a panegyric upon bourgeois achievement that has no equal in economic literature … No reputable "bourgeois" economist of that or any other time – certainly not A. Smith or J. S. Mill – ever said as much as this. Observe, in particular, the emphasis on the *creative* role of the business class that the majority of the most "bourgeois" economists so persistently overlooked. (Schumpeter 1949, 209–210, emphasis in original)

Whereas almost all economists committed the mistake of treating science and technology as "*independent* factors," Schumpeter observed, Marx's *Manifesto* presented scientific and technological innovations as "products of the bourgeois class culture." And this is why he insisted on repeating that "by no modern defender of the bourgeois civilization has anything like this been penned, never has a brief been composed on behalf of the business class from so profound and so wide a comprehension of what its achievement is and of what it means to humanity" (Schumpeter 1949, 210). And insofar as the state also needed to be taken into account, and especially what Schumpeter designated as "the contributions of non-bourgeois bureaucracies," he also praised Marx for showing that this should not be seen, as it was by "the economists of all times" as well as by "political science itself," as representing some metaphysical entity to be called "The Common Good" and a not less metaphysical "state" ... sailing in the clouds and exempt from and above human struggles and group interests ... It was, therefore, a major scientific merit of Marx that he hauled this state down from the clouds and into the sphere of realistic analysis. (Schumpeter 1949, 208–209)

By sharp contrast, the discussion of the *Manifesto* in Thomas Piketty's much celebrated recent book – although very much in the Schumpeterian tradition in lamenting that the discipline of economics should have cut itself off from historical and sociological analysis – not only misses what Schumpeter stressed ("the bourgeoisie cannot exist without continually revolutionizing the instruments of production") but goes so far as to claim that "Marx totally neglected the possibility of durable technological progress and steadily increasing productivity" (Piketty 2014, 10). In doing this, Piketty betrays precisely what Schumpeter criticized other economists for, that is, mistakenly treating technology as an *independent* factor – in Piketty's words, "a force that can to some extent serve as a counterweight to the process of accumulation and concentration of private capital" (Piketty 2014, 10).

This seems to be at the root of some of the more confusing aspects of Piketty's book. His suggestion that the advanced European countries which rejected communist revolutions and "explored, other, social democratic avenues" were able to use this independent factor of technology as a counterweight to capital would appear to contradict the main thesis of his book, which is primarily concerned with demonstrating the inevitable reproduction of inequality that has come with the survival of capitalism. And this confusion may well be why the progressive tax proposals that he calls on capitalist states to take up now at the end of the book seem to be so badly in need of being "hauled down from the clouds and into the sphere of realistic analysis," as Schumpeter put it. Leaving aside such problems, Piketty's divergence from Schumpeter on how to read the *Manifesto* rests on the much greater weight the former gives to passages in the *Manifesto* that refer to the likely collapse of capitalism by virtue of the bourgeoisie having already cut the ground under its own feet.

While recognizing that "Marx wrote at a time of a great political fervor, which at times led him to issue hasty pronouncements," Piketty wants to stress the extent to which Marx "decided on his conclusions in 1848 before embarking on the research needed to justify them," and that for "the next two decades Marx labored over the voluminous treatise that would justify this conclusion" about the collapse of capitalism (Picketty 2014, 9). Interestingly, Schumpeter also contended that – even though Marx "by 1847 was hardly an economist at all: it was during the 1850's that he became one, and one of the most learned ones who ever lived" – Marx's program of research over the following decades was "quite set" in the *Manifesto* and its "*vision* that the capitalist process not only creates the 'proletariat' but also by virtue of its inherent logic steadily deteriorates its condition" (Schumpeter 1949, 211–212). The difference with Piketty is that Schumpeter emphasizes much more Marx's ongoing concern with, and contribution to, understanding the ongoing revolutionary dynamic of capitalism; it was not only what Piketty calls his "prediction of the apocalyptic end of capitalism" that drove Marx's research agenda.

Of course, it is not only among non-Marxist economists like Schumpeter and Piketty (who, unlike most of his fellow economists today, at least directly engages with Marx) that one finds this difference. It appears in another form in the continuing disagreements among Marxists today over how much emphasis to put on "The Law of the Tendency of the Rate of Profit to Fall" which was the title of Part III of Volume III of *Capital* (CW 37: esp. 209) that was published (in 1894) only after Marx's death. Crucial to these disagreements is the question of whether Marx specifically recognized that one of the most important "counteracting tendencies" to this were new technologies, such as were in fact developed and applied in the context of intensified capitalist competition among larger units of capital. This could be seen as yielding, in the terms of Marx's formula for the tendency, a changing technical composition of capital that could increase the productivity of labor by more than enough to offset the effects on profits of a rise in the organic composition of capital (Smith and Butovsky 2012; Albo et al. 2010). Of course, the heat generated by this debate among Marxists varies with how important one thinks it is for our interpretation of the world today whether Marx was right or wrong about this so-called "law." As Sweezy aptly put it in a letter to Baran in 1956: "Formulas are the opium of the economists, and they acted that way on Marx too. Vide the chapter on the falling rate of profit which tries as hard as any of the market stuff to squeeze knowledge out of tautologies" (Sweezy 2014, 3).

It is certainly notable, however, that even while he was quite diffident about how much else in the *Manifesto* remained relevant in the 1870s (see Chapter 4 in this volume), Marx was still in no doubt that its passages on the bourgeoisie as a revolutionary class had stood the test of time. This was clearly seen when in 1875 he angrily penned his *Critique of the Gotha Programme* of the German Social Democratic Workers Party. He was particularly critical of the notion that, in comparison with the laboring class, "all other classes are only a reactionary mass." Marx saw this formulation as concealing the difference between the backward looking landlord classes' roots in pre-capitalist social relations and the modern bourgeoisie which the *Manifesto* had designated as playing such "a highly revolutionary role in history." And notably, against the claim in the Gotha Programme that the bourgeoisie was a "reactionary mass," Marx was content simply to quote the *Manifesto*: "Of all the classes which today oppose the bourgeoisie, the only *truly revolutionary class* is the proletariat. The other classes come to the fore and then decline to extinction with large-scale industry." And he then immediately goes on to say, in his *Critique of the Gotha Programme*: "The bourgeoisie is understood here to be a revolutionary class – the bringer of large-scale industry – contrasting with the feudal and lower middle classes, which want to retain the whole social hierarchy, the products of outdated modes of production" (CW 24: 88–89; Sperber 2013, 526).

PARTIES AND PROLETARIATS

This brings us directly to the other unique contribution of the *Manifesto* – its vision of the revolutionary potential of the proletariat. The power of that vision was what led the *Manifesto* to be brought back from relative obscurity to be deployed as a key educational and organizational aid by the German Social Democratic Workers Party – the model for the great working-class parties that emerged in the last quarter of the nineteenth century. Neither the Communist Leaguers who had commissioned the *Manifesto* in London in 1847 as part of "their historic mission to change the world," let alone the eighteen members with Marx in the Brussels branch, nor even the great many *quarante-huitards* (i.e. the '48ers) that soon crowded the streets "with their beards, flowing cravats and broad-brimmed hats" (Gabriel 2011, 109, 132) qualified as a party in the sense that this would come to be understood from the 1870s onward. It is highly significant that when the Communist League broke up in 1850 amidst a factional dispute, Marx defined the issue behind the fatal split as the difference between his side's materialism and the other side's idealism in their approach to revolutionary time:

The materialist standpoint of the *Manifesto* has given way to idealism. The revolution is seen not as the product of realities of the situation but as the result of an effort of will. Whereas we say to the workers: You have 15, 20, 50 years of civil war to go through in order to alter the situation and to train yourselves for the exercise of power, it is said: We must take power *at once*, or else we may as well take to our beds. Just as the democrats abused the word "people" so now the word "proletariat" has been used as a mere phrase. To make this phrase effective it would be necessary to describe all the petty bourgeois as proletarians and consequently in practice represent the petty bourgeois and not the proletarians. The actual revolutionary process would have to be replaced by revolutionary catchwords. (CW 10: 626, emphasis in original)

Marx's timeline here for party building was remarkably prescient. The new working-class parties that emerged over the following fifteen, twenty, fifty years, with the mass memberships that they built up over these decades, premised their activities, as Engels put it in 1895, on the understanding that "the time of surprise attacks, of revolutions carried through by small conscious minorities at the head of unconscious masses, is past ... The history of the last fifty years has taught us that ... in order that the masses may understand what is to be done, long persistent work is required" (CW 27: 520). This long patient process of organization-building and mass popular education was based on the premise, as Engels continued in the same text, that "where it is a question of a complete transformation of the social organisation, the masses themselves must also be in it, must themselves already have grasped what is at stake, what it is they are going for, body and soul" (CW 27: 520).

The ongoing appeal of the *Manifesto* during this long process, in fact, was that even though it was written to be of use in the 1848 insurrections, its conception of "the organization of the proletariat into a class" spoke directly to the very different approach that was taken by the mass working-class parties of the mid to late nineteenth century. This can be seen from the way the *Manifesto* articulated its vision of a revolutionary working class alongside the case it made on the "highly revolutionary role" of the bourgeoisie. The argument that in calling into existence these modern proletarians the bourgeoisie had produced "its own gravediggers" (CM 246) did not rest on any notion that these modern proletarians carried revolutionary consciousness in their genes (although it became quite fashionable, in the confused intellectual climate on the left in the 1980s and 1990s, to argue that the classical Marxists thought this). The argument was rather that as the bourgeoisie surmounted each of the crises it produces by "preparing more comprehensive and devastating crises and diminishing the means of preventing them," it was not only thereby forging "the weapons which bring its death; it has also produced the men who will wield these weapons – modern workers, *proletarians*" (CM 241). After pointing to the basic debility of wage labor in capitalism, wherein through the use of machinery and the division of labor work had "lost all the characteristics of autonomy, and hence all attraction for the workers" (CM 242), the *Manifesto* also addressed the apparent growing pauperization of the worker with each successive capitalist crisis, so that the modern worker, "instead of advancing with industrial progress, sinks ever deeper beneath the circumstances of his own class. The worker becomes a pauper, and pauperism develops more quickly than population and wealth" (CM 245).

Piketty (2014, 9) interprets this to be the sole basis of what led Marx to expect that "sooner or later would unite the workers into revolt," and thinks it is enough to discount this by pointing out that "by the last third of the 19th century wages finally began to increase." But in fact it was not poverty that made the working class uniquely revolutionary among history's subordinate classes in Marx's eyes; it was rather the capacity of the working class to organize more and more effectively. When the first section of the *Manifesto* concluded with the resounding claim that the bourgeoisie was producing "its own grave-diggers" (CM 246), and that its "downfall and the victory of the proletariat are equally unavoidable," (CM 246) this was not because the workers had been impoverished but rather because "industrial progress, involuntarily and irresistibly promoted by the bourgeoisie, replaces the isolation of the workers through competition with their revolutionary unity through close association" (CM 245). The conditions for such organization were in part established by the bourgeoisie itself, as it brought many workers together in crowded factories and cities, and subjected them to similar conditions of life. It also provided means of communication that laid the basis for contact among workers of different localities, whereby they connected together their numerous local struggles against low or fluctuating wages, against appalling working conditions and despotism in production, against restraints on freedom of association for workers and against their own exclusion from the new structures of representative government that the bourgeoisie had fashioned for itself in relation to the state.

This looked so familiar by the late nineteenth century that the predictions in the *Manifesto* concerning the political implications of the capacity of the working class for organization have long appeared to be, if anything, remarkably sober. It had recognized, after all, that "from time to time, the workers are victorious, but only temporarily." What it had insisted on was that the "real fruit of their battle lies not in some immediate success but a unity amongst workers that gains ever more ground. It should be noted moreover, that even here, *pace* Piketty, Marx hardly ignored the importance of technological development, stressing how much this was furthered "by improved communications, which are generated by large-scale industry . . . which put workers from different localities in touch with one another," (CM 243) and by comparing how long it "took the burghers of the Middle Ages . . . with their country lanes" to unify their class, with what could now be "accomplished by modern proletarians in a few years with railways" (CM 243).

But the most important point in the *Manifesto*, which is perhaps still far too little recognized, was Marx's formulation of what really constituted a class struggle. It was only insofar as "the many local struggles of a general similar character" were unified "into a national struggle" that he designated workers' struggles as "a class struggle." And it is notable that even in immediately adding that "every class struggle, however, is a political struggle," it was only following the organization of the class in this sense that the concept of political party emerges in this passage of the *Manifesto* timeline, and when it is introduced, it is once again with remarkable sobriety: "This organisation of the proletarians into a class, and hence a political party, is disrupted time and again by competition among the workers themselves. But it always rises up again, more resolute, more powerful" (CM 243–244).

But no less notable, having just said here that the organization of the proletariat into a political party *follows from* its previous formation into a class, the second section of the *Manifesto* opens by stressing the initial role of political parties in class formation: "The immediate aim of the communists is the same as that of all other all proletarian parties: formation of the proletariat into a class" (CM 246). The insight that political parties themselves have a critical role in the formation of the working class has enormous implications for understanding whether that class in fact becomes revolutionary or not. The question becomes whether such parties, as they emerge out of the limited degree and form of working-class identity and solidarity that develops spontaneously and through trade-union organization within capitalism, can transform that identity and solidarity into a force that can realize the possibility of revolution. The realization of the vision in the *Manifesto* of working-class revolutionary potential thus is conditional on what these parties did, and what new parties successive to them might still do.

This has enormous bearing on how we should interpret what was clearly incorrect about what the *Manifesto* had to say about working-class formation. The notion in the *Manifesto* that age and sex differences would have "no social validity any more for the working class" (CM 242) was plainly wrong. And the same applies to the question of the persistence of religious, racial, ethnic and national identities. But this only brings us back to the role that the *Manifesto* expected parties themselves to play in the formation of the proletariat into a class. Insofar as working-class organizations either ignored or institutionalized these differences and identities, rather than recognized them and drew them into a common class struggle, it could be said, in the terms stated in the *Manifesto*, that they were engaged in processes of class formation that impeded the realization by the working class of its revolutionary potential. Indeed, the *Manifesto* explicitly insisted that united action to overcome such differences was "one of the first conditions for freeing the proletariat" (CM 250). This was just another way of restating the primary communist aim of the "formation of the proletariat into a class," conceived in the broadest possible way (Panitch and Leys 1998, 41–42). In any case, precisely because it was traversing such virgin terrain, the anticipation in the *Manifesto* of class formation and struggle through the agency of mass working-class parties, which developed only decades later, should hardly be taken as providing the last word on the subject.

Marx's own attempt at this famously took place mostly through his role in the formation of what became known as the First International in 1864. And it was the limited breadth of class formation through it due to the limitations of trade unions associated with it that perhaps concerned him most in subsequent years. As he put it to the delegates at the meeting of the International in 1866:

Apart from their original purpose, they must now learn to act deliberately as organising centres of the working class in the broad interests of its complete emancipation. They must aid in every social and political movement tending in that direction … They must convince the world at large that their efforts, far from being narrow and selfish, aim at the emancipation of the proletariat. (Marx 2014, 47–48)

This remained far too little theorized in the Marxist tradition, as Lukács pointed out in 1922 in observing that the idea of the revolutionary party was usually "seen purely in technical terms rather than as one of the most important intellectual questions of the revolution … no really vital theoretical energy seemed to be left over for the task of anchoring the problem of organisation in communist theory" (Lukács 1971, 295). And this was also the issue that concerned Gramsci most, i.e. the determining role and proper organizational form of the mass party in the creation of the collective will for fundamental change in the working class itself (Gramsci 1971, 14–15). In the past few decades of intellectual disillusionment with working-class parties, the classic texts of Marxist politics have been pilloried for assuming that the working class was innately revolutionary; but nothing like a serious historical analysis which would actually try to explain what these parties did and did not do in relation to forming the political and ideological identities of the working class was undertaken by post-Marxist critics (Laclau and Mouffe 1985; Panitch 1989, 17–21; Panitch, 2008).

Failing to take the question of the party's role in class formation and identity at all seriously has been the most surprising aspect of the vast literature that has been produced in the past few decades on the strategic lessons that must be gleaned from how and why the working class has failed to be the fount of socialist change. The classic texts of Marxist politics have instead been pilloried for assuming that the working class was innately revolutionary; but the actual work that socialist parties did (or did not do) in relation to forming the political and ideological identities of the working class has hardly been examined. It is, of course, possible to read the *Manifesto* in a manner that sees it as portraying political practice in terms of parties playing out nothing but pure Jacobin-style vanguardism; or, at the other extreme, as being nothing but the bearers of innate revolutionary aspirations of working-class people. But such readings miss that dialectical dimension of it which saw class organization and struggle neither in terms of the formation of a self-contained crack-troop of revolutionaries nor in terms of the merely passive representation of pre-formed class consciousness, but rather as the very arena in which hegemonically oriented class identity and consciousness were going to be formed.

CLASSES AND STRUGGLES

The link between class formation, class consciousness, class struggle and revolution is not located in the allegedly reductionist minds of those who produced the *Manifesto*. It lies in the nature of capitalism. The two central conditions of the bourgeoisie's existence – and continuing revolutionary role – are competition, including competition among workers on the one hand, and the exploitation of people who must sell their capacity to labor on the other. And both competition and exploitation remain key to understanding life in the twenty-first century.

Witnessing how far the concentration and centralization of capital had gone by the turn of twentieth century, a great many Marxists proclaimed that a monopoly stage of capitalism had already displaced an earlier stage of competitive capitalism. They were wrong. The tendency of the competitive dynamics in capitalism to lead to the concentration and centralization of capital was indeed one of Marx's great insights, but he understood this in terms of reframing the nature of competition, which, far from eliminating it, *intensified* it even in what he called "large-scale industry." What the twentieth-century notion of monopoly capital underplayed was the extent to which competition revolved not so much around the number of firms in an industry, but around the mobility of capital on the one hand, and around the uneven development of technology as well as pressures for valorization arising in large-scale industry from both fixed costs and labor costs on the other. Even amidst the concentration of capital in a few giant industrial firms, firms remained intensely competitive with one another, if not always over prices, then over profitability, market share and the capacity to attract new capital. Corporations in entirely different sectors compete with each other today, and in fact have blurred what was traditionally understood by a *sector* of the economy. Facilitated by the lowering of transportation and communication costs, new value chains across companies and countries have been introduced, through which competition among corporations has intensified as well as among ever more numerous suppliers around the globe competing to join their value chains.

As for the working class in the twenty-first century, the effects of ongoing competition on it are all too palpable. And here too Marx's understanding of the asymmetric impact of competition on the capitalist class and the working class remains highly relevant. This was indeed what Marx was getting at when he insisted that workers, no less than peasants, do not form a class insofar as they have merely local interconnections. This was why Marx was right to reserve the term "class struggle" in the *Manifesto* for the processes that "centralise the many local struggles of a generally similar character into a national struggle, a class struggle" (CM 243). Marx was also acutely aware, however, that this "organisation of proletarians into a class" even in this sense was itself "continually being upset again by the competition among the workers themselves" (CM 243). For the fact was that from the moment that a capitalist, in bringing workers together under one roof, established the conditions for those workers to potentially overcome competition among themselves, the institutional forms through which they did so had ambivalent effects on class formation. As craft unions tried to take wages out of competition by organizing across capitalist firms, the exclusions of other workers became embedded in workers' own institutional forms. Later, industry-wide union organizations created broader solidarities but this institutionalized sectoral class formation. Such institutionalized divisions within working classes were always partially offset by the way working-class communities spanned craft and sectoral identities.

While economic competition destroyed particular companies, the survival of the fittest tended to strengthen the capitalist class as a whole. In contrast, it often impelled workers to identify with their employer and regard other workers as competitors, which undermined solidarity and weakened the working class. Taking wages out of competition for most workers in an industrial sector certainly involved unions deliberately acting as organizing centers which, even if it was not directed at workers' complete emancipation, deployed a broader definition of the working class than had craft unions. But as corporations in entirely different sectors have come to compete with each other around the globe, this has had an enormous impact on sectoral unions, and dramatically shifted the balance of class forces in favor of capital. Moreover, the specific occupational impacts of the capitalist restructuring this has involved – the growth of precarious work, the expansion of services relative to industrial production, the shift to smaller workplaces – tended to both increase inequalities within the working class and make organizing workers into unions much more difficult. No less significant has been the spatial restructuring wrought by competition in our time. As capital relocated at home or abroad, it established

economic, cultural and political linkages which generally contributed to bringing capitalists closer together. Capitalist globalization has at the same time
vastly increased the size of the global proletariat, but as this has happened,
the intergenerational and community foundations for creating class identity
often tended to be undermined.

There is no end to history in this respect either, however. Capitalist restructuring in our time has led the old industrial unions to undertake organizing
drives in the service sectors, indeed even in the universities. The feminization of
trade unions is contributing to this, and sometimes goes so far as to become the
basis for overcoming very old divisions between highly skilled and less skilled
female workers such as nurses and cleaners in hospitals. There are also new
institutional forms of class organization, from the Workers Action Centers in
the USA, which, in linking class, ethnic, racial and local identities, have become
central to campaigns for increasing minimum wages; to the New Trade Union
Initiative, which organizes precarious workers in India; to the dramatic new
developments taking place in the institutional structures of the South African
working class.

CONCLUSION

At the core of the Marxist vision of socialism is the transcendence of class society.
Although this is seen as taking place through the agency of the working class, it
involves the transcendence of the working class itself in order to realize the diverse
potentials of humanity. Unless and until working-class organizational capacities
are redeveloped so as realize this goal, there should be no illusions about the
transformative potential of socialist strategies. This returns us to the most difficult
question, which is whether and how working classes can actually become the
gravediggers of capitalism. The largely unresolved tension in Marx's political
writings, from the *Manifesto* onward, between his conception that the working-
class party followed the proletariat's prior organization into a class, and his
alternative conception of the determining role of parties in the "formation of
the proletariat into a class" (CM 246), remains unresolved in socialist strategy
today. It will probably never be resolved. But the role parties or movements play
in forming common class identities and perceptions of interest is such a crucial
determinant of realizing revolutionary possibilities precisely because it pertains to
whether what they do is directed or not at undermining these conditions of the
bourgeoisie's continued existence. Only with such a conception of what it means
for parties to aim at "the formation of the proletariat into a class" can we
conceive of that class realizing its revolutionary potential.

REFERENCES

Albo, Greg, Leo Panitch, and Sam Gindin. 2010. *In and Out of Crisis: The Global
    Financial Meltdown and Left Alternatives.* Oakland: PM Press.

Gabriel, Mary. 2011. *Love and Capital.* London: Little Brown.

Gramsci, Antonio. 1971. *Selections from the Prison Notebooks*, eds. Quintin Hoare and Geoffrey Nowell-Smith. London: Lawrence and Wishart.

Laclau, Ernesto, and Chantal Mouffe. 1985. *Hegemony and Socialist Strategy.* London: Verso.

Lukács, Georg. 1971. "Towards a Methodology of the Problem of Organisation." In Georg Lukács, *History and Class Consciousness: Studies in Marxist Dialectics.* London: Merlin, 295–342.

Marx, Karl. 2014. "Instructions for Delegates of the Provisional Council: The Different Questions." *The International after 150 Years*, eds. George C. Comninel, Marcello Musto, and Victor Wallis, *Socialism and Democracy.* 28(2): 39–43.

Panitch, Leo. 1989. "Capitalism, Socialism and Revolution: The Contemporary Meaning of Revolution in the West." *Socialist Register 1989.* London: Merlin.

Panitch, Leo. 2008. *Renewing Socialism: Transforming Democracy, Strategy and Imagination.* London: Merlin.

Panitch, Leo, and Colin Leys. Eds. 1998. "The Political Legacy of the Manifesto." *Socialist Register 1998.* London: Merlin.

Panitch, Leo, and Sam Gindin. 2012. *The Making of Global Capitalism: The Political Economy of the American Empire.* New York: Verso.

Piketty, Thomas. 2014. *Capital in the Twenty-First Century.* Cambridge: Harvard University Press.

Schumpeter, Joseph. 1949. "The Communist Manifesto in Sociology and History." *Journal of Political Economy.* 57: 199–212.

Smith, Murray E. G., and Jonah Butovsky. 2012. "Profitability and the Roots of the Global Crisis." *Historical Materialism.* 20(4): 39–74.

Sperber, Jonathan. 2013. *Karl Marx: A Nineteenth-Century Life.* New York: Norton.

Sweezy, Paul. 2014. "The Baran-Sweezy Letter Project, Letter Two: Paul M. Sweezy to Paul A. Baran, November 23, 1956." *Monthly Review.* 65 (March): 38–41.

8

Hunting for Women, Haunted by Gender: The Rhetorical Limits of the *Manifesto*

Joan C. Tronto

How revolutionary can a revolutionary text be? How revolutionary must its rhetoric be?[1] The *Communist Manifesto* is surely a revolutionary text of the first order. Not only is it *about* the "series of revolutions" in history (CM 238), it is an extended speech act fomenting revolution among the working class. To and of the proletariat, its rhetoric soars. "They have nothing to lose but their chains" and "a world to win" (CM 260). But how exactly does the *Manifesto*'s rhetoric work for revolution? What rhetorical strategies did Marx and Engels use to convince real men and women, as workers, to devote themselves to revolutionary change? What traditional beliefs did they leave in place? This chapter answers these questions by closely examining the men and women – real and spectral – that the *Manifesto* described and addressed. It reveals some of the profoundly gendered assumptions and traditional beliefs about women at work in this otherwise revolutionary text.

Women make only cameo appearances in the *Manifesto*. They appear here and there as workers, as part of the scandalous "community of wives" and in other minor roles. This was not because Marx and Engels were unfamiliar with, or unwilling to hold, radical ideas about women and their place in society. They were attentive to such topics in the work of, among others, Fourier and Saint-Simon. Women's roles in Saint-Simonian thought had been debated and worked out in great detail throughout the 1820s and 1830s (Moses 1984; Cohen 1991). Women were prominent behind the scenes in the anti-slavery movement in the United Kingdom. Engels and Marx were involved in setting up a democratic organization in Brussels in the fall of 1847 with Lucien-Leopold Jottrand (Engels to Jottrand, CW 38:132), who was committed to changing "the abnormal situation of women in our societies" (Bouyssy and Fauré 2003, 303). In *The Holy Family*, Marx and Engels frequently addressed women's status and defended women writers. There, in a discussion of Eugene Sue's novel *Les Mystères de Paris*, Marx quoted Fourier's progressive views on the treatment of women. Helen Macfarlane, the first translator of the *Manifesto* into English,[2] was a Chartist who argued for women's equal treatment (Black 2004). Writing in 1868, Marx expressed pride in the fact that women were involved in the International and opined that "everyone who knows anything of history also knows that great social revolutions are impossible without the feminine ferment" (CW 43: 184). Nevertheless, as forward looking as Marx and Engels might have been, not least on subjects such as divorce and suicide, navigating the gravitational pull of traditional and changing ideas about women was a task with which radicals in the mid-nineteenth century had to wrestle. George Sand herself discussed the needs for women's changing status, but she refused to accept a nomination for the National Assembly in 1848, saying that women's suffrage was a distraction (Walton 1994; Fauré 2002, 304). While some have found Marx and Engels to be feminists or proto-feminists in their time (Carver 1998), surely they do not look so feminist from the standpoint of the twenty-first century.

Feminists all over the world and from many political positions have drawn inspiration from Marx and Engels; they have written in praise of them and built some of their most insightful critiques of social theory through their encounters with them. Early feminists drew revolutionary inspiration from Marx and Engels (Mitchell 1966 and 1973; Rowbotham 1972; Vogel 1983), and it would be difficult to imagine the shape of feminist theory without its reliance upon and reactions to Marxist thought (Eisenstein 1978; Brock 1988; W. Brown 1988; Jaggar 1988; Di Stefano 1991; H. Brown 2012; Himmelweit *et al.* 2013).

The aim of this chapter is not to review or to engage this extensive literature, but to achieve a more modest goal: namely, to think about the women and gendered imagery in the *Manifesto* to help address the relationship between rhetoric and revolution. Focusing on the actual and spectral women who appear in this text requires, as well, that they be placed in relationship with the actual and spectral men who appear in the text. Instead of measuring the text against any more recent feminist yardsticks, this chapter considers Marx and Engels's own framing of their goal in this text: to persuade workers that class struggle was inevitable and that they had "a world to win" in joining this struggle (CM 260). How far could they go in rejecting conventional attitudes towards women and gender and still be persuasive? In reality, they were able to go far in challenging a standard belief of the time that women were mainly immoral. But what they could not surrender was the assumption that women (and children) require protection. This protection was resituated in the proletariat to be sure, but a gendered analysis may help explain why it remained the task of "workingmen" to create a revolution.

We are used to framing the "world to win" as one in which the exploitation of workers has ended. But this chapter uncovers another side to the revolutionary call in the *Manifesto* by lingering closer to the men, women and gender dynamics that occupy and haunt the text. Analysis of these gender dynamics reveals frameworks of gender difference and protection.

BOURGEOIS AND PROLETARIANS

The first people who appear in the *Manifesto* are people of "different orders" from earlier historical epochs who lived in more complex class-differentiated statuses (CM 237). They were quickly displaced, though, by the "modern bourgeoisie," themselves a product of a "long process of development." This bourgeoisie is transformed from a product of world history into an actor in world history. Marx and Engels refer to them not as "they" but as "it," that is, a class that revolutionizes economic production and the material conditions of everyone's lives. Thus, "for exploitation cloaked by religious and political illusions, it has substituted open, unashamed, direct, brutal exploitation" (CM 239).

Moreover, "the bourgeoisie has not only created the weapons which bring it death; it has also produced the men (*die Männer*) who will wield these weapons – modern workers, *proletarians*" (CM 241; cf. CW 5: 468). At first, these proletarians have no human qualities left to them: "the worker becomes a mere appendage to the machine" (CM 241–242). How might an appendage to a machine become a revolutionary? It requires an appeal to the manhood of the proletarians themselves. As the text unfolds, it becomes clear that this is not only the manhood one needs to live in freedom, but the manhood one needs to protect one's nearest and dearest. At this point, the bourgeoisie exit the stage as the focus turns to the workers themselves.

PROLETARIANS OR WORKINGMEN?

In the first explicit appearance of women in the *Manifesto*, Marx and Engels have begun to explain the effects of modern factory work on the workers. Women are simply, along with children, "pressed *en masse* in a factory," and "organised like an army" where "differences of age and sex have no social validity any more for the working class" (CM 242). This assertion is telling; it is not worth condemning the irrelevance of differences by "age and sex" unless one is drawing upon the sympathy of readers to find such a situation abhorrent. In this situation, moreover, workers simply "cost more or less according to age and sex" (CM 242), and women cost less. Thus, "the labour of men is more and more displaced by that of women." This objection – namely, that not distinguishing men, women, and children by anything but their cost is objectionable – also presumes that there is something wrong with making men, women and children labor in the same way.

One of the specters invoked in this way is the ongoing argument about the morality of women working in paid employment (Albistur and Armogathe 1977; Berg 2002; DeGroat 2002; Honeyman and Goodman 2002). Although women had begun to enter this industrial army, and even outnumbered men in some settings (Gane 1998), older discussions about the moral dangers of women working outside of the household continued to arise throughout the first half of the nineteenth century. For some, the treatment of women was not outrageous because they were economically exploited. Rather, they were exposed to the moral risks of becoming less feminine and of being in sexually dangerous settings. Some argued that men, as overseers, might exploit women, while others argued that simply being around men who were not family members might prove morally corrupting. Of course, middle class women were not expected to work, but the proper role for working class women in paid employment outside of the home was an issue that attracted public attention. Starting from an assumption about a fairly rigorous distinction between public and private life, it was scandalous to think that men and women would work in the same place. The presumption was that, working outside of the home, women would be without the protection of male family members, and thus subject to abuse from these men, or that the women themselves, given their circumstances, would become coarser and lose their virtue, "to become contaminated and lost" (*The Union* 2001b, 528). Others believed that working-class women could be used to undo the brutality of working-class men. But no one doubted the harmful effects of working outside of the home on women's moral capacities. Of course, this had already happened in practice in many of the places where women worked, including in coal mines, where the Mines Commissioners wrote that it was "scarcely possible for girls to remain modest who are in the pits" (Mort 2002, 48). E. W. Binney, a geologist, averred in an 1842 report, published in the radical journal *The Union*, that the corruption extended to the men as well, finding "the moral and intellectual condition of the working colliers in a much worse state where females are employed in mines" (*The Union* 2001a, 504). Many manufacturers attracted the labor of unmarried women by advertising that they would be working in a moral, single-sex workplace. This contributed to the ongoing sex segregation (and drop in wages) that made working conditions worse in the nineteenth century. *The Union* began by noting "the influence of woman, as the first and most impressive educator of man," means that it is of "paramount importance, that women should be placed and trained as to ensure the transmission of a pure and elevated character to the embryo men and women committed to her charge" (*The Union* 2001a, 501). That working-class women, treated brutally by their husbands (*The Union* 2001b), would not fulfill this role is obvious. And not only was this a problem for women, but also for working-class men, whose manhood was challenged by their working wives. Consider Engels's observation in *The Condition of the Working Class in England*:

> In many cases the family is not wholly dissolved by the employment of the wife, but turned upside down. The wife supports the family, the husband sits at home, tends the children, sweeps the room and cooks ... This condition, which unsexes the man and takes from the woman all womanliness, without being able to bestow upon the man true womanliness, or the woman true manliness ... is the last result of our much-praised civilisation. (CW 4: 438–439)

Thus, the discussion in the nineteenth century about women workers was only partly about their exploitation in economic terms. As suggested by *The Union*, if men were paid more money, women and children would not have to work, producing better lives for them all. Economic degradation was tied to a poor quality of family life. Mentions of women workers in the *Manifesto* occur in light of, and rely upon, this context. Marx and Engels were taking advantage of these associations in their condemnation of bourgeois life for producing such situations.

Marx and Engels thus knew that proletarians were not always the same as "workingmen." Of course, this distinction even shows up in the history of the translation of the *Manifesto* into English. In 1850, Helen Macfarlane translated the famous last line as "Proletarians of the world unite," and this was reproduced in *Woodhull & Claflin's Weekly* of 1871 when the *Manifesto* first appeared in an American publication. The "authorized" Moore and Engels translation from 1888, which remained widely circulated by International Publishers, changed "proletarians" to "workingmen." Carver's translation agrees with the original translation. Nevertheless, whether proletarians include women or not, the discussion of working women in the *Manifesto* does not treat them as being in the same circumstance as workingmen. Traditional attitudes towards male leadership underpin the discussion of women as workers.

THE FAMILY AND THE "COMMUNITY OF WIVES"

The general narrative about the need for men to be able to protect their wives and children emerges even more strongly in the section of the *Manifesto* that puts bourgeois and proletarian men and women into families. Once again, Marx and Engels make the rhetorical move not only of wishing for freedom, but of restoring to workers something that has been taken away from them: the family itself.

Marx and Engels mention the destruction of the proletarian family in several places. The first mention comes at the end of the first section on "Bourgeois and Proletarians," where they first explained the misery of the proletariat. While most of this discussion is in the plural, referring to "the proletariat," they switch to the masculine singular to describe the family. They write, "the circumstances for the old society to exist are already abolished in the circumstances of the proletariat. The proletarian [*Der Proletarier*] is without property; his relationship [*sein Verhältnis*] to his wife and children no longer has anything in common with bourgeois family relations" (CM 244; CW 4: 472).

In his first two preparatory documents that led to the *Manifesto*, that is, "Draft of a Communist Confession of Faith" and "Principles of Communism" (both from 1847), Engels had been compelled to address the question about the association of communists with a "community of women." In those earlier two texts, Engels was willing to disown the radical ideas of other socialists. In the draft confessional, Engels writes,

Question 20: Will not the introduction of community of property be accompanied by the proclamation of the community of women?

Answer: By no means. We will only interfere in the personal relationship between men and women or with the family in general to the extent that the maintenance of the existing institution would disturb the new social order. Besides, we are well aware that the family relationship has been modified in the course of history by the property relationships and by periods of development, and that consequently the ending of private property will also have a most important influence on it. (CW 6: 102–103)

In the first sentence, Engels tries to minimize communist interference with the family. In the second, he allows that the institution of family is related to private property, and thus, will probably change. But the upshot of this answer is to prevent the bourgeoisie from saddling communists with "the community of women."

When Engels revised this text into the "Principles of Communism," the argument was framed differently. Now the question posed is a more general one about the family, and the horror of a "communist community of women" arises later in the discussion:

Question 21: What influence will the communist order of society have upon the family?

Answer: It will make the relation between the sexes a purely private relation which concerns only the persons involved, and in which society has no call to interfere. It is able to do this because it abolishes private property and educates children communally, thus destroying the twin foundation of hitherto existing marriage – the dependence through private property of the wife upon the husband and of the children upon the parents. Here also is the answer to the outcry of moralizing philistines against the communist community of women. Community of women is a relationship that belongs altogether to bourgeois society and is completely realized today in prostitution. But prostitution is rooted in private property and falls with it. Thus instead of introducing the community of women, communist organisation puts an end to it. (CW 6: 354)

Engels here makes several important points. He ties bourgeois family structure to two dimensions, one about wives who are dependent and the second about children who are dependent. This argument seems to preview the claims that Engels will make much later in 1884 in *The Origin of the Family, Private Property, and the State* (CW 26: 129–276). This claim is quite novel; by decades, it predates Marx's engagement with anthropological writings about the family and Engels's longer published version. The question of "community of women" is now abrogated to the concerns of "moral philistines," and the rebuttal is tied, as it is in the *Manifesto*, to another group of women: namely, prostitutes. Engels has turned the tables and argued that rather than creating a community of women, communism will end it.

Although this paragraph could have been simply imported into the *Manifesto*, the argument there is different. It appears in the second section called "Proletarians and Communists," a section that is distinct from the rest of the *Manifesto* in using the first and second person to make its points. For example, Marx and Engels address their audience as "you" and exclaim: "it horrifies you that we wish to transform private property" (CM 248). After a discussion of property and education, they return to the second person: "But do not argue with us while you judge the abolition of bourgeois property by your bourgeois conceptions of freedom, education, justice, etc." (CM 248). This establishes their rhetorical point that the bourgeoisie has no moral grounds on which to judge the communists. And, then, dramatically: "Transformation of the family! Even the most radical of the radicals flares up at this infamous proposal of the communists" (CM 249).

At this point, Marx and Engels had many rhetorical strategies available to them. They could simply have denied that this was their view. Indeed, in a number of places Marx and Engels deplored the ways in which utopian socialists have sensationalized family transformation (e.g. CM 258). Yet, perhaps because of such sensationalism, Marx and Engels thought they could not avoid this question. And it is perhaps the most rhetorically powerful way to call out bourgeois hypocrisy. They began by turning first to children and education. "But, you say, we transform the dearest relations of all when we move child-rearing from the domestic sphere and into the social." In response, "Communists did not discover the effects of society on child-rearing" (CM 249). "Even more revolting" is the bourgeois reliance on the tender bonds with children while "all proletarian family ties are severed as a consequence of large-scale industry, and children are simply transformed into articles of trade and instruments of labour" (CM 249).

As in Engels's "Principles of Communism," having now dealt with the family as a unit, Marx and Engels turn to the bourgeois accusation about wives: "But you communists want to introduce common access to women, protests the whole bourgeoisie in chorus" (CM 249). Here communists are addressed in the second person by the "chorus" of the bourgeoisie. This discussion is not directed to the individual bourgeois man as "you," but he is the actor in these next paragraphs, behaving in a way that is dismissive and immoral. Marx and Engels begin by explaining that since the bourgeois man sees wives as "instruments of production," he would assume that wives would be, like other such instruments, socialized. "He does not suspect that the point here is to transform the status of women as mere instruments of production." But the next point is still more telling. As a direct response to the claim about a "community of wives," they write that such a community "has almost always existed."

The trope of the "community of wives" was not unknown in nineteenth-century thought and practice (Sargent 1983). Some of the experimental socialist communities of the time practiced "free love." Conservative commentators condemned this, of course, arguing that even utopians like Thomas More had preserved the family intact (see, e.g., *Catholic Encyclopedia*, 2014).

For the next two paragraphs, the discussion shifts from wives to prostitutes, the other women held in "community":

Our bourgeois, not content with having the wives and daughters of the proletariat at their disposal, not to mention legally sanctioned prostitutes, take the greatest pleasure in reciprocal seduction of married women ... Bourgeois marriage is really the community of married women. (CM 249)

In condemning the bourgeois man, Marx and Engels remind their readers of the dangers of sexual predation for women as workers. This move is deft; these spectral victims forestall the argument that women should not work outside of the home at the same time that it invokes this danger. Their next point continues to reinforce the immoral behavior of bourgeois men as they seduce the wives of others. They add, sarcastically, that "at the very most communists might be reproached for wanting to replace a hidden community of women with a sanctioned, openly avowed community of women" (CM 249). While this might seem to concede too much, it actually reiterates a main theme of the *Manifesto* and of its second section, namely, that the bourgeoisie only see the world from their own self-serving perspective. Marx and Engels then invoke the spectral presence of the prostitute. They assert, as their final point, that "with the transformation of the current relations of production, the community of women emerging from those relations, i.e. sanctioned and unsanctioned prostitution, will disappear" (CM 249). All defensiveness has disappeared. Proletarian daughters and wives, bourgeois wives and prostitutes have all been lumped together as the victims of the sexually voracious and revolting bourgeois man.

Rhetorically, not only have Marx and Engels shown the bourgeoisie to be hypocritical and immoral, but they have also positioned themselves to be the defenders of women, from the lowly prostitute to the woman worker to the bourgeois wife. Prurient interests in the sexual practices of communists have been inverted into concerns for the safety and virtue of almost all other women in society. It was a progressive move for Marx and Engels not to condemn prostitutes, but this point is consistent with arguments that they made elsewhere in their writings (Rowbotham 1972; Brown 2012). Others were not so kindly disposed. Consider Proudhon: "Why is it that, independent of economic and political causes that attach themselves to it, prostitution is incomparably greater in women than in men" (in Moses 1984, 155). By 1848, prostitution was a titillating social problem, not to be discussed in public but already the subject of scientific study (Bernheimer 1989). Indeed, Sheila Rowbotham (1972) has argued that Europeans were obsessed with the question. A number of social reformers had begun to turn their attention to the problem. Marx and Engels had been, in previous writings, more sympathetic to the plight of prostitutes than most, echoing the line that we find in "Principles" that women who became prostitutes did not really have any alternatives before them (Plaut and Anderson 1999).

These passages about wives and prostitutes expose the hypocrisy of bourgeois claims to be the defenders of morality in familial affairs. The passage is not about the desirability of a sexual revolution or family transformation; it is about undermining the authority of the male bourgeois householder. As for bourgeois women, they have, in rhetorical effect, been reduced to prostitutes by another name, or those seduced by bourgeois men. Thus, Marx and Engels answer the scandalous charge against communists – that they would change the family structure – by condemning hypocritical bourgeois morality (Rowbotham 1972). Whether or not this is a satisfying answer, it does make clear that the problem of exploitation is not the only moral issue that should move proletarian men to act. Marx and Engels acknowledge later in the *Manifesto* that there are "critical elements" in the thoughts of utopian socialists. Among them, they list "the transformation of the family." But as the foregoing passage makes clear, any such speculation on the nature of future families has "only a purely utopian import" (CM 258).

The closest thing to an actual discussion of transforming the family in the *Manifesto* occurs in one of the points of the first steps for Communists to take. In advocating a public form of upbringing for children, Marx and Engels seem to argue for a more fitting account of what families would actually do. Weikart argues that given the broader meaning of *Erziehung* than the English term "education," the *Manifesto* is actually making a more radical claim for transforming the family and substituting the public care of children (Weikart 1994, 665), a point that is more consistent with Engels's description of a public education system in "Principles of Communism" that would begin "as soon as they [children] are old enough to do without the first maternal care, in national institutions and at the expense of the nation" (CW 6: 351). Neither the specific points of action contained in the *Manifesto*, nor anything else that Marx or Engels had specifically written, or would write, calls for a deliberate transformation of the family's structure; family structure will change as a result of economic changes. Engels did speculate in *Origins* that when marriage is no longer linked to property relations, family will return to a kind of monogamy based on real love (CW 26: 186–189), but this is not a "community of wives and children." It is as if Marx and Engels felt compelled to answer this charge, since other communists had tainted the entire belief system with their familial transformations. Everyone in their audience would be familiar with the scandalous ideas of Saint-Simon and Fourier, and familiar with the approaches to "free love" in experimental socialist communities such as Harmony, which Engels had written about in 1844–1845 (CW 4: 214–228). (Engels later remarked that "It is a peculiar fact ... that with every great revolutionary movement the question of 'free love' comes to the foreground" (in Weikart 1994, 657).) Haunted by the "free love" distraction, Marx and Engels turned this concern upside down. Using a critique unusual for its *ad hominem* character, their rhetorical strategy is persuasive not for its appeal to liberation but for its appeal to proletarian men's capacities to protect women.

WOMEN AS POLITICAL ACTORS

The third, and penultimate, section of the *Manifesto* is devoted to distinguishing the approach of Marx and Engels from other socialists and communists. Until this point, women have primarily appeared as if they were auxiliaries to men's activities. When we turn to the final issue for discussion – the possibility for women to act politically, both as members of the working class movement and on their own – spectral women from the past and future haunt the text.

It should not surprise us that there are but few women in this section of the text. In the 1840s, it was virtually unheard of for a woman to speak in public. At the World Anti-Slavery Conference in London in 1840, for example, women were not permitted to be seated (much less speak) on the floor of the convention. Marx and Engels do not devote much attention to the concerns of women as actors or political activists, but neither do they make statements about women's "natural place" in the household. Nor do they venture an overt claim about women as a different species or about their incapacity for political action. This treatment is thus consistent with others' claims about Marx and Engels's proto-feminism.

Consider, also, the question of women's suffrage. English Chartists and French *réformistes* had argued for the franchise for women by this time. Although Engels later wrote disparagingly of suffrage as a concern for bour-geois women (CW 47: 312; see Hunt 2010: 19), Marx and Engels did not consider it frivolous in 1848. So, women's suffrage is conspicuous by its absence from their list of the "*social grievances*" that "conservative or bourgeois soci-alism" might want to address: "Included in it are economists, philanthropists, humanitarians, do-gooders for the working classes, charity organizers, animal welfare enthusiasts, temperance union workers, [and] two-a-penny reformers of multifarious kinds" (CM 256). Were this claim written later in their lives, women would surely be among these humanitarians, do-gooders, temperance union workers and animal welfare enthusiasts. But in 1848 these organizations were still almost exclusively male and the activities of women limited to domes-tic political tasks such as writing letters and soliciting funds (Ritvo 1987; Barrow 2003).

As Marx and Engels continued their critique of alternative socialists, they criticized their rejection of political and revolutionary action. They acknowl-edged that there were "critical elements" in imagining "future society," includ-ing "transformation of the conflict of interest between town and country, transformation of the family, of private appropriation, of wage-labor," and so forth (CM 258). They concluded this critique by observing that these osten-sible socialists were "bitterly opposed to all political activity by the workers" (CM 258). Hence, they observe, "The Owenites in England oppose the Chartists, the Fourierists in France oppose the *réformistes*" (CM 259). Although Owenites and Fourierists considered themselves "pro women," so too were arguments for women's suffrage made among the Chartists; and there were French *réformistes* such as Flora Tristan arguing for the inclusion of women in *political* action to change the balance of power.

The absence of a sustained engagement with women's political activity might be explained by the insufficient importance of suffrage to the authors of the

Manifesto. On the other hand, they might have simply been leaving the question of the franchise to another day or discussion (though Engels later took a dim view of suffragists because he considered their cause a bourgeois one (Hunt 2010, 19)). Or, then again, it could be that they did not mention women's suffrage here, but saw it as part of the necessary, broader "victory for democracy" (CM 251).

Since actual political actors and activists do appear in abundance in the last two sections of the *Manifesto*, perhaps we should again notice the absence of women. In reality, they are writing treatises, engaging in politics and even aiding revolts (including the Cracow insurrection of 1846, mentioned in the *Manifesto* when Appolonia Jagiello took part dressed as a male soldier (Hale 1853, 704 ff.)). But these activities did not show up in the *Manifesto*.

One key woman who appears only as a specter in the *Manifesto* is Flora Tristan, otherwise known to Marx and Engels. Tristan is not mentioned in biographies of Marx by David McLellan (1973), Fritz Raddatz (1979) or Jonathan Sperber (2013); and she receives only one passing mention by Leopold (2007, 31, n. 68). Yet Maximilien Rubel (1946a; 1946b) argued early in his illustrious scholarly career that Marx and Engels owed much in thinking about class consciousness and the capacity of a class to work on its own behalf politically to Tristan.

In 1843 Flora Tristan (Strumingher 1988) published her book *The Workers' Union* (Tristan 2007). The daughter of a Peruvian nobleman and a French woman who married in Spain, Tristan was considered illegitimate in France and so found herself without money. As a young woman, she worked as a lithographer. After bearing three children, she left her brutal husband and went to Peru to demand her patrimony, but none was forthcoming. Despite her lack of formal education, she began to write travel books and novels to support herself, and in 1840 published *Promenades dans Londres*, which explored the conditions of working-class people in London. By 1843, when she wrote *The Workers' Union*, workers' organizations were banned in France. The book advocated an international union of all workers. "Listen to me," she began the text, soon insisting that "now the day has come when one must *act*, and it is up to you and *only* you to act in the interest of your own cause" (Tristan 2007, 37–38). The economic analysis is not very sophisticated. Tristan argued that since some did not work, society was insufficiently productive, and shortages produced selfishness. "If tomorrow [society] were to produce an abundance of everything, selfishness would disappear" (Tristan 2007, 124). Situating the problem this way, the solution she calls for is for a "right to work," and, indeed, an insistence that everyone must work. From there, other causes of the economic crisis, such as the separation of countryside from city, could be resolved. Note, then, that while Tristan recognizes the political power of the bourgeoisie, she does not see the economic system of exploitation as the main enemy. Instead, she advocates the creation of a Workers' Union. The main goals of the union were twofold: first, to create a *politically* powerful organization that could influence the state. Describing 1789 as the emergence of the bourgeoisie and 1830 as its rise to power, she continues:

This bourgeois-owners class represents itself in the legislature and before the nation, not to defend its own interests, for no one threatens them, but to impose its conditions and command upon 25 million proletarians. In a word, it is both counsel and judge, just like the feudal lords it triumphed over ... In turn, the workers, the vital part of the nation, must create a huge union to assert their unity!" (Tristan 2007, 58)

Second, the Union would achieve prominence, she argues, through the creation of an institutional Workers' Palace. Functioning locally everywhere, the Workers' Palace, for example, would house the elderly and infirm and school the children of workers. In a way, the call in the *Manifesto* for "free public education for all children" seems to echo this idea (CM 251). Her demand for workers to act for their own benefit distinguishes her from the "feudal socialists" derided in the *Manifesto*. And she was an outspoken advocate for recognizing the needs of, and roles to be played by, women and women workers, noting that there were five million French men and two million French women who were workers.

Marx and Engels were familiar with Tristan's writings. Indeed, they had defended her against the left-Hegelians who considered themselves the rightful arbiters of leftist thought. In *The Holy Family*, for example, there is an extended defense of Tristan against the attacks of "Herr Edgar" Bauer (CW 4: 19–20). And perhaps her ideas were more influential in helping Marx and Engels discover their ideas about class consciousness than most scholars allow. In *The German Ideology*, they too had called for a "union" – an international association of workers with local branches – as a step prior to revolution. Indeed, the Communist League, for which Marx and Engels would write the *Manifesto*, had seven "lodges" in German cities in 1847 (Raddatz 1979, 74). As in Tristan's writings, the role of the Workers' Union was to create solidarity and an opportunity for workers to organize their struggle.

After she published *The Workers Union*, Tristan spent the last year of her life lecturing on these ideas. She kept notes about her experiences, and, when published, they revealed her surprise at the difficulty of organizing and transforming workers to make revolution their cause. *The Workers' Union*, moreover, addresses the other issue raised in this chapter: the moral grounding of the call for revolution. Tristan's appeal was only partly about ending exploitation; she was also interested in providing a decent life for workers and their families.

There might be many reasons why Tristan's ghost remains hauntingly in the shadows of the *Manifesto*. She does not conceive of the struggle on the same terms: her view of the economy is pre-Marxist, as it were. But her account of a worker-oriented society seems to capture a transition to workers' agency before, or along with, the seizing of state power. But her focus is not on this "victory," but on the creation of public institutions by, for and of the workers themselves. The call to end exploitation is the main theme of the *Manifesto*.

Nevertheless, Tristan's non-economic and unscientific socialism has also recognized the importance of protection – or the provision of care for the vulnerable – as a centrally important issue in motivating workers to change.

A MASCULINIST MANIFESTO?

Another specter of women and gender lurks around the *Manifesto*. It concerns the ultimate prospects for action by working class men and women. As Margaret Cohen (1991) observed, the question of how to conceive of the working class was unanswered before the *Manifesto*. Both women and workers were treated, in traditional views, as passive and incapable of action. Edgar Bauer's critique of Tristan blamed her for a misunderstanding, namely for presuming that workers are capable of action, whereas Bauer presumed that they are not. Indeed, Bauer presumed, as Marx and Engels observed, that "Flora Tristan is an example of the feminine dogmatism which must have a formula" (CW 4: 19). Actually, Marx and Engels took an opposite view, that women – like workers – can think and act politically. It is no wonder that Marx and Engels used this occasion to level a sexist volley against Bauer, claiming that his sort of critical philosophy "is and remains an old woman – faded, widowed *Hegelian* philosophy which paints and adorns its body, shriveled into the most repulsive abstraction, and ogles all over Germany in search of a wooer" (CW 4: 20). Marx and Engels therefore used sexist language to criticize Bauer's sexist position. It is not clear, then, how strongly they meant to defend Tristan's ideas against Bauer's attack, or if the association of women with workers was the more problematic step to which they objected.

As the ambiguity in their critique of Bauer reflects, Marx and Engels lived in a milieu that fully accepted the ideology that women were soft and emotional, among other deficits, and thus incapable of action. Feuerbach, whom Marx and Engels were reading carefully in the 1840s, had thoroughly embraced this ideology, making gendered bodies a key element of his "materialist" world view. In mid-nineteenth-century Germany, "the specific qualities assigned to the genders were structured around the putatively internal, passive domestic, dependent and emotive character of women and the putatively external, competitive, public, independent, and rational character of men" (Plumley 2003, 88). The Abbé Sièyes, the provocateur of "the third estate," had argued that it was inappropriate to ask women to be agents of change, since they only were "passive citizens." "Women, at least in the present state of society, children, aliens, and those who contribute nothing to the support of the public establishment should exert no active influence on public affairs" (Sewell 1994, 176–177).

There was another change emerging here: the emergence of two genders and thus of two accounts of moral and emotional life (Lacquer 1992). As men were seen as ostensibly more scientific, women were being perceived as more emotional and sensual (Thomson 2008, 245). But when this gendered dichotomy was expanded to the possibilities for action as well, it began again to impinge upon what Marx and Engels thought was possible for the proletariat to do.

So we arrive at the final feminine specter in the *Manifesto*. What if, as countless writers at the time thought, working-class people were simply too poorly educated, too unintelligent, *too feminized*, to act (Cohen 1991)? That women were treated as almost a different species was laid bare in Proudhon's *Qu'est-ce que la propriété?* "Between woman and man there may exist love, passion, ties of custom and the like; but there is no real society. Men and women are not companions. The difference of the sexes places a barrier between them, like that placed between animals, by a difference of race" (in Moses 1984, 152). Tristan had understood how difficult it was to convince workers to take the step that she had urged: to act in their own interests. Perhaps this fear haunted Marx and Engels, too. Such views were widespread among other socialists as well. Saint-Simonians portrayed "both workers and women as the passive victims of physical and moral suffering" (Cohen 1991, 257). Marx and Engels use the language of suffering only in one place in the *Manifesto*, and that is to characterize how utopian socialists think about "the class that suffers most," asserting that "only from the point of view of the most suffering class does the proletariat exist for them" (CM 27). That Marx and Engels felt the need to refute this point invites the speculation that it was an argument that was abroad. Perhaps workers did not know how to act on their own behalf. How then would a revolution happen?

Adding this obviously gendered dimension to the problem may help to explain why the insistence on the inevitability of revolution was a theme sounded in the *Manifesto*. It may help to explain why Marx and Engels had written, in *The German Ideology*, that a revolution was necessary to transform workers so that they would lose "everything that still clings to it [the proletariat] from its previous position in society" (CW 5: 88). Perhaps Marx and Engels did not want workers to be understood in gendered terms, and so they only referred to men. In a fanciful letter to "Dr Marx," as if she were writing in 1851, Sheila Rowbotham chides him for the absence of the discussion of women political actors:

While I can understand that you were forced to compress your thoughts in the *Manifesto*, the exclusion of all reference to women's part in our own emancipation presents us as all weakness and working men as all strength. You thus deny the efforts women have made through association to put equality and democracy into practice in Europe, and by omission set back the cause for the abolition of all privileges of sex, race, birth, caste and wealth for which we too have sacrificed so much. (Rowbotham 1998, 7)

If the accusation here is true, as it would indeed appear, then the depth of the so-called woman question has been misjudged. It is not that Marx and Engels did not want the concerns of women to enter the political agenda after the concerns of men. It is that they did not want the concerns of all proletarians to be mistaken as womanish.

CONCLUSION

We are used to thinking of exploitation as the moral and political problem to be solved by the revolutionary action counseled by the *Manifesto*. But simply pointing out that there are exploited or suffering people has, only rarely, been a ground for abolishing an existing social order. There is a difference between the perspectives of "experts," often from the upper class, explaining and pre-scribing how people (including the inadequate lower classes) should live, and those who look at the world from the standpoint of the lower classes. Marx and Engels do the latter here, transforming the proletariat into an agent of historical change. The exploitation narrative is the clearest and most powerful narrative in the text.

Yet this chapter has revealed a second narrative for change, one based on traditional gender roles and arguing that working men had to be able to protect their women and children. In this regard, the spectral women becoming exploited in the factories and mines play a powerful role, as does the destruction of any traditional basis for the family among the proletariat. Although the *Manifesto* exalted the revolutionary role of the bourgeoisie in tearing down old social forms, it becomes clear from their lament for traditional families among the working class that Marx and Engels also meant to gain support from proletarian men eager to assume the traditional mantel of defenders of their families.

Narratives about the morality of the family also play out here in this way as well. Marx and Engels were well aware of the traditional views of the household and family, and they exploited these traditional views *against the bourgeoisie*. As in the curious passage about "the community of wives," Marx and Engels implicitly asked: How can any group whose own behavior is so immoral be treated as superior, more knowledgeable or fitter to rule?

In this chapter, by looking more closely at women and how they needed to be protected, and at the various men who would protect them, it becomes clear that Marx and Engels were making two appeals to workers to convince them to become revolutionaries. They would lose their chains and end their exploita-tion. But the *Manifesto* also implicitly promises that the proletarians' "world to win" would remain a gendered world in which men were recognizably mascu-line, and fully capable of action, and so not womanish. The specter of a gender and sexual revolution remained for the future.

REFERENCES

Albistur, Maite, and Daniel Armogathe. 1977. *Histoire du féminisme français: de l'empire napolónien à nos jours*. Paris: Éditions des Femmes.
Barrow, Margaret. 2003. "British Women's Temperance League." In *Alcohol and Temperance in Modern History: An International Encyclopedia*, eds. Jack S. Blocker, David M. Fahey, and Ian R. Tyrrell. Santa Barbara, CA: ABC-CLIO, 114–116.

Berg, Maxine. 2002. "What Difference Did Women's Work Make to the Industrial Revolution?" In *The European Women's History Reader*, eds. Fiona Montgomery and Christine Collette. London: Routledge, 100–105.

Bernheimer, Charles. 1989. *Figures of Ill Repute: Representing Prostitution in Nineteenth-Century France*. Cambridge, MA: Harvard University Press.

Black, David. 2004. *Helen Macfarlane: A Feminist, Revolutionary Journalist, and Philosopher in Mid-Nineteenth-Century England*. Lanham, MD: Lexington Books.

Boussy, Maite, and Christine Fauré. 2003. "1848 in Paris." In *Political and Historical Encyclopedia of Women*, ed. Christine Fauré. English eds. London: Routledge, 294–317.

Brock, Gillian. 1988. *Necessary Goods: Our Responsibilities to Meet Others' Needs*. Lanham, MD: Rowman & Littlefield.

Brown, Heather. 2012. *Marx on Gender and the Family: A Critical Study*. Chicago: Haymarket Books.

Brown, Wendy. 1988. *Manhood and Politics: A Feminist Reading in Political Theory*. Totowa, NJ: Rowman & Littlefield.

Carver, Terrell. 1998. *The Postmodern Marx*. State College, PA: Pennsylvania State University Press.

Catholic Encyclopedia. 2014 [1907–1912]. *Communism*. www.catholic.org/encyclopedia/view.php?id=3209. (Accessed August 12, 2014).

Cohen, Margaret. 1991. "'The Most Suffering Class': Gender, Class, and Consciousness in Pre-Marxist France." *Boundary* 18(2): 22–46.

DeGroat, Judith A. 2002. "The Public Nature of Women's Work: Definitions and Debates during the Revolution of 1848." In *The European Women's History Reader*, eds. Fiona Montgomery and Christine Collette. London: Routledge, 124–128.

DiStefano, Christine. 1991. *Configurations of Masculinity: A Feminist Perspective on Modern Political Theory*. Ithaca, NY: Cornell University Press.

Eisenstein, Zillah R. 1978. *Capitalist Patriarchy and the Case for Socialist Feminism*. New York: Monthly Review Press.

Fauré, Christine. 2002. "Rights or Virtues: Women and the Republic." In *Republicanism: A Shared European Heritage*, eds. Martin van Gelderen and Quentin Skinner. Cambridge: Cambridge University Press, 125–137.

Gane, Mike. 1998. "The *Communist Manifesto*'s Transgendered Proletarians." In *The Communist Manifesto: New Interpretations*, ed. Mark Cowling. Edinburgh: Edinburgh University Press, 132–141.

Hale, Sarah Josepha Buell. 1853. *Woman's Record; or Sketches of All Distinguished Women, from "The Beginning" till A.D. 1850*. New York: Harper and Brothers.

Himmelweit, Susan, Christina Santos, Almudena Sevilla, and Catherine Sofer. 2013. "Sharing of Resources Within the Family and the Economics of Household Decision Making." *Journal of Marriage* 75(3): 625–639.

Honeyman, Katrina, and Jordan Goodman. 2002. "Women's Work, Gender Conflict, and Labour Markets in Europe, 1500–1900." In *The European Women's History Reader*, eds. Fiona Montgomery and Christine Collette. London: Routledge, 79–99.

Hunt, Tristram. 2010. "Introduction." In Friedrich Engels, *The Origin of the Family, Private Property, and the State*. New York: Penguin, 3–30.

Jaggar, Alison M. 1988. *Feminist Politics and Human Nature*. Lanham, MD: Rowman & Littlefield.

Lacquer, Thomas. 1992. *Making Sex: Body and Gender from the Greeks to Freud.* Cambridge, MA: Harvard University Press.

Leopold, David. 2007. *The Young Karl Marx: German Philosophy, Modern Politics, and Human Flourishing.* New York: Cambridge University Press.

McLellan, David. 1973. *Karl Marx: His Life and Thought.* New York: Harper & Row.

Mitchell, Juliet. 1966. "Women: The Longest Revolution." *New Left Review.* 40: 11–37.

Mitchell, Juliet. 1973. *Woman's Estate.* New York: Vintage.

Mort, Frank. 2002. *Dangerous Sexualities: Medico-Moral Politics in England since 1830.* London: Routledge & Kegan Paul.

Moses, Claire G. 1984. *French Feminism in the 19th Century.* Albany: State University of New York Press.

Plaut, Eric A., and Kevin Anderson. 1999. *Marx on Suicide.* Evanston, IL: Northwestern University Press.

Plumley, Ryan. (2003) "Feuerbach and Gender: The Logic of Complementarity." *History of European Ideas.* 29(1): 85–105.

Raddatz, Fritz J. 1979. *Karl Marx, A Political Biography.* Boston, MA: Little Brown and Company.

Ritvo, Harriet. 1987. *The Animal Estate: The English and Other Creatures in the Victorian Age.* Cambridge, MA: Harvard University Press.

Rowbotham, Sheila. 1972. *Women, Resistance, Revolution: A History of Women and Revolution in the Modern World.* New York: Vintage.

Rowbotham, Sheila. 1998. "Dear Dr Marx: A Letter from a Socialist Feminist." In *Socialist Register 1998: The Communist Manifesto Now*, eds. Leo Panitch and Colin Leys. New York: Monthly Review Press, 1–17.

Rubel, Maximilien. 1946a. *Flora Tristan et Karl Marx.* London: Internationale echo; Ideen en gebeurtenissen uit alle landen.

Rubel, Maximilien. 1946b. "Flora Tristan et Karl Marx." *La Nef: Revue Mensuelle.* 14: 71–76.

Sargent, Lyman Tower. 1983. "Utopia and the Family: A Note on the Family in Political Thought." In *Dissent and Affirmation: Essays in Honor of Mulford Q. Sibley*, eds. Arthur L. Kalleberg, J. Donald Moon, and Daniel R. Sabia. Madison: University of Wisconsin Press, 106–117.

Sewell, William H. 1994. *A Rhetoric of Bourgeois Revolution: The Abbé Sieyes and What is the Third Estate?* Durham, NC: Duke University Press.

Sperber, Jonathan. 2013. *Karl Marx: A Nineteenth-Century Life.* New York: W.W. Norton.

Strumingher, Laura S. 1988. *The Odyssey of Flora Tristan.* New York, NY: Peter Lang.

The Union. 2001a. "Employment of Females in Mines, May 1842." In *Women and Radicalism in the Nineteenth Century*, ed. Mike Sanders. New York: Routledge, 501–506.

The Union. 2001b. "The Women of the Working Classes, January 1843." In *Women and Radicalism in the Nineteenth Century*, ed. Mike Sanders. New York: Routledge, 525–540.

Thomson, Ann. 2008. *Bodies of Thought: Science, Religion, and the Soul in the Early Enlightenment.* New York: Oxford University Press.

Tristan, Flora. 2007. *The Workers' Union.* Bloomington, IL: University of Illinois Press.

Vogel, Lise. 1983. *Marxism and the Oppression of Women: Toward a Unitary Theory.* New Brunswick, NJ: Rutgers University Press.

Walton, Whitney. 1994. "Writing the 1848 Revolution: Politics, Gender, and Feminism in the Works of French Women of Letters." *Society for French Historical Studies.* 18(4): 1001–1024.

Weikart, Richard. 1994. "Marx, Engels, and the Abolition of the Family." *History of European Ideas.* 18(5): 657–672.

PART III

INTELLECTUAL LEGACY

9

The *Manifesto* in Political Theory: Anglophone Translations and Liberal Receptions

James Farr and Terence Ball

Despite its brevity, immediacy and hasty composition in 1848, the *Manifesto of the Communist Party* was elevated to its prominence by the end of the century as the urtext of a Marxist canon. In due course, it also found a place in the broader canon of Western political thought. Not only did the *Manifesto* sarcastically and brilliantly enter the terrain of political theory, it subsequently became the subject of critical receptions by political theorists and philosophers down to our time. These receptions – not to mention Marx*ism*[1] – gave the *Manifesto* an extended, influential life well beyond 1848 and canonized it as essential reading in an age of ideologies.

In this chapter, we consider the legacy of the *Manifesto* in political theory via its reception history. We begin by giving notice to such political theory that exists in the *Manifesto* itself, especially its embrace of freedom foretold, and to its translations into English in 1850 and 1888. We then turn to our principal task of reception history, namely, to consider across four periods the Anglophone liberal reception of the *Manifesto* by some of the major theorists of the last century: Bertrand Russell, John Dewey, Sidney Hook, Isaiah Berlin, Karl Popper and John Rawls. While a fuller study would consider a longer list – and indeed there are more theorists than these in the pages that follow – we trust that the liberal political theorists we have chosen to emphasize need no strained justification in the space allowed in this *Cambridge Companion*. By dint of fame and influence, their critical scrutiny of the *Manifesto* aided and abetted its influence outside Marxist circles, for good or ill. Indeed, they helped canonize the work as a great dark star in the ideological firmament of the twentieth century. From Russell to Rawls, these thinkers found in the *Manifesto* an adversarial ideology that brilliantly – and thus all the more dangerously – propagandized a radical, communist alternative to their respective views of individual freedom, political power and the course of history. At the same time, they also reveal the great variety of examples of "liberalism," an ideological colligation we use reservedly.

Thus, the reception history of the *Manifesto* reveals political theory as ideology-critique.

Understanding the reception of a work in political theory is not far removed, in our view, from understanding the whys and wherefores of its original composition. Indeed, the composition of a work of political theory is invariably engaged in the reception of earlier works. Marx clearly had Engels's and his own recent works to hand, as well as documents from the newly formed Communist League and all the socialists criticized in section III. His composition of the *Manifesto* depended in considerable part, then, on the reception of this earlier material. This is a prime example why the history of political thought is an essential feature of political theory, no matter how contemporary. Furthermore, understanding a text's composition and/or reception might be thought of in different but complementary ways. A text composed *or* received, in whole or part, is a complex answer to a question (Collingwood 1939), a conjectural solution to a problem (Popper 1972), or an act of doing something in writing (Skinner 2002). As composition and in its reception, the *Manifesto* should be approached as an assemblage of questions and answers, problems and solutions, speech and action.[2]

POLITICAL THEORY IN THE MANIFESTO

The *Manifesto* is as political a work as could be imagined. It was a masterpiece of propaganda when published days before the Revolutions of 1848, and it remains a masterpiece of rhetoric.[3] Designed to motivate proletarian action, it dramatically underscored the power, exploitation and liberation then at work. The *Manifesto* also does its political work by way of a theory of history that is simultaneously a sociological theory of class conflict and an economic theory of productive forces. The theory is barely outlined, and sketched in bold, grand, even grandiose strokes. No time for details, a world to win! For all that, there is scarcely any political theory in the *Manifesto* – if by "political theory" we mean the traditional exercise since antiquity of providing fundamental principles of justice, sovereignty or rights. Marx simply "did not write a comprehensive or even exemplary work of political theory" (Carver 1996, ix). Of course, it is not that Marx – with or without Engels – did not engage political theory, say, as critiques backed by humanist, democratic, and/or communist convictions. Works such as "On the Jewish Question," *The Critique of Hegel's Philosophy of Right, The Poverty of Philosophy, The Holy Family* and *The German Ideology* were all composed within the five years preceding the *Manifesto*. And then there was all that came after, as Marxism or Marxist political thought.

If we lower the bar imposed by the traditional exercise of theorizing politics, the *Manifesto* makes decisive incursions onto the terrain of political theory in three ways. First, there is the sarcastic deflation of bourgeois hypocrisies that parade as universal ideals. Justice "is merely the will of your class, raised to the status of law" (CM 248). Law, in turn, is a bourgeois prejudice, like religion and morality (CM 245). The state "is merely a device for administering the common affairs of the whole bourgeoisie" (CM 239). Freedom, the most hallowed of the "boasts" of the bourgeoisie, is really but "a single freedom – conscienceless free trade," "the freedom to buy and sell" (CM 239, 247).

Second, the *Manifesto* not only unleashes savage criticism against the bourgeois order but against its competitors in the "socialist and communist literature" (CM 252–259). Continuing the scolding of reformers, leftists and "true socialists" begun in *The Holy Family* and *The Poverty of Philosophy*, section III of the *Manifesto* lays bare for its readers the shallow, mindless, speculative, utopian or contradictory character of the platforms and promises of many self-described friends of the proletariat. This was an intended overturning of – and a speech act against – the political theories of Saint-Simon, Proudhon, Fourier, Owen and Sismondi, by name, as well as Babeuf, Blanqui, Cabet, Grün, Weitling, Ruge, Hess and others, by innuendo.[4]

Third, for all the mockery of bourgeois freedom, the *Manifesto* compressed into one sentence a visionary credo that was the cell form of a new political theory for a new political world: "In place of the old bourgeois society with its classes and class conflicts there will be an association in which the free development of each is the condition for the free development of all" (CM 252–259). The meaning of this credo was not altogether clear on its face, despite its apparent simplicity, and later readers sometimes transposed "each" and "all," making it sound ostensibly more collectivist or egalitarian. But it is in fact "each" before "all" in an association dedicated to "free development." Further light is shed on this core creedal sentence from Engels's two catechistic documents that preceded the *Manifesto*, namely, "Principles of Communism" (1847) and, before that, "Draft of a Communist Confession of Faith" (1847). (Engels encouraged Marx to write the final version and "to abandon the catechetical form and call the thing Communist *Manifesto*" (CW 38: 149).) In "Principles," Engels said "association" was contrasted with and would replace social relations based on "competition" (CW 6: 348). And the question "What is the aim of the Communists?" in his draft catechism was answered: "To organise society in such a way that every member of it can develop and use all his capabilities and powers in complete freedom and without thereby infringing the basic conditions of this society" (CW 6: 96). The *Manifesto* and its two then-unpublished predecessors strongly implied that the "capabilities and powers" in question pertained principally to "production," in the broadest sense. Thus the productive powers of each member of the non-competitive, post-capitalist association were to be freely developed, and this was a condition for the free development of the productive powers of all other members. The general vision morphed into *Capital* as a "society ... treated as production by freely associated men" (CW 35: 90). "Freedom," pronounced volume 3, "can only consist in socialised man, the associated producers" (CW 37: 807).

As important as these incursions onto the terrain of political theory were, they would hardly have sufficed to make the *Manifesto* what it has come to be. "The *Communist Manifesto* is now a principal *dramatis personae* of the monumental history of Western political thought" (Isaac 2012, 17). This outcome was the shared work not only of Marx and Engels, but of translators, editors, pamphleteers, biographers, political theorists and historians of political thought. Then, too, there was all the non-literary, non-preserved work of poster readers, alehouse agitators, union organizers, proletarian rousers and countless others. In short, it was the reception of the *Manifesto* that made it the monument of political theory that has never gone out of print and is still reissued and read today.

TRANSLATION AS RECEPTION

The Anglophone reception of the *Manifesto* began with its initial translation into English in 1850. Engels had begun his own translation soon after the German original was published in London (CW 6: 698). Although he failed to complete the task, he offered suggestions to Helen Macfarlane, whose translation appeared in 1850 in *The Red Republican*, the Chartist organ edited by George Julian Harney.[5] This translation was later reprinted in the heady days of 1871 in *Woodhull & Claflin's Weekly*. Despite its avowed communism, the *Manifesto* thus appeared to its first English readers as a species or fellow traveler of republicanism (Macfarlane) or the "new socialism" (Woodhull).

The Authorized English Translation – as it announced itself – appeared in 1888, five years after Marx's death. Engels brought the translation to fruition in a stand-alone pamphlet, relying upon a draft penned by his friend Samuel Moore, co-translator of *Capital*. Unlike 1848 or 1871, the politics prompting the translation were more textual, concerning the apparent need to vanquish unauthorized editions. Engels announced in his preface that in the period since the 1871 reprint – which he called a "translation" of "1872" – "at least two more English translations, more or less mutilated, have been brought out in America, and one of them had been reprinted in England" (CW 26: 516). But the reference is unclear or incorrect, and it appears likely that the politics of authorization turned upon the building of a canon of works by Marx *and* Engels, under Engels's own imprimatur. Precisely because of his authority, the translation of 1888 became the anointed, standard one ever since, for Marxists and non-Marxists alike.

Reception history of the *Manifesto* recognizes and honors the 1888 translation precisely because it was the one that most Anglophone theorists received and commented upon. However, it also notes recent re-translations (especially Draper 2004; Findlay 2004; and Carver 1996)[6] as proof of the *Manifesto*'s continuing life and relevance (Carver 1998). Furthermore, it needs acknowledging that the Moore/Engels translation is "in places quite free and occasionally misleading" (Stedman Jones 2002, 191). Some translated passages are "extremely literal" and others "boldly revisionary" (Draper 2004, 83). The bold revisions are intriguing but puzzling. Engels's "authorized" preface quoted the preface to the 1872 German edition, signed by Marx and Engels, to underscore that the *Manifesto* was "a historical document which we have no longer any right to alter" (CW 23: 175; CW 26: 519). Yet the new translation of 1888 altered passages in literarily striking ways. Macfarlane's Gothic opener – "A frightful hobgoblin stalks throughout Europe" – became "a specter" "haunting Europe." "All that is solid melts into air" dramatically replaced "Everything fixed and stable vanishes." And at least one alteration proved threateningly consequential, as well: the fall of the bourgeoisie and "the victory of the proletariat are equally inevitable."

FROM THE FIRST INTERNATIONAL THROUGH THE GREAT WAR

Beyond translation, the Anglophone reception of the *Manifesto* began in books *about* socialism or utopias by authors and for readers who were usually neither socialists nor utopians. Drily academic and biographically sketchy, the underlying tone of these books was one of skepticism or condemnation. Yet, for all that, they did increase the visibility of the *Manifesto* and Marx himself. Marx even assisted the author of one of the first of these books, *Utopias; or, Schemes of Social Improvement from Sir Thomas More to Karl Marx* (Kaufman 1879).[7] This was Moritz Kaufman, an English clergyman, who claimed that "the hazy conceptions of the earlier authors of utopias have been crystallized into hard dogma" in the *Manifesto* (258). He paraphrased the threatening pronouncements about the proletariat rising, opining, "no wonder Marx was considered a dangerous subject after this" (229). He thanked Marx in print for sending information about the First International (247 n.); indeed, Marx offered corrections to the final two chapters devoted to him and the International Workingmen's Association (IWA)(CW 45: 435). Kaufman then ordained him "the real Pope of the Socialist World" (248). The IWA and "the leading features of the theory of Marx" also figured in *Communism and Socialism in their History* (1880) by Theodore Dwight Woolsey, an American theorist of "the state" and former president of Yale. In this anti-communist tome, the *Manifesto* was quoted specially regarding bourgeois marriage and the community of women. "This malignity" was too much for Woolsey, who added: "As for these words we only ask, how a man could be believed in any statement afterward, who would send forth stuff in the world" (Woolsey 1880, 152–153). Less fulminating was the Scottish journalist John Rae in *Contemporary Socialism* (1884), though this future biographer of Adam Smith framed his presentation in terms of Marx's "mistaken zeal" for workers' internationalism and the "threats to individuality" posed by his writings. But Rae nonetheless hailed the *Manifesto* as "the first public declaration of the International Socialist Democracy that now is," before describing in four full pages its principal claims about class struggle, state power and proletarians uniting (Rae 1884, 105, 107, 129–132).

In the 1890s through the Great War, authors of higher caliber in the history of political thought played key roles in the reception of the *Manifesto*. Two stand out: Bertrand Russell and John Dewey. Their initial comments and citations were sympathetic, as each at the time leaned toward gradualist socialism. In our short and selective history, they also display two opposing ways that the *Manifesto* was received and exerted its influence in non-Marxist circles. Russell thought it contained "Marx's system" in its essentials. *Capital* simply "added bulk and substance to the theses of the *Communist Manifesto*" (Russell 1918, 13). As such, it was central in Russell's subsequent discussions over many years. Dewey, on the other hand, cited the *Manifesto* a mere handful of times, for example in *Ethics* (Dewey and Tufts 1906). But it was spectrally present in the background – a case of "conspicuous exclusion" (Berger 1988; Dietz 2002, 190–193) – whenever Dewey wrote at greater length about Marx, Marxism or "the economic interpretation of history." Of the two, Dewey's reading is the more characteristic of reception. Although infrequently cited, the *Manifesto* dominated liberal criticism.

Dewey lectured on ethics at the turn of the last century, where Marx appears as having "interpreted history from a materialistic standpoint." He thought their philosophies close, but "would not say that the economic process is the cause of all other social phenomena but rather that it is the key, from the standpoint of method" (Dewey 1991, 373). Dewey also bristled against class violence that, like the methodological point, would return later in stronger objections when he wrote about Marx (with the *Manifesto* in the background).

But the more important reception in this period came from Russell, then a Fabian socialist. Indeed, Russell's long career (that would earn him a Nobel Prize in Literature in 1950) began with *German Social Democracy* (Russell 1895).[8] Laying out "the theoretical basis of Social Democracy," he provided an exegesis of the *Manifesto*, "which is almost unsurpassed in literary merit ... For terse eloquence, for biting wit, and for historical insight, it is, to my mind, one of the best pieces of political literature ever produced" (10). The diagnoses of the socio-economic ills found in that work were, on the eve of the twentieth century, even more apt than they were when the *Manifesto* was first published, thus giving it an even greater freshness and immediacy (12). "In this magnificent work, we have already all the epic force of the materialistic disdain of morals and religion, its reduction of all social relations to the blind action of impersonal productive forces" (13–14). In the *Manifesto*, "the essential points of [Marx's] doctrine are stated with a force and eloquence which his later work nowhere attains" (14). That seminal work was "the imaginative and poetical aspect of Marx's system," which Russell contrasted with "the dry and tedious details of his economic theory," much of which turned out to be false (15).

More than two decades after *German Social Democracy*, Russell, then a Guild Socialist with anarchist sympathies, published *Proposed Roads to*

Freedom (1918). One of the three roads proposed was Marxist socialism (alongside anarchism and syndicalism). Published during the still-unconsummated Russian Revolution and at the end of the Great War, his book had a particular urgency. He claimed that in the *Manifesto*, "for the first time Marx's system is set forth" (Russell 1918, 8) with three undergirding themes: "the materialistic conception of history," the increasing "concentration of capital" and "the class war" (Russell 1918, 9–10). "All these ideas are contained in the 'Communist Manifesto,' a work of the most amazing vigor and force, setting forth with terse compression the titanic forces of the world, their epic battle and the inevitable consummation" (Russell 1918, 10).

For Russell, the worm in the apple was Marx's and the *Manifesto*'s view of the state. "The attitude of the Manifesto to the State is not altogether easy to grasp," although it is clear that "the first step for the proletariat must be to acquire control of the State." What happens once they, or rather the proletarian vanguard, control the state poses potential problems. The interim state that Marx calls the "dictatorship of the proletariat" will, initially at least, be more powerful than the bourgeois state it replaces. Although Marx and Engels "cannot themselves be accused of any glorification of the State," it is less clear that self-proclaimed followers in Russia and elsewhere will not be so inclined (Russell 1918, 12–13). This proved a prophetic suspicion in the longer arc of Russell's political development.

THE RUSSIAN REVOLUTION THROUGH THE SECOND WORLD WAR

The creation of the Soviet Union in the wake of the Russian Revolution dramatically transformed the Anglophone reception of Marx, Marxism and the *Manifesto*. Where previously there had been the IWA and socialist alliances – not to mention Czarist Russia – now there was a unified (or unifying) communist state identifying itself *as* Marxist. Ideological reactions to this monumental development varied considerably in the English-speaking world, as it did everywhere, between and among socialists, democrats, liberals, conservatives and pragmatists. But curiosity brought travelers who were familiar enough with the "prophecies" of the *Manifesto* about where a revolution would break out to know that semi-feudal Russia was not even a remote candidate; Russell went in 1920, Dewey in 1928, and Sidney Hook in 1929. Russell was appalled, looking back later. Everything "was totally contrary to what any person of a liberal outlook would desire. I thought the regime hateful and certain to become more so. I found the source of evil in a contempt for liberty and democracy which was a natural outcome of fanaticism" (Russell 1956, 8). Writing from "Soviet Russia" in praise of the cooperatives and schools, Dewey nonetheless said it was "unlike the society which orthodox Marxian formulae call for," and, like his reaction to the *Manifesto*, he decried the official propaganda about "the necessity of class war and of world revolution by violence" (Dewey 1988a, 223, 250). Hook, Dewey's brilliant

student and a scholar-activist, was at the time attempting to solve the problems posed by his ideological hybridization of pragmatism and Marxism. He
went to Moscow at the invitation of David Ryazanov, director of the Marx-
Engels Institute and editor-in-chief of the monumental *MEGA* (*Marx-Engels
Gesamtausgabe*), to research the vast manuscript holdings being assembled
there. Hook was one of the first Western scholars to have access to these
manuscripts (Phelps 1997, 47), including the preparatory materials by Engels
for the *Manifesto*. As he later remembered (Hook 1987, 121), "no one but
very advanced students could approach the holy precincts of Marxism"
represented by the "institute's incomparable collection." Indeed, his host
Ryazanov was the author of *The Communist Manifesto of Karl Marx and
Frederick Engels*, first published in Russian in 1922 and then translated into
German in 1928 and English in 1930. His "explanatory notes" were (and
remain) the most extensive ever written on the *Manifesto*. On the political
front, Hook was then more hopeful for the outcome of the Soviet experiment
than were Dewey and especially Russell. But "he had begun to see a darker
side to Soviet society while he was there" (Phelps 1997, 49). Stalin would
ensure it by, among other things, stopping publication of the *MEGA* and
ordering its eminent editor shot.

As a result of his research Hook wrote two very important books –
Towards the Understanding of Karl Marx: A Revolutionary Interpretation
(1933) and *From Hegel to Marx* (1936). The *Manifesto* – "undoubtedly
the most influential political pamphlet of all time," as he put it later (Hook
1948, 6) – loomed large in both works. Unlike Russell, however, Hook did
not find a "system" in the *Manifesto* or, indeed, in Marx's writings as a whole.
He found "critiques" consistent with the fighting spirit and rhetoric of the
Manifesto, as well as a "unity" in method, not doctrine or dogma. Hook
shared this insight with two unorthodox Marxist influences, Georg Lukacs
and Karl Korsch. And he excitedly communicated it to Dewey during his
travels abroad. "I have come to the conclusion that in its original form Marx's
thought was not in the least an expression of a system but rather a thorough
criticism ... It was Engels who attempted for good but insufficient reasons to
make a system out of Marx. But Marxism is no more a system than is
pragmatism" (quoted in Farr 1999, 272).

The status of the *Manifesto* – with the names Marx *and* Engels on the title
page – was thus one of Hook's problems, given his desire to separate Marx from
Engels and method from system. As a consequence, Hook simply quoted Marx as
sole author and underscored the "revolutionary philosophy of the *Communist
Manifesto*" that he associated with Marx in *Towards the Understanding*
(1933, 26) as distinguished from the "scientism" inherited from Engels. This
revolutionary philosophy eschewed determinism, reductionism and inevitabilism.
It rejected a Leninist "reflection" epistemology (according to which "ideas" are
"reflections" of material reality), insisting that ideas were instead pragmatic
"plans of action." It was also a philosophy of freedom – the freedom of "socialized

man, the associated producers," as argued in *Capital*, echoing the *Manifesto* (1933, 186). In short, Marx's revolutionary philosophy could be characterized as socialist pragmatism or pragmatist socialism.

While Hook in the mid-1930s labored away on his ideological hybrid, Dewey distanced his pragmatism and socialist-leaning liberalism from Marxism. His version of Marxism, however, was actually what Hook had said of Engels and his scientistic legacy. More damningly to Dewey, Marxism was the state philosophy of an increasingly totalitarian Soviet Union, as well as the orthodox ideology embraced by "Communist spokesmen in speech and press" in the United States. Dewey stated it, painfully, in "Why I Am Not a Communist," his contribution to a symposium with Hook and Russell (who also contributed an essay of the same title). Reflecting his own mistreatment, Dewey assailed American Communists for "the hysteria of their denunciations, their attempts at character assassination of their opponents, [and] their misrepresentation of the views of the 'liberals'" (Dewey 1934, 56). Moreover, Dewey also could not abide the preaching of violent class war and the crowing about the "inevitable" victory of the working class. In the symposium, Russell now found "so much hate in Marx" and his "Sacred Book" (Russell 1934, 52–53). Hook criticized capital "C" Communists but otherwise defended "communism without dogmas" and underscored the ideological centrality of the *Manifesto*'s view of "the free development of each is the condition for the free development of all" (Hook 1934, 69).

This immediate background influenced what Dewey wrote about the *Manifesto* when he cited it directly, as for example in *Liberalism and Social Action* (1935) – "a book," Hook claimed, "which may very well be to the twentieth century what Marx and Engels' *Communist Manifesto* was to the nineteenth" (Hook 1940, 158). "In orthodox communist literature, from the *Communist Manifesto* of 1848 to the present day," Dewey wrote in 1935, "we are told that the bourgeoisie, the name for a distinctive class, has done this and that," including the creation of a proletariat that will be its undoing as "class struggle of veiled civil war will finally burst into open revolution" (Dewey 1987, 54–55). More often, as noted earlier, Dewey did not mention the *Manifesto* by title, but it was present, if only spectrally, governing his understanding and objections to orthodox Marxism. This was especially the case in *Freedom and Culture* (1939), a work which, given its title, could and should have addressed what Marx had written about "the free development of each" being "the condition for the free development of all." In place of this, Dewey criticized and rejected a doctrine that was, in his words, "uniformitarian," "absolutistic," "monistic" and "monolithic" (Dewey 1988b, 116–135; see Farr 1999, 277–281). A fleeting reading of the *Manifesto* could find sentences to support the epithets, especially in the 1930s when Marxist orthodoxy had been reduced to phrases. But then, as G. D. H. Cole (1934, 4) had observed of orthodox phraseology: "Only idiots learn the *Communist Manifesto* and the key passages of *Das Kapital* by heart, and conceive themselves to have unlocked the secrets of the capitalist system as it now exists."

In this crucial period, a new genre of academic writing proved to be an influential medium for the reception of the *Manifesto* – the textbook history of major figures in the history of political thought. This genre came into its own with William A. Dunning's *A History of Political Theories* in three volumes (1902, 1905 and 1920). In the section on "Marxist Doctrine," the *Manifesto* was given pride of place, for in it "is embodied the whole substance of the doctrine, so far as concerns political theory" (Dunning 1920, 372). Dunning was a quite conservative liberal who, as a Columbia University historian, was a critic of Reconstruction in the American South. He emphasized that, in the *Manifesto*, "economic facts determine the forms of political life," and class struggle is made the "clue to all history" (Dunning 1920, 372). Dunning took note of the "concrete projects" and "program of action" at the end of the second section. And he quoted – with an interventionist bracket that signaled his confusion or criticism – the closing line about freedom: after "warring classes" cease, there will be "an association in which the free development of each [individual?] is the condition for the free development of all" (Dunning 1920, 375). He editorialized: "This somewhat jaunty evasion of a serious dilemma is out of touch with Marxist doctrine" (Dunning 1920, 375). In 1925, Robert Murray (with the assistance of Michael Oakeshott in the second edition of 1929) added to the genre and stated that the *Manifesto* "contains all the essential points of his system, but the argument is used to work up to a climax, which is a call to action" (Murray [1925] 1929, 383). He continued, spiritedly:

In it Marx raised a standard. He was a Mahdi preaching a holy war, a Peter the Hermit preaching a crusade for the recovery of the holy city from the infidels who had impiously taken possession of it. Only the name of that holy city is Wealth, the infidels are the capitalists... It is a call to arms, and there is more life in it than in the chilly and incompatible doctrine of... "scientific" Socialism. (Murray 1929, 383–340)

With premature finality, Murray concluded by saying that the doctrine in the *Manifesto* "has not withstood the elements; it has been falsified by the course of events and has crumbled away" (Murray 1929, 389).

Generations of university students and general readers got their Marx and *Manifesto* this way. From Yale Professor Francis Coker they would learn that "the doctrine of class struggle is stated most succinctly in the *Communist Manifesto*, but it dominates all Marx's writings" (Coker 1934, 48). Coker was generous enough to allow that, beneath the economic trappings, Marx's "ultimate interest was in liberated and cultivated individuals" and "a society in which the full and free development of every individual forms the ruling principle" (Coker 1934, 61). The most sustained treatment of Marx, if not the *Manifesto*, was by George Sabine in *A History of Political Theory* (1937), the exemplar of the textbook genre. Students and readers were treated to lengthy disquisitions on "economic determinism" and "dialectical materialism" (Sabine 1937, 686–693). They learned that Hook was wrong to separate Engels from Marx, and that "in any case the version of dialectic which Professor Hook attributes to Marx seems to me no more valid than Engels's" (Sabine 1937, 697 n). But "the importance of Marx's economic interpretation of history [in the *Manifesto*] can hardly be exaggerated" (Sabine 1937, 703). Indeed, "Marx was the most important social philosopher in the whole of the nineteenth century" (Sabine 1937, 703). Thirteen years later, in the revised edition, this estimate changed a bit. The economic interpretation of history was now "one of the most important additions made to social theory in the nineteenth century" (Sabine 1950, 781). The reasons for the revision had to do, as Sabine admitted in his new preface, with his more forceful conviction of the rectitude of "liberalism" (seeing "in that tradition the most hopeful prospect for social and political improvement by peaceful means" (Sabine 1950, ix)), after the bracing realities of the Second World War, the imperialism of Soviet Russia and the onset of the Cold War.

Another liberal historian of political thought and indeed one of the twentieth century's most eminent historians of ideas – Isaiah Berlin – contributed greatly to the Anglophone reception of the *Manifesto* on the eve of war (both hot and cold) by way of biography. *Karl Marx: His Life and Environment* (1939) – now remarkably in its fifth edition (2013) – made Marx's ideas and the *Manifesto* accessible to English speakers in an unprecedented way. It appeared originally in 1939 in the Home University Library of Modern Knowledge, a series that aimed to further the education, and especially the self-education, of workers and citizens in England and elsewhere. As a biographical study his book was not altogether kind to Marx the man, whom Berlin viewed as overbearing, offensive and dogmatic (Berlin 1939, 11–12). But Marx the author of the *Manifesto* elicited very different reactions. Berlin wrote of the *Manifesto* in glowing terms. It is, he wrote,

> very nearly a work of genius ... No other modern political movement or cause can claim to have produced anything comparable with it in eloquence or power. It is a document of prodigious dramatic force; in form it is an edifice of bold and arresting historical generalizations, mounting to a denunciation of the existing order in the name of the avenging forces of the future, much of it written in prose which has the lyrical quality of a great revolutionary hymn, whose effect, powerful even now, was probably greater ninety years ago. (Berlin 1939, 143–144)

Contextualizing the *Manifesto* to the events of 1848, Berlin summarized in three extensive paragraphs its historiography, phraseology and glimpses of political theory. He paraphrased freely and evocatively: "The past is gone, the classes which belonged to it have long been decisively defeated by the march of history," while the bourgeoisie faced crises that forced it "to exhaust itself in feeding its servants instead of feeding on them" (Berlin 1939, 146). He loosely parsed Marx's view of freedom: "True personal freedom rests on a basis of power of independent action, of which the artisan, the small trader, the peasant, has long been deprived under capitalism" (Berlin 1939, 146). This "true personal freedom" appears to reflect Berlin's "inchoate liberal allegiances" more than Marx's view of a future association of freedom for each and all, but it helps us see Berlin's writing of the influential biography as a deliberate action "to join the swim of the major ideological current of his age" (Ignatieff 1998, 70–71). "Berlin's *Marx*," it is fair to say, "was in many ways a vehicle for the construction of his own moral positions and historical identity" (Toews 2003, 175; also Carver 2007). Its readers sized up two men, two competing ideologies. For all that, Berlin viewed the *Manifesto* as an unmatched work of propaganda for Marx's brand of revolutionary socialism. "No summary can convey the quality of its opening or closing pages. As an instrument of destructive propaganda it has no equal anywhere; its effect upon succeeding generations is unparalleled outside religious history; had its author written nothing else, it would have ensured his lasting fame" (Berlin 1939, 148). The *Manifesto*'s propaganda and destructiveness – felt so keenly by Berlin in 1939 – would continue to ensure Marx's "lasting fame" well into the era of the Cold War.

THE COLD WAR TO 1989

The *Manifesto* would lose little if any of its power to attract readers, both sympathetic and critical, after the Second World War and beyond. It turned one hundred years old in 1948 during the height of the Cold War when its Anglophone reception at first echoed the ideological debates of the interwar years. This is evident in one of the most important books in the history of the *Manifesto*'s reception.

Karl Popper was already famous as a philosopher of science when, having fled Austria, he performed his "war work" by writing *The Open Society and Its Enemies* (1945). (Russell performed his war work by publishing his *History of Western Philosophy* in 1945, with a chapter on Marx.) As if anticipating the criticism that such work was of little help in the fight against fascism, Popper confessed that he wrote the two-volume work because of his "expectation that Marxism would become a major problem" (Popper 2013, xxxix).[9] His solution (aimed at Plato and Hegel, as well) was a fierce and sustained refutation of Marx's "grandiose philosophical system" (341), which Popper took pains to logically "reconstruct" when he thought it needed it ("preserving as much of the original theory as possible" (364)). The *Manifesto* was deemed philosophically and empirically central to the system, not merely a rhetorical gesture; and it was quoted or cited some three dozen times. Even that number understates its "presence." A former socialist (Hacohen 2000), Popper was by 1945 a social democrat, a believer in "piecemeal social-engineering," and a liberal – a so-called cold-war liberal. As such, he was decidedly anti-communist and anti-Marxist. But he was not anti-Marx. In contrast to Berlin (with whom he would later correspond about "positive" freedom), Popper expressed regard for

Marx's personal traits of sincerity, open-mindedness, and a burning desire to help the oppressed (294). He was also, like Berlin, able to find much to admire in Marx's theorizing. In the *Manifesto* and elsewhere, Marx protected the autonomy of sociology against "psychologism" (322) – the doctrine that all social phenomena must be explained by referring to the intentions of individuals – which Popper deemed "an extremely valuable advance in the methods of social science" (317). Marx was resolutely theoretical *and* practical, making him "one of the first philosophers to develop the views which later were to be called 'pragmatism'" (296). (Doubtless this would have pleased Hook if not Dewey a decade earlier, though no longer.) In the *Manifesto*, "Marx's *idea* 'Workers of all countries, unite!' was of the greatest significance down to the eve of the Russian Revolution" (318). Indeed, the theory behind the idea – that "history is the history of class struggle," repeatedly quoted or noted by Popper – could be understood, favorably, as an example of "institutional analysis," that is, the social "mechanism by which ... power is controlled" (401).

More importantly, however, the author of the *Manifesto* was a "false prophet" who needed to be "attacked" (294) on methodological as well as political grounds. Misleading "scores of intelligent people," Marx was "responsible for the devastating influence of the historicist method of thought within the ranks of those who wish to advance the cause of the open society" (294). Historicism entailed a strong version of determinism (struggling against the "activism" of the *Manifesto*'s dual message). It claimed to "foretell" the future development of society that offered scores of people "a form of escape" into illusions of "a future paradise" under socialism (349). This is why Marx's false prophecy was also "utopian," despite Popper's acknowledgment of the criticism of "utopian socialists" in section III of the *Manifesto* (682, n. 6). To attempt to bring about a socialist paradise would not only be inconsistent with the prophecy that it was going to happen anyway but would require wholesale social change – not piecemeal but "utopian social engineering" (338). The ten practical measures at the end of the second section were admirably "interventionist," though most of them (like progressive taxation, abolition of inheritance, state-owned industries and free education) had been largely realized in democratic countries (350). This proved that actually existing, non-socialist countries could intervene and improve the welfare of their people. The coming of communist society was not prophesied correctly, and still less was it inevitable. Despite those camp followers who were "blinded by the glare of a preconceived system," this showed (to Popper's satisfaction) that "not only is Marxism a bad guide to the future, but it also renders its followers incapable of seeing what is happening before their own eyes, in their own historical period, and sometimes even with their own co-operation" (351). On matters of method and politics, page after page Popper was relentless.

As for freedom, *The Open Society and Its Enemies* opened up a related political-theoretical front in attacking the *Manifesto*. Popper was actually of two minds. One mind believed "Marx loved freedom, real freedom," not the spiritual version of Hegel (313). This then inspired the surprising claim, coming as it did from a cold-war liberal, that "Marx was ultimately an individualist" (335; cf. 682, n. 2). He cared for actual individuals who suffered from capitalist "crimes" and "cruel exploitation" (330–331). The other mind thought that Marx misunderstood freedom, including its "paradox" that, when "unfettered," it "defeats itself" (333–334). In this context, Popper twice quoted (and elsewhere gestured to) the "prophecy" in the *Manifesto* of a classless future association in which, as he put it, "the free development of each is the *warrant* for the free development of all" (349, 696, n. 4, emphasis added). He then condescended: "It is a beautiful belief, but it is an aesthetic and romantic belief; it is a wishful 'Utopianism'" (696, n. 4). The structure and cadence of the *Manifesto*'s line on freedom, however, resonated with Popper when, later in the Cold War and thinking himself "the last laggard of the Enlightenment," he articulated his liberal view that "true freedom of thought is impossible without political freedom. Political freedom becomes thus a condition for the full use of his reason by each individual person" (Popper 1992, 204, 208).

In 1948, the *Manifesto* enjoyed a centennial reception in a number of books and articles. Of particular note was Hook's "The Communist Manifesto 100 Years After" (Hook 1948), written for *The New York Times Magazine*, an outlet of considerable prestige and prominence. For a decade, Hook had distanced himself (politically, if not as a scholar) from his writings on Marx and his own "communism without dogmas." But he was most certainly by then – as were Berlin, Russell and Dewey – a staunch anti-communist resolutely rejecting Stalinism, the Soviet Union and communist parties all across the globe. The review's paraphrase underneath the title virtually advertised what he was doing in writing the review: "Enduring interest is found in a critique of capitalism which Communists have misused." Hook was praising Marx and his *Manifesto* in such a way as to discredit Communists. But the praise was both genuine and astonishing. It suggested the considerable respect that Hook still felt for the author and the *Manifesto*, "undoubtedly the most influential political pamphlet of all time." "No one can read it without being stirred by its rhetoric . . . Its very exaggerations give it force." Hook called Marx's sketch of history "a miracle of compression." He took special notice of Marx's "handsome compliments to capitalists" for all the revolutionary changes they had achieved. Marx's large-scale predictions had failed; indeed, fascism had been as potent a reaction to economic distress as socialism. But there was a marked prescience in the list of ten measures since Western democracies had realized most of them. Hook underscored the rationalist, humanist and democratic character of Marx's beliefs about freedom. Here was a political-theoretic issue that revealed "an even greater difference between the Communists of the *Manifesto* and the totalitarian Communists of today," namely, "the fervent belief of the former in personal and civil freedom." Marx was particularly fervent: "His Socialist ideal was a society in which 'the free development of each is the condition of the free development of all'" (all references to Hook 1948, 6–7, 38). Thanks to

Hook's op-ed, the *Manifesto* caught the attention of a wide readership, to judge by the correspondence Hook received. It was "an amazing response," he wrote to one of his correspondents who included a major book publisher, a perennial Socialist candidate for New York office, a college student who wanted references for his senior thesis on how Russian Communists modified Marx, a famous psychologist of propaganda, an irate citizen demanding proof that Marx thought revolution might come without violence and the International Broadcasting Division of the U.S. Department of State requesting permission to use the article "for the purpose of furthering the Government's aim to portray, to the peoples of other countries, a full and fair picture of American life" (Sidney Hook Collection, box 49, folder 13, Hoover Institution Archives).

In this context, Berlin rejoined the ideological and scholarly "swim" by putting out a second edition of *Karl Marx: His Life and Environment* (1948) and by investigating the concept of "freedom" in its history. "Historical Inevitability" (1954) and "Two Concepts of Liberty" (1958) proved to be two of his most important essays. In both, Berlin took up two themes of the *Manifesto* that in 1950 he had already heralded as "a unique polemical masterpiece" and "the most arresting exposition of [Marx's] views" (Berlin 1996, 98). The title of the first essay called up the specter of the *Manifesto* with its prophetic claim about the "inevitability" of the fall of the bourgeoisie and the victory of the proletariat. According to the doctrine of historical inevitability, human beings were mere playthings of or appendages to (in T. S. Eliot's words, used by Berlin as an epigram) "those vast impersonal forces" that are "beyond the control of individuals" (Berlin 2002a, 98). Berlin counted class and history among those forces, but there were others like race, culture and "the Spirit of the Age." The former pair picked out "Marx and Marxists," though Berlin admitted that, unlike Gobineau, Carlyle or Hegel, they were "more ambiguous," presumably because of the revolutionary agitation that characterized their propaganda and manifesto. But, on balance, they were guilty of the view that "men do as they do, and think as they think, largely as a 'function of' the inevitable evolution of the class as a whole" (Berlin 2002a, 99). Besides a fallacious claim of inevitability, Berlin also saddled Marx and the Marxists with an erroneous entailment, namely, "the elimination of the notion of individual responsibility" (Berlin 2002, 115). This raised from a different angle the problem of freedom that Berlin took up in "Two Concepts of Liberty" where he contrasted the "positive liberty" of "self-mastery" with the "negative liberty" of choice without obstacles. The *Manifesto*, like the whole of Marx's canon, inclined to the former, whereas liberals like Berlin (though not those like Popper) hewed to the latter.

Berlin would continue his investigations into freedom, Marxism and the history of ideas as the Cold War wound down and scholarly studies of Marx proliferated. He brought out two more editions of *Karl Marx: His Life and Environment*. The gloss he had originally given the *Manifesto* remained essentially the same, but other elements changed. In the third edition (1963), he admitted that the "most important" omission in previous scholarship – Marxist, non-Marxist and his own – was "the relation between the alienation and the freedom of men." With the *Economic and Philosophic Manuscripts* in hand – and with eyes now newly focused on the *Manifesto* – he set about repairing that omission while at the same time shifting much of the blame to Engels for the "more mechanistic and crudely deterministic" heritage of Marxism (Berlin 1963, 267). In place of his earlier decree that the *Manifesto* was "very nearly the work of genius," he now hailed it as "the greatest of all socialist pamphlets" (Berlin 1963, 163). In the fourth edition (1978) he confessed he had been too influenced by Marxist orthodoxy in his original analysis of 1939; and he went even further in trying to answer the question, "What kind of freedom?" was being promised about a communist future. At long last, he grappled with the famous phrase, "the free development of each is the condition for the free development of all." But, he added, "if men are themselves the product only of objective conditions ... then the concept of human freedom, whether in its social or individual aspects, is clearly in need of explanation" (Berlin 1978, 103–104).

Berlin's views of freedom – and of other conceptions central to modern liberalism – were influential on the most prominent liberal of the late twentieth century, John Rawls. Rawls selectively cited Berlin and Marx in his magnum opus, *A Theory of Justice* (1971), as well as in *Justice as Fairness: A Restatement* (2001). Despite a tantalizing note in the former about the communal development of individual capacities (Rawls 1971, 424–425 523–525 n. 4), it is only in the latter work that Rawls directly addressed "Marx's critique of liberalism" (Rawls 2001, 176–177). However, he had been lecturing on Marx's critique since the early 1970s and examining his students about the "analysis of historical change in the *Communist Manifesto*" (Little 2010). When published posthumously, *Lectures in the History of Political Philosophy* (Rawls 2007) joined the genre of textbook histories of political thought that typified an earlier era of reception and had continued ever since. Marx was the only non-liberal, though the range of liberals was quite broad to include Hobbes, Locke, Hume, Rousseau, Mill and Sidgwick. It became clear how sympathetically Rawls had read (and taught) Marx, as well as how seriously he had taken Marx's challenge to liberalism. Three long chapters covered questions of justice, freedom and communism. He also contrasted "central command socialism" as associated with the "discredited" system in the former Soviet Union with what he called "liberal socialism" in an ideology-bending manner (Rawls 2007, 323). The *Manifesto* was quoted only twice, on the pauperization of the working class and the self-undermining "heroism" of the bourgeoisie preparing the way for the "victory of the proletariat" (Rawls 2007, 339). But, in the manner of Dewey's reading, its presence (or, rather, conspicuous absence) suffused the discussion, as when Rawls contrasted Marx from the utopian socialists and when canvassing interpretations (that he had come to abandon) of Marx's apparent dismissal of justice as a time- and class-bound conceit, in the spirit of "your justice is merely the will of your class raised to the status of law" (CM 248) and eternalized to boot. The *Manifesto*'s vision of an association of freely developing communists seems quite inspirational in the final chapter that concluded: "There is a unity of theory and practice: we all understand why we do what we do, and what we do realizes our natural powers under conditions of freedom" (Rawls 2007, 372). While Marx was not a "liberal socialist," neither was he a Soviet-styled command socialist. His vision of planning in a communist society was "public and democratic," and it was, in its own way, "certainly just" (Rawls 2007, 371). In a Rawlsian light, one might – as Reiman (2012) recently has – imagine yet another ideological hybrid, a "Marxian liberalism."

1998 AND THE CAPITALIST FUTURE

There can be no definitive conclusion to the Anglophone liberal reception history of the *Manifesto*. The reception continues apace. In 2013 alone, when we began this chapter, the fifth edition of Berlin's *Karl Marx: His Life and Environment* appeared, as did a new one-volume edition of Popper's *Open Society and Its Enemies*. New or renewed editions of the *Manifesto* came out. *Karl Marx: A Nineteenth-Century Life* emerged as the latest biography, judging the *Manifesto* "the most renowned of Marx's writings" and "a literary masterpiece: compact, pithy, elegant, powerful, and sarcastically amusing all at once" (Sperber 2013, 200, 203). And now here is this *Cambridge Companion to the Communist Manifesto*. The last quarter-century of reception has taken the ideological measure of 1989 when the Berlin Wall came down and, then in 1991, the break-up of the Soviet Union with the end of its state ideology. In 1998, the *Manifesto* reached its 150th anniversary with an outpouring of scholarly and journalistic reflection that attested to its continuing importance and influence. *The New Yorker* magazine, to choose an unlikely source, hailed "the return of Karl Marx" as "the next big thinker," not least for predicting the globalization of capital in the *Manifesto*, making it "worth reading as long as capitalism endures" (Cassidy 1997, 251, 256). The works of the Anglophone liberal political theorists covered here – Russell, Dewey, Hook, Berlin, Popper, Rawls and others – may also retain their worth as long as capitalism endures. If so, their pages will do their part to keep the *Manifesto* alive, both ideologically and critically.

REFERENCES

Andréas, Bert. 1963. *Le Manifeste Communiste de Marx et Engels: Histoire et Bibliographie, 1848–1918*. Milan: Feltrinelli.

Berger, Harry. 1988. "Conspicuous Exclusion in Vermeer: An Essay in Renaissance Pastoral." In Harry Berger, *Second World and Green World: Studies in Renaissance Fiction-Making*. Berkeley, CA: University of California Press.

Berlin, Isaiah. 1939. *Karl Marx: His Life and Environment*. London: Butterworth.

Berlin, Isaiah. 1963. *Karl Marx: His Life and Environment*, 3rd edn. London: Oxford University Press.

Berlin, Isaiah. 1978. *Karl Marx: His Life and Environment*, 4th edn. Oxford: Oxford University Press.

Berlin, Isaiah. 1996 [1950]. "Socialism and Socialist Theory." In *The Sense of Reality*, ed. Henry Hardy. New York: Farrar, Strauss, and Geroux, 77–115.

Berlin, Isaiah. 2002a [1954]. "Historical Inevitability." In *Liberty*, ed. Henry Hardy. Oxford: Oxford University Press, 94–165.

Berlin, Isaiah. 2002b [1958]. "Two Concepts of Liberty." In *Liberty*, ed. Henry Hardy. Oxford: Oxford University Press, 166–217.

Berlin, Isaiah. 2013. *Karl Marx*, 5th edn, ed. Henry Hardy. Princeton: Princeton University Press.

Carver, Terrell. Ed. 1996. *Marx: Later Political Writings*. Cambridge: Cambridge University Press.

Carver, Terrell. 1998. "Re-Translating the *Manifesto*: New Histories, New Ideas." In *The Communist Manifesto: New Interpretations*, ed. Mark Cowling. New York: New York University Press, 51–62.

Carver, Terrell. 2007. "Berlin's Karl Marx." In *The One and the Many: Reading Isaiah Berlin*, eds. George Crowder and Henry Hardy. Amherst, NY: Prometheus, 31–46.

Cassidy, John. 1997. "The Return of Karl Marx: The Next Big Thinker." *New Yorker*, October 20.

Coker, Francis. 1934. *Recent Political Thought*. New York: D. Appleton-Century.

Cole, G. D. H. 1934. *What Marx Really Meant*. London: Alfred A. Knopf.

Collingwood, R. G. 1939. *An Autobiography*. Oxford: The Clarendon Press.

Dewey, John. 1934. "Why I Am Not a Communist." In *The Meaning of Marx*, ed. Sidney Hook. New York: Farrar and Rinehart, 54–56.

Dewey, John. 1987 [1935]. *Liberalism and Social Action*. In *Later Works, 1935–1937*, vol. 11. Carbondale: Southern Illinois University Press, 1–66.

Dewey, John. 1988a [1928]. "Impressions of Soviet Russia." In *Later Works, 1927–1928*, vol. 3. Carbondale: Southern Illinois University Press, 203–250.

Dewey, John. 1988b [1939]. *Freedom and Culture*. In *Later Works, 1938–1939*, vol. 13. Carbondale: Southern Illinois University Press, 63–188.

Dewey, John. 1991 [1901]. *Lectures on Ethics, 1901–1911*, ed. Donald Koch. Carbondale: Southern Illinois University Press.

Dewey, John, and James H. Tufts. 1932 [1906]. *Ethics*. New York: Henry Holt.

Dietz, Mary G. 2002. *Turning Operations: Feminism, Arendt, and Politics*. New York: Routledge.

Draper, Hal. 2004. *The Adventures of the Communist Manifesto*. Alameda, CA: Center for Socialist History.

Dunning, William A. 1920. *A History of Political Theories from Rousseau to Spencer*. New York: Macmillan.

Farr, James. 1999. "Engels, Dewey, and the Reception of Marxism in America." In *Engels after Marx*, eds. Manfred Steger and Terrell Carver. University Park: Pennsylvania State University Press, 261–287.

Findlay, L. M. Ed. 2004. *The Communist Manifesto*. Peterborough, ON: Broadview Press.

Hacohen, Malachi Haim. 2000. *Karl Popper: The Formative Years, 1902–1945*. Cambridge: Cambridge University Press.

Hook, Sidney. 1933. *Toward the Understanding of Karl Marx: A Revolutionary Interpretation*. New York: The John Day Company.

Hook, Sidney. 1934. "Communism without Dogmas." In *The Meaning of Marx*, ed. Sidney Hook. New York: Farrar and Rinehart, 63–89.

Hook, Sidney. 1940 *John Dewey: An Intellectual Portrait*. New York: The John Day Company.

Hook, Sidney. 1948. "The Communist Manifesto 100 Years After." *The New York Times Magazine*, February 1.

Hook, Sidney. 1987. *Out of Step: An Unquiet Life in the 20th Century*. New York: Harper Row.

Ignatieff, Michael. 1998. *Isaiah Berlin: A Life*. New York: Henry Holt.

Isaac, Jeffrey C. Ed. 2012. *The Communist Manifesto*. New Haven, CT: Yale University Press.

Kaufman, Moritz. 1879. *Utopias; or, Schemes of Social Improvement from Sir Thomas More to Karl Marx*. London: C.K. Paul and Co.

Little, Daniel. 2010. "Rawls on Marx, December 1972." http://understandingsociety. blogspot.com/2010/03/rawls-on-marx-december-1973.html. (Accessed May 25, 2015).

Macfarlane, Helen. 2014. *The Red Republican: Essays, Articles, and Her translation of the Communist Manifesto*, ed. David Black. London: Unkant.

Murray, Robert. 1929 [1925]. *The History of Political Science from Plato to the Present*. New York: D. Appleton.

Phelps, Christopher. 1997. *Young Sidney Hook: Marxist and Pragmatist*. Ithaca, NY: Cornell University Press.

Popper, Karl R. 1972. *Objective Knowledge: An Evolutionary Approach*. Oxford: Oxford University Press.

Popper, Karl R. 1992 [1959]. "What Does the West Believe In?" In Karl R. Popper, *In Search of a Better World: Lectures and Essays from Thirty Years*, trans. Laura Bennett. London: Routledge, 204–222.

Popper, Karl R. 2013 [1945]. *The Open Society and Its Enemies*. Princeton: Princeton University Press.

Rae, John. 1884. *Contemporary Socialism*. New York: Charles Scribner's Sons.

Rawls, John. 1971. *A Theory of Justice*. Cambridge, MA: The Belknap Press.

Rawls, John. 2001. *Justice as Fairness: A Restatement*. Cambridge, MA: The Belknap Press.

Rawls, John. 2007. *Lectures on the History of Political Philosophy*, ed. Samuel Freeman. Cambridge, MA: The Belknap Press.

Reiman, Jeffrey. 2012. *As Free and as Just as Possible: The Theory of Marxian Liberalism*. London: Wiley-Blackwell.

Russell, Bertrand. 1895. *German Social Democracy*. London: Longmans, Green, and Company.

Russell, Bertrand. 1918. *Proposed Roads of Freedom*. London: George Allen and Unwin.

Russell, Bertrand. 1934. "Why I Am Not a Communist." In *The Meaning of Marx*, ed. Sidney Hook. New York: Farrar and Rinehart, 52–53.

Russell, Bertrand. 1956. *Portraits from Memory and Other Essays*. London: Allen and Unwin.

Sabine, George. 1937. *A History of Political Theory*. New York: Henry Holt.

Sabine, George. 1950. *A History of Political Theory*, rev. edn. New York: Henry Holt.

Skinner, Quentin. 2002. *Visions of Politics, vol. 1: Regarding Method*. Cambridge: Cambridge University Press.

Sperber, Jonathan. 2013. *Karl Marx: A Nineteenth-Century Life*. New York: Liverwright-Norton.

Stedman Jones, Gareth. Ed. 2002. *The Communist Manifesto*. London: Penguin.

Toews, John E. 2003. "Berlin's Marx: Enlightenment, Counter-Enlightenment, and the Historical Construction of Historical Identities." In *Isaiah Berlin's Counter-Enlightenment*, eds. Joseph Mali and Robert Wokler. Philadelphia: American Philosophical Society, 163–176.

Woolsey, Theodore Dwight. 1880. *Communism and Socialism in Their History and Theory*. New York: Charles Scribner's Sons.

10

The Specter of the *Manifesto* Stalks Neoliberal Globalization: Reconfiguring Marxist Discourse(s) in the 1990s

Manfred B. Steger

In April 1993, less than fourteen months after the official dissolution of the Soviet Union, a pertinent academic conference was held at the Center for Ideas and Society at the University of California, Riverside. Critical of the proliferation of "hasty postmortems of Marxism" in both neoliberal academic circles and the mainstream media, co-conveners Bernd Magnus and Stephen Cullenberg consciously entitled the conference, "Whither Marxism? Global Crises in International Perspective." Designed as a multinational and multidisciplinary gathering, the event attracted leading scholars eager to assess the seemingly dire prospects of Marxist and socialist traditions in the wake of the unexpected communist collapse of 1989. In particular, Magnus and Cullenberg (1995, 8–9) asked Jacques Derrida, the conference's invited keynote speaker, as well as the other participants, to consider the following questions in light of the changing social, political, philosophical and economic dimensions of the global community. Have we indeed reached the "end of history," as Francis Fukuyama (1989; 1992) argued, where pluralistic democracies and capitalist economies reign supreme? Has the collapse of communism also spelled the death of Marxism, and of Marx as an important philosopher and political thinker? What is living and what is dead in Marxism? And, perhaps most importantly, how should intellectuals in the Marxist tradition respond, theoretically and politically, to the hegemonic narrative of the "irrelevance of Marxism"?

Derrida did not disappoint his audience. Delivered in two parts on successive days of the conference, his plenary address, "Specters of Marx: The State of the Debt, the Work of Mourning, and the New International," constituted the French philosopher's first sustained and systematic engagement (in print) with Marxist theory. What made this philosophical encounter even more noteworthy was Derrida's rare willingness to engage explicitly with the explosive political context of the death of Soviet communism and the uncertain future of

Marxism. A year later, excerpts of his long lecture were published in abridged form in *New Left Review* and drew considerable public attention (Derrida 1994a). A full-fledged book version bearing the same title appeared soon thereafter (Derrida 1994b). While some commentators on the radical left derided Derrida's deconstructionist lecture as "the ultimate poststructuralist fantasy" (Eagleton 1995, 39) or "idealized avant-gardism" (Harvey 1995, 16), *Specters of Marx* also received abundant academic praise, in addition to racking up very impressive sales figures.

For the purposes of this chapter, there is no need to rehash Derrida's arguments in much detail. However, two of his points are of great relevance here. First, the French philosopher turned emphatically to Marx and Engels's *Communist Manifesto*. He embraced their 1848 pamphlet as a key text through which he – and other contemporary intellectuals of the radical left – ought to ponder not only the fate of Marxism but also make sense of how the crisis in the former Soviet bloc affected the ways in which scholars and politicians around the world recalibrated their intellectual and political projects. As Derrida explained:

Upon rereading the *Manifesto* and a few other great works of Marx, I said to myself that I knew of few texts in the philosophical tradition, perhaps none, whose lesson seemed more urgent *today* ... No text in the tradition seems as lucid concerning the way in which the political is becoming worldwide, concerning the irreducibility of the technical and the media in the current of the most thinking thought – and this goes beyond the railroad and the newspapers of the time whose powers were analyzed in such an incomparable way in the *Manifesto*. (Derrida 1994a, 32)

Second, the French philosopher recognized more clearly than most left commentators at the time how deeply the post-1989 "manic triumphalism" had already pervaded "the expressly political discourse of the 'political class', media discourse, and intellectual, scholarly, or academic discourse" (Derrida 1994a, 38–39). Neoliberalism's message that Marxism – both in theory and practice – was finished and had nothing relevant to offer had gone mainstream and was quickly becoming commonsense. Carrying the free-market gospel of Friedrich Hayek, Milton Friedman, Margaret Thatcher and Ronald Reagan to the four corners of the earth, this dominant discourse was anchored in what Derrida, in reference to the popular thesis of the "end of history" (Fukuyama 1989, 3–4), called the "neo-evangelistic dogma" of the "universalization of Western liberal democracy as the final form of human government." In this regard, the following passage of Derrida's lecture deserves to be cited in full:

No one, it seems to me, can *contest* the fact that a dogmatics is attempting to install its worldwide hegemony in paradoxical and suspect conditions. There is today in the world a *dominant* discourse, or rather one that is on the way to becoming dominant, on the subject of Marx's work and thought, on the subject of Marxism (which is perhaps not the same thing), on the subject of the socialist International and the universal revolution, on the subject of the more or less slow destruction of the revolutionary model in its Marxist inspiration, on the subject of the rapid, precipitous, recent collapse of societies that attempted to put into effect at least in what we will call for the moment, citing once again the *Manifesto*, "old Europe," and so forth. This dominating discourse often has the manic, jubilatory, and incantatory form that Freud assigned to the so-called triumphant phase of mourning work. The incantation repeats and ritualizes itself, it holds forth and holds to formulas, like animistic magic. To the rhythm of a cadenced march, it proclaims: Marx is dead, communism is dead, very dead, and along with it its hopes, its discourse, its theories, and its practices. It says: long live capitalism, long live the market, here's to the survival of economic and political liberalism! (Derrida 1994a, 38)

To break neoliberalism's spell, Derrida called for the formation of a "New International," which he conceived as an "alliance without institution" among groups of the global radical left. Anchored in the revolutionary message of the *Manifesto*, such a New International would "continue to be inspired by at least one of the spirits of Marx or of Marxism" (Derrida 1994a, 53). Although he never employed the rising concept "globalization" in his lecture or subsequent book, Derrida's language was rife with synonyms and related phrases such as "the way in which the political is becoming worldwide," "worldwide economic and social field," "worldwide market," "new stage of geopolitics," "global system" and so on. With hindsight, then, one could plausibly argue that one of the most significant achievements of the *Specters of Marx* texts lies in their author's ability to set the thematic stage for a crucial task that would fall more and more heavily on the shoulders of Marxist intellectuals as the decade progressed: the adaptation of their theory to the new discursive and political landscape of "globalization." Their willingness to engage with the most remarkable "discursive event" of the 1990s (Wodak and Meyer 2009, 5–6) might enable leading voices of the radical left to defend the core message of Marxism more effectively from the relentless onslaught of post-1989 neoliberal triumphalism.

Highlighting the significance of the Roaring Nineties in the history of the global left, this chapter opens by setting the thematic stage with a brief genealogy of the keyword "globalization" – from its earliest usages before World War II to its proliferation at the *fin de siècle*. This preliminary section is important because it traces the evolution of *several* currents of meanings. Hence, it was not preordained that economistic understandings would rise to dominance in the 1990s. The subsequent main section offers a critical analysis of a key text penned by a leading Marxist intellectual during this crucial decade: David Harvey's "Globalization in Question" (1995). As my examination of the article shows, its author responded to the hegemonic neoliberal narrative of the "death of Marxism" by reconfiguring the beleaguered Marxist political discourse(s) around the rising keyword "globalization." Thus challenging the dominant discourse of "market globalism" on its own ideological turf (Steger 2008; 2009), Harvey and other intellectuals on the radical left made a strong case for the continued relevance of the spirit of the *Manifesto* in the post-Cold War context of "global capitalism."

Before drawing this introductory section to a close, let me offer three important clarifications. First, my selection of Harvey's "Globalization in Question" showcases but one influential example among the numerous writings on the subject produced by Marxist intellectuals around the globe in the 1990s.[1] Second, throughout this chapter, I use such concepts as "Marxist discourse(s)," "Marxist intellectuals" and "radical left" quite loosely. Rather than applying a narrow litmus test to determine what "really" counts as "Marxist," I employ these terms in reference to those narratives and authors that draw significant theoretical and political inspiration from the ideas and works of Karl Marx and Friedrich Engels – and especially from the *Manifesto*. Third, I am fully aware of the fact that Marxist writers in the 1990s held a broad range of views on the impact of the post-1989 global changes and the future of Marxism. They endorsed diverse and sometimes conflicting political strategies. Hence, I am quite sympathetic to the suggestion that the new Marxist "globalization literature" emerging during this decade could be usefully divided into different thematic categories and theoretical currents (Hosseini 2006, 9–10; Doran 2008).

In this chapter, however, I am not concerned with offering an overview and subsequent categorization of the positions expressed in these texts. Rather, my interest lies in presenting and analyzing the various rhetorical maneuvers employed by Marxist intellectuals in their engagement with the keyword. Ultimately, this chapter seeks to contribute to a better understanding of how the ideological contest over the meanings of "globalization" became a powerful catalyst in the revision of the theoretical and political discourse(s) of the radical left.

A BRIEF GENEALOGY OF "GLOBALIZATION"

When "globalization" took the world by storm in the Roaring Nineties, it carried meanings that related predominantly to the spheres of *economics* and *business*. The normative articulation of these meanings occurred primarily in positive terms that celebrated the global spread of free-market capitalism facilitated by the information and communication technologies (ICT) revolution that followed in the wake of the Cold War. But "globalization" had already been in use for half a century and its associated meanings had actually been far broader than those foregrounded in these economistic views of the 1990s. As Raymond Williams (1983) has pointed out, the history of the meaning construction of what he called "keywords" has often remained rather obscure. "Globalization" is no exception. Moreover, while the meanings of other pivotal keywords such as "economics," "culture" or "modernity" evolved rather slowly over many decades, and even centuries, and built upon a relatively continuous meaning base, "globalization" – the concept, not the process – has had a very short and discontinuous career (Steger and James 2014).

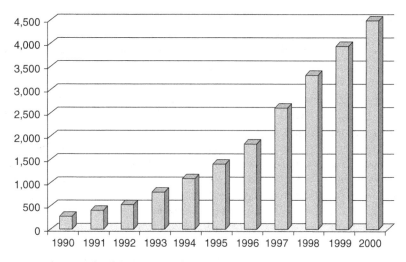

FIGURE I The use of "globalization" between 1990 and 2000
Source: JSTOR: www.jstor.org. Accessed July 7, 2014.

The discursive explosion of the concept at the end of the twentieth century is even more astonishing when one considers that the term "globalization" entered general dictionaries for the first time in 1961, in the *Merriam-Webster Third New International Dictionary*. By the late 1990s, however, thousands of books and articles had been authored that dealt with objective aspects of the phenomenon such as the intensification of world trade or the apparent loss of power of nation-states. In the digital age, it has become much easier to track the proliferation of "globalization" through such mammoth databases as Google's *Ngram*, which collates information from nearly 5.2 million digitized books available free to the public for online searches. Figure 1 shows the dramatic increase of publications containing references to the keyword during the 1990s as measured by JSTOR, a digital library established in 1995 that offers full text searches for almost 2,000 academic periodicals across a broad swath of disciplines.

As noted, however, earlier uses of the term tended to involve a broad web of understandings. These variously signified universalizing processes such as inter-regional connections, the act of being systematic, a childhood development phase and the dynamics of linking the entire world together. Ongoing colla-borative research efforts on the genealogy of "globalization" have revealed the existence of four distinct genealogical branches in the meaning formation of the keyword prior to its dramatic takeoff phase in the 1990s (Steger and James 2014). The first current is rooted in the fields of education and psychology; the second in culture and society; the third in politics and international relations; and the fourth in economics and business.

The educational branch appears to be the oldest of the four and relates primarily to the universalization of knowledge. In 1930, the first use of "globalization" in the English language occurred in William Boyd's classic textbook, *The History of Western Education* (1921). For the Scottish educator, the term denoted not only a certain conceptual holism but also an entirely new approach to education: "Wholeness ... integration, globalization ... would seem to be the keywords of the new education view of mind: suggesting negatively, antagonism to any conception of human experience, which overemphasizes the constituent atoms, parts, elements" (Boyd and MacKenzie 1930, 350). In other words, "globalization" had hardly anything to do with "whole worldness" since it addressed the issue of human learning processes running from the global to the particular.

In fact, Boyd and his collaborators originally acquired the term by translating the French term *globalisation* (not *mondialisation*!) as used by Jean-Ovide Decroly (1929). Referring to a "globalization function stage" in childhood development, the Belgian educational psychologist placed his new concept at the center of his early twentieth-century "New Education" movement. It was connected to a holistic pedagogical system for teaching children to read – *la méthode globale* ("whole language teaching") – which is still used in Belgian and French schools bearing Decroly's name. By the 1990s, however, this education/psychology meaning trajectory had either largely dried up or mutated into its more contemporary denotation of a political pedagogy calling for the "study of globalization" as part of a project to rejuvenate educational systems worldwide (Snyder 1990). In the twenty-first century, "globalization" has also become a keyword in transdisciplinary writings exploring the dramatic changes impacting higher education worldwide (Odin and Manicas 2004; Neubauer 2013; Wildavsky 2010).

Projecting cultural and sociological meanings, the second evolutionary branch of "globalization" originated in the 1940s. The first instance of this usage seems remarkable for both its unusual context and the form with which it was delivered. In 1944, Lucius Harper, the African-American editor of the *Chicago Defender* – which was at the time probably the most influential black newspaper in the United States, with an estimated readership of 100,000 – published an article that quoted from a letter written by a black U.S. soldier based in Australia. In the letter, the G.I. refers to the global impact of American sociocultural views about "negroes":

> The American Negro and his problem are taking on a global significance. The world has begun to measure America by what she does to us [the American Negro]. But – and this is the point – we stand in danger ... of losing the otherwise beneficial aspects of globalization of our problems by allowing the "Bilbos in uniform" with and without brass hats to spread their version of us everywhere. (Harper 1944, 4)

"Bilbos in uniform" was a reference to Theodore G. Bilbo (1877–1947), a mid-century governor and U.S. senator from Mississippi renowned for his avid advocacy of segregation and affinity for the racist practices of the Ku Klux Klan. As David Runciman (2013, 13–16) explains, Bilbo echoed Hitler's *Mein Kampf* in asserting that merely "one drop of Negro blood placed in the veins of the purest Caucasian destroys the inventive genius of his mind and strikes palsied his creative faculties." At the time, the elected representatives of the segregated South successfully blocked any federal legislative attempt to clamp down on lynching, insisting that such practices were something that "Northerners could never understand" and should, therefore, remain a matter of state regulation. However, it is difficult to assess the wider impact of Harper's use of "globalization." No other article employing the keyword was published in the *Chicago Defender* for decades.

A second early instance of using the concept in a cultural sense is not quite as compelling but more perplexing. In 1951, Paul Meadows, an American sociologist whose name is missing in the contemporary pantheon of "global studies pioneers," contributed an extraordinary piece of writing to the prominent academic journal *Annals of the American Academy of Political and Social Science*. Meadows's article stands out for reasons that will become readily apparent:

> The culture of any society is always unique, a fact which is dramatically described in Sumner's concept of *ethos*: "the sum of the characteristic usages, ideas, standards and codes by which a group is differentiated and individualized in character from other groups." With the advent of industrial technology, however, this tendency toward cultural localization has been counteracted by a stronger tendency towards cultural universalization. With industrialism, a new cultural system has evolved in one national society after another; its global spread is incipient and cuts across every local ethos. Replacing the central mythos of the medieval Church, this new culture pattern is in a process of "globalization," after a period of formation and formulation covering some three or four hundred years of westernization. (Meadows 1951, 11)

That passage is worth quoting at length, not only because it is one of the first pieces of writing to use "globalization" in the contemporary sense of the concept, but because Meadows's analysis employs the keyword in a *conductive* relation with terms such as "localization," "universalization" and "Westernization." Meadows's act of putting "globalization" in inverted commas suggests that he was quite self-conscious about using the term relationally. It is perplexing that the synergy formed between the meaning clusters such as "globalization," "localization" and "culture" would remain dormant for decades until it reappeared regularly during the 1980s and 1990s in the writings of socio-cultural globalization pioneers such as Roland Robertson (1992), Mike Featherstone (1990), Anthony Giddens (1990) and Arjun Appadurai (1996).

The third branch of the formation of the keyword is rooted in the fields of politics and international relations (IR). In 1965, American political scientist Inis Claude published an article on the future of the United Nations. Treating universalization and globalization as the same phenomenon, he mentioned the latter only once, in passing, under the heading "The Movement Toward Universality." Claude argued that, "the United Nations has tended to reflect the steady globalization of international relations" (Claude 1965, 837). Three years later, with no reference to the political scientist, an extraordinary article appeared that had the potential of changing the entire field of IR. George Modelski's essay (1968) linked "globalization" to "world politics" in general. Although his seminal contribution to the evolution of the keyword had surprisingly little impact, the Anglo-American political scientist offered a remarkably robust and dynamic definition of globalization:

A condition for the emergence of a multiple-autonomy form of world politics arguably is the development of a global layer of interaction substantial enough to support continuous and diversified institutionalization. We may define this process as globalization; it is the result of the increasing size, complexity and sophistication of world society. (Modelski 1968, 389)

Indeed, Modelski's formulation prefigured the vigorous and highly contested political debates of the 1990s involving the intensifying nexus among globalization, the weakening of the nation-state (Ohmae 1996), the rise of nongovernmental organizations and transnational corporations and the new political framework of "global governance."

The fourth genealogical branch of the keyword favored meanings associated with economics, trade and business. In the post-Cold War context, the economic aspects of "globalization" were usually discussed in conjunction with the ICT revolution in a way that bolstered the discursive ascent of neoliberal triumphalism. The initial economic usage of the term, however, occurred in the late 1950s in connection with the extension of the European Common Market and a possible "globalization of [trade] quotas" (Anonymous 1959). In 1962, François Perroux, a French political economist, used the keyword akin to the contemporary dominant understanding by relating it directly to the formation and spread of increasingly integrated economic markets on a planetary scale. As the research of French sociologist Stéphane Dufoix (2013, 2) shows, Perroux was the first to coin the influential phrase of the *"mondialisation de certains marchés"* ("globalization of some markets").[2]

This expression, of course, was destined to become the title of a famous 1983 *Harvard Business Review* article penned by the Harvard marketing professor Theodore Levitt, whose "The Globalization of Markets" (1983) injected "globalization" into public discourse for good. Three decades later, Thomas Friedman, the American neoliberal "globalization guru," would adopt one of the essay's sub-headings as the title of his bestseller *The World Is Flat* (2005). Thus, Levitt's seminal contribution laid the foundation for the neoliberal depiction of globalization as an "inevitable" techno-economic process destined to give birth to a "global market for standardized consumer products on a previously unimagined scale of magnitude." But the description of what the Harvard Business School dean considered "indisputable empirical trends" was inseparable from his neoliberal ideological prescriptions. For example, he insisted that multinational companies had no choice but to transform themselves into global corporations capable of operating in a more cost-effective way by standardizing their products. The necessary elimination of costly adjustments to various national markets depended, according to Levitt, on the swift adoption of a "global approach." What he had in mind was the willingness of CEOs to think and act "as if the world were one large market – ignoring superficial regional and national differences … It [the global corporation] sells the same things in the same way everywhere" (Levitt 1983, 92–102). This ode to economic homogenization spawned hundreds of similar pieces in business magazines and journals that sought to convince leading companies to "go global." The advertising industry, in particular, set about creating "global brands" by means of worldwide commercial campaigns. Hence, it is hardly surprising that the founder of the advertising giant "Saatchi and Saatchi" was one of Levitt's most fervent disciples.

Hence, as the 1980s drew to a close, the public interpretation of "globalization" was falling disproportionately to global power elites enamored with the neoliberal views expressed in Levitt's essay. This global phalanx consisted mostly of corporate managers, executives of large transnational corporations, corporate lobbyists, prominent journalists and public-relations specialists, cultural elites and entertainment celebrities, academics writing for large audiences, high-level state bureaucrats and political leaders. They marshaled their considerable material and ideal resources to sell the public on the alleged benefits of the liberalization of trade and the global integration of markets: rising living standards, reduction of global poverty, economic efficiency, individual freedom and democracy and unprecedented technological progress. When communism came crashing down in the early 1990s (as in the Soviet case) or transformed itself into a state capitalist one-party system (as in the case of China and Vietnam), the "inevitable globalization of markets" economistic mantra deepened and merged seamlessly with a political-ideological triumphalism that celebrated the irrevocable relegation of Marxism to the dustbin of history.

It took some time for Marxist intellectuals to process these epochal changes and respond effectively to their ideological opponents' deafening charge of drifting into historical irrelevance. But when they finally began to engage with the new post-Cold War realities of capitalism-gone-global, they channeled the main thrust of their attack at the dominant neoliberal meaning construction of "globalization." Although most left critics shared their adversaries' heavily economistic usage of the new buzzword, they insisted on drawing a crucial distinction between what they saw as the two fundamentally different manifestations of the process: "globalization-from-above" (or "corporate globalization"), linked to the neoliberal dynamics of global capitalism; and "globalization-from-below" (Brecher, Costello and Smith, 2000), associated with those incipient "alter-globalization" forces that would eventually emerge in full force on the world stage at the 1999 "Battle of Seattle." Engaging in the discursive strategy that corresponded to the core message of Derrida's *Specters of Marx*, many of these writers celebrated Marx and Engels's *Communist Manifesto*. They understood it not just as a brilliant piece of political rhetoric of largely historical significance but, more importantly, as an extremely timely text capable of inspiring what Richard Appelbaum and William Robinson (2005) would some years later call "critical globalization studies."

RECONFIGURING MARXIST DISCOURSE(S)

In the early 1990s, David Harvey emerged as the perhaps most insightful and innovative thinker among those Marxist intellectuals who were spearheading the charge against neoliberal market globalism. Remarkably, the British political geographer has managed to retain his pivotal role as a leading critic of global capitalism up to its most recent phase following the 2008 Global Financial Crisis and the Great Recession (Harvey 2011; 2014). Published precisely at the historical moment when Eastern European communism was coming apart at the seams, Harvey's study *The Condition of Postmodernity* (1989) laid the theoretical foundation for his 1995 article that will be examined here shortly as a key text in the collective effort of the radical left to revise Marxist discourse(s) for the global age. In his 1989 book Harvey famously introduced the term "time-space compression" to capture the crucial role of geographical and spatial dynamics in the creation of a novel "turbo-charged capitalism" (Luttwak 2000) that neoliberal triumphalists celebrated as "the globalization of free markets."

Second, Harvey had drawn attention to capitalism's growing ability to speed up the production, circulation and exchange of commodities by harnessing new information and communication technologies to its intensifying efforts to overcome spatial and political barriers. Finally, while he had acknowledged the intellectual and aesthetic appeal of postmodernism in the 1980s – particularly its appreciation of discontinuity, plurality and difference – Harvey explained this new paradigm largely as a cultural response to the disruptive time-space compression inherent in the latest phase of capitalism. Thus reasserting the primacy of economics over culture, he also reaffirmed both the theoretical power and political relevance of "grand narratives" such as Marxism that had been the prime targets of poststructuralist critics since the 1970s (Harvey 1989, 114–115).

Six years after the publication of *The Condition of Postmodernity*, Harvey faced a drastically altered landscape dominated by the free-market globalization narrative of neoliberal triumphalists. Grasping the significance of this new ideological context "signaled primarily by all the 'posts' that we see around us (e.g. postindustrialism, postmodernism)," Harvey's seminal essay focuses on the theoretical and political implications (and consequences) of these "important changes in western discourses" for the socialist movement in general and the Marxist tradition in particular. From the start, the author flags the central position of "globalization" in the postcommunist political vocabulary by explicitly acknowledging that it has "become a key word for organizing our thoughts as to how the world works" (Harvey 1995, 1).

Harvey considers this discursive shift to be important for the left's political development in at least two principal ways. First, it put pressure on radicals like himself to critically reevaluate both the relevance and efficacy of conventional Marxist concepts such as "imperialism," "colonialism" and "neocolonialism." Conceding that these terms "have increasingly taken a back seat to 'globalization' as a way to organize thoughts and to chart political possibilities," he even goes so far as to say that anti-capitalist movements can no longer hope to "recapture the political initiative by reversion to a rhetoric of imperialism and neocolonialism, however superior the political content of those latter terms might be" (Harvey 1995, 15). Second, the dominance of neoliberal meanings associated with "globalization" has operated as a "powerful deterrent" by shrinking the room for political manoeuver and amplifying a sense of "powerlessness on the part of national, regional, and local working-class movements" (Harvey 1995, 1). Perhaps most famously expressed in Margaret Thatcher's cynical quip, "There is No Alternative" (to neoliberalism), the horror of facing an unstoppable juggernaut had plunged many progressives into fatalism and despair.

Given the severe political price exacted by the keyword and its associated neoliberal baggage, the radical left was facing a difficult decision. Should it reject or abandon the term altogether, or, as Harvey advises, "take a good hard look at what it incorporates and what we can learn, theoretically and politically, from the brief history of its use" (Harvey 1995, 1)? Determined to provide politically useful answers to this quandary, Harvey embarked on a careful analysis of "globalization" that took the *Manifesto* as its point of departure. But why the *Manifesto*? Portraying "globalization" as a *process* rather than a political-economic *condition* that has recently come into being – as asserted by most neoliberals – he notes that globalization processes have always been integral to capitalist development because "the accumulation of capital has always been a profoundly geographical and spatial affair" (Harvey 1995, 2) In other words, since its inception in the sixteenth century following the European capture of the Americas (CM 238), capitalism has thrived on the opportunities created by geographical expansion, spatial reorganization and, most importantly, uneven geographical development.

This is where the *Manifesto* comes in. For Harvey, Marx and Engels were the first modern thinkers to recognize capitalism's perennial need to provide a "spatial fix" to its inherent contradictions. Such a remedy involved, crucially, the creation of a global historical geography of capital accumulation, which allowed the bourgeoisie to "get a foothold everywhere, settle everywhere, establish connections everywhere" (CM 239). Although he concedes that the *Manifesto* never fully resolved its linguistic ambivalence involving its authors' "spatial thinking" and their less helpful temporal-diachronic narrative, Harvey emphasizes the former. In other words, the contemporary relevance of this text lies in Marx and Engels's insights into the geographical dynamics of capital accumulation and class struggle on a *worldwide* scale. To bolster his argument, Harvey provides a long citation from the *Manifesto*:

Through the exploitation of the world market the bourgeoisie has made the production and consumption of all countries cosmopolitan. It has pulled the national basis of industry right out from under the reactionaries, to their consternation. Long established national industries have been destroyed and are still being destroyed daily. They are being displaced by new industries – the introduction of which becomes a life-and-death question for all civilized nations – industries that no longer work up indigenous raw materials but use raw materials from the ends of the ends of the earth, industries whose products are consumed not only in the country of origin but in every part of the world. In place of the old needs satisfied by home production we have new ones, which demand the products of the most distant lands and climes for their satisfaction. In place of the old local and national self-sufficiency and isolation we have a universal commerce, a universal dependence of nations on one another. As in the production of material things, so also with intellectual production. The intellectual creations of individual nations become common currency. National partiality and narrowness become more and more impossible, and from the many national and local literatures a world literature arises. (CM 239–240)

As it turned out, this "globalization passage" from the first section of the *Manifesto* would be cited over and over again by various progressive intellectuals as "irrefutable confirmation" that Marx should be seen as "the theorist of globalization *avant la lettre*" (Tomlinson 1999, 76). It was also paraded as "clear evidence" for the relevance of this most famous of all Marxist texts in the age of globalization.[3] As Michael Löwy puts it, "In many respects, the *Manifesto* is not merely up-to-date – it is even more relevant today than it was 150 years ago. Let us take as an example its diagnosis of *capitalist globalization*" (Löwy 1998, 17). Harvey (1995, 2) concurs: "If this is not a compelling description of globalization, then it is hard to imagine what would be. And it was, of course, precisely by way of this analysis that Marx and Engels derived the global imperative 'working men of all countries unite' as a necessary condition for an anticapitalist and prosocialist revolution." Indeed, his strong emphasis on the geographical sophistication of the founders allows the British thinker to dispute quite effectively the potent "Marx is dead" charge of neoliberal triumphalists. Far from relegating it to the dustbin of history, the rise of globalization made the Marxist tradition more relevant in the global age than ever before. For Harvey and scores of other left intellectuals writing in the 1990s, the *Manifesto*, in particular, showcases how well Marxism is equipped to deal both theoretically and politically with the profound geographical reorganization of capitalism that has been unfolding under the narrative banner of "globalization" since the collapse of Soviet communism.

But Harvey goes beyond the mere delivery of an effective blow to the triumphalist ambitions of Francis Fukuyama and his neoliberal acolytes.

Derived from his geographical reading of the *Manifesto* and other seminal texts by Marx and Engels, his spatial critique of globalization as a novel political-economic condition or system – as depicted by neoliberals – allows him to exorcize the post-1989 specter of fatalism that had been stalking the radical left since 1989. Harvey's message is clear: rather than contemplating their imminent demise, progressives around the world ought to feel good about this "historic opportunity to seize the nettle of capitalism's geography, to see the production of space as a constitutive moment within (as opposed to something derivatively constructed by) the dynamics of capital accumulation and class struggle" (Harvey 1995, 5). His redefinition of globalization as an ongoing "process of production of uneven temporal and geographical development," allows him to charge the radical left with its most pressing political task: the reorganization of its material struggles – both locally and globally – in step with revised ("spatialized") Marxist discourse(s). Such a unified promotion of critical-alternative narratives of "globalization" would, according to Harvey, serve to expose the "violence and creative destruction of uneven geographic development ... just as widely felt in the traditional heartlands of capitalism as elsewhere" (Harvey 1995, 12).

Overall, then, Harvey endows the Marxist "grand narrative" with a new lease on life by stressing its capacity to debunk the spatial foundations of the neoliberal globalization myth. Such new discursive strategies allow the left to challenge the dominant paradigm of market globalism on its own terms without having to forsake its Marxist heritage. And, as Harvey (1995, 8) emphasizes time and again, discursive reconfigurations can have a tremendous political impact: "that shift of language can have some healthy political consequences, liberating us from the more oppressive and confining language of an omnipotent process of globalization."

Still, the thesis of the continued relevance of a recalibrated Marxist narrative in the global age raises at least one troubling objection. If capitalism's globalization dynamics – now no longer celebrated as the liberalization and global integration of markets but assailed as the bleak outcomes of "uneven geographical development" – indeed stretch back to the Industrial Revolution and beyond, then what, if anything, is actually qualitatively new enough about globalization in its current phase to justify the concession of "contemporary shifts" and "social changes?" Much to his credit, Harvey does not hesitate to address the problem head on:

While everyone will, I think, concede the quantitative changes that have occurred, what really needs to be debated is whether these quantitative changes are great enough and synergistic enough when taken together to put us in a qualitatively new era of capitalist development, demanding a radical revision of our theoretical concepts and our political apparatus (to say nothing of our aspirations). (Harvey 1995, 11)

But Harvey's argument in favor of what he calls a "limited qualitative shift" fails to overcome the old Marxist idealism/materialism binary. For this reason, his answer might not be entirely convincing – especially for critics of Marx's theoretical framework of historical materialism. Harvey's approach strains to avoid Marxist orthodoxy as it seeks to straddle a philosophical middle ground that allots some agency to the ideological superstructure. While he asserts that there has not been a fundamental shift in the capitalist mode of production and its associated social relations, he also concedes the existence of a significant discursive shift brought on by globalizing capitalism's accelerated "uneven spatio-temporal development."

As previously noted, Harvey's *The Condition of Postmodernity*, too, largely followed this theoretical route by explaining the rise of postmodernism as a cultural response to the disruptive time-space compression inherent in the latest phase of capitalism. Six years later, Harvey again employs the same logic in his conceptual efforts to create space for the possibility of political action originating in the superstructural realm of discourse. But this cannot be done without ceding some philosophical terrain to neoliberal idealists like Fukuyama, who relish the power of ideas and discourses. On the upside, this philosophical concession puts Harvey in the favorable position of mixing his strong defense of the continued relevance of Marxist principles with his recognition of the need to revise Marxist discourse(s):

If there is any real qualitative trend it is towards the reassertion of nineteenth-century capitalist values coupled with a twenty-first-century penchant for pulling everyone (and everything that can be exchanged) into the orbit of capital while rendering large segments of the world's population permanently redundant in relation to the basic dynamics of capital accumulation. This is where the powerful image, conceded and feared by international capital, of contemporary globalization as a "brakeless train wreaking havoc" comes into play. (Harvey 1995, 12)

Harvey (1995, 12) ultimately concedes that the philosophical limitations of his modified historical materialism highlight the discursive task of "reformulating both theory and politics." Still, he insists that his proposed modification of the meaning of "globalization" from a desirable neoliberal condition or system of globally integrated markets to one of "uneven spatio-temporal development of capitalism" contains abundant opportunities for political organizing and action. After all, the current time-space compression of global capitalism comes not just with unprecedented gains for the wealthy, but with all its accompanying evils such as people's enhanced vulnerability to violence, increasing unemployment and inequality, collapse of services and degradation in living standards and environmental qualities. In his quest for a "formulation of an adequate politics" he brilliantly utilizes Raymond Williams' notion of an alliance of "localized militant particularisms" (quoted in Harvey 1995, 16). Harvey connects this concept to his demands for greater theoretical flexibility and recognition of political and cultural diversity. What he has in mind is the resurrection of "one of the historical strengths of the Marxist movement," namely the commitment to "synthesize localized struggles with divergent and multiple aims" into a more universal anti-capitalist movement with a global aim. However, such a rosy interpretation of the Marxist tradition as a decentralized and pluralistic "movement of movements" sounds rather odd when considering the recent historical context of the demise of Soviet-style communism (Harvey 1995, 13).

Harvey (1995, 15–16) must have felt that his audience needed more convincing on this point, for he rushes headlong into a rather intriguing discourse on socialist political leadership. As expected, he strongly disavows the authoritarian avant-gardism of Soviet-style communist parties. What is more surprising is the hard-hitting criticism he reserves for "unconstrained postmodern eclecticism." Charging postmodernism with promoting "idealized avant-gardism," he quotes approvingly from Terry Eagleton's vitriolic review of *Specters of Marx*, in which Eagleton refers to Derrida's vision of a leaderless New International as "a dissent beyond all formulable discourse, a promise which would betray itself in the act of fulfillment, a perpetual exciting openness to a Messiah who had better not let us down by doing anything as determinate as coming" (Eagleton 1995, 37). Yet Harvey struggles to endow his desired democratic model of a "socialist avant-garde" with the kind of concreteness that he accuses Derrida of withholding from his readers. It is only in the penultimate paragraph of his remarkable essay that Harvey (1995, 16) offers his readers a fleeting glimpse of what "the work of synthesis and organizing anti-capitalist struggles on the variegated terrain of uneven geographical development" might actually look like in practice. Like many of his fellow radicals who reconfigured Marxist discourse(s) in this trying decade of neoliberal triumphalism, Harvey sees a new model of political organization in the Zapatista Army of National Liberation, whose powerful appeal to resist the "violence of neoliberal globalization" was resonating with progressives worldwide. With hindsight, Harvey's nod to the "Zapatistas" proved to be an inspired choice given their subsequent influential role in the formation of the "alter-globalization movement" and the 2001 creation of the World Social Forum (Steger et al. 2013).

CONCLUDING REMARKS

My decision to devote the bulk of this chapter to an analysis of "Globalization in Question" might create the impression that Harvey's essay almost single-handedly accomplished the difficult task of reconfiguring Marxist discourse(s) around the new buzzword "globalization." Nothing could be further from the truth. While this essay certainly represents one of the finest specimens in this endeavor, it was merely one instance among many in the collaborative effort of the radical left to respond more effectively to the ideological claims of market globalism that had saturated the public discourse in the 1990s. To pick another example, Bob Sutcliffe's "The *Communist Manifesto* and Globalization" (1998) offers exquisite insights into the reasons for the difference between the optimism of the authors of the *Manifesto* and the pessimism of many on the current left who blame "globalization" for most ills of the planet, not to mention the dire prospects for socialism. Löwy's "How Up-to-date is the *Communist Manifesto?*" (1998), too, represents a fine example that follows in Harvey's footsteps by reclaiming the *Manifesto* for the new kind of critical spatial thinking that both authors regard as an essential weapon in the discursive battle with the proponents of "capitalist globalization."

Writing for leading contemporary Marxist periodicals such as *Rethinking Marxism, Socialism and Democracy* and *Monthly Review*, most of these thinkers were critical journalists or academics representing a wide range of disciplines. They took a variety of positions and expressed a broad range of views within the spectrum of the radical left. Most of their publications shared the same elements identified in our analysis of Harvey's essay: close attention to the centrality of "globalization" in current political discourse; an emphasis on the relevance of the *Manifesto* for our global age; the introduction of critical-alternative meanings of globalization; an enhanced role for geography and spatial thinking; various suggestions for how to reconfigure Marxist discourse(s); and expressions of sympathy for a more decentralized, locally embedded and diverse "global network" of anti-capitalist actors. While is true that the majority of these writers hail from the global North, the 1990s and early 2000s also witnessed a remarkable upsurge of pertinent contributions from the global South, such as Walden Bello's "De-Globalizing the Domestic Economy (1999), Chu Van Cap's "Marx and Engels on Economic Globalization" (2002) and Claudio Katz's "The *Manifesto* and Globalization" (2001).

By the first years of the new century, the Marxist engagement with "globalization" had become intense enough to convince publishers to take their chances on the publication of new primary source anthologies bearing such suggestive titles as *Marx on Globalisation* (Renton 2001). Moreover, the argument that the *Manifesto* should serve as a key text for an alternative conception of globalization found strong resonance. Young alter-globalization activists, in particular, showed a strong interest in Marxist thought. In the United Kingdom alone, nearly 100,000 copies of the *Manifesto* were sold between 1996 and 1997, which represented a significant increase from previous years (Renton 2001, 19). In 2000, Chinese scholars organized an international seminar on "The *Manifesto of the Communist Party* and Globalization" at Beijing University (People's Online Daily 2000). In the same year, Harvard University Press released Michael Hardt and Antonio Negri's *Empire* – a neo-Marxist account of globalization hailed by sympathetic reviewers as the *Manifesto* for our time. The tremendous intellectual and commercial appeal of *Empire* quickly transcended the narrow walls of the ivory tower, drawing its authors into the glaring public spotlight that only rarely shines on political and literary theorists. Figure 2 confirms the upswing in the academic use of "Communist Manifesto" in the late 1990s when it equaled or surpassed the high numbers of presumably negative references during the collapse years of Eastern European communism.

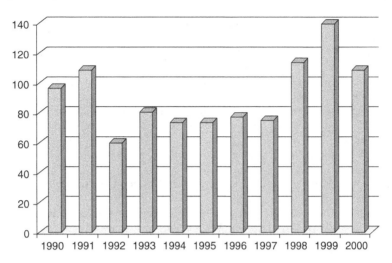

FIGURE 2 The use of "Communist Manifesto" between 1990 and 2000
Source: JSTOR; www.jstor.org. Accessed July 8, 2014.

Taken together, then, these pieces of evidence point to an astonishing feat accomplished by the radical left during a decade that many considered would see its ultimate demise. Remarkably, Marxist intellectuals managed to articulate the rising global imaginary in new ways that challenged hegemonic neoliberal definitions and understandings of "globalization" as the "liberalization and global integration of markets." Far from dissolving into nothingness, the specter of the *Manifesto* was actually stalking neoliberal globalization. As they flowed into the self-understanding of the fledgling alter-globalization movement at the beginning of the new century, recalibrated Marxist discourse(s) contributed to a new optimism on the left, perhaps best reflected in the popular slogan of the newly minted World Social Forum: "Another World Is Possible."

REFERENCES

Amin, Samir. 1996. "The Challenge of Globalisation." *Review of International Political Economy.* 3(2): 216–259.
Anonymous. 1959. "European Communities." *International Organization.* 13(1): 174–178.
Appadurai, Arjun. 1996. *Modernity at Large: The Cultural Dimensions of Globalization.* Minneapolis: University of Minnesota Press.
Appelbaum, Richard P., and William I. Robinson. Eds. 2005. *Critical Globalization Studies.* London and New York: Routledge.
Beck, Ulrich. 2000. *What Is Globalization?* Cambridge: Polity Press.

Bello, Walden. 1999. "De-Globalizing the Domestic Economy." *Social Development Review*. 3(2): 3–7.

Brecher, Jeremy, Tim Costello, and Brendan Smith. Eds. 2000. *Globalization from Below*. Boston: South End Press.

Burbach, Roger, Orlando Nunez, and Boris Kagarlitsky. 1996. *Globalisation and Its Discontents: The Rise of Postmodern Socialisms*. London: Pluto Press.

Boyd, William. 1921. *The History of Western Education*. London: Adam & Charles Black.

Boyd, William, and M. M. MacKenzie. Eds. 1930. *Towards a New Education*. London: A. Knopf.

Cap, Chu Van. 2002. "Marx and Engels on Economic Globalization." *Nature, Society, and Thought*. 15(2): 241–245.

Claude, Ines L. 1965. "Implications and Questions for the Future." *International Organization*. 19(3): 835–846.

Cooper, Caryl A. 1999. "The Chicago Defender: Filling in the Gaps for the Office of Civilian Defense, 1941–1945." *The Western Journal of Black Studies*. 23(2): 111–117.

Decroly, Jean-Ovide. 1929. *La Fonction de Globalisation et l'Enseignement*. Brussels: Lamertin.

Doran, Christine. 2008. "Review Essay: Globalization, Dead or Alive?" *Globality Studies Journal*. http://globality.cc.stonybrook.edu/?p=95. (Accessed September 20, 2014).

Derrida, Jacques. 1994a. "Specters of Marx: The State of the Debt, the Work of Mourning, and the New International." *New Left Review*. 205: 31–58.

Derrida, Jacques. 1994b. *Specters of Marx: The State of the Debt, the Work of Mourning, and the New International*. London and New York: Routledge.

Dufoix, Stéphane. 2013. "Between Scylla and Charybdis: French Social Science Faces Globalization," unpublished manuscript.

Eagleton, Terry. 1995. "Jacques Derrida: Specters of Marx." *Radical Philosophy*. 73:35–37.

Featherstone, Mike. 1990. *Global Culture: Nationalism, Globalization and Modernity*. London: Sage Publications.

Foster, John Bellamy. 2000. "Marx and Internationalism." *Monthly Review*. 52(3). http://monthlyreview.org/2000/07/01/marx-and-internationalism. (Accessed September 20, 2014).

Friedman, Thomas. 2005. *The World Is Flat: A Brief History of the Twenty-First Century*. New York: Farrar, Straus & Giroux.

Fukuyama, Francis. 1989. "The End of History?" *National Interest*. 16:1–19.

Fukuyama, Francis. 1992. *The End of History and the Last Man*. New York: The Free Press.

Giddens, Anthony. 1990. *The Consequences of Modernity*. Cambridge: Polity Press.

Greider, William. 1997. *One World, Ready or Not: The Manic Logic of Global Capitalism*. New York: Simon and Schuster.

Harper, Lucius C. 1944. "He Is Rich in the Spirit of Spreading Hatred." *Chicago Defender*. 15: 1–4.

Harvey, David. 1995. "Globalization in Question." *Rethinking Marxism*. 8(4): 1–17.

Harvey, David. 1989. *The Condition of Postmodernity*. London: Basil Blackwell.

Harvey, David. 2011. *The Enigma of Capital and the Crisis of Capitalism*. Oxford: Oxford University Press.

Harvey, David. 2014. *Seventeen Contradictions and the End of Capitalism*. Oxford: Oxford University Press.

Hersh, Jacques, and Ellen Brun. 2000. "Globalisation and the Communist Manifesto." *Economic and Political Weekly.* 35(3): 105–108.

Hosseini, Hamid. 2006. "From Communist Manifesto to Empire: How Marxists Have Viewed Global Capitalism in History." *Review of Radical Political Economics.* 38(1): 7–23.

Katz, Claudio. 2001. "The *Manifesto* and Globalization." *Latin American Perspectives.* 28(5): 85–96.

Levitt, Theodore. 1983. "The Globalization of Markets." *Harvard Business Review.* (May–June): 92–102.

Löwy, Michael. 1998. "Globalization and Internationalism: How Up to Date Is the Communist Manifesto?" *Monthly Review.* 50(6): 16–27.

Luttwak, Edward. 2000. *Turbo-Capitalism: Winners and Losers in the Global Economy.* New York: Harper Perennial.

Magnus, Bernd, and Stephen Cullenberg. Eds. 1995. *Whither Marxism? Global Crises in International Perspective.* London and New York: Routledge.

Modelski, George. 1968. "Communism and the Globalization of Politics." *International Studies Quarterly.* 12(4): 380–393.

Neubauer, Deane E. Ed. 2013. *The Emergent Knowledge Society and the Future of Higher Education.* London and New York: Routledge.

Odin, Jaishree, and Peter Manicas. 2004. *Globalization and Higher Education.* Honolulu: University of Hawai'i Press.

Ohmae, Kenichi. 1996. *The End of the Nation-State: The Rise of Regional Economies.* New York: The Free Press.

People's Daily Online. 2000. "Marx, Engels Predict Globalization in Communist Manifesto." http://english.peopledaily.com.cn. (Accessed September 20, 2014).

Perroux, François. 1962. "The Conquest of Space and National Sovereignty." *Diogenes.* 10(1): 1–16.

Renton, David. Ed. 2001. *Marx on Globalisation.* London: Lawrence & Wishart.

Robertson, Roland. 1992. *Globalization: Social Theory and Global Culture.* London: Sage Publications.

Runciman, David. 2013. "Destiny vs. Democracy" *London Review of Books.* 35(8): 13–16.

Singer, Daniel. 1999. *Whose Millennium? Theirs or Ours?* New York: Monthly Review Press.

Snyder, Richard C. 1990. *Thinking, Teaching, Politicking about the Globalization of the World: Toward a Synthesis and Possible Future Strategy.* Washington, DC: ERIC Clearinghouse. http://catalogue.nla.gov.au/record/5538423. (Accessed September 20, 2014).

Steger, Manfred B. 2008. *The Rise of the Global Imaginary: Political Ideologies for the French Revolution to the Global War on Terror.* Oxford: Oxford University Press.

Steger, Manfred B. 2009. *Globalisms: The Great Ideological Struggle of the Twenty-First Century.* Lanham, MD: Rowman & Littlefield Publishers.

Steger, Manfred, James Goodman, and Erin Wilson. 2013. *Justice Globalism: Ideology, Crises, Policy.* London: Sage Publications.

Steger, Manfred, and Paul James. 2014. "A Genealogy of 'Globalization': The Career of a Concept." *Globalizations.* 11(4): 417–434.

Sutcliffe, Bob. 1998. "The *Communist Manifesto* and Globalization." *Socialism and Democracy.* 12(1): 213–219.

Sweezy, Paul. 1997. "More (or less) on Globalization." *Monthly Review.* 49(4). http:// monthlyreview.org/1997/09/01/more-or-less-on-globalization. (Accessed September 20, 2014).

Tabb, William. 1997. "Globalization Is an Issue; The Power of Capital Is the Issue." *Monthly Review.* 49(2). http://monthlyreview.org/1997/06/01/globalization-is-an-issue. (Accessed September 20, 2014).

Tomlinson, John. 1999. *Globalization and Culture.* Chicago: University of Chicago Press.

Waters, Malcolm. 1995. *Globalization.* London and New York: Routledge.

Wildavsky, Benjamin. 2010. *The Great Brain Race: How Global Universities Are Reshaping the World.* Princeton: Princeton University Press.

Williams, Raymond. 1983. *Keywords: A Vocabulary of Culture and Society.* New York: Oxford University Press.

Wodak, Ruth, and Michael Meyer. Eds. 2009. *Methods of Critical Discourse Analysis.* London: Sage.

Wood, Ellen Meiksins. 1997. "Back to Marx." *Monthly Review.* 49(2). http:// montlyreview.org/1997/06/01/back-to-marx. (Accessed September 20, 2014).

Decolonizing the *Manifesto*: Communism and the Slave Analogy

Robbie Shilliam

In this chapter, I will engage with the *Communist Manifesto* through the sensibilities of what has been called the "Black Radical Tradition." This tradition finds its source in the lived struggles of peoples of African heritage, especially those in the diaspora, from slavery days until the present. Its intellectual provenance is the theorization and narration of racial order – especially, but not only, that of white supremacy. Those who work in the tradition differ in the personal and intellectual depth of their engagement with Marxism and communism; however, on the whole, a sympathetic yet critical outlook defines this engagement (see Kelley 2002; Rabaka 2009). In his seminal book, *Black Marxism*, Cedric Robinson explores the nature of this engagement – both theoretically and historically – and its necessarily critical appreciation of Marxism (Robinson 2001). This chapter will adopt Robinson's orientation in order to decolonize the *Manifesto*.

Most historical readings of the *Manifesto* focus on the political upheavals following the French Revolution, the growing economic consequences of industrialization and the uprooting of extant agricultural systems in Europe, and especially in France and Germany (see, e.g., Levin 1981; Cunliffe 1982; Moss 1998; Shilliam 2006). Other commentators – some from a postcolonial bent, some Marxist – have acknowledged the Eurocentric nature of the text, its unilinear narrative and its ambivalences regarding the broader imperial and colonial context of the making of the world market (see especially Mitchell 2000; Anderson 2010). Kevin Anderson (2010), following on from the pioneering work of Theodor Shanin (1983), has explored how Marx's investigations after the *Manifesto*, in contrast, seem to increasingly grapple with both non-European contexts and different temporalities of world development. Similarly, it is now established that Marx and Engels took great interest in the American Civil War and ultimately understood the conflict in terms of plantation slavery versus capitalist industrialization (Symposium 2011).

My purpose in this chapter is to show that the engagement with plantation slavery exists in the *Manifesto* itself, yet as a recessive trait; I follow the Ashis Nandy-inspired approach to critiquing the canons of classical political economy led by Blaney and Inayatullah (2009). The dominant narrative of the class struggle of the European proletariat is given life by making him (and it is "him") an analogue of the enslaved African laborer of the American plantations. This analogical lexicon makes the racial oppression that is the rule of the world market a recessive narrative. The proletariat are animated through the slave analogy; however, precisely because this animation requires the proletariat to take on a universalizing political force, the enslaved laborer must lose her/his presence in the flow of world history. An insightful cognate argument has been made recently by James Edward Ford III (2010) regarding Marx's use of the "slave" in his *Capital* volumes.[1] Rather than Marx, Engels is the key interlocutor of my discussion. And rather than *Capital*, the key texts that I will engage with are those by Engels leading up to and including the *Manifesto*.

I start by framing my argument through the Black Radical Tradition expressed eloquently by Cedric Robinson's sympathetic critique of Marxism. I clarify the importance of racial rule and European colonial expansion as nonderivative features of the capitalist world market. I then tease out the dominant and recessive narratives in the *Manifesto*, the former predicated upon the rise of industrial wage-labor in Europe, the latter predicated upon the technologies of colonial rule through the world market. I focus on the way in which the argument of the *Manifesto* politicizes the European waged worker through an analogy with African enslaved laborers in the American plantations. It is this analogical lexicon that makes the world market recede and the industrial landscape of Europe proceed to the fore.

Subsequently I illuminate the genealogy of the slave analogy by reference to Engels's engagement with Tory radicals and Chartists in England. I show how their analogical discourse apprehends plantation slavery as a warning sign of the future social effects of industrialization in England. Specifically, the destruction of paternal authority in the plantations promises a destruction of the common law compact so that anarchy will burst forth from the factories. I then textually chart how Engels uses this apprehension to animate the English working class with a unique political consciousness so that it ultimately frames his communist credo, and henceforth finds its way into the *Manifesto*. Finally, I use the contention between Marcus Garvey's "race first" program and the Communist International's "class first" program to draw out the political stakes that ride on the slave analogy. I end by briefly imagining a decolonized *Manifesto*.

THE BLACK RADICAL TRADITION AND MARXISM

Robinson re-narrates the making of the capitalist world market by positioning the racial order of Atlantic slavery at its dynamic center. Rather than accepting the traditional Marxist narrative that capitalism had forged a new European order, Robinson argues that capitalism should be understood more in terms of the re-weaving of the world market with the extant fabrics of the European feudal order (Robinson 2001, 10, 24–25). Crucially, this implies, for Robinson, that extant practices of European civilization – especially slavery and the differentiation of rights and privileges on the basis of blood – are used to reorder the world market by European powers. In this movement, existing differences – be they cultural, regional or social – are racialized; indeed, race is used to rationalize the "domination, exploitation and extermination of Non-Europeans" (Robinson 2001, 23, 26–27). Robinson distinguishes four moments in the development of European racialism. Two take place within this rewoven world market, the last being colonial practices of "plantocratic slavery" and the "formation of industrial labor and labor reserves" (Robinson 2001, 67).

Because the Marxist narrative posits capitalism as a rupture from – rather than as a continuation of – feudal order, Robinson argues that class analysis does not fundamentally address the deeper determining structures of racial rule. Hence Marxism finds its limitations in the understanding of race consciousness, that is to say, the "persistence of racialism in Western thought" (Robinson 2001, 66). Alternatively, he points out that historically what allowed enslaved Africans to creatively survive the plantation system was "the ability to conserve their native consciousness of the world from alien intrusion, the ability to imaginatively re-create a precedent metaphysic" (Robinson 2001, 309). Robinson suggests that this "Africanity of our consciousness" is culturally inherited by the Black Radical Tradition of thought in order to bear witness to the "unacceptable standard of human conduct" practiced under "racial capitalism" (Robinson 2001, 308). The Tradition, argues Robinson, always realized that:

something of a more profound nature than the obsession with property was askew in a civilization that could organize and celebrate – on a scale beyond previous human experience – the brutal degradations of life and the most acute violations of human destiny. (Robinson 2001, 308)

The Black Radical Tradition therefore challenges traditional Marxist narratives that posit class and capitalist exploitation as the most deeply determining dialectic of world order, while race and racial oppression are ascribed derivative status *vis-à-vis* that dynamic. In this respect, some intellectuals, such as Charles Mills, have argued that even the term "racial capitalism" still implies that capitalism is a system of class exploitation facilitated by a mechanism of racial oppression. Mills favors the term "white supremacy" to indicate that the racial ordering of social life is not an addition to, but rather is the fundamental dynamic of, modernity (see Mills 2003, *passim.*). Robinson does use the term "racial capitalism" in passing; however, the notion of a global racial ordering of oppression that "white supremacy" implies is in keeping with the intellectual purpose of *Black Marxism.*

This tells us that the core phenomenon to be addressed is not so much the alienation of the worker from the fruits of his/her labor power but rather, as Aimé Césaire (2007) puts it, the "thingification" (*chosification* in French) of personhood through enslavement and its lasting racial legacies. In other words, while the industrial factory system alienates labor power (and its results) from the laborer via the technology of waged work, plantation slavery alienates the entire body and labor power of the person via the technology of racialization. Therefore, the problem of dehumanization lies at the heart of the Black Radical Tradition and its critical engagement with Marxism. And this is why the Tradition is sensitive to the cultural, psychological and even spiritual determinants of racial oppression that are not simply derivative of the experience of class exploitation through the labor-capital relation and its attendant class rule (see West 1993; Bogues 2003). Even Manning Marable, convinced that racial oppression serves a "larger class objective" (1995, 217), nevertheless acknowledges that the politics immanent in this objective point back to dehumanization and not simply alienation:

The cultural history of black Americans is, in part, the struggle to maintain their own group's sense of identity, social cohesion and integrity, in the face of policies which have been designed to deny both their common humanity and particularity. (Marable 1995, 227)

I shall now use the sensibilities of the Black Radical Tradition to draw out a tension in the text of the *Manifesto* that is created in the attempt to contain the coordinates of the world-market – and its associated dynamics of colonial expansion, racial oppression and dehumanization – within the neat walls of Western Europe's industrial factory system and its monologic dynamic of class antagonism situated in waged work. I shall show how this tension is manifested through the analogizing of the industrial waged worker with the enslaved plantation laborer.

THE RECESSIVE MANIFESTO

The dominant narrative in the *Manifesto* is the decay of feudalism and the eruption of a new society with the appearance of two new classes – the bourgeoisie and the proletariat. This society purifies the dynamic of class struggle to a degree heretofore unexperienced in world history (CM 238; on the plurality of socialist agendas and programs in Germany itself, see Robinson 2001). As a purifier of the motion of human history, Marx and Engels prophesy that bourgeois society will give birth to a higher form of universal society that might even transform the fundamental dynamic of class struggle itself. Large-scale industry is identified as the arena wherein this singular class antagonism plays out through the exploitative nature of wage work and the concomitant accumulation by the bourgeoisie of capital through the sanctity of private property. The Communists appear as a "working-class party" whose "theoretical insights" into the class struggle demand the abolition of private property and the conquest of political power by the proletariat (CM 246). Germany is proclaimed as the society most ripe for such a revolution, because the starkness of its class antagonism is more marked there than even in advanced England or France. The dominant narrative is – as has been well commented upon – unilinear and monological, in that capitalist class antagonism is universalized over time to subsume all other social forces and entities into its global architecture. Indeed, this is why Marx and Engels posit the proletarian as the truly revolutionary class – all other exploited classes "decline to extinction" with the expansion of the industrial landscape (CM 244).

However, the *Manifesto* does admit to another world in existence, with antagonisms and struggles that are other than the industrial kind. Entangled with the narrative of the world-historical uniqueness of bourgeois society is a recessive story of the "world market." In fact, it is just as much here, as in the industrial landscape, that the grand narrative unfolds. The world market is articulated by Marx and Engels as a colonial endeavor of European ruling classes in which the colonization of America marks a signal episode (CM 237–238). In fact, they give multiple explications as to the causal weight of this colonially induced world market *vis-à-vis* the development of modern bourgeois society. For example, the world market quickens this Eurocentric development and "prepares" its way (CM 237–238). But at the same time, it is through colonial and/or imperial expansion that the bourgeois conquer national markets, and not via the inner driving force of capitalist class antagonism (CM 238–239). Indeed, the famous statement, "cut-price commodities are the heavy artillery with which it batters down all Chinese walls" (CM 240), should not to be taken as a metaphor of industrial expansion: it is, in fact, a reference to the imperial Opium Wars of 1839–1842.

Moreover, while the world market inaugurates and facilitates the political dominance of the bourgeoisie, its significance for the dominant narrative of the *Manifesto* does not stop there. For bourgeois society does not seem to be universalized through the immanent working out of its historically unprecedented class antagonism. Rather, it is the colonial and imperial practices of the world market that stitch together once parochial and national-based struggles into a universal struggle (CM 240). Nevertheless, the very praxis of the *Manifesto* is centered upon the inherent universality of the capitalist dialectic between bourgeoisie and proletariat – capital and labor – in terms of its purification of all struggles heretofore in world history (see Ahmad 1998). This dialectic being inherently universal, proletarians – according to the communists – are not simply struggling for control over their own factories, communities or nations; rather, "they have a world to win" (CM 260). Yet if the very political technologies and instrumentalities of the world market owe no special allegiance to the capital-labor dialectic, how can Marx and Engels present the struggle over wage work in the European-industrial context as a universalizing political force?

The recession of the world market in order to clear space for the industrial landscape of Europe is facilitated in Marx and Engels's narrative through a lexicon of analogy. In the key passages that depict the political nature of the struggle over labor, Marx and Engels analogize the enslaved African of the plantations of the Americas with the waged worker of the industrial factories of Western Europe. Indeed, Marx and Engels use this analogy to make the argument that the latter are oppressed even more intensely than the former. Factory workers are not only the "chattel servants" of the bourgeois class as a whole, but are also "hourly and daily enslaved by the machine, by the overseer, and above all by the individual bourgeois manufacturer himself" (CM 242). Moreover, every oppressed class must at least be able to "scrape a slave-like existence" (CM 245). However, due to the wage contract and the exigencies of crises-prone markets, the bourgeois class, unlike the slave-master, cannot assure "its slave any kind of existence within his slavery" (CM 245). Even the laborer's family – that provider, in the last instance, of care – is "torn" apart by bourgeois rule (CM 239). It is for this reason that the proletariat *must* be revolutionary. And whilst they have a world to win, they have "nothing to lose but their chains" (CM 260; on this phrase see also Gordon 2000).

Marx and Engels are empirically mistaken on the issue of what would later be termed "basic needs." Most enslaved populations in the plantation societies of the Americas could not reproduce themselves (exceptions include the relatively marginal case of the American South), hence the consistent "importing" of new enslaved labor (Vann Woodward 1983, 91). But empirics aside, the point is that Marx and Engels, after having proclaimed in their dominant narrative the historically unique and universal significance of the dialectic of private property and waged work, nevertheless animate that struggle through an analogy with a non-waged struggle between capital and labor. Colonial forms of oppression that constitute the world market – specifically the enslavement of Africans – breathe life into the exploitation of wage workers in the European industrial landscape such that the latter become the universal class of salvation while the former are consigned to the museum of modes of production.

It could be protested that in the German text, it is *Knecht* that Marx and Engels use, which, unlike *Sklave* (slave), denotes a more general type of servitude, albeit one that still connotes a sub-human quality. Perhaps, then, my argument as to the importance of plantation slavery in the Americas is an error borne from translation into English.[2] Nevertheless, in the section that follows I shall argue that the genealogy of this analogy is tied to Engels's sojourn in England and his engagement with the political discourses over industrialization at the time. Engels's writings on the English working class are important not just because they were influential on Marx's own critique of political economy but also because they constitute one of the first applications of post-Hegelian philosophy to the "facts" of industrialization (Henderson 1976, 73; Carver 1990, 124–132). And in the political discourses *en vogue* in England during Engels's first sojourn, the purposeful analogizing of enslaved Africans with English factory workers was fundamental to the lexicon. It is this analogy that finds its way into the *Manifesto*; it is this analogy that subsumes the world market under English industry; and that enables enslaved African laborers to recede into the past while European factory workers come to the fore of world history.

THE SLAVE ANALOGY IN BRITISH POLITICAL DISCOURSE

By the early nineteenth century it had become an established practice to use slavery as an analogue device for moral argumentation concerning the condition of English subjects. During the English Revolution, the Restoration and beyond, both royalists and anti-royalists compared political liberty and despotism through tropes of enslavement, biblical and otherwise (Hudson 2001, 563, 566; Skinner 2002, vol. 2, 286–307). For example, John Locke and William Blackstone used slave analogies to refer to all kinds of threats to the flowering of common law, whether in the guise of the Norman Conquest or the ersatz French absolutism of the Stuarts (Locke 1993, 5; Michals 1993–1994, 208–209). However, the rise of plantation slavery in the English/British American colonies engendered a new intensity to this practice of analogising. These stakes were laid out clearly in the "Somersett case" of 1772.

Somersett, an enslaved person, had been brought to England with his master, had promptly escaped but was recaptured (Drescher 1987, 16–19). A group of abolitionists subsequently applied for *habeas corpus*, arguing that no slaves could be permitted to exist on English soil lest the traditional liberties of common law be uprooted and despotism return to the polity (Davis 1975, 375, 392). Justice Mansfield ruled that Somersett should indeed be freed because there was no precedent for the return of a slave from English shores. However, his ruling was not a categorical outlawing of slavery, because at stake also was the paternal authority of the property-owning man over his servants. And the rights of the *pater familias* were as much a compact of common law as were the rights of private property (see especially Michals 1993–1994). Similarly, James Beattie, a moral philosopher and abolitionist, attempted to distinguish between the immoral condition of enslavement and the deeper paternal principle of servitude: "[the slave] cannot be bought or sold; but if he has bound himself by contract to serve his master for a certain length of time, that contract, like those entered into by apprentices, and some other servants, will be valid" (Beattie 1790, 165).

The fundamental problem that presented itself to Beattie and others was that commercial law – the British law that applied to the world market – enabled plantation slavery, while common law – the domestic law of Britain – did not. The Somerset case clarified the danger that the former law posed to the latter, that is, commercial law sought to render all property relations utterly alienable and mobile, hence upsetting the very source of English liberty encoded in common law, namely the rights of the *pater familias* transmitted through patriarchal inheritance. The slave master had usurped the paternal authority of the male slave; and it was evident to some that factory owners, in employing children and women, were usurping the paternal authority of male servants (for an extended argument along these lines, see Shilliam 2012b).

By the 1830s, as Joseph Persky has insightfully detailed, Tory radicals ("compassionate Conservatives") were using the image of the free and paternal yeoman to contest the ills of slavery – both real and the "waged" variant found in Yorkshire (Persky 1998, 646; see for example Engels, *The Condition of the Working Class in England*, CW 4: 477–478). Tory radicals drew comparisons between, on the one hand, the overseers of England's satanic mills with their child laborers and, on the other hand, plantation owners and their slaves in the colonies. Both forms of exploitation, argued Tory radicals, had displaced and disintegrated paternal authority within the poor family (Davis 1975, 460; Persky 1998, 641–642). In plantation slavery they therefore gleaned not the pre-commercial past but rather the terrible prospects of commercial society in Britain. If servants could not be fathers, then the grand chain of paternalism would be severed, common law ousted and true anarchy reign. Thus Richard Oastler, a Tory radical who had started out his political life as a follower of William Wilberforce, declared the horror of "child slavery." He described the groups of workers arriving at factories as "shiploads" being brought to "plantations." "There is Slavery at home," Oastler proselytized, ". . . as demoralising, as debasing, and as killing as West India Slavery! – aye and much more so!" (cited in Boime 1990, 40).

Concurrently, Chartist newspapers of the 1830s and 1840s, for which Engels was later a foreign correspondent, decried Britain's imperial and colonial ventures, especially the Opium Wars that were then battering down "all Chinese walls" (CM 240; see Guan 1987; Vargo 2012). But particular attention was often paid to the abolition of slavery in the Caribbean and the attempts at self-determination, including a three-part biographical sketch of Toussaint L'Ouverture, leader of the 1791 anti-slavery revolution in Haiti, and the coining of one cooperative effort by "native labourers" to purchase their former plantation as a "chartist land plan of Guinea" (Vargo 2012, 245). Indeed, just like the Tory radicals, the Chartist movement availed itself of the slavery analogy, and also in order to remonstrate against the evil of the factory system (Vargo 2012, 247). Both groups utilized this analogical discourse in debates over the "ten hours" movement, the issues of which were later to form the substance of Marx's chapter in *Capital*, vol. 1. on "The Working Day" (CW 23: 239–306). In commenting upon the extinction of the handloom weaver, and thus the extinction of the family economy, Peter Murray McDougall argued: "I would rather be the slave of the West Indies and possess all the physical benefits of real slavery than be the white factory slave of England and possess all the hardships of an unreal freedom" (cited in Turley 1991, 177). In this respect, what becomes evident in much of the Chartist analogical discourse is less a trans-racial/national solidarity, and more a strategy to use plantation slavery to sharpen sympathy for factory workers in England (Mays 2001). This is congruent with the analogical strategies deployed by Tory radicals, even if the political aims of each group were different.

It is true that Engels's awareness of the Americas as a colonial landscape predates his first sojourn in Manchester. Writing to his sister in 1842, Engels mentioned that he would see the play *Columbus* by Karl Werder. The play presented Columbus as a man driven by the enlightenment spirit of discovery and knowledge accumulation, but also as a man compromised by the need to collaborate with state power, and, by these means, even to be complicit in slave trading (Engels to Marie Engels, January 5, 1842, in CW 2: 538; Zantop 1997, 178–179). Nevertheless, Engels's key influence regarding plantation slavery is owed to his engagement in England with the parallel analogical discourses of the Tory radicals and Chartists (Persky 1998, 646; see for example Engels, *The Condition of the Working Class in England*, CW 4: 477–478).

In this respect, Engels imbibes a comparative morality predicated upon the difference between the (domestic) servant and (colonial) slave, and the intimacy engendered by this comparison in the apprehension that plantation-like conditions were being introduced into England by the entrenchment of the non-familial industrial factory system. In short, the racial oppression of enslaved plantation laborers inflected the class exploitation of industrial waged workers. The notion of the wage slave was certainly a product of Tory radicals. However, the accompanying apprehension that plantation slavery – a practice of the world market – was the future prospect of industrial practices in Britain was overtaken in Engels's writings by a related sensibility garnered from the Chartists: wage slaves were more dehumanized than "real existing" slaves. As a tool to sharpen attention on the plight of waged workers in "free" Albion, this assessment also imbibed a long-standing abolitionist sensibility that enslaved Africans were fundamentally human, but neither effectively nor efficiently so (see, e.g., Geggus 1985). With this sensibility, the enslaved would diminish in significance from a sign of the future global commercial compact to a relic of the pre-modern past (on these temporal issues in general, see Quijano 2000, 550–551). We shall now examine how these strategies were employed in Engels's writings pre-1848. And we shall see how they prefigured many of the key tropes and rhetorical devices of the *Manifesto* itself.

ENGELS AND THE SLAVE ANALOGY

In his 1844 *Outlines of a Critique of Political Economy*, Engels makes an intimate connection between the factory and plantation; both are economic practices that "yield nothing in inhumanity and cruelty to ancient slavery" (CW 3: 420). Whilst this statement suggests the co-constitutive relationship of the world market and European industrialism, Engels's interlocutory intent is to highlight the hypocrisy of the bourgeois defense of private property through their proselytizing of British freedoms. Enthusiastically citing Thomas Carlyle's repudiation of industrialization, Engels then reverses the flow of influence between world-market slavery and domestic industry imputed by the Tory radicals. In other words, the hypocritical defense of private property by the English bourgeoisie disseminates outward as part of their re-ordering of the world market (see also Engels, *Condition of England*, CW3: 444–468); indeed, by "dissolving nationalities," bourgeois rule "universalises enmity." Engels then takes the end point of commercial society in Britain prophesied by Tory radicals through the slave analogy – that is, the dissolution of the family – and universalizes it as an effect not of enslavement but of industrialization. The final step of this global bourgeois project, claims Engels, is to dissolve the family and replace it with the despotic rule of the factory owner. Hence the "last vestige of common interests" – a "community of goods disappears" (Engels, *Outlines of a Critique of Political Economy*, CW 3: 424).

Engels argues that "the philanthropic Tories were right when they gave the [factory] operatives the name *white slaves*" (Engels, *The Condition of the Working Class in England*, CW 4: 474; my emphasis). That he does not translate this English phrase into German is proof of his conceptual debts to the Tory radicals and Chartists.[3] Engels goes on to argue that "the slavery [*Sklaverei*] in which the bourgeoisie holds the proletariat chained is nowhere more conspicuous than in the factory system. Here ends all freedom in law and in fact" (CW 4: 467). Indeed, "disguised slavery" allows for the bourgeois affirmation of political freedom. Here Engels pre-empts Marx's understanding of "double freedom" as the condition that historically *distinguishes* industrial wage work from all other prior forms of exploitation; that is, formal political freedom combined with an ironic substantive "freedom" from direct access to the means of production (CW 35: 179). In Engels, this condition is explicated not as an immanent critique of wage work, but through an analogy to enslaved labor. Moreover, Engels goes on to argue that it is precisely this contradictory condition of freedom that cultivates in the English proletariat a political consciousness. In effect, the principle of freedom, affirmed in the midst of oppression and experienced by the "white slaves," will "one day see to it that this principle is carried out" (Engels, *The Condition of the Working Class in England*, CW 4: 474). Some years later, C. L. R. James would return this argument to the historical experience and prospects of enslaved Africans and their descendants in the Americas (James 1993).

Engels clarifies his sociological prognosis of the radical potential of the English wage worker, again, by virtue of the slave analogy. The worker is the "slave" of the property-holding class, and in fact this "slave ... is sold like a piece of goods, rises and falls in value like a commodity" (Engels, *The Condition of the Working Class in England*, CW 4: 379). Here, as in most of the book, the German original deploys the term *Sklave* (as well as *Sklaverei*) rather than *Knecht*. Engels thus draws out the radical sociality of the wage worker by intentionally *likening* him to a slave. In fact, he goes on to imply that the wage worker is more immiserated than the enslaved plantation laborer because the former has to sell himself not once but every day, and, further, the bour-geoisie as a class have no responsibility to ensure his basic needs (Engels, *The Condition of the Working Class in England*, CW 4: 379). As we have seen, these arguments derive directly from both the Tory radicals' and the Chartists' con-cerns over the effect of industrial factories upon the working class *pater famil-ias*. And they shall be repeated in the *Manifesto* (CM 249). Through the slave analogy, then, Engels presents the English working class as the most immiser-ated and thus most potentially radical class at this juncture of world history.

At this point we are faced with the resonance *and* discord between the Marxist notion of alienated labor power and Cesaire's notion of the thingified laborer. It is the latter that presents the most radically and fully commodified entity – and through the laws of the world market. Yet, via analogy, this radicality is poured into the English proletariat, bypassing any analysis of the immanent effects arising from the systematic alienating of (only) labor power. In this respect, and not withstanding or belittling the principled stance on abolition taken by the Chartists and by Marx and Engels, the slave analogy works to segregate the world market from the English industrial factory system, and, ultimately, to consign one of the occupants of the former sphere – enslaved peoples of the American plantations – to a mute, pre-modern condition. Once a sign of the future of commercial society, the enslaved are now historically superseded through an analogical device.

I argue that the slave analogy preys vampirically upon real living enslaved peoples. It drains them so much that it makes of them specters, a haunting presence in narratives and tropes throughout European writings of the late eighteenth and nineteenth centuries.[4] For example, soon after the deployment of the slave analogy, Engels, in ethnographic mode, notes the prevalence of peddlers on street corners selling ginger beer or nettle beer. "Two cooling effervescent drinks," Engels explains in a footnote, "the former made of water, *sugar* and some ginger" (Engels, *The Condition of the Working Class in England*, CW 4: 385 n.*). And it is the factory workers of the *cotton* districts, who, for Engels, form the "nucleus of the labour movement" (Engels CW 4: 528). Back in Prussia, one year after the publication of *The Condition of the Working Class in England,* Engels explicates the many relations of production and exchange in the world market that a product passes through before it reaches the consumer. Cotton from North America passes to exporters, to speculators in Liverpool, to manufacturers in Rotterdam, to printers and to consumers. However, the initial laborers in this global commodity chain are absent from Engels's narration. All we know is that a bale of cotton, produced in North America, "passes from the *hands of the planter* into those of the agent" (Engels, "Speeches in Elberfeld," CW 4: 246–247, emphasis added).

Engels's attribution of a historically unprecedented agency to the wage-working class via the slave analogy is subsequently parsed through Marx's post-Hegelian philosophy to form the guiding grand narrative of the manu-scripts collected as *The German Ideology*, which, prefiguring the *Manifesto*, gives rise to a chaotic grand narrative of world markets and industrial factory landscapes, where, within the cracks of the chaos, flows the molten lava of an apparently universalizing and purifying social force – the immiserated wage worker. By the time Engels sketches out his "Draft of a Communist Confession of Faith" in 1847 (CW 6: 96–103) he has retained the affect of the slave analogy but disavowed what the analogy emerged from: the contemporaneous intimacy between enslaved laborers and wage workers, as conceived even by Tory radicals and Chartists. The slave now represents the historical archaeology of the proletarian.

In the "Draft Confession," Engels presents a historically unparalleled relationship between big capitalists and the proletariat – the "completely propertyless" (CW 6: 100). True, says Engels, a working class has always existed. For example, he writes in the slightly later "Principles of Communism" that in "days of antiquity," workers "were the slaves [*Sklaven*] of those who owned them, just as they even still exist in backward lands and even in the southern part of the United States" (CW 6: 343).[5] In this comparison, the American South that the enslaved inhabit at present is consigned to the past (see Hindess 2007). How, then, is the proletariat different from this pre-modern slave, asks Engels? Engels repeats the arguments made in *The Condition of the Working Class in England*: "the slave [*Sklave*] is sold once and for all, the proletarian has to sell himself by the hour" (CW 6: 100). Furthermore, "the slave [*Sklave*] is counted a *thing* [*Sache*] and not a member of civil society; the proletarian is recognized as a *person*, as a member of civil society" (CW 6: 100; emphasis in original). Here, again, Engels refers to the distinction between things and persons, thingification and alienation.

Moreover, even if it is the slave that exhibits a far more fundamental commodification of labor and self, Engels provides the comforting partial truth that the slave might be able to secure basic needs more successfully than the proletarian (CW 6: 100). The most intense contradiction of the commercial age, therefore, is imputed to lie in the condition of the latter. Indeed, Engels clarifies the consequences of commercial crises as the need to abolish private property. Yet for him, private property is a peculiar manifestation of the industrial revolution, not of the world market and plantation slavery (CW 6: 343). In any case, the proletarian "stands at a higher stage of development" of society than the slave [*Sklave*], for when the slave is freed, he becomes a proletarian (CW 6: 100). The world market is now purified of slave labor by the industrial factory system: "large scale industry, by creating a world market, has so linked up the peoples of the earth, and especially the civilized peoples, that each people is dependent on what happens to another" (CW 6: 351–352). The revolution will take place globally, enacted by the proletariat, the truly universal class, because they have nothing left to lose. Except, perhaps, their very personhood?

Marx uses Engels's "Draft Confession" in order to partially frame the argument of the *Manifesto*. Retrieving this genealogy of the slave analogy in Engels's thought therefore illuminates that crucial part of the *Manifesto* where the ambivalent term *Knecht* is used to sharpen the radical and world-shaking potency of the proletariat in their struggles over factory life. Perhaps in the *Manifesto, Knecht* made more dialectical sense to Marx than *Sklave*. After all, the *Herr* (master)/*Knecht* (servant/sub-human) pairing had already been deployed in Hegel's influential *Phenomenology of Spirit*. Susan Buck-Morss has argued that Hegel's dialectic of self-consciousness, represented by the struggle between *Herr* and *Knecht*, was influenced by the contemporaneous Haitian Revolution (Buck-Morss 2000). This claim has drawn much critical consideration (see, e.g., Fischer 2004, 24–33). However, my argument is that plantation slavery exerts another influence on the *Manifesto*, one that explicitly engages with enslavement and abolition.[6] It is the influence of the slave analogy cultivated by Radical Tories and Chartists that propels Engels to politicize the conditions of the factory worker (rather than just sympathize with this in a Kantian fashion). Marx then supports this politicization with a German philosophical frame.

COMMUNISM AND GARVEYISM

In order to draw out the political stakes of this argument I shall finish by returning to the Black Radical Tradition and considering its evolving relationship to communism in the early twentieth century. A key question was posed by this tradition in the era immediately following the legal emancipation of Africans across the Americas: what of the ongoing quest for personhood and re-humanization in a world market structured through white supremacism? It was Marcus Garvey, along with Amy Ashwood and Amy Jacques Garvey, who developed the most influential philosophical and political platform (initially in Jamaica) that sought to address such a question. Through the Universal Negro Improvement Association (UNIA) and African Communities League, the Garveys galvanized, for the first time in the history of the United States, a mass public movement of descendants of enslaved Africans, much to the exasperation of the Communist International.

The Garveys' platform was race – not class – first; and although each chapter of the UNIA embedded itself in particular local contexts, the focus upon collective economic self-reliance and political self-organization had avowedly pan-African coordinates. Garvey impelled his constituencies to retrieve their personhood on the world stage, and while in philosophical and symbolic terms this calling was heavily masculinized, the UNIA had a historically pronounced percentage of offices – senior and junior – filled by women. Inextricably woven into these substantive activities was a focus upon the redemption of black humanity, both spiritually and psychologically. Marcus Garvey entreated his constituencies to sight their God "through the spectacles of Ethiopia," since humanity was created in the image of God (Garvey 1967, vol. 1, 34). And late in his life, to a Nova Scotia audience in Menelik Hall (named in honor of Haile

Selassie I), Garvey articulated a principle he had long held: "We are going to emancipate ourselves from mental slavery because whilst others might free the body, none but ourselves can free the mind" (Garvey 1937, 791).

The UNIA grew as a mass movement of at least one million members, and extended across the Americas into Europe, Africa and even as far as Australia. Concurrent to the rise of the UNIA, of course, was the emergence of the Comintern onto the world stage, buoyed by the Bolshevik triumph of 1917. Antonio Gramsci described the Russian Revolution as "against Capital," meaning against the expectations of the volumes of Marx's *Capital* – and, harking back to the *Manifesto*, argued that the universal class to drive forward a new stage of human existence would be the proletariat of "civilized" countries (Gramsci 1917). The revolution that brought a communist party to state power had in fact occurred in a predominantly peasant society with no real bourgeois leadership and a minute – if concentrated – industrial factory system. This "backward" context, though, was also the source of intellectual strength among the Bolsheviks.

One year before the inauguration of the UNIA, Lenin had written a suggestive piece on "Russians and Negroes." Unlike Engels's "Draft Confession" and "Principles" of 1847, Lenin, critical of his own society's backwardness, effectively retrieved the contemporaneous entanglement of plantation slavery and factory waged labor. Lenin noted that serfdom in Russia had been legally abolished in 1861, just a few years before the American emancipation proclamation (Lenin 1975, 343). Moreover, "Negroes," argued Lenin, "still bear ... the cruel marks of slavery," because "capitalism cannot give either complete emancipation or even complete equality" (Lenin 1975, 344). Although Lenin here follows Engels's notion of contradictory freedom, he does not do so at the price of historically or philosophically segregating enslaved labor and waged work.

George Padmore, the famous Trinidadian Marxist and Pan-Africanist, was later to comment on the progressiveness of the Bolshevik awareness of the racial and ethnic heterogeneity of empires (Padmore 1972, 291–293). Indeed, the Russian Empire had been internally structured almost as heterogeneously as the world market itself. Furthermore, by the end of the Second World War, Harold Moody, the African-Jamaican convener of the London-based coalition, the League of Coloured Peoples, was positively inclined towards the proclaimed (if not actual) equality of races and nations under the Soviets. By no means a Marxist or communist himself, Moody nevertheless argued that "the whole future of this British commonwealth of nations rests upon the fact as to whether she is big enough to follow Russia's brilliant example" (Moody 1944, 22).

In 1919 the Comintern had started to extend its influence into the United States and subsequently set for itself the task of recruiting the most immiserated group of people – the Negroes whom Lenin in 1913 suggested *could* be considered a nation (Lenin 1975, 543; Kelley 1994; Baldwin 2002). However, this nation had already been announced – and was already being organized – by the

Garveys. The contention between manifestos for "race first" and "workers of the world unite" was extremely complex and shifting, and by no means did it exhibit a straightforwardly personal black-versus-white dynamic. For example, the Programme of the African Blood Brotherhood (1922) decried Garvey's "grandeur" as impractical. And by 1922 the Brotherhood was intimately organizing with the Comintern and also attempting to steal membership away from the UNIA (see Robinson 2000, 215–218). Conversely, in 1925, the Workers (Communist) Party of America issued a demand for the immediate release of Marcus Garvey from his jail cell in Atlanta, and supported "the full and free intercourse of American negroes with their brothers of the African continent" (Workers Party of America 1925, 142).

Nevertheless, with the admission that there would be no imminent world revolution, and with the rise of Stalin, the Comintern's relationship to the black struggle in the United States became more and more instrumentalized and perfidious. Garvey's own platform, while not socialist, was socialistic in its pursuit of collective self-reliance; however, Garvey was always (correctly) suspicious that the Comintern would use the black struggle for its own purposes. And, most importantly, the Comintern never managed to orchestrate a mass movement of African Americans along the lines of "workers of the world unite." But Garvey's "race first" program had. Two famous (black) Trinidadian Marxists – Padmore and C. L. R. James – provide testimony of Garvey and of Garveyism's influence and of its challenge especially to black Marxists.

Both James and Padmore had been influenced by Garveyism in their formative years in Trinidad. James remembers, on behalf of himself and Padmore, how they had both read Garvey's paper *The Negro World* (James 1973; Martin 1976, 261). James also remembers the great strike of Trinidadian waterfront men in 1919, all of whom were Garveyites, "even if they didn't say" (James 1980). By the later 1930s both Marxists were heckling the "petty-bourgeois" Garvey from the audience at Speakers' Corner in London's Hyde Park (Dhondy 2001, 55). And in 1940, James described Garvey as a fascist similar to Hitler. Nevertheless, James also argued that Garveyism had to be studied by Marxists in that it constituted the "first great eruption of the Negro people" (James 1940). Along these lines, James acknowledged that "no revolution is ever made except when the masses have reached this pitch of exaltation, when they see a vision of a new society" (James 1940). Similarly, after the Second World War Padmore reflected on Garvey's "fanatical racialism" (Padmore 1972, 89), but also judged him to be "the greatest black prophet and visionary since Negro Emancipation" (cited in Martin 1976, 263).

Hence both James and Padmore had to acknowledge the political efficacy of race consciousness, despite their broadly class-based analyses. But more than that, Garvey's sensibility towards "race first" infiltrates both James's and Padmore's *oeuvres*, albeit more clandestinely in the former. James was a committed Hegelian Marxist, framing much of his work around the dialectic of freedom as expressed in association and labor. However, he was to place the enslaved laborer in the Caribbean plantations at the heart of the narrative that he spun from this dialectic (James 2001). In this endeavor, the consciousness of race, racism, enslavement and liberation played a crucial part, if, nevertheless, these were in contention with James's Marxist sensibilities (on this issue see Shilliam 2012a). Padmore was much more of a political worker than James, consistently agitating against European imperialism in Africa both before and after he left the Communist Party in response to Stalin's sacrifice of Africa to Europe on the eve of the Second World War (Lewis 2009). So whereas James articulated the issue of African enslavement and liberation through a philosophical register, Padmore did so in a directly political one. He subsequently came to see in Pan-Africanism the space wherein peoples of African heritage – at home and abroad – could "attain freedom under … a banner of their own choosing" (Padmore 1972, 16). Crucially, in both authors, the analogy of slavery is insufficient for addressing the problem of freedom from oppression. Both must acknowledge Garvey, because it is the praxis of Garveyism and not communism which disavows the lexicon of analogy and so ensures that the descendants of enslaved Africans take their place as contemporaneous – lively – agents in the struggle over world order.

CONCLUSION

The *Manifesto* conjures up a breathtaking image of an inter-connected world populated by a diverse set of peoples spread over a geographical mosaic that is scarred with the brutality of oppression, exploitation and immiseration. The many suffer the few – as they always have – and yet the *Manifesto* prophesies that soon enough the mosaic will be rearranged as a new humanity forges itself in resistance to such brutality. What must be acknowledged is the fact that due to this imaginary, many Marxists and communists have been emboldened to stand on a principled anti-racist platform in front of sometimes virulently racist societies. Indeed, the strength of the vision in the *Manifesto* vision is that we can all emplot ourselves in it. Still, only some will be sanctified by its prophetic movement as saviors.

To decolonize the *Manifesto* is to redeem the prophecy. And to embark on this path one must disavow its analogical lexicon, the grammatical structure that animates some by draining many others of their life force. I have argued that the *Manifesto* animates the wage workers of Europe's factories as analogues to the enslaved African laborers of America's plantations. Henceforth, the *Manifesto* makes of the enslaved a "worthy sacrifice," at the epistemological level, for the progress of European civilization (Dussel 1993, 75). And this epistemological sacrifice bears political consequences. What would happen, though, if we apprehended liberation through a non-analogical – decolonializing– apprehension of that mosaic world presented in the *Manifesto*? I argued above that the most logical extension of the right of private property in English commercial law lay in turning African captives into laboring things for sale upon the world market. One could say, in this respect, that the most intense contradiction of the commercial age lies in the retrieval of personhood for those whose exploitation and oppression derives from the white supremacist structuring of that age (Winter 2003). Forward, then, to a *Manifesto* colored human.

REFERENCES

African Blood Brotherhood. 1922. Programme of the African Blood Brotherhood. www. marxists.org/history/international/comintern/sections/britain/periodicals/communist_review/1922/06/african.htm. (Accessed November 1, 2012).

Ahmad, Aijaz. 1998. "The Communist Manifesto and the Problem of Universality." *Monthly Review* 50(2): 12–23.

Anderson, Kevin B. 2010. *Marx at the Margins: On Nationalism, Ethnicity, and Non-Western Societies.* Chicago: University of Chicago Press.

Baldwin, Kate A. 2002. *Beyond the Color Line and the Iron Curtain: Reading Encounters Between Black and Red, 1922–1963.* Durham, NC: Duke University Press.

Baucom, Ian. 2005. *Specters of the Atlantic: Finance Capital, Slavery, and the Philosophy of History.* Durham: Duke University Press.

Beattie, James. 1790. *Elements of Moral Science.* Edinburgh: T. Cadell and William Creech.

Blaney, David L., and Naeem Inayatullah. 2009. *Savage Economics: Wealth, Poverty, and the Temporal Walls of Capitalism.* Basingstoke: Routledge.

Bogues, Anthony. 2003. *Black Heretics, Black Prophets: Radical Political Intellectuals.* New York: Routledge.

Boime, Albert. 1990. "Turner's Slave Ship: The Victims of Empire." *Turner Studies* 10(1): 34–43.

Buck-Morss, Susan. 2000. "Hegel and Haiti." *Critical Inquiry* 26(4): 821–865.

Carver, Terrell. 1990. *Friedrich Engels: His Life and Thought.* New York: St. Martin's Press.

Césaire, Aimé. 2007. *Discourse on Colonialism.* Princeton, NJ: Princeton University Press.

Cunliffe, John. 1982. "Marx's Politics – The Tensions in the Communist Manifesto." *Political Studies* 30(4): 569–574.

Davis, David Brion. 1975. *The Problem of Slavery in the Age of Revolution.* Ithaca, NY: Cornell University Press.

Dhondy, Farrukh. 2001. *CLR James.* London: Weidenfeld & Nicolson.

Drescher, Seymour. 1987. *Capitalism and Antislavery: British Mobilization in Comparative Perspective.* New York: Oxford University Press.

Dussel, Enrique. 1993. "Eurocentrism and Modernity." *Boundary 2* 20(3): 65–76.

Fischer, Sybille. 2004. *Modernity Disavowed: Haiti and the Cultures of Slavery in the Age of Revolution.* Durham: Duke University Press.

Ford, James Edward III. 2010. "From Being to Unrest, from Objectivity to Motion: The Slave in Marx's Capital." *Rethinking Marxism* 23(1): 22–30.

Garvey, Marcus. 1937. "Speech by Marcus Garvey, Menelik Hall, Sydney, Nova Scotia, 1 Oct 1937." In *The Marcus Garvey and Universal Negro Improvement Association Papers. Vol. VII, November 1927-August 1940,* ed. Robert A Hill. Berkeley, CA: University of California Press, 1991. 788–794.

Garvey, Marcus. 1967. *Philosophy and Opinions of Marcus Garvey or Africa for the Africans: Two Vols in One*, ed. Amy Jacques Garvey. London: Frank Cass.

Geggus, David. 1985. "Haiti and the Abolitionists: Opinion, Propaganda and International Politics in Britain and France, 1804–1838." In *Abolition and Its Aftermath – The Historical Context, 1790–1916*, ed. D. Richardson. London: Frank Cass. 113–140.

Gordon, Lewis R. 2000. *Existentia Africana: Understanding Africana Existential Thought*. New York: Routledge.

Gramsci, Antonio. 1917. "The Revolution against Capital." www.marxists.org/archive/gramsci/1917/12/revolution-against-capital.htm. (Accessed November 1, 2012).

Guan, Shijie. "Chartism and the First Opium War." *History Workshop Journal* 24(1) (21 September 1987): 17–31.

Henderson, W. O. 1976. *The Life of Friedrich Engels*. London: Frank Cass.

Hindess, Barry. 2007. "The Past Is Another Culture." *International Political Sociology* 1(4): 325–338.

Hudson, Nicholas. 2001. "'Britons Never Will Be Slaves': National Myth, Conservatism, and the Beginnings of British Antislavery." *Eighteenth-Century Studies* 34(4): 559–576.

James, C. L. R. 1940. "Marcus Garvey." *Labor Action* 4(11). www.marxists.org/archive/james-clr/works/1940/06/garvey.html. (Accessed November 1, 2012).

James, C. L. R. 1973. "Transcript of Speech: Reflections on Pan-Africanism." www.marxists.org/archive/james-clr/works/1973/panafricanism.htm. (Accessed November 1, 2012).

James, C. L. R. 1980. "*Interview. By Ken Ramchand.*" www.marxists.org/archive/james-clr/works/1980/09/banyan.htm. (Accessed November 1, 2012).

James, C. L. R. 1993. *American Civilization*. Cambridge, MA.: Blackwell.

James, C. L. R. 2001. *The Black Jacobins: Toussaint L'Ouverture and the San Domingo Revolution*. London: Penguin Books.

Kelley, Robin D. G. 1994. "Africa's Sons with Banner Red." In Robin D. G. Kelley, *Race Rebels: Culture, Politics and the Black Working Class*, New York: The Free Press. 103–122.

Kelley, Robin D. G. 2002. *Freedom Dreams: The Black Radical Imagination*. Boston: Beacon Press.

Lenin, V. I. 1975. "Russians and Negroes." In *Collected Works*. Moscow: Progress Publishers. 543–544.

Levin, Michael. 1981. "Deutschmarx: Marx, Engels, and the German Question." *Political Studies* 29(4): 537–554.

Lewis, Rupert. 2009. "George Padmore: Towards a Political Assessment." In *George Padmore: Pan-African Revolutionary*, eds. Fitzroy Baptiste and Rupert Lewis. Kingston: Ian Randle Publishers. 148–161.

Locke, John. 1993. *Two Treatises of Government*. London: J.M. Dent.

Marable, Manning. 1995. *Beyond Black and White: Transforming African-American Politics*. London: Verso.

Martin, Tony. 1976. *Race First: The Ideological and Organizational Struggles of Marcus Garvey and Universal Improvement Association*. Westport, CT: Greenwood Press.

Mays, Kelly J. 2001. "Slaves in Heaven, Laborers in Hell: Chartist Poets' Ambivalent Identification with the (Black) Slave." *Victorian Poetry*, 39(2): 137–163.

Michals, Teresa. 1993–1994. "'That Sole and Despotic Dominion': Slaves, Wives, and Game in Blackstone's Commentaries." *Eighteenth-Century Studies* 27(2): 195–216.

Mills, C. Wright. 2003. *From Class to Race: Essays in White Marxism and Black Radicalism.* Lanham, MD: Rowman & Littlefield.

Mitchell, Timothy. 2000. "The Stage of Modernity." In *Questions of Modernity*, ed. T. Mitchell, 1–33. London: University of Minnesota Press.

Moody, Harold. 1944. "Editorial." League of Coloured Peoples Newsletter. November. National Archives UKBL/025NWLT194411.

Moss, Bernard. 1998. "Marx and the Permanent Revolution in France: Background to the Communist Manifesto." *Socialist Register* 34: 147–168.

Padmore, George. 1972. *Pan-Africanism or Communism.* New York: Anchor Books.

Persky, Joseph. 1998. "Wage Slavery." *History of Political Economy* 30(4): 627–651.

Quijano, Anibal. 2000. "Coloniality of Power, Eurocentrism, and Latin America." *Nepantla: Views from the South* 1(3): 533–580.

Rabaka, Reiland. 2009. *Africana Critical Theory: Reconstructing the Black Radical Tradition, from W.E.B. Du Bois and C.L.R. James to Frantz Fanon and Amilcar Cabral.* Lanham, MD: Lexington Books.

Robinson, Cedric J. 2000. *Black Marxism: The Making of the Black Radical Tradition.* London: University of North Carolina Press.

Robinson, Cedric J. 2001. *An Anthropology of Marxism.* Aldershot: Ashgate.

Shanin, Teodor. 1983. *Late Marx and the Russian Road: Marx and 'the Peripheries of Capitalism'.* London: Routledge & Kegan Paul.

Shilliam, Robbie. 2006. "Marx's Path to Capital: The International Dimension of an Intellectual Journey." *History of Political Thought* 27(2): 349–375.

Shilliam, Robbie. 2012a. "Civilization and the Poetics of Slavery." *Thesis Eleven* 108(1): 99–117.

Shilliam, Robbie. 2012b. "Forget English Freedom, Remember Atlantic Slavery: Common Law, Commercial Law and the Significance of Slavery for Classical Political Economy." *New Political Economy* 17(5): 591–609.

Skinner, Quentin. 2002. *Visions of Politics, vol. 2: Renaissance Virtues.* Cambridge: Cambridge University Press.

Symposium on Karl Marx and the US Civil War. 2011. *Historical Materialism* 19(4): 33–206.

Turley, David. 1991. *The Culture of English Anti-Slavery: 1780–1860.* London: Routledge.

Vann Woodward, C. 1983. *American Counterpoint: Slavery and Racism in the North/South Dialogue.* Oxford: Oxford University Press.

Vargo, Gregory. 2012. "'Outworks of the Citadel of Corruption': The Chartist Press Reports the Empire." *Victorian Studies* 54(2): 227–253.

West, Cornel. 1993. "The Dilemma of the Black Intellectual." *The Journal of Blacks in Higher Education* 2: 59–67.

Workers Party of America. 1925. "Declaration by the Central Executive Committee, Workers (Communist) Party of America." In *The Marcus Garvey and Universal Negro Improvement Association Papers. Vol. VI. September 1924-December 1927*, ed. Robert A. Hill. Berkeley, CA: University of California Press, 1989. 141–143.

Wynter, Sylvia. 2003. "Unsettling the Coloniality of Being/Power/Truth/Freedom: Towards the Human, After Man, Its Overrepresentation – An Argument." *CR: The New Centennial Review* 3(3): 257–337.

Zantop, Susanne. 1997. *Colonial Fantasies: Conquest, Family, and Nation in Precolonial Germany, 1770–1870.* Durham, NC: Duke University Press.

The *Manifesto* in a Late-Capitalist Era: Melancholy and Melodrama

Elisabeth Anker

The *Communist Manifesto* continues to shape the trajectory, rhetoric and desires of leftist critical theory in a late-capitalist era. Contemporary critical theorists, including Giorgio Agamben, Michael Hardt and Antonio Negri, employ the language of the *Manifesto* to articulate their political critiques of globalization, transnational capitalism and biopolitics, and to delineate possible resistances to the crises of our era. These scholars draw on the *Manifesto* not only to utilize its methodology for their critiques of the present, but also, I argue, because the *Manifesto* has come to represent a set of broken promises about the emancipation from capitalism. These promises include not only the overcoming of class domination, but also the promise that that the very practice of critical thought can be a means to freedom and an expression of moral rightness. The *Manifesto*, in contemporary critical theory, comes to represent what leftist political critique has desired and lost in a late-capitalist era: the guarantee of imminent freedom, the clear virtue of leftist political positions and the promise of the left's destiny as the harbinger of revolutionary emancipation.

Contemporary theorists reappropriate the *Manifesto* as a way of disavowing the losses that it has come to represent. This dynamic recapitulates what Walter Benjamin (2005) once called "left melancholy." According to Benjamin, left melancholy describes a condition in which critiques of the present are disabled by their attachments to lost objects and failed promises. Melancholy is a refusal to acknowledge one's desire to repossess something that has been loved and lost. Contemporary critical theory is melancholic when it disavows its attachments to the failed but still-loved promise of leftist political-theoretical critique: that its methods can accurately scrutinize and help overcome the brutality of capitalism, and that it can provide direct means to freedom and moral rightness. Contemporary left melancholy draws on the analytic methods of the *Manifesto* as a way to hold on to its lost promises, but in doing so it undercuts the capacity to critically grasp the objects it places under scrutiny.

More surprisingly, contemporary theory becomes melancholic by incorporating the particular *melodramatic* narrative, style and promise of the *Manifesto*. It mimics the melodramatic style of the *Manifesto* in a melancholic effort to hold on to and revivify the losses that the *Manifesto* is pressed to represent. The rhetorical form that left melancholy takes in an era of late capitalism, then, is not primarily the melancholic traits of sadness and self-loathing but the *melodramatic* traits of moral self-righteousness, galvanizing sentiment and binary diagnostics of oppression. The *Manifesto*, I argue, is a melodrama: it portrays dramatic events using moral binaries of good and evil, innocent victims, heightened affects of pain and suffering, race-to-the-rescue chases, grand gestures and astonishing feats of courage. It offers a story about the suffering of virtuous people, overwhelmed by nefarious forces, who overcome their domination, and it thematizes broad political and social conflict through heightened representations of unjust persecution. Contemporary left theorists mimic the manifesto, implicitly or explicitly, when they dramatically interrogate oppressive social structures through a heightened moral drama of good and evil, in which the forces of empire and administered capitalism are arrayed as evil villainy, and the proletariat and other marginalized, weak and vulnerable people across the globe – as well as those who write about inequality on their behalf – are positioned as pure protagonists. It confers moral clarity on the complex and often unaccountable powers organizing politics and subjectivity, bestows an impeccable virtue upon people who live in conditions of subjugation, organizes its critique through narrative cycles of pathos and action, and often, though not always, assures readers that heroic emancipation will conquer the villainous source of oppression.

While the intention behind new melodramatic appropriations of the *Manifesto* is to galvanize audiences for radical social change in the way that the *Manifesto* did more than a century earlier, their melancholic use of melodramatic conventions also limit their capacity to depict the distinct challenges and unintended effects of political life in the present. Their melodramas are underpinned by a refusal to acknowledge the loss of left political theory's guarantee that it necessarily provides a means to revolutionary freedom, as well as the loss of intrinsic moral virtue implicitly granted to its practitioners. Contemporary theorists incorporate the melodrama of the *Manifesto* as a way to offer an affectively charged narrative that lucidly reveals the violence of contemporary oppression. Yet their critical capacities and effective diagnostics are curtailed by the melodramatic style that works to disavow the losses of present politics. The current appropriation of the melodramatic form of the *Manifesto* thus occludes Marx's and Engels's own counsel that the possibility of radical transformation is diminished when nostalgia for the past furnishes the blueprint for the future. It burdens revolutionary desire with the structural and imaginative limitations of outdated and moralized material and ideal conditions.

This chapter analyses the melancholic and melodramatic uses of the *Manifesto* in late-capitalist critical theory in three parts. It begins by analyzing the melodramatic structure and form of the *Manifesto*. It then moves to examine Benjamin's concept of left melancholy and its application to the contemporary moment. In the third part, it combines these analyses to examine "left melodrama" – how the texts of Agamben, Hardt and Negri melancholically recapitulate the melodrama of the *Manifesto* in an effort to sustain the promises of freedom and equality it represents.

THE MANIFESTO AS MELODRAMA

In order to see how current appropriations of the *Manifesto* melancholically reappropriate its melodramatic style, I first examine the *Manifesto* as a melodrama. The genre of melodrama, while varying to a certain degree across time, place and medium, generally refers to set of cultural conventions that portray events through a narrative of victimization and retribution, and a character triad of villain, victim and hero (Elsaesser 1987; Books 1995; Williams 2001).[1] Their stories are organized in cycles of injury and action, of suffering and strength, until a hero rescues the victim and usually triumphs over the villain. For the purposes of this chapter, I utilize a core set of conventions that are generally present throughout melodrama's different iterations, while being attentive to how melodrama manifests differently in different texts and historical moments, in particular noting its differences in the *Communist Manifesto, Empire* and *Homo Sacer*. As Steve Neale (1993) among others notes, melodrama references a set of generic conventions yet it also shifts and evolves; the term "melodrama" means different things at different historic moments and social spaces, as can be demonstrated by its varied definitions in Rousseau's origination of the term, its use in the 1920s American film industry and again in 1980s feminist film and theater studies.

Melodramas encourage visceral responses in their readers and audiences by depicting wrenching and perilous situations that cultivate affective connections to victims, and sometimes to the heroes who rescue them (Gledhill 1987; Berlant 2008). Using a morally polarizing worldview, melodramas signify goodness in the suffering of victims, and evil in the cruel ferocity of antagonists. The victim's injury organizes the melodrama narrative and defines its social critique by dramatizing what causes and contributes to the injury. Many melodramas promise a teleology of change that can rectify the social injuries they diagnose (Anker 2005). They valorize the powerless and vilify the powerful, even though the types of characters who are powerless or powerful can shift radically in different texts and historic junctures; within melodramas, human actions are often dictated by social position; indeed, individual characters are often the metonymic substitute for economic or social classes (Gerould 1980).

Melodramatic cultural forms, particularly theater, have aligned with left politics for more than two centuries. Melodrama arose as a theatrical genre form that justified the French revolution by telling heightened stories of toppled evil aristocrats, and offering common folk as virtuous protagonists (Elsaesser

1987; Brooks 1995; Buckley 2006). They moralized unequal social-economic relations, connecting poverty with virtue and wealth with venality. One French melodramatist even claimed that his plays instigated the 1848 Revolution (Gerould 1994, 186). Indeed, Jean-Jacques Rousseau invented the term "melodrama," and posthumously inspired melodramatic critiques of unjust authority and class inequality in revolutionary France (Rousseau 1990, 497). The imbrication of melodrama and revolution is well-documented by theater historians and literature scholars, as many Euro-American leftists have at key points turned to melodrama "as the most effective means of conveying revolutionary sentiments to mass audiences" (Gerould 1994, 185). Yet in addition to melodrama's better-known leftist theatrical and film affiliations, I contend that melodrama also contributes to the political critique that structures the *Communist Manifesto*. Karl Marx and Friedrich Engels can be considered melodramatists in penning their challenge for collective emancipation.[2]

The *Manifesto* takes shape through a melodramatic narrative that connects revolutionary heroism with the social victimization of the proletariat, in order both to illuminate the violence of industrial capital and to reveal its imminent overcoming. Reading the *Manifesto* as melodrama shows how the text illuminates class oppression by molding historical relations into stark binaries, detailing the unjust suffering of the proletariat, promising the triumph of heroism, highlighting the moral righteousness of the oppressed and employing all of these tropes with the aim of affectively motivating its reader into undertaking revolutionary action. The presumable intentions of the *Manifesto* – to point to the economic forces that drive political and historical development, to motivate radical action to establish an equal, sustainable and meaningful species-wide human existence – also turn the complex dynamism of history into a melodramatic unfolding. The *Manifesto* promises the radical overcoming of economic domination, and, like most melodramas, insists that rightness will eventually prevail. Even for all of Marx's and Engels's claims to the contrary, they still reassure their readers that the world is just: oppression will be eradicated and the oppressed will triumph.

Marx and Engels begin section I of the *Manifesto* as such:

The history of all society up to now is the history of class struggles.
    Freeman and slave, patrician and plebian, lord and serf, guild-master and journeyman, in short, oppressor and oppressed stood in continual conflict with one another, conducting an unbroken, now hidden, now open struggle, a struggle that finished each time with a revolutionary transformation of society as a whole, or with the common ruin of the contending classes. (CM 237)[3]

From the outset of the text, Marx and Engels reconfigure the history of social relations into various binary oppositions, which all become an opposition of "oppressor and oppressed." This opposition is not particularly civilizational, nor does it seem to partake in longstanding Greek/barbarian distinctions based on superiority. And neither does it seem to be a product of an ontological friend/enemy antagonism, even though Carl Schmitt melodramatically describes it as such: "This antithesis concentrates all antagonisms of world history into one single final battle against the last enemy of humanity" (1996, 74). Rather, this is a distinction that is specifically based on power. It is what Marx and Engels explicitly describe as having become a "simplified" polarity, juxtaposing two options: powerful and powerless, in which power is determined by economic production (CM 238). For the authors, the modern industrial era has tidied the pre-modern clutter of human relationships into "two great hostile encampments, into two great classes directly mutually opposed – bourgeoisie and proletariat" (CM 238). They create their contemporary moment as a sharpening of hostility down to solitary and stark distinctions. These two classes do not merely face each other, but they do so, as the authors state above, "directly." This language heightens the back-and-forth drama of this clash of power – what Linda Williams calls melodrama's "dialectic of pathos and action" (2001, 30) – that is part of melodrama's affective engagement with its readers. For Marx and Engels, relations of power, even "political power in its true sense," is "the organized power of one class for oppressing another" (CM 252). These first sentences inaugurate history as a dramatic narrative story about power antagonisms – a building up and compressing of myriad human relationships into one model with two possible positions.

The analysis of this power antagonism does not rest there, however; if read through the generic conventions of melodrama, it is moralized. The binary Marx and Engels identify is "oppressor and oppressed" (CM 237). Another way to explain this might be to say that it is a distinction based upon villainy and victimization; in melodrama, the experience of oppression by an oppressor is depicted by categories of victim and victimizer, with victimization intensified by the unjustness of the injury. Oppression marks the inverse link between power and moral virtue, so that more of one entails less of the other (Anker 2005). If we understand moralization as the overt making of absolute moral claims, then the authors do not explicitly moralize their distinction, nor is their critique reproachful or self-satisfied (Bennett and Shapiro 2002). However, they do interpret history by drawing on distinctions that have deep-seated moralistic connotations. They do not make direct claims of goodness for the proletariat, but they do describe the proletariat's condition in heightened language that gestures to an organizing structure of good and evil, and they frame events in a cyclical narrative of victimization and overcoming. In these ways, the *Manifesto* signals the melodramatic claim that powerlessness marks virtue.

In arguing that the bourgeoisie acquires power by conquering all other classes, Marx and Engels diagnose one primary mover of modern history, one that subtends and subsumes other forces: capital. They isolate capital in order to draw attention to its pervasive force, and they place it above and in control of other social forces, which become its derivatives. Capital, and the bourgeoisie as the capitalist class, produces the political, social and familial dilemmas that the *Manifesto* diagnoses. Even the state is wholly in the service of modern industry.

The bourgeoisie puts an end to all other human relations besides those based on exchange and labor; dramatically, it has "pitilessly severed" feudal ties, leaving only "naked self-interest," "unfeeling 'hard cash'" (CM 239). Its actions are quite violent: toward all other human relations, it has "obliterated," "drowned," "stripped the sanctity" and "torn" away their organizing power using "open, unashamed, direct, brutal exploitation" (CM 239). In undoing feudal structures, the bourgeoisie produces a system that resolves human worth into exchange value, and generates power for the few at the expense of the working masses. Capital is everywhere, destroying everything, harming everyone. Melodrama's "metaphors of unfreedom," in Thomas Elsaesser's words, are well suited for revealing and depicting capital's breathtaking violence (1987, 67). Marx and Engels inform the reader that this power has created more massive and colossal productive forces than in all preceding generations combined. It has subjected nature, burst its own fetters and cannibalized all other forms of human relationship.

The bourgeoisie absorbs responsibility for the horrors the authors depict; as the generative force of these injustices, it compels, batters down, creates the world in its own image. The description of villainy in the *Manifesto* makes it easy to champion its overcoming; the bourgeois villain becomes an identifiable target to mobilize against, the singular and clear agent of evil. Marx and Engels may be simplifying power intentionally in the *Manifesto* in order to shed light on the then-underexamined role of capital in social suffering, and to emphasize the disregarded conditions of the proletariat. In other texts they portray power and capital in significantly more complex ways. Yet presented in this way and in this text, the isolation of capital comes at the price of diminishing other important generative forces of history and social life, and quite possibly of limiting the possibilities for thinking about how to overcome the plight of the working class. This isolation antecedes the left's current problem of narrowing the varied phenomena of power, and may contribute to – though it is not solely responsible for – the determinism that haunts contemporary analysis. With one singular source of accountability, analytic focus is directed at only one aspect of society.

Writing in the 1940s, literary critic Wylie Sypher (1948) argued that Marx uses melodramatic tropes throughout *Capital*. Sypher suggested that Marx's particular uptake of the Hegelian dialectic draws partly from melodrama's Manichean moral binary. For Sypher, the social conventions of the nineteenth century were saturated with melodramatic ways of viewing the world; Marx is a product of his time period, and though not intentionally employing melodramatic conventions he would have been hard pressed to fully extricate himself from melodrama's pervasiveness as a worldview. Though Sypher's claims for melodrama's saturation may be overdrawn, his analysis supports how the *Manifesto* can be read to employ melodrama's moralistic tropes in its depiction of revolution. The initial paragraphs of the *Manifesto* draw upon the moral horrors of capital to presage the communist revolution, and shape how readers interpret the rest of the powerful first section.

Marx and Engels render in melodramatic detail the suffering of capital's victims: they emphasize the proletariat's dehumanization, as "devalued" by their burdensome and monotonous toils; they are, in body and soul, "enslaved by the machine" (CM 242). Horrifyingly abject, they are not only without property but also without supportive family relations, without nation, without law, morality, religion. Stripped of all organizing forces save capital, "the proletariat is [modern industry's] particular product" (CM 244). The *Manifesto* both denaturalizes economically produced suffering and makes the weak harbingers of emancipation. Because the proletariat is so stripped, their needs are selfless, aligned with all of humanity. The heroic possibility of human emancipation thus lies with them. They become what Karl Löwith calls the "universal human function of the proletariat," as their self-emancipation will necessarily emancipate all humanity (Löwith 1993, 110). Their abjection is exactly what makes them capable of a world-historic heroism.

After describing the power of villainy and the victimization that it inflicts, the *Manifesto* moves along the melodramatic narrative trajectory and turns to the victim's heroic overcoming. At the end of section I, Marx and Engels write of the struggle coming "to a head," the classic heightening of suspense, the race-to-the-rescue, last-minute tension that makes melodrama such an affectively engaging mode (CM 244). In their analysis, heroic overcoming will occur by the very victims of capital's cruel and violent logic. Victims become the heroes and perform their own rescue; as Sheldon Wolin writes, "not only is revolution to destroy the rule of capital, but the experience is to transform the worker into a heroic actor of epic stature" (Wolin 2004, 434). As the proletariat's numbers grow and its strength concentrates, the future collision between the two classes fulfills the narrative promise, a teleology of revolution providing freedom in/and equality. The melodramatic cycle whereby the injustice of victimization legitimates the violence of heroism is here made manifest in the authorization of revolution.

Combined with the detailing of villainy, this explanation of victimization and heroism intends to engender, viscerally, a new affective charge. It aims to motivate the desire, and the difficult work, for revolutionary change. The horrors endured by the proletariat inform the readers of the *Manifesto* that this suffering is unjust, cruel and yet eradicable. Film theorist Jane Gaines emphasizes melodrama's ability to motivate revolutionary sentiment; she argues:

> Theatrical melodrama has historically been the preferred form of revolutionary periods for precisely its capacity to dichotomize swiftly, to identify targets, to encapsulate conflict, and to instill the kind of pride that can swell the ranks of malcontents. Revolutionary melodrama can be depended upon to narrate intolerable historical conditions in such a way that *audiences wish to see wrongs "righted," are even moved to act upon their reaffirmed convictions, to act against tyranny and for the people."* (Gaines 1996, 59–60, emphasis added)

Gaines, drawing from Sypher, argues that readers of Marx, "like the melodrama audience, see patterns of injustice laid out before us, and we are appalled" (Gaines 1996, 60). Melodrama's affective power, what literary theorist Peter Brooks calls melodrama's "excess" and Williams calls its "pathos," makes melodrama so politically powerful for mobilizing large-scale transformations, and can help explain the widespread transnational and transhistorical effects of the *Manifesto*. The *Manifesto* ends with a galvanizing call to action: "Proletarians have nothing to lose ... but their chains. They have a world to win. *Proletarians of all countries unite!*" (CM 260; emphasis in original). Having been shown the cruelties and exploitations of industrial capitalism, and asked to reinterpret their own experience through its injustices, readers are energetically summoned to fight for revolution.

THE MANIFESTO AND LEFT MELANCHOLY

New modes of political critique incorporate the affective force, explanatory power and moral rightness of the *Manifesto* by drawing on its melodramatic conventions. They detail heightened scenes of unjust victimization, employ cycles of pathos and action, divide social formations into moral binaries of protagonists and antagonists and promise a heroic overcoming of global injustice and transnational networks of inequality. They intend to re-galvanize the twenty-first-century political imagination in the way that the *Manifesto* did in the nineteenth and early twentieth centuries. Their use of melodrama positions the *Manifesto* to stand as proof of the left's moral virtue, heroic promise and capacity to instigate substantive freedom. Yet it seems instead to reveal a melancholic relationship to the present era, in which revolutionary possibility seems out of reach, in which capitalism continues to extend through across much of the globe and continues to cannibalize alternative and more equitable structures of social organization, in which neoliberal and biopolitical powers deepen the devaluation of human existence unable to be captured by profit. The contemporary use of melodrama is thus different from the melodrama of the *Manifesto*, as it is motivated by disavowed loss; it uses melodrama to recapture the specific losses that the *Manifesto* comes to represent. To argue that, I next turn to analyzing the melancholy that underpins this appropriation before reading how the work of contemporary critical thinkers appropriates the *melodramatic* genre conventions melancholically.

"Left melancholy" is a term first coined by Walter Benjamin, who used it in a brief essay that critiqued left intellectuals whose writings seemed to reflect desires for the comforts of the present rather than the revolution their texts claimed to support. He derided the way their condemnations of society derived from habitual modes of criticism, rather than a real desire for change, and became reflex responses imposed upon difficult problems. Erich Kastner, the particular Weimar-era writer who served as an exemplar of this broader condition, was "as incapable of striking the dispossessed with his rebellious accents as he is of touching the industrialists with his irony" (Benjamin 2005, 423–424). Kastner's routinized forms of scrutiny betrayed a longing for the comfort of past sureties that precluded insight into present configurations of power and inequality, and thus stifled possibilities for more radical political action.

Benjamin titled the critique "Left Melancholy," though he did not provide an explicit definition of the term in the text. It is provocatively contoured, however, as a "clenched fist in papier-mâché": a figure that outwardly gestures to revolutionary desire yet is reified, inanimate, frozen in place at the same time that it has no inside material (Benjamin 2005, 424). Its core contains only "empty spaces," "hollow forms," an inner void where melancholy holds on to dead objects instead of engaging the world of animate life – even and especially when that world is increasingly oppressive, commodified, fascist and in desperate need of radical social transformation to real equality and freedom (Benjamin 2005, 425).

Benjamin's term 'left melancholy' seems to imply not only the act of holding on to dead objects – the more conventional way of interpreting melancholy after Sigmund Freud – but the frightening act of deadening live subjects in its grasp. In *The Origin of German Tragic Drama*, where Benjamin engages more directly in the concept of melancholy, he describes it in one iteration as "the deadening of the emotions ... [that] can increase the distance between the self and the surrounding world to the point of alienation from the body" (Benjamin 2003, 140). Melancholy's deadening work creates distance between the self and the world it places under investigation, an act that can potentially provoke distantiation and enable innovative criticism, but that also harbors the dangerous threat of devitalizing that very world. In melancholy, "the utensils of active life are lying around unused on the floor, as objects of contemplation" (Benjamin 2003, 140). Melancholy, in this regard, is a form of contemplation that makes alien the things in the world; in the particulars of left melancholy, this making-alien turns active material into unused, inert objects. Melancholy, for Benjamin, is always a product of the historical moment it inhabits. Its operations and source of sadness are temporally shifty; indeed, it is one aim of the *Origins of German Tragic Drama* to investigate the constellation of interpretations for how melancholy has been differently situated. Benjamin connects "Left Melancholy" to the work in *The Origins of German Tragic Drama* when writing that left melancholy is the latest development of two thousand years of melancholia. Left melancholy's deadening of revolutionary reflexes is inescapably situated in, and a product of, its time period. Perhaps, then, the making dead of live things provides an accurate reflection of the historical moment Benjamin analyzes: it is the work of commodification and alienation, of capital's turning the world and its inhabitants into dead objects. Left melancholy, possibly, encapsulates this turn, revealing the true story of the violence in which it is situated, of a life lived through processes that turn all things into commodities and numbers, that render live things dead for efficiency and profit.

In "Left Melancholy" Benjamin similarly describes Kastner's intellectual movement as accomplishing "the transposition of revolutionary reflexes ... into objects of distraction, of amusement, which can be supplied for consumption" (Benjamin 2005, 424). Left melancholy is akin to a process of reification, as habituated forms of leftist scrutiny drain the vitality and energetics of both the melancholic and the objects he holds on to, vitality necessary for sustaining the critical push for freedom in a dark and dangerous time. Diminishing revolutionary potential, left melancholy reflects the outward trappings that signify work for social change while its animating core is inert, empty and lifeless.

The term "left melancholy" gained attention again at the turn of the millennium, in an essay by Wendy Brown which asked how Benjamin's analysis could supply a diagnosis for leftist critical theory in a neoliberal, late-capitalist era. In "Resisting Left Melancholy" Brown (1999) argues that loss now saturates leftist intellectual inquiry, as left academics must contend with the loss of legitimacy for Marxism and socialism, the loss of a unified movement and method and the loss of viable alternatives to counter the nexus of liberal-capitalism. These losses originate in part in leftist critical analysis, which has had difficulty accounting for recent formations of power in late capitalism and thus has become ineffective in challenging them. For Brown, the difficulty in analyzing contemporary power is traceable to new iterations of left melancholy. She addresses the unanswered questions from Benjamin's piece by examining the content of the losses that left melancholy clings to, and by asking how left melancholy accomplishes its deadening work. Addressing the latter question first, she suggests that deadening arises from the conventional methodologies of left critical theory: economic determinism, totalizing social analysis and a teleology of human emancipation have each proven inadequate or unsustainable for grappling with contemporary political economy. Significant historical shifts have changed how politics and the economy operate and interconnect with individuals since the mid-nineteenth century, but leftist modes of critique have often been unable to keep pace with them. Drawing from Stuart Hall (1988), Brown argues that attachments to older forms of critique narrow and devitalize the current dynamics they scrutinize, and thus impede discovery of the unexpected and particular. A more effective analysis would require a break with certain methods and assumptions that had conventionally defined what it meant to be part of the academic left.

Yet attachments to outdated forms of critique are only one part of the problem, and they had already been confronted in the late twentieth century by key interventions from feminist, queer and postcolonial theory, among other modes of inquiry. More influential, Brown suggests, is the loss that underpins the attachments: "In the hollow core of all these losses, perhaps in the place of our political unconscious, is there also an unavowed loss – the promise that left analysis and left commitment would supply its adherents a clear and certain path toward the good, the right, and the true?" (Brown 1999, 22). Melancholy, in Freud's "Mourning and Melancholia," is defined as the loss of what cannot be loved, the disavowed desire for something that has left or abandoned the subject. It is the refusal to acknowledge that a "love object" has been lost, or that one had desired this lost object in the first place (Freud 1959). Incorporating Freud's analysis, Brown argues that left melancholy is formed by the refusal to acknowledge the desire for what the left has lost in a new era that has weakened and cannibalized leftist political power: the faith that leftist theoretical analysis and political commitment can provide a direct means to truth, moral virtue and human freedom. This "hollow core" of loss, perhaps the core of Benjamin's papier-mâché fist, underpins left critical theory, and because unacknowledged it continues to inhibit the academic left's reckoning with the present; it weakens and marginalizes leftist inquiry. The refusal to relinquish these desires, let alone acknowledge them, marks the refusal to grapple with the failed promise of inevitable emancipation, or, as Hall puts it, the refusal to abandon the guarantee that leftist theory can "rescue us from the vicissitudes of the present" (Hall 1988, 4). Sustaining leftist commitments paradoxically requires that critical theory grapple directly with the left's losses and failures.

Since Brown made her analysis, the topics, range and methods of left analysis have further expanded and reoriented crucial aspects of critical thought. Widespread criticisms of post-9/11 politics reinvigorated leftist critical and political theory in Euro-American thought and remobilized its sustained commitment to social transformation. Influential authors such as Giorgio Agamben have written trenchant political critiques of contemporary domination that do not privilege only class or capital in diagnosing experiences of unfreedom. Others, such as Michael Hardt and Antonio Negri, have used multidisciplinary analyses to delineate complex formations of power and energize revolutionary sentiment. Yet the attachments animating left melancholy are still present in their particular modes of left theoretical work, though they have been reinscribed in new form. Left melancholy thus continues to shape a type of left political-theoretical inquiry, but the loss it holds on to manifests in different form to that which Brown and Hall diagnose, even as it draws from the dynamics they identify.

Twenty-first-century left melancholy attaches to a *particular* love object. Freud's analysis of melancholy can help to interpret the nature of this object. Freud makes clear that the lost "object" – his psychoanalytic term for describing what or who is desired – can be a person, a group identity, an abstraction, a country or an ideal (Freud 1959, 1990). I retain Freud's term "object" to describe what has been lost in left melodrama because the term attends to the psychic dimension of the losses I examine. I therefore use "object" as a specific reference to the psychoanalytic valence of melancholy, and do not intend it to mark a broad or quotidian use of the term.

The melancholic not only refuses to acknowledge that it has lost or been abandoned by the object it loves; it also takes on the characteristics of the lost love object. The melancholic subject incorporates the disavowed lost object into itself in order to hold on to what it has lost (Butler 1997). Melancholy, therefore, includes both a disavowal of loss, and a part of the self that turns into that very object, so that the self begins to mimic the lost object of its desire. Through incorporation, the melancholic refuses to let its object go.

The lost object, in current left melancholy, is the *Manifesto*. The *Manifesto* is situated as a paradigmatic text weighted with representing the set of losses articulated above. It is a text that provoked the promise and the dream of radical social transformation, that augured revolution, indeed that founded left praxis, all of which often failed or were lost or out of reach in an era of late capital. Most important, this text galvanized millions of people, and its widespread appeal, explosive moral power and emancipatory guarantee engendered a century or more of transnational solidarity toward the project of human freedom.

In certain strands of contemporary critical theory, the *Manifesto* has become the "hollow core," the lost and deadened object. Its style and terms of analysis are reabsorbed into contemporary political inquiry as a way of fending off the losses it represents. The *Manifesto* is "lost" to the degree that it stands in for the failed twinned promises of leftist critical theory: inevitable emancipation and unwavering moral rightness. It has come to represent a former era when leftist political critique seemed unquestionably vital and promising, when the moral virtue of left critique seemed valid, when the freedom it envisioned seemed imminent. Indeed, the *Manifesto,* when situated in this way, becomes the instantiation of those guarantees. The logic of the *Manifesto* as the lost love object conjures up a past era when the left's moral certitude seemed self-evident, and aims to recover the possibility that a single text can energize populations for the collective pursuit of human freedom. The *Manifesto* has also come to represent these failed promises because the very collective movements it helped to engender often only entrenched the oppression they intended to overcome.

While this new form of left melancholy still interprets politics through older leftist frameworks, including monocausality, teleology and moral certainty, it displaces the earlier analytic targets of capital, revolution, immanent dialectic and the working class onto different targets. And, more strikingly, left melancholy now adopts the galvanizing melodramatic form the *Manifesto* uses to tell its story. Left melancholy thus ironically draws upon the melodramatic narrative form of the *Manifesto*, incorporating it into its very constitution. Left melodrama is a complex phenomenon: it sustains older leftist critical modes such as monocausality when positing a singular and clear accountability for oppression (usually in the character of a villain); its villainization and victimization of various economic/political positions maintains simplified antagonisms for interpreting social change; its teleology of heroic overcoming of oppression revives the guarantee that critical theory inevitably guides toward freedom. It even insists that the practice of critical theory is itself an expression of virtue. When melodrama organizes contemporary critical inquiry in this way, disavowed loss sustains left melancholy in melodramatic form. The melodrama of the *Manifesto* is melancholically absorbed into some of the most popular recent critical theory, particularly the work of Agamben, Hardt and Negri. In the rest of this essay, I examine how the melodramatic tropes of the *Manifesto* melancholically inhabit contemporary critical theory.

LEFT MELODRAMA AND CONTEMPORARY APPROPRIATIONS OF THE MANIFESTO

Left melodrama can be found in some of the most important and influential critical theory circulating at the outset of the twenty-first century, including Giorgio Agamben's *Homo Sacer* and *States of Exception*, and Michael Hardt and Antonio Negri's collaborative works *Empire* and *Multitude*. (I am not suggesting that these books could be exclusively explained through recourse to melodrama, but instead intend to show what can be illuminated when we read their projects as melodrama.) These texts critique global inequalities in economic, state and bureaucratic power by attending to key factors that produce them, including the work of biopolitics and sovereign power in producing the poor and marginalized as abject humans, and the work of transnational capital and the forces of empire in generating massive worldwide inequality.

Agamben's work interrogates individuals' relationship to the state through the concept of "bare life": human bodies that become bereft of social value, bodies that can be killed with impunity because their death lacks social or political recognition. The sovereign power of the state is the ultimate arbiter for conferring bare life, as it can except itself from the law and designate bare life, *homo sacer*, at will. *Homo sacer* is a provocative and valuable concept for analyzing certain contemporary problems; it critically interrogates how humans have been subject to state violence while stripped of legal protection and political recognition (Agamben 2005). For Agamben, critical analysis of bare life is the primary tool with which to interpret contemporary power. It "has thus offered the key by which not only the sacred texts of sovereignty but also the very codes of political power will unveil their mysteries" (Agamben 1998, 8). Offering methodological heroism, Agamben suggest that the very study of *homo sacer* promises to reveal the analytic truth of our historical moment and the horrors that will occur if its warnings about abjection remain unheeded. And it may soon face an omnipotent villain; Agamben ominously warns in *Homo Sacer* that if left unchecked, state power as the permanent state of exception "will soon extend itself over the entire planet" (Agamben 1998, 27).

Yet is the state really the only arbiter of power in contemporary life, as Agamben seems to claim? In Agamben's melancholy melodrama, the state is both monolithic and sovereign. Agamben's accountability, similarly to Marx and Engels's melodrama, points one sensationalistic finger of blame for social suffering: most contemporary forms of abjection become effects of the sovereign state. The texts draw clear lines of accountability for the suffering of bare life onto a villain whose motives are transparent: control, dehumanization and domination. Agamben's melodrama marks social binaries akin to Marx and Engels's binary between "oppressor and oppressed"; here the antagonism is between *homo sacer* and the sovereign state, victims and villains; even as his work aims to dispel antagonistic models with nuanced readings of indistinction, his descriptions instate new binaries in this effort. In some sense, the state of exception has become capital, the great force of domination leftist scholars can safely and rightly align, without reservation, against. Perhaps part of Agamben's popularity is that he has given critical theorists a new enemy against which to mobilize in opposition.

The Nazi death camp functions in Agamben's argument as the archetype and epitome of the relationship of sovereignty and bare life, and it models modern individuals' relationship to the state. Agamben's treatment of the camp, which he calls "the hidden paradigm" of all modern biopower, weakens his analysis of late capitalism by diminishing the heterogeneity of power, the dynamism of juridicality, the multifaceted and nonlinear directionality of accountability for contemporary unfreedom and the existing forms of nonsovereign politics (Agamben 1998, 123). If political life is captured only by the state of exception, and power is an all-encompassing form of dehumanizing sovereignty – one that seems to apply as much to Nazi death camps as to the suburbs – then all modern individuals become lumped together, categorized without differentiation as innocent victims of a villainous entity that has full control over human life. And like the melodrama of the *Manifesto*, this diagnosis of victimization is moralized: Agamben takes pains to assure his readers that *homo sacer* "is the protagonist of this book" (Agamben 1998, 27). And later, like the "universal human function" of the *Manifesto*, Agamben argues: "if today there is no longer any one clear figure of the sacred man, it is perhaps because we are all virtually *homines sacri*" (Agamben 1998, 115).

It is at the juxtaposition of these two claims that the melancholic "hollow core" of this argument shines through. Everyone is a victim of sovereignty; "we" are all *homo sacer,* "the protagonist of this book." Everyone who lives in a late-modern moment, who aligns politically and morally against the sovereign state, against indefinite detention, is a besieged protagonist. As we are all *homines sacri* living in a state of exception, we are all innocent victims, free of complicity with oppression, harm and violence effected in our world. This claim, that all readers are protagonists, nourishes the disavowal of the desire for moral rightness. Agamben's critique moves solely outward, against a force so sovereign and omnipotent that all can disclaim responsibility for the political horrors his texts depict. Unlike the *Manifesto*, however, Agamben's virtuous protagonists have significantly diminished agency over their conditions of domination. The perhaps unintended effect of this move is that individuals are left somewhat bereft of the capacity to shape society. It offers up victims but denies a readily available hero, and thus undoes the guarantee that freedom will be imminent. Aside from his hopes that humans might create a nonsovereign politics, Agamben's modern individuals passively wallow in the state of exception, the flip side perhaps to passive protagonism of the *homines sacri.*

This is where *Empire*, the book hailed as a "*Communist Manifesto* for the twenty-first century," steps in (Žižek 2001). A different form of left melodrama that more explicitly draws on the *Manifesto*, Hardt and Negri sew politics, culture and the economy into a complex yet unified tapestry of global society dominated by the machinations of empire. Empire is they key diagnostic lens for analyzing the forces at play in new millennium. It is, not unlike capital in the *Manifesto*, "the political subject that effectively regulates these global exchanges, the sovereign power that governs the world" (Hardt and Negri 2001, xi). It operates as a sovereign agent that organizes, but supersedes, myriad variations of power and economy in order to permeate varied registers of civil society and govern them all. As the prime mover, empire is "the idea of a single power that overdetermines them all, structures them in a unitary way, and treats them under one common notion of right that is decidedly postcolonial and postimperialist" (Hardt and Negri 2001, 9). The primary antagonism of "oppressor and oppressed" in *Empire* and *Multitude* is between empire and the multitude, the villain and the victim of this melodramatic story. The multitude, like the proletariat in the *Manifesto*, is a "radical counterpower" comprised of marginalized and suffering groups across the globe whose very existence signifies revolutionary promise (Hardt and Negri 2001, 66). Hardt and Negri see signs of revolution at the unraveling margins of society, in various resistances to surveillance, war, corporate domination and government hegemony, among other forces. They examine local resistance efforts in different and unaligned sectors of the multitude, and argue that these efforts combined become harbingers of a more total social transformation. With empire as the "parasitical," "single power" of oppression, all forms of challenge presage human emancipation (Hardt and Negri 2004, 336, 339).

The antagonism between empire and multitude carries explanatory power for late capitalism, just as the antagonism between capital and the proletariat did in the *Manifesto*, by connecting many different conditions of domination into a unifying force of the multitude, and by connecting different forms of domination as the unifying force of empire. Its melodrama highlights the moral rightness of the dominated, and promises that they will overcome their conditions of unfreedom. Like Agamben's analysis, in which the reader is likened to *homo sacer*, Hardt and Negri's analysis implicitly encourages its readers to identify as a member of the multitude. On this point see Nealon (2009, 41): "Though [Hardt and Negri] caution that this socialization does not mean that all struggles are alike, or that all exploitation is equally intense, their stance clearly makes room for the affect-workers of the northern literary academy to imagine themselves in alliance with the exploited of the global south."

The left melodrama of both analyses places its readers as victims of the horrifying forces they depict, and thus as harbingers for a new emancipatory project. The optimistic analysis and melodramatic rhetoric of Hardt and Negri's books have captured public imagination, reaching across academic audiences to a broader public readership thirsting for social change in the wake of neoliberal globalization. Yet Hardt and Negri's narrative of victimization and heroism, description of a "single power" as the agent of oppression and prophetic over-coming of social suffering function like Agamben's analysis to deaden the dynamics of geopolitical landscape. Their analytic frame tidies the messiness, confusions and contingencies of various forms of political life, narrows what formations of power and politics can be understood within its terms, and revivifies the promise in the *Manifesto* that emancipation from domination is imminent. The aim of *Multitude,* like the aim of the *Manifesto*, is in part to mobilize the multitude as a collective historical force fighting contemporary empire, but, as Terrell Carver describes it, "the enterprise as a whole is much more about updating than it is about announcing anything radically new to the world, as Marx and Engels pointedly did" (Carver 2006, 352). The authors' argument becomes, as Timothy Brennan states, "everything for new-ness provided newness is polite enough to appear in familiar forms" (Brennan 2005, 204).

Hardt and Negri's melodrama is thus an expression of melancholy because of how its structure is organized by loss. *Empire* demonstrates a form of political analysis too rooted in the disavowed loss of past promises of revolutionary emancipation to fully grasp the newness of the present. Melodramatic genre forms often harbor a backward focus, in that their critiques of injustice stem from a desire to recapture an idyllic lost past, rather than to postulate a new and unknowable future (Brooks 1995). The injury that jumpstarts melodramatic narratives often marks the loss of a past state of virtue that will be recaptured by righting the victim's injury and re-establishing a prior state of moral rightness. Melodramas aim to reestablish a virtuous world that was seemingly destroyed by villainy, in which goodness, rightness and truth are easily identifiable and ever-present (Anker, 2014). This is the lost promise that left melodrama aims to recover. Referring to melodrama's backward gaze, film scholar Christine Gledhill contends that

melodrama's challenge lies not in confronting how things are, but rather in asserting how things ought to be. But since it operates within the frameworks of the present social order, melodrama conceives "the promise of human life" not as a revolutionary future, but as a return to a "golden past": less how things ought to be then how they should have been. (Gledhill 1988, 21)

For Gledhill, melodramas often dramatize the forces of revolution but from within the boundary of the dominant social/economic/political order in which they are deployed. In this sense, melodramatic idealizations of the past eventually recoil social critique and reassert the *status quo*. Brennan captures this dynamic in the quote above, in how *Empire*'s premise of radical transformation in the future looks suspiciously like nineteenth-century revolutionary promise in the *Manifesto*.

Melodramas in *Empire* and *Multitude* incorporate the emancipatory guarantee of the *Manifesto*, while refusing to evaluate the methods, promises and style it uses to secure that guarantee. Indeed, their melancholy melodrama may even deaden the social critique in the *Manifesto* by turning its forceful analysis into the empty papier-mâché fist that Benjamin so feared. Though they take into account the historic particularities of contemporary globalization, current political events and recent identity politics, *Empire* and *Multitude* still search for a past ideal to ground their vision of the future. Using the *Manifesto* as that ideal, they put forth immanent revolution, the moral virtue of their protagonists/ readers, clear lines of social accountability and, as John Brenkman puts it, a "root thesis" (Brenkman 2007, 66), a common aim in Marxian theory to find a root cause that carries explanatory power for all social ills. The lost ideal, in these texts, is therefore less the possibility of freedom or the *Manifesto per se*, than the guarantee that emancipation is imminent and that moral virtue is necessarily conferred upon those who desire it.

It is important to note that melodrama *in* the *Manifesto* operates differently from the melancholic appropriation *of* the *Manifesto* in two ways. First, the sufferers in the melodramatic story are not free of responsibility for creating or overcoming injustice. The agency of heroic emancipation is in a complex relationship to teleology: revolution is forthcoming but requires the action of the workers and the communist party. The overcoming of capital is both inevitable and yet must be nourished by collective political action. Both the weapons that will destroy capitalism and the people who wield them are called into being by capitalist forces. While the final source of emancipation is not fully worked out in the *Manifesto*, or perhaps it is more accurate to say that the process of emancipation is *purposely* ambiguous and multifaceted, it still relies in part upon the agency of the dispossessed and the communist party. After all, the bourgeoisie does not provide its own grave, but instead "its own grave-*diggers*" (CM 246, emphasis added).

Second, the analysis in the *Manifesto*, unlike left melodrama, is not motivated by loss. Marx and Engels uproot melodrama's conventional backward-looking inspiration and forcibly turn its focus forward, to an unknown and unknowable future. The frustration and excitement of the text, indeed its necessity, is that it intentionally does not flesh out what a non-bourgeois, communist, post-revolutionary future will look like. For Marx and Engels, any concrete description of the future would inevitably be colored by the framework of the present, and thus would diminish the possibility of motivating truly radical change. As Benjamin noted of Marx and Engels, in not charting the future, therefore, they choose not to limit its transformative possibilities (Benjamin 1968). This is not to say that Marx and Engels understand the future to have limitless possibility, but that they make a strategic effort not to offer a systematic vision of the post-revolutionary future. Gledhill suggests that most melodramas are motivated by a normative vision of the past that often serves to structure and limit future visions (Gledhill 1987). Marx and Engels, by contrast, refuse to posit an ideal past that can be recaptured. They begin the text by interpreting history through cycles of violence that staunch nostalgia for any past epoch. Instead, the *Manifesto* only gestures to the eventual dissolution of economic inequality, and allows the vision of the future to be open-ended, unconstrained by the limited imaginaries of the past that shape the present.

This chapter reads melodrama in the *Manifesto* in order to draw out why melodrama may appeal to certain segments of contemporary political theory as a mode of analysis. There are certainly examples of contemporary critical theory that challenge left melancholy. They include political critique that avows the loss of moral righteousness and sees it as mark of strength that can engender innovative and vital political diagnoses, and work that emphasizes the tragic dimension of politics, highlighting the inescapable losses, and losers, inherent to all forms of political inquiry and collective self-governance. It includes, among many others, Wolin (2008), Connolly (1995), Johnston (2007), Brown (2001), Kaufman-Osborn (2008), Butler (2004), Gilroy (2006) and Borradori (2004). These modes of political theory work through the problem of melancholy because they explicitly avow responsibility, loss or a refusal of self-purity as starting conditions for critical interrogation.

Of course, reading the *Manifesto* as melodrama could not exhaust the varied cultural modes and rhetorical devices that structure its logic and shape its worldwide effects; to claim the *Manifesto* as fully explainable in this way would be its own form of melodrama. Much of the text does not conform to melodramatic conventions, and even disrupts its melodramatic elements: its forward-looking vision, its refusal to ground critique in the loss of a past ideal, its ambiguity in detailing the agency of heroic emancipation and the proletariat's complex relation to overcoming the villainy of capital – as both its conqueror and inheritor – all disrupt conventional melodramatic tropes. The *Manifesto* is thus *not* a melancholic text, and refuses to generate a lost past ideal as a model for the future. Yet the current re-uptake of its melodrama works in this way. The melancholic appropriation of the melodramatic style of the *Manifesto* functions to disavow – by holding on to – the failed guarantee of imminent freedom, and also to reassure the contemporary critical theorists of their moral rightness in the face of the left's weakness and defeats in an neoliberal and late-capitalist era. While this certainly does not mean that contemporary thinkers should refuse the inspiration, the message or the import of the *Manifesto*, it suggests that melancholic incorporation of the melodramatic tenets of the *Manifesto* limits the critical salience of contemporary critical theory in its attempts to scrutinize the violence of empire, the unaccountable effects of state and corporate power and the intensifying administration of human life.

REFERENCES

Agamben, Giorgio. 1998. *Homo Sacer: Sovereign Power and Bare Life*. Trans. Daniel Heller-Roazen. Stanford, CA: Stanford University Press.
Agamben, Giorgio. 2005. *States of Exception*. Trans. Kevin Attell. Chicago, IL: University of Chicago Press.

Anker, Elisabeth. 2005. "Villains, Victim and Heroes: Melodrama, Media and 9/11." *Journal of Communication.* 55(1): 22–37.

Anker, Elisabeth. 2014. *Orgies of Feeling: Melodrama and the Politics of Freedom.* Durham, NC: Duke University Press.

Benjamin, Walter. 1968. "Theses on the Philosophy of History." In *Illuminations*, trans. Harry Zohn. New York: Schocken, 253–264.

Benjamin, Walter. 2003. *The Origin of German Tragic Drama.* Trans. John Osborne. London: Verso.

Benjamin, Walter. 2005. "Left-Wing Melancholy." In *Walter Benjamin: Selected Writings*, eds. Howard Eiland and Michael Jennings, vol. 2, Pt. 1. Cambridge, MA: Harvard University Press, 423–427.

Bennett, Jane, and Michael J. Shapiro. 2002. "Introduction." In *The Politics of Moralizing*, eds. Jane Bennett and Michael J. Shapiro. London: Routledge, 1–10.

Borradori, Giovanna. 2004. *Philosophy in a Time of Terror: Dialogues with Jürgen Habermas and Jacques Derrida.* New York: Columbia University Press.

Brenkman, John. 2007. *Cultural Contradictions of Democracy: Political Thought since September 11.* Princeton, NJ: Princeton University Press.

Brennan, Timothy. 2005. *Wars of Position: Cultural Politics of Left and Right.* New York: Columbia University Press.

Brooks, Peter. 1995. *The Melodramatic Imagination: Balzac, Henry James, Melodrama and the Mode of Excess.* New Haven, CT: Yale University Press.

Brown, Wendy. 1999. "Resisting Left Melancholy." *Boundary 2* 26(3): 19–27.

Brown, Wendy. 2001. *Politics Out Of History.* Princeton, NJ: Princeton University Press.

Buckley, Matthew. 2006. *Tragedy Walks the Streets: The French Revolution in the Making of Modern Drama.* Baltimore, MD: Johns Hopkins University Press.

Butler, Judith. 1997. *The Psychic Life of Power: Essays in Subjection.* Stanford, CA: Stanford University Press.

Butler, Judith. 2004. *Precarious Life: The Powers of Mourning and Violence.* London: Verso.

Carver, Terrell. 1999. "The Engels-Marx Question." In *Engels after Marx*, eds. Manfred B. Steger and Terrell Carver. University Park, PA: Pennsylvania State University Press, 17–36.

Carver, Terrell. 2006. "Less Than Full Marx ..." *Political Theory* 34(3): 351–356.

Connolly, William E. 1995. *The Ethos of Pluralization.* Minneapolis, MN: University of Minnesota Press.

Elsaesser, Thomas. 1987. In *Home is Where the Heart Is: Melodrama and the Woman's Film*, ed. Christine Gledhill. London: British Film Institute, 43–69.

Freud, Sigmund. 1959 [1917]. "Mourning and Melancholia." In *Collected Papers*, vol. 4, trans. Joan Rivière. New York: Basic Books, 152–170.

Freud, Sigmund. 1990. *Group Psychology and Analysis of the Ego 1922.* Trans. James Strachey. New York: W.W. Norton.

Gaines, Jane. 1996. "The Melos in Marxist Theory." In *The Hidden Foundation: Cinema and the Question of Class*, eds. David James and Rick Berg. Minneapolis, MN: University of Minnesota Press, 56–71.

Gerould, Daniel. 1994. "Melodrama and Revolution." In *Melodrama: Stage, Picture, Screen*, eds. Jacky Bratton, Jim Cook, and Christine Gledhil. London: British Film Institute, 185–198.

Gilroy, Paul. 2006. *Postcolonial Melancholia.* New York: Columbia University Press.

Gledhill, Christine. 1987. "The Melodramatic Field: An Investigation." In Christine Gledhill, *Home is Where the Heart Is: Studies in Melodrama and the Woman's Film.* London: British Film Institute, 5–39.

Hall, Stuart. 1988. *Hard Road to Renewal: Thatcherism and Crisis of the Left.* London: Verso.

Hardt, Michael, and Antonio Negri. 2001. *Empire.* Cambridge, MA: Harvard University Press.

Hardt, Michael, and Antonio Negri. 2004. *Multitude.* Cambridge, MA: Harvard University Press.

Johnston, Steven. 2007. *The Truth about Patriotism.* Durham, NC: Duke University Press.

Kaufman-Osborn, Timothy. 2008. "We Are All Torturers Now: Accountability after Abu-Ghraib." *Theory and Event* 11(2).

Löwith, Karl. 1993. *Max Weber and Karl Marx.* London: Routledge.

Mulvey, Laura. 2009. *Visual and Other Pleasures.* New York: Palgrave Macmillan.

Neale, Steve. 1993. "Melo Talk: On the Meaning and Use of the Term 'Melodrama' in the American Trade Press." *The Velvet Light Trap.* 32: 66–89.

Nealon, Chris. 2009. "Reading on the Left." *Representations* 108: 22–50.

Pryzbos, Julia, and Daniel Gerould. 1980. "Melodrama in the Soviet Theater." In *Melodrama*, ed. Daniel Gerould. New York: New York Literary Forum 7, 75–92.

Rousseau, Jean Jacques. 1990 [1774]. "Lettre à M. Burney, sur la Musique, avec Fragments d' Observations sur Alceste." In *Collected Writings of Rousseau*, vol. 7, ed. Roger Masters. Dartmouth, NH: Dartmouth College, 491–505.

Schmitt, Carl. 1996. *The Concept of the Political.* Trans. George Schwab. Chicago, IL: University of Chicago Press.

Sypher, Wylie. 1948. "The Aesthetic of Revolution: The Marxist Melodrama." *Kenyon Review* 10(3): 431–441.

Williams, Linda. 1998. "Melodrama Revised." In *Refiguring Film Genres*, ed. Nicke Browne. Berkeley, CA: University of California Press, 42–88.

Williams, Linda. 2001. *Playing the Race Card: Melodramas of Black and White from Uncle Tom to OJ Simpson.* Princeton, NJ: Princeton University Press.

Wolin, Sheldon. 2004. *Politics and Vision: Continuity and Innovation in Western Political Thought, expanded edn.* Princeton, NJ: Princeton University Press.

Wolin, Sheldon. 2008. *Democracy Incorporated: Managed Democracy and the Specter of Inverted Totalitarianism.* Princeton, NJ: Princeton University Press.

Žižek, Slavoj. 2001. "Have Michael Hardt and Antonio Negri Rewritten the Communist Manifesto for the Twenty-First Century?" *Rethinking Marxism* 13(3–4), 190–198.

PART IV

THE TEXT IN ENGLISH TRANSLATION

Manifesto of the Communist Party (1848)[1]
Translated from the first edition by Terrell Carver (1996)

A spectre stalks the land of Europe – the spectre of communism. The powers that be – Pope and Tsar, Metternich and Guizot, French Radicals and German police – are in holy alliance for a witchhunt.

Where is the opposition that has not been smeared as communistic by its enemies in government? Where is the opposition that has not retaliated by slandering more progressive groups and reactionary opponents alike with the stigma of communism?

Two things follow from this fact.

I. Communism is already recognised as a force by all the European powers.

II. It is high time for communists to lay before the world their perspectives, their goals, their principles, and to counterpose to the horror stories of communism a manifesto of the party itself.

For this purpose communists of various nationalities have gathered together in London and have drawn up the following manifesto, for publication in English, French, German, Italian, Flemish and Danish.

I. BOURGEOIS AND PROLETARIANS

The history of all society up to now is the history of class struggles.

Freeman and slave, patrician and plebeian, lord and serf, guildmaster and journeyman, in short, oppressor and oppressed stood in continual conflict with one another, conducting an unbroken, now hidden, now open struggle, a struggle that finished each time with a revolutionary transformation of society as a whole, or with the common demise of the contending classes.

In earlier epochs of history we find almost everywhere a comprehensive division of society into different orders, a multifarious gradation of social rank. In ancient Rome we have patricians, knights, plebeians, slaves; in the middle ages feudal lords, vassals, guildmasters, journeymen, serfs, and again in almost all of these classes further fine gradations.

Modern bourgeois society, which arose from the demise of feudal society, has not transcended class conflict. It has merely established new classes, new conditions of oppression, new forms of struggle in place of the old.

Our epoch, the epoch of the bourgeoisie, is distinguished by the fact that it has simplified class conflict. Society as a whole is tending to split into two great hostile encampments, into two great classes directly and mutually opposed – bourgeoisie and proletariat.

From the serfs of the Middle Ages arose the petty traders of the first towns; from this class of petty traders the first elements of the bourgeoisie developed.

The discovery of America and the voyages round Africa provided fresh territory for the rising bourgeoisie. The East Indian and Chinese market, the colonisation of America, the colonial trade, the general increase in the means of exchange and of commodities, all gave to commerce, to sea transport, to industry a boost such as never before, hence quick development to the revolutionary element in a crumbling feudal society.

The feudal or guild system in industry could no longer satisfy the increasing demand from new markets. Small-scale manufacture took its place. The guildmasters were squeezed out by the middle ranks in industry; the division of labour between different guild corporations gave way to the division of labour within the individual workshop itself.

But markets were ever growing and demand ever rising. Even small-scale manufacture no longer sufficed to supply them. So steam power and machinery revolutionised industrial production. In place of small-scale manufacture came modern large-scale industry, in place of the middle ranks of industry came industrial millionaires, the generals of whole industrial armies, the modern bourgeois.

Large-scale industry has established a world market, for which the discovery of America prepared the way. The world market has given an immeasurable stimulus to the development of trade, sea-transport and land communications. This development has produced in turn an expansion of industry, and just as industry, commerce, sea-trade and railways have expanded, so the bourgeoisie has developed, increased its capital, and pushed into the background all pre-existing classes from the Middle Ages onwards.

So we see how the modern bourgeoisie is itself the product of a long process of development, a series of revolutions in the modes of production and exchange.

Each of these stages of development of the bourgeoisie was accompanied by a corresponding political advance. From an oppressed class under the rule of feudal lords, to armed and self-administering associations within the medieval city, here an independent urban republic, there a third estate taxable by the monarchy, then in the era of small-scale manufacture a counterweight to the nobility in the estates-system or in an absolute monarchy, in general the mainstay of the great monarchies, the bourgeoisie – with the establishment of large-scale industry and the world market – has finally gained exclusive political control through the modern representative state. The power of the modern state is merely a device for administering the common affairs of the whole bourgeois class.

The bourgeoisie has played a highly revolutionary role in history.

Where it has come to power the bourgeoisie has obliterated all relations that were feudal, patriarchal, idyllic. It has pitilessly severed the motley bonds of feudalism that joined men to their natural superiors, and has left intact no other bond between one man and another than naked self-interest, unfeeling 'hard cash'. It has drowned the ecstasies of religious fervour, of zealous chivalry, of philistine sentiment in the icy waters of egoistic calculation. It has resolved personal worth into exchange-value, and in place of countless attested and hard-won freedoms it has established a single freedom – conscienceless free trade. In a word, for exploitation cloaked by religious and political illusions, it has substituted open, unashamed, direct, brutal exploitation.

The bourgeoisie has stripped the sanctity from all professions that were hitherto honourable and regarded with reverence. It has transformed the doctor, the lawyer, the priest, the poet, the man of science into its paid workforce.

The bourgeoisie has torn the pathetic veil of sentiment from family relations and reduced them to purely monetary ones.

The bourgeoisie has revealed how the brutal exercise of power, which reactionaries admire so much in the middle ages, was suitably complemented by the dullest indolence. Uniquely it has demonstrated what human activity can accomplish. It has executed marvels quite different from Egyptian pyramids, Roman aqueducts and Gothic cathedrals; it has carried out expeditions quite different from barbarian invasions and crusades.

The bourgeoisie cannot exist without continually revolutionising the instruments of production, hence the relations of production, and therefore social relations as a whole. By contrast the first condition of existence of all earlier manufacturing classes was the unaltered maintenance of the old mode of production. The continual transformation of production, the uninterrupted convulsion of all social conditions, a perpetual uncertainty and motion distinguish the epoch of the bourgeoisie from all earlier ones. All the settled, age-old relations with their train of time-honoured preconceptions and viewpoints are dissolved; all newly formed ones become outmoded before they can ossify. Everything feudal and fixed goes up in smoke, everything sacred is profaned, and men are finally forced to take a down-to-earth view of their circumstances, their multifarious relationships.

The need for a constantly expanding outlet for their products pursues the bourgeoisie over the whole world. It must get a foothold everywhere, settle everywhere, establish connections everywhere.

Through the exploitation of the world market the bourgeoisie has made the production and consumption of all countries cosmopolitan. It has pulled the national basis of industry right out from under the reactionaries, to their consternation. Long-established national industries have been destroyed and are still being destroyed daily. They are being displaced by new industries – the introduction of which becomes a life-and-death question for all civilised nations – industries that no longer work up indigenous raw materials but use raw materials from the ends of the earth, industries whose products are consumed not only in the country of origin but in every part of the world. In place of the old needs satisfied by home production we have new ones which demand the products of the most distant lands and climes for their satisfaction. In place of the old local and national self-sufficiency and isolation we have a universal commerce, a universal dependence of nations on one another. As in the production of material things, so also with intellectual production. The intellectual creations of individual nations become common currency. National partiality and narrowness become more and more impossible, and from the many national and local literatures a world literature arises.

Through rapid improvement in the instruments of production, through limitless ease of communication, the bourgeoisie drags all nations, even the most primitive ones, into civilisation. Cut-price commodities are the heavy artillery with which it batters down all Chinese walls, with which it forces undeveloped societies to abandon even the most intense xenophobia. It forces all nations to adopt the bourgeois mode of production or go under; it forces them to introduce so-called civilisation amongst themselves, i.e. to become bourgeois. In a phrase, it creates a world in its own image.

The bourgeoisie has subjected the country to the rule of the town. It has created enormous cities, vastly inflated the urban population as opposed to the rural, and so rescued a significant part of the population from the idiocy of living on the land. Just as it has made the country dependent on the town, so it has made the undeveloped and semi-developed nations dependent on the civilised ones, peasant societies dependent on bourgeois societies, the East on the West.

Increasingly the bourgeoisie is overcoming the dispersal of the means of production, of landed property and of the population. It has agglomerated the population, centralised the means of production, and concentrated property in a few hands. The necessary consequence of this was political centralisation. Provinces that were independent or scarcely even confederated, with different interests, laws, governments and taxes, were forced together into one nation, one government, one legal system, one class interest nationally, one customs zone.

In scarcely one hundred years of class rule the bourgeoisie has created more massive and more colossal forces of production than have all preceding generations put together. The harnessing of natural forces, machinery, the application of chemistry to industry and agriculture, steamships, railways, the telegraph, clearance of whole continents for cultivation, canalisation of rivers, whole populations conjured up from the ground – what earlier century foresaw that such productive powers slumbered in the bosom of social labour.

This is what we have seen so far: the means of production and trade that formed the basis of bourgeois development were generated in feudal society. At a certain level of development of these means of production and trade, the relations in which feudal society produced and exchanged, the feudal organisation of agriculture and small-scale manufacture, in a word feudal property relations, no longer corresponded to the forces of production already developed. They impeded production instead of advancing it. They became just so many fetters. They had to be sprung open, they were sprung open.

In their place came free competition along with a complementary social and political constitution, the economic and political rule of the bourgeois class.

A similar movement is going on before our very eyes. The bourgeois relations of production and trade, bourgeois property relations, modern bourgeois society, which has conjured up such powerful means of production and trade, resembles the sorcerer who could no longer control the unearthly powers he had summoned forth. For decades the history of industry and commerce has been but the history of the revolt of modern productive forces against modern relations of production, against property relations that are essential for the bourgeoisie and its rule. It suffices to mention the commercial crises, returning periodically with ever increasing severity, that place the very existence of bourgeois society in question. In these crises a large portion of the current product as well as previously generated forces of production are regularly destroyed. During these crises an epidemic breaks out in society, one which would seem a paradox to all earlier epochs – the epidemic of overproduction. Society is suddenly thrust back into a condition of temporary barbarism; a famine, a general war of annihilation appears to have cut off all means of life; industry and commerce appear to be destroyed, and why? Because there is too much civilisation, too many goods, too much industry, too much commerce. The forces of production available to society no longer serve for the advancement of bourgeois civilisation and the bourgeois relations of property; on the contrary, the forces of production have become too powerful for these relations, they are impeded by them, and as soon as they overturn this impediment, they bring the whole of bourgeois society into disorder and endanger the existence of bourgeois property. Bourgeois relations have become too narrow to encompass the wealth they produce. – And how does the bourgeoisie surmount these crises? On the one hand through the enforced destruction of a mass of productive forces; on the other through the capture of new markets and a more thoroughgoing exploitation of old ones. How exactly? By preparing more comprehensive and devastating crises and diminishing the means for preventing them.

The weapons used by the bourgeoisie to strike down feudalism are now turned against the bourgeoisie itself.

But the bourgeoisie has not only forged the weapons which bring it death; it has also produced the men who will wield these weapons – modern workers, *proletarians*.

As the bourgeoisie, i.e. capital develops, so in direct proportion does the proletariat, the class of modern workers who live only so long as they find work, and who find work only so long as their labour increases capital. These workers, who must sell themselves piecemeal, are a commodity like any other article of commerce and equally exposed to all the vicissitudes of competition, to all the fluctuations of the market.

Because of the extensive use of machinery and the division of labour, the work of the proletarians has lost all the characteristics of autonomy and hence all attraction for the workers. The worker becomes a mere appendage to the machine, and only the simplest, most monotonous, most reflex-like manual motion is required. The costs occasioned by the worker are limited almost entirely to the subsistence which he requires for his maintenance and the reproduction of his race. The price of a commodity, and therefore of labour, is equal to its costs of production. As the repulsiveness of a task increases, so the wage declines proportionately. Moreover as machinery and the division of labour become more widespread, the amount of work rises proportionately, whether through lengthening working-hours, or increasing the work demanded in a given time, or accelerating the speed of machines, etc.

Modern industry has transformed the small workshop of the patriarchal master craftsman into the huge factory of the industrial capitalist. Workers, pressed together *en masse* in a factory, are organised like an army. They become the common foot soldiers of industry under the command of a full hierarchy of officers and commanders. They are not only the chattel servants of the bourgeois class and the bourgeois state, they are hourly and daily enslaved by the machine, by the overseer, and above all by the individual bourgeois manufacturer himself. The more openly this despotism proclaims gain to be its ultimate aim, the more petty, hateful and embittering it is.

As manual work requires fewer skills and less exertion, that is, the more modern industry has developed, so the labour of men is more and more displaced by that of women. Differences of age and sex have no social validity any more for the working class. They are merely instruments of labour which cost more or less according to age and sex.

Once the exploitation of the worker by the factory owner comes to an end, he receives his wages in cash, and other sections of the bourgeoisie beset him in turn, the landlord, the shopkeeper, the pawnbroker, etc.

The lower middle classes, small workshop proprietors, merchants and rentiers, tradesmen and yeoman farmers of the present, all these classes will descend into the proletariat, in part because their small capital is not sufficient for the scale of large industry and so succumbs to the competition of larger capitals, in part because their skills are devalued by the new modes of production. There are recruits to the proletariat from all classes in the population.

The proletariat goes through various stages of development. Its struggle with the bourgeoisie begins with its very existence.

At the outset there are struggles mounted by individual workers, then the workers in a factory, then workers in one trade at a particular site, against the individual bourgeois who exploits them directly. They direct their assaults not only against the bourgeois relations of production but against the instruments of production themselves; they destroy imported commodities that compete with theirs, they smash up machines, they put factories to the torch, they seek to regain the lost status of the medieval workman.

At this stage the workers form a mass dispersed over the whole country and disunited through competition. The purpose behind their own unification is not yet a massive organisation of workers, rather this is a consequence of the unity of the bourgeoisie, which must set the whole proletariat in motion in order to achieve its own political purposes, and for the moment it can do so. At this stage the proletariat does not struggle against its enemies, but rather against the enemies of its enemies – the remnants of absolute monarchy, the great land-owners, the non-industrial bourgeoisie, the small traders. The whole movement of history is concentrated in the hands of the bourgeoisie; every victory so gained is a victory for the bourgeoisie.

But with the development of industry the proletariat not only increases; it is forced together in greater masses, its power grows and it feels it more. The interests, the circumstances of life within the proletariat become ever more similar, while machinery increasingly obliterates different types of labour and forces wages down to an almost equally low level. The increasing competition of the bourgeois amongst themselves and the crises emerging therefrom make the worker's wage ever more fluctuating; the incessant improvements in machinery, which develops ever more quickly, makes their whole livelihood ever more uncertain; the confrontations between individual workers and individual bourgeois increasingly take on the character of confrontations between two classes. As a result the workers begin to form coalitions against the bourgeois; they unite in order to protect their wages. They establish continuing associations themselves in order to make provision in advance for these occasional rebellions. Here and there the struggle breaks out into riots.

From time to time the workers are victorious, but only temporarily. The real result of their battles is not some immediate success but a unity amongst workers that gains ever more ground. This is furthered by improved communications, which are generated by large-scale industry, and which put workers from different localities in touch with one another. But this unity is all that is needed to centralise the many local struggles of a generally similar character into a national struggle, a class struggle. Every class struggle, however, is a political struggle. And the unity, which took the burghers of the Middle Ages centuries with their country lanes, is being accomplished by modern proletarians in a few years with railways.

This organisation of the proletarians into a class, and hence into a political party, is disrupted time and again by competition amongst the workers themselves. But it always rises up again, stronger, more resolute, more powerful. It compels the recognition of workers' individual interests in legal form by taking advantage of divisions within the bourgeoisie itself. Thus the Ten Hours Bill in England was passed.

On the whole, clashes within the old society advance the development of the proletariat in many ways. The bourgeoisie becomes involved in a constant battle; at first against the aristocracy; later against a part of the bourgeoisie itself, those whose interests contradict the advance of industry; and always against the bourgeoisie in foreign countries. In all these struggles it finds it necessary to appeal to the proletariat, to enlist its aid, and thus to draw it into political action. Hence it supplies the proletariat with its own materials for development, i.e. weapons for use against the bourgeoisie itself.

Moreover, as we have seen, there are whole sections of the ruling class dumped into the proletariat as a result of the advance of industry, or at least threatened in their essential circumstances. These also transmit to the proletariat a mass of materials for self-development.

Finally at the time when the class struggle comes to a head, the process of dissolution within the ruling class, within the whole of the old society, takes on such a violent and striking character that a part of the ruling class renounces its role and commits itself to the revolutionary class, the class that holds the future in its hands. As in the past when a part of the nobility went over to the bourgeoisie, so now a part of the bourgeoisie goes over to the proletariat, in particular, a part of the bourgeois ideologists who have worked out a theoretical understanding of the whole historical development.

Of all the classes which today oppose the bourgeoisie, the only truly revolutionary class is the proletariat. The other classes come to the fore and then decline to extinction with large-scale industry, whereas the proletariat is its particular product.

The middle classes, the small manufacturer, the shopkeeper, the artisan, the peasant, they all struggle against the bourgeoisie in order to secure their existence as middle classes against economic ruin. Hence they are not revolutionary, but conservative. Moreover they are reactionary for they seek to turn back the tide of history. If they are revolutionary, it is because they recognise that they face a descent into the proletariat, so they defend their future interests, not just their present ones, and they abandon their own standpoint in order to adopt that of the proletariat.

The lumpen proletariat, that passive dung heap of the lowest levels of the old society, is flung into action here and there by the proletarian revolution, though by its whole situation in life it will be readier to sell itself to reactionary intrigues.

The circumstances necessary for the old society to exist are already abolished in the circumstances of the proletariat. The proletarian is without property; his relationship to his wife and children no longer has anything in common with bourgeois family relations; modern industrial labour, modern servitude to capital, which is the same in England as in France or America as in Germany, has stripped him of any all national characteristics. The law, morality, religion, are for him so many bourgeois prejudices that hide just as many bourgeois interests.

Up to now all the classes that seized power for themselves have sought to assure their hard-won position by subjecting the whole of society to their own economic terms. The proletarians can only seize the productive powers of society by abolishing their own former mode of appropriation and hence all former modes of appropriation. The proletarians have nothing of their own to secure; they will have to destroy all former private security and private assurances.

All previous movements were movements of minorities or in the interest of minorities. The proletarian movement is the independent movement of the vast majority in the interests of that vast majority. The proletariat, the lowest stratum of present-day society, cannot lift itself up, cannot raise itself up, without flinging into the air the whole superstructure of social strata which form the establishment.

The struggle of the proletariat against the bourgeoisie is at the outset a national one in form, although not in content. Naturally the proletariat of each country must first finish off its own bourgeoisie.

In outlining phases in the development of the proletariat in the most general terms, we traced the more or less hidden civil war within existing society up to the point where it breaks out into open revolution, and the proletariat establishes its rule through the forcible overthrow of the bourgeoisie.

As we have seen, all society up to now has been based on conflict between oppressing and oppressed classes. But for a class to be oppressed, there must be assured conditions within which it can at least scrape a slave-like existence. The serf rose to be a member of the medieval commune during the period of serfdom just as the petty trader rose to bourgeois status under the yoke of feudal absolutism. The modern worker, by contrast, instead of advancing with industrial progress, sinks ever deeper beneath the circumstances of his own class. The worker becomes a pauper, and pauperism develops more quickly than population and wealth. It should now be obvious that the bourgeoisie is incapable of continuing as the ruling class of society and of enforcing its own conditions of life on society as sovereign law. It is incapable of ruling because it is incapable of assuring its slave any kind of existence within his slavery, because it is forced to let him sink into a condition where it must feed him, instead of being fed by him. Society cannot live under it any longer, i.e. its life is no longer compatible with society itself.

The essential condition for the existence and for the rule of the bourgeois class is the accumulation of wealth in the hands of private individuals, the formation and expansion of capital, and the essential condition for capital is wage-labour. Wage-labour rests exclusively on the competition of workers amongst themselves. Industrial progress, involuntarily and irresistibly promoted by the bourgeoisie, replaces the isolation of the workers due to competition with their revolutionary unity due to close association. The development of

large-scale industry pulls from under the feet of the bourgeoisie the very foundations on which they produce goods and appropriate them. Above all it
produces its own gravediggers. Its downfall and the victory of the proletariat
are equally unavoidable.

II. PROLETARIANS AND COMMUNISTS

What is the general relation between communists and proletarians?

Communists are not a separate party as opposed to other workers' parties.

They have no interests apart from those of the whole proletariat.

They do not declare any special principles for shaping the proletarian
movement.

Communists are distinguished from the rest of the proletarian parties only
in that, on the one hand, in the various national struggles of the proletarians
they raise and highlight the common interests of the whole proletariat, independent of nationality, and on the other hand, in the various stages of development through which the struggle between proletariat and bourgeoisie
proceeds, they always represent the interests of the movement as a whole.

Communists are therefore in practice the most resolute and thrusting section
of the working class parties of every country; they have an advantage over the
general mass of the proletariat in terms of a theoretical insight into the conditions, progress and general result of the movement.

The immediate aim of the communists is the same as that of all the other
proletarian parties: formation of the proletariat into a class, overthrow of
bourgeois rule, conquest of political power by the proletariat.

The theoretical propositions of the communists are in no way founded on
ideas or principles invented or discovered by this or that reformist crank.

They merely express in general terms the factual relations of an existing class
struggle, a historical movement that is proceeding under our own eyes. The
abolition of existing property relations is not distinctively communist.

All property relations have been subject to continuous historical change, to
continuous historical variation.

The French revolution, for example, abolished feudal property in favour of
bourgeois property.

What is distinctively communist is not the abolition of property in general
but the abolition of bourgeois property.

But modern bourgeois private property is the final and most complete
expression of the production and appropriation of products which rests on
class conflict, on the exploitation of individuals by others.

In that sense communists can sum up their theory in a single phrase: the
transformation of private property.

We communists have been reproached with wanting to abolish property that
is personally acquired or produced oneself, property that forms the basis of
personal freedom, activity and independence.

Property that is hard won, dearly acquired, well deserved! Are they talking here of petty traders, small farmers and their property, which preceded the bourgeois form? We do not need to abolish it, as the development of industry has abolished it and does so daily.

Or are they talking of modern bourgeois private property?

But does wage-labour, the labour of the proletarian, create property for him? Not at all. It creates capital, i.e. property which exploits wage-labour, which can increase only on condition that it produces new wage-labour to be exploited afresh. Property in its present form develops within the essential conflict between capital and labour. Let us consider both sides of this conflict. To be a capitalist is not just to have a purely personal position in the process of production but a social one.

Capital is a social product and can only be set in motion by an activity common to many members of society, in the last instance only by the activity common to all members of it.

Capital is therefore not a personal power but a social one.

If capital is converted into social property belonging to all members of society, personal property is not therefore converted into social. Only the social character of property is converted. It loses its class character.

Now we come to wage-labour.

The average price of wage-labour is the minimum wage, i.e. the sum total of the means of life necessary for subsistence as a living worker. What the wage-labourer appropriates through his own activity merely suffices to reproduce a bare existence. We want in no way to abolish this personal appropriation of the products of labour used for the reproduction of life itself, an appropriation that leaves no pure surplus that could give power over another's labour. We want instead to transform the miserable character of this appropriation through which the worker merely lives in order to increase capital, and only in so far as it suits the interest of the ruling class.

In bourgeois society living labour is merely a means to increase accumulated labour. In communist society accumulated labour is but a means to broaden, to enrich, to promote the whole life of the worker.

Therefore in bourgeois society the past rules over the present, and in communist society the present over the past. In capitalist society it is capital that is independent and personalised, while the living individual is dependent and depersonalised.

And the bourgeoisie calls the transformation of these relationships the transformation of individuality and freedom! And rightly so. Of course this concerns a transformation of bourgeois individuality, independence and freedom.

Under the current bourgeois relations of production freedom means free trade, freedom to buy and sell.

But if bargaining disappears so does free bargaining. The expression free bargaining, like all the other boasts of freedom by our bourgeoisie, means anything only in contrast to restricted bargaining, in contrast to the suborned

burgher of the middle ages, but not in contrast to the communist transformation of bargaining, the bourgeois relations of production and the bourgeoisie
itself.

It horrifies you that we wish to transform private property. But in your
existing society private property has been transformed for nine-tenths of its
members; it exists precisely in that it does not exist for nine-tenths. You
reproach us for wanting to transform a type of property which presupposes
the propertylessness of the vast majority of society as a necessary condition.

In a word you reproach us for intending to transform your property. That is
exactly what we want.

From the moment that labour can no longer be turned into capital, money,
rent, in short, into a monopolisable power in society, i.e. from the moment that
personal property can no longer be turned into bourgeois property, from that
moment, clearly, the individual person is transformed.

Thus you confess that by a person you understand nothing except the
bourgeois, the bourgeois property-holder. And this person is to be transformed
as well.

Communism deprives no one of the power to appropriate products in
society; it merely removes the power to subjugate the labour of others through
this appropriation.

It has been objected that with the transformation of private property, all
activity will cease and a general idleness will spread.

According to this view bourgeois society ought to have collapsed into idleness long ago; for those who work do not gain and those who gain, do not work.
The whole idea amounts to the tautology that as soon as there is no more
capital, there will be no more wage-labour.

All the objections which are directed at the communist mode of appropriation and production of material products have been extended to the appropriation and production of intellectual products. To the bourgeois the
disappearance of class property denotes the disappearance of production itself,
and in just the same way the disappearance of class-bias in education denotes
the disappearance of education altogether.

The bourgeois regrets the loss of this education, but for the vast majority it is
only training to act as a machine.

But do not argue with us while you judge the abolition of bourgeois property
by your bourgeois conceptions of freedom, education, justice, etc. Your ideas
themselves are products of the relations of bourgeois production and property,
just as your justice is merely the will of your class raised to the status of law, a
will whose content is established in the material circumstances of your class.

The biased conception by which you transform your relations of production
and property from historical relations that emerge in the course of production
into eternal laws of nature and reason is a conception you share with all the
ruling classes that have previously come and gone. What you grasp in the case of

ancient property, what you grasp in the case of feudal property, you will never grasp in the case of bourgeois property.

Transformation of the family! Even the most radical of the radicals flares up at this infamous proposal of the communists.

What is the basis of the contemporary bourgeois family? Capital and private gain. It is completely developed only for the bourgeoisie; but it finds its complement in the enforced dissolution of the family among the proletarians and in public prostitution.

The bourgeois family naturally declines with the decline of its complement, and the two disappear with the disappearance of capital.

Do you object that we want to transform the exploitation of children by their elders? We admit this offence. But, you say, we transform the dearest relations of all when we move child-rearing from the domestic sphere into the social.

And is your education not determined by society as well? Through the social relations with which you are brought up, through the more or less direct or indirect interference of society by means of schools, etc.? Communists did not discover the effect of society on child-rearing; they merely alter its character, rescuing it from the influence of the ruling class.

Bourgeois phrases about the family and child-rearing, about the deeply felt relationship of parent to child, become even more revolting when all proletarian family ties are severed as a consequence of large-scale industry, and children are simply transformed into articles of trade and instruments of labour.

But you communists want to introduce common access to women, protests the whole bourgeoisie in chorus.

The bourgeois sees in his wife a mere instrument of production. He hears that the instruments of production are to be utilised in common and naturally cannot think otherwise than that common use is equally applicable to women.

He does not suspect that the point here is to transform the status of women as mere instruments of production.

Anyway nothing is more laughable than the moralising dismay of our bourgeois concerning the community of women allegedly sanctioned by communists. Communists do not need to introduce the community of women; it has almost always existed.

Our bourgeois, not content with having the wives and daughters of the proletariat at their disposal, not to mention legally sanctioned prostitutes, take the greatest pleasure in reciprocal seduction of married women.

Bourgeois marriage is really the community of married women. At the very most the communists might be reproached for wanting to replace a hidden community of women with a sanctioned, openly avowed community of women. In any case it is self-evident that with the transformation of the current relations of production, the community of women emerging from those relations, i.e. sanctioned and unsanctioned prostitution, will disappear.

Communists have been further criticised for wanting to abolish the nation and nationalities.

Workers have no nation of their own. We cannot take from them what they do not have. Since the proletariat must first of all take political control, raise itself up to be the class of the nation, must constitute the nation itself, it is still nationalistic, even if not at all in the bourgeois sense of the term.

National divisions and conflicts between peoples increasingly disappear with the development of the bourgeoisie, with free trade and the world market, with the uniform character of industrial production and the corresponding circumstances of modern life.

The rule of the proletariat will make them disappear even faster. United action, at least in the civilised countries, is one of the first conditions for freeing the proletariat.

To the degree that the exploitation of one individual by another is transformed, so will the exploitation of one nation by another.

As internal class conflict within a nation declines, so does the hostility of one nation to another.

The denunciations of communism from the religious, philosophical and ideological points of view do not merit detailed discussion.

Does it require a profound insight to grasp that men's presumptions, views and conceptions alter according to their economic circumstances, their social relations, their social existence?

What else does the history of ideas demonstrate than that the products of the intellect are refashioned along with material ones? The ruling ideas of an age were always but the ideas of the ruling class.

In speaking of ideas which revolutionise the whole of society, we merely express the fact that within the old society the elements of a new one have formed, that the dissolution of the old ideas stays in step with the dissolution of the old conditions of life.

When the ancient world was in decline, the ancient religions were conquered by Christianity. When Christian concepts were defeated in the eighteenth century by the ideas of the Enlightenment, feudal society fought a life and death struggle with the then revolutionary bourgeoisie. The ideas of religious freedom and freedom of inquiry merely expressed the rule of free competition in the moral realm.

However, it may be said, religious, moral, philosophical, political and legal ideas, etc. have been modified in the course of historical development. Religion, morality, philosophy, politics, the law are always maintained through these changes.

Besides, there are eternal truths, such as freedom, justice, etc., which are common to all social circumstances. But communism abolishes eternal truths, it abolishes religion and morality, instead of maintaining them, and it therefore contradicts all historical development up to now.

What does this objection amount to? The history of all society up to now was made through class conflicts which took different forms in different epochs.

But whatever form it has taken, the exploitation of one part of society by another is a fact common to all past centuries. Hence it is no wonder that the social consciousness of all the centuries past, in spite of all its multiplicity and varying aspects, takes on certain common forms. These are forms, forms of consciousness, which finally vanish only with the total disappearance of class conflict.

The communist revolution is the most radical break with traditional property relations, so it is no wonder that in its process of development there occurs the most radical break with traditional ideas.

But let us put by the bourgeois objections to communism.

We have seen above that the first step in the workers' revolution is the advancement of the proletariat to ruling class, victory for democracy.

The proletariat will use its political power to strip all capital from the bourgeoisie piece by piece, to centralise all instruments of production in the hands of the state, i.e. the proletariat organised as ruling class, and to increase the total of productive forces as rapidly as possible.

Naturally this can only be effected at first by means of despotic incursions into the rights of private property and into bourgeois relations of production, hence through measures which appear economically inadequate and unsustainable, but which drive the course of development past that stage and are essential means for overturning the mode of production as a whole.

These measures will naturally vary according to the country.

For the most advanced countries the following could be very generally applicable:

1) Expropriation of property in land and investment of rents in state enterprises.
2) A sharply progressive system of taxation.
3) Abolition of inheritance.
4) Confiscation of the property of all emigrants and rebels.
5) Centralisation of credit in the hands of the state through a national bank with public capital and a guaranteed monopoly.
6) Centralisation of all means of transport in the hands of the state.
7) Expansion of nationalised factories, instruments of production, newly cultivated lands and improvement of agriculture according to a common plan.
8) Equal obligation to labour for all, establishment of industrial armies, particularly for agriculture.
9) Managerial unification for agriculture and industry, progressively eliminating the conflicting interests of town and country.
10) Free public education for all children. Elimination of factory work for children in its present form. Associating education with material production, etc.

When in the course of development class distinctions have disappeared, and all production is concentrated in the hands of associated individuals, then the public power loses its political character. Political power in its true sense is the organised power of one class for oppressing another. If the proletariat necessarily unites as a class in its struggle against the bourgeoisie, makes itself into a ruling class through revolution, and as a ruling class forcibly transforms the old relations of production, then it will transform, along with these relations of production, the underlying conditions for class conflict and for classes in general, hence its own supremacy as a class.

In place of the old bourgeois society with its classes and class conflicts there will be an association in which the free development of each is the condition for the free development of all.

III.   SOCIALIST AND COMMUNIST LITERATURE

1)   Reactionary Socialism

a)   *Feudal Socialism*

Because of their historical position the French and English aristocracies had the job of writing pamphlets against modern bourgeois society. In the French revolution of July 1830 and in the English reform movement these aristocracies were once more beset by the hateful upstarts. There could no longer be any question of a serious political struggle. A literary battle was the only thing left. But even in the literary domain the old phrases of the restored monarchy had become impossible. To arouse sympathy the aristocrats had to appear to forego their interests, and to formulate their indictment of the bourgeoisie only in terms of the interests of the exploited working class. Thus they prepared their revenge – daring to sing slanderous songs against their new master and to whisper more or less malign prophecies in his ear.

In this way feudal socialism arose, half lamentation, half lampoon, half echo of the past, half menace of the future, striking the bourgeoisie at its very core through bitter, witty, biting judgements that were always comic because of a total incapacity to grasp the course of modern history.

They waved the proletarian begging bowl order to unite the people under their flag. But as often as the aristocracy succeeded, the people espied the old feudal arms on their hind quarters and deserted with loud and irreverent laughter.

A section of the French legitimists and the Young England movement gave the best exhibition of this spectacle.

When the feudalists point out that their mode of exploitation takes a form different from that of bourgeois exploitation, they still forget that they did their exploiting under wholly different and now superseded circumstances and conditions. When they demonstrate that under their rule the modern proletariat did not exist, they forget that the modern bourgeoisie was a necessary offspring of their social order.

In any case they conceal the reactionary character of their criticisms so little that their main complaint about the bourgeoisie emerges in these terms, that under their regime a class has developed, one that will explode the whole social order.

They berate the bourgeoisie more for creating a revolutionary proletariat than for merely producing a proletariat as such.

In political practice they support all the repressive legislation against the working class, and in ordinary life, in spite of all their inflated talk, they comfort themselves by picking golden apples and by swapping truth, love and honour for speculation in wool, beetroot and spirits.

The parson was always hand in glove with the feudal lord, and clerical socialism was always so with the feudalists.

Nothing is easier than to give to Christian asceticism a socialist tinge. Has not Christianity declaimed against private property, against marriage, against the state? Has it not preached their replacement by charity and poverty, celibacy and mortification of the flesh, monasticism and the organised church? Saintly socialism is but the holy water with which the priest blesses the fulminations of the aristocrat.

b) Petty-bourgeois Socialism

The feudal aristocracy is not the only class that was ruined by the bourgeoisie, not the only class whose conditions of life withered and died in modern bourgeois society. The suburban burghers of the middle ages and the small-holding peasantry were the precursors of the modern bourgeoisie. In the less industrial and commercially developed countries this class still just rubs along next to the rising bourgeoisie.

In countries where modern civilisation has developed, a new petty-bourgeoisie has formed, fluctuating between proletariat and bourgeoisie, and always renewing itself as a complement to bourgeois society, but whose members are continually being dumped into the proletariat as a result of competition, who themselves – as modern industry develops – see the time approaching when they will disappear as an independent part of modern society and will be replaced in trade, in small-scale manufacture, in agriculture by managerial classes and domestic workers.

In countries such as France where the peasant classes make up far more than half the population it was natural for writers who supported the proletariat against the bourgeoisie to use the standards of the petty-bourgeoisie and small peasantry in their criticism of the bourgeois regime and to espouse the workers' party from the standpoint of the petty bourgeoisie. Petty-bourgeois socialism was formed in this way. Sismondi is the high point of this literature not only in France but also in England.

This type of socialism dissected with great perspicuity the conflicts inherent in modern relations of production. It exposed the hypocritical apologetics of economists. It demonstrated incontrovertibly the destructive consequences of the use of machinery and the division of labour, the concentration of capital and of land ownership, the production of surplus goods, crises, the necessary ruin of the small trader and peasant, the poverty of the proletariat, anarchy in production, flagrant disparities in the distribution of wealth, the industrial fight to the death between one nation and another, the dissolution of traditional morality, of traditional family relationships, of traditional national identities.

In its positive programme this type of socialism either wants to restore the traditional means of production and trade, and along with them traditional property relations and traditional society, or it wants to force modern means of production and trade back into the confines of traditional property relations that are now being – and must be – dismantled. In either case it is reactionary and utopian in equal measure.

Guild socialism for artisans and patriarchal relations in agriculture are the last word here.

In its later development this tendency petered out in a pusillanimous hangover.

c) German or True Socialism

The socialist and communist literature of France, which originated within the constraints imposed by the bourgeoisie in power, and which is the literary expression of the struggle against their rule, was imported into Germany at a time when the bourgeoisie had just begun its struggle against feudal absolutism.

German philosophers, semi-philosophers and wordsmiths eagerly occupied themselves with this literature and simply forgot that with the importation of these writings from France, the circumstances of French economic life were not imported into Germany at the same time. Set against German conditions, the French literature lost all immediate practical significance and took on a purely literary cast. That literature could only appear as idle speculation concerning the true society or the realisation of the human essence. Thus for the German philosophers of the eighteenth century the demands of the first French revolution only made sense as demands of 'practical reason' in general, and the public expression of the will of the French revolutionary bourgeoisie signified in their eyes the law of pure will, of will as it had to be, of the truly human will.

The definitive task of the German literati consisted in bringing the new French ideas into line with their traditional philosophical outlook, or rather in appropriating the French ideas for themselves from their own philosophical point of view.

This appropriation took place in the same way that foreign languages are learned, through translation.

It is well known how monks transcribed absurd lives of the Catholic saints over the manuscripts on which the classical works of ancient pagans were inscribed. The German literati reversed this with secular French literature. They write their philosophical nonsense under the original French. For example, under the French critique of monetary relations they wrote 'externalisation of the human essence', under the French critique of the bourgeois state they wrote 'transformation of the reign of abstract generality', etc.

This insertion of their philosophical phrases beneath the French discussions they dubbed 'philosophy of the deed', 'true socialism', 'German science of socialism', 'philosophical foundation of socialism', etc.

The literature of French socialism-communism was thus punctiliously emasculated. And since it ceased in German hands to express the struggle of one class against another, so the German 'true socialist' was conscious of superseding French one-sidedness, of having substituted for true requirements the requirement of truth, for the interests of the proletariat the interests of the human essence – of man in general, of man belonging to no class or to any actuality at all, but to the misty realm of philosophical fantasy.

This German socialism, which pursued its lumbering scholastic exercises so earnestly and solemnly and trumpeted itself so blatantly, gradually lost its pedantic innocence.

The struggle of the German, particularly the Prussian bourgeoisie against feudalism and absolute monarchy, in a word, the liberal movement, grew more earnest.

Thus the 'true socialists' were offered a much sought after opportunity to put forward socialist demands in opposition to current politics, to hurl traditional anathemas against the liberals, against the representative state, against bourgeois competition, bourgeois freedom of the press, bourgeois justice, bourgeois freedom and equality, and to preach to the masses how they had nothing to gain from this bourgeois movement and everything to lose. German socialism forgot at just the right time that French criticism, whose mindless echo it was, itself presupposed modern bourgeois society, along with the material conditions corresponding to it and the complementary political constitution, the very things for which the struggle in Germany was so earnest.

This served the absolutist regimes in Germany, with their following of clergy, schoolmasters, country squires and bureaucrats, as a welcome scarecrow to frighten off the rising bourgeoisie.

This marked a sweet revenge for the bitter whipping and buckshot with which the same regimes belaboured the uprisings of the workers.

Though 'true socialism' formed a weapon in the hands of the governments against the German bourgeoisie, it also represented a reactionary interest directly, the interest of German philistines. In Germany the petty bourgeoisie forms the real social basis of existing circumstances, but it is a relic of the sixteenth century, albeit one that is ever-changing into different forms.

To preserve this class is to preserve existing circumstances in Germany. The industrial and political rule of the bourgeoisie threatens it with certain ruin, on the one hand as a consequence of the concentration of capital, on the other, from the rise of the revolutionary proletariat. 'True socialism' appeared to kill two birds with one stone. It spread like an epidemic.

The gown, worked from speculative cobwebs, embroidered with flowery speeches, saturated with damp, sticky sentiment, this extravagant gown, with which German socialists cover their few scraggy eternal truths, merely increased the sale of their wares to the public.

For its part German socialism recognised its vocation ever more clearly, as the highfalutin representative of petty-bourgeois philistinism.

It proclaimed the German nation to be the model nation and the German petty philistine to be the model man. To his every dirty trick it gave a hidden, higher, socialist interpretation which meant the opposite. It drew the ultimate conclusion when it directly opposed the crudely destructive programme of communism, and announced that it was impartial and above all class struggles. With very few exceptions everything that is ostensibly socialist and communist now circulating in Germany comes from this malodorous and boring domain.

2)   Conservative or Bourgeois Socialism

A part of the bourgeoisie wants to redress *social grievances* in order to assure the maintenance of bourgeois society.

Included in it are economists, philanthropists, humanitarians, do-gooders for the working classes, charity organisers, animal welfare enthusiasts, temperance union workers, two-a-penny reformers of multifarious kinds. This form of bourgeois socialism has been worked up into whole systems.

For example, take Proudhon's *Philosophy of Poverty*.

The socialist bourgeois want the living conditions of modern society without the struggles and dangers necessarily arising from it. They want existing society with the exception of the revolutionary elements bent on destroying it. They want the bourgeoisie without the proletariat. The bourgeoisie naturally views the world in which it rules as the best. Bourgeois socialism works this comforting conception up into a more or less complete system. By requiring the proletariat to realise this system in order to reach a new Jerusalem, bourgeois socialism requires the proletariat to remain in present-day society but to cast off its spiteful conceptions of it.

A second less systematic and more practical form of this socialism sought to discredit every revolutionary movement in the eyes of the working class by proving how only a change in the material relations of life, in economic relations, might be of use to them, not this or that political change. By change in the material relations of life this form of socialism by no means understands the abolition of bourgeois relations of production, which is only possible by revolutionary means, but rather administrative reforms presupposing the present relations of production; hence changing nothing in the relationship of capital and wage-labour, but at best reducing the costs to the bourgeoisie of their political rule and simplifying their state administration.

Bourgeois socialism only reaches a suitable expression when it turns into a mere figure of speech.

Free trade! in the interests of the working class; protective tariffs! in the interests of the working class; prison reform! in the interests of the working class, which is the final, the only sincere word of bourgeois socialism.

Ultimately its socialism consists in maintaining that the bourgeois are bourgeois – in the interests of the working class.

3) Critical-Utopian Socialism and Communism

We are not referring here to the literature which has expressed the demands of the proletariat in all the great modern revolutions (like the writings of Babeuf, etc.).

The first attempts by the proletariat to assert its own class interests directly were made in times of general upheaval, in the period of the overthrow of feudal society; these attempts necessarily foundered on the undeveloped condition of the proletariat itself, as well as on the lack of material conditions for its emancipation, conditions which are only the product of the bourgeois epoch. The revolutionary literature which accompanied these first stirrings of the proletariat is necessarily reactionary in content. It teaches a general asceticism and a crude egalitarianism.

Proper socialist and communist systems, the systems of Saint-Simon, Fourier, Owen, etc., emerged in the first undeveloped period of struggle between proletariat and bourgeoisie which we have outlined above. (See 'Bourgeoisie and Proletariat' [sic].)

The founders of these systems, to be sure, see the conflict between classes as well as the active elements of dissolution in prevailing society itself. But they discern on the side of the proletariat no historical autonomy, no political movement of its own.

Since the development of class conflict proceeds in step with the development of industry, they discover few material conditions for the emancipation of the proletariat, and they search for a social science based on social laws in order to create these conditions.

In place of activity in society they have to introduce their personally invented forms of action, in place of historical conditions for emancipation they have to introduce fantastic ones, in place of the gradually developed organisation of the proletariat into a class they have to introduce a specially contrived organisation of society. The approaching events of world history resolve themselves into propaganda and practical execution of their plans for society.

They are indeed conscious in their plans of generally supporting the interests of the working classes as the class that suffers most. Only from the point of view of the most suffering class does the proletariat exist for them.

The undeveloped form of the class struggle, as well as their own circumstances in life, leads however to the belief that they are far above the conflicting classes. They want to improve the circumstances of all members of society, even the best placed. Hence they continually appeal to the whole of society without distinction, even by preference to the ruling class. Anyone needs but to understand their system in order to recognise it as the best possible plan for the best possible society.

Hence they reject all political action, particularly all revolutionary action; they want to reach their goal by peaceful means and seek through the power of example to pave the way for the new social Gospel through small-scale experiments, which naturally fail.

In a time when the proletariat is still highly undeveloped and hence comprehending its own position in a fantastic way, these fantastic images of future society correspond to its first deeply felt for a general reorganisation of society.

But the socialist and communist writings also consist of critical elements. They attack all the fundamental principles of existing society. Hence they have offered material that is very valuable for the enlightenment of the workers. Their positive proposals concerning future society, e.g. transformation of the conflict of interest between town and country, transformation of the family, of private appropriation, of wage-labour, the proclamation of social harmony, the conversion of the state into a mere agency for administering production – all these proposals merely point towards the end of class conflict which had in fact only just begun to develop, which they only knew in its first formless and undefined stage. Hence these proposals themselves still have only a purely utopian import.

The significance of critical utopian socialism and communism stands in an inverse relationship to historical development. To the extent that the class struggle develops and takes shape, this fantastic transcendence of the class struggle, this fantastic attack on the class struggle, loses all practical worth, all theoretical justification. Though the originators of these systems were revolutionary in many senses, their disciples have in every case formed reactionary sects. They adhere to the original views of their mentors in firm opposition to the historically progressive development of the proletariat. Consequently they seek to dull the class struggle further and to ameliorate conflict. They still dream of an experimental realisation of their social utopias, the establishment of individual phalansteries, the foundation of home colonies, the building of a little Icaria – pocket editions of the new Jerusalem – and to erect all these castles in the air, they must appeal to the philanthropy of the bourgeois heart and purse. Gradually they fall into the category of the reactionary or conservative socialism depicted above, and distinguish themselves only by their more systematic pedantry, fantastic faith in the miraculous effects of their social science.

Hence they are bitterly opposed to all political activity by the workers which could only happen through blind disbelief in the new Gospel.

The Owenites in England oppose the Chartists, the Fourierists in France oppose the *réformistes*.

IV.   RELATION OF COMMUNISTS TO THE VARIOUS OPPOSITION PARTIES

After Section 2 the relation of the communists to the already constituted working-class parties is self-evident, hence their relation to the Chartists in England and the agrarian reformers in North America.

They struggle for the attainment of the immediate aims and interests of the working class, but within the current movement they also represent the future. In France the communists ally themselves to the social-democratic party against the conservative and radical bourgeoisie, without giving up the right to criticise the phrases and illusions flowing from the revolutionary tradition.

In Switzerland they support the radicals without losing sight of the fact that this party consists of contradictory elements, in part of democratic socialists in the French sense, in part of radical bourgeois.

In Poland the communists assist the party which works for an agrarian revolution as a precondition for national emancipation. This is the party which brought the Cracow insurrection of 1846 to life.

In Germany the communist party struggles in common with the bourgeoisie against absolute monarchy, feudal landholding classes and the petty-bourgeoisie as soon as the bourgeois revolution breaks out.

But they never cease for a moment to instil in the workers as clear a consciousness as possible concerning the mortal conflict between bourgeoisie and proletariat, so that German workers may straightaway turn the social and political conditions, which the bourgeoisie must introduce along with its rule, into so many weapons against the bourgeoisie itself, so that after the overthrow of the reactionary classes in Germany, the struggle against the bourgeoisie begins straight away.

Communists direct their attention chiefly to Germany, because Germany is on the eve of a bourgeois revolution, and because it carries out this upheaval under more advanced conditions of European civilisation in general and with a much more developed proletariat than England in the seventeenth century and France in the eighteenth; thus the bourgeois revolution in Germany can be merely the immediate prelude to a proletarian revolution.

In a word communists everywhere support every revolutionary movement against existing social and political conditions.

In all these movements they emphasise the property question, which may have taken a more or less developed form, as the basic question for the movement.

Finally communists work everywhere for the unification and mutual understanding of democratic parties of all countries.

Communists disdain to make their views and aims a secret. They openly explain that their ends can only be attained through the forcible overthrow of all social order up to now. Let the ruling classes tremble at a communist revolution. Proletarians have nothing to lose in it but their chains. They have a world to win.

Proletarians of all countries unite!

Manifesto of the German Communist Party (1848)[1]
First English translation (abridged) by Helen Macfarlane (1850)

A frightful hobgoblin stalks throughout Europe. We are haunted by a ghost, the ghost of Communism. All the Powers of the Past have joined in a holy crusade to lay this ghost to rest, – the Pope and the Czar, Metternich and Guizot, French Radicals and German police agents. Where is the opposition which has not been accused of Communism by its enemies in Power? And where the opposition that has not hurled this blighting accusation at the heads of the more advanced oppositionists, as well as at those of its official enemies? Two things appear on considering these facts. I. The ruling Powers of Europe acknowledge Communism to be also a Power. II. It is time for the Communists to lay before the world an account of their aims and tendencies, and to oppose these silly fables about the bugbear of Communism, by a manifesto of the Communist Party.

CHAPTER I

Bourgeois and Proletarians

Hitherto the history of Society has been the history of the battles between the classes composing it. Freemen and Slaves, Patricians and Plebeians, Nobles and Serfs, Members of Guilds and journeymen, – in a word, the oppressors and the oppressed, have always stood in direct opposition to each other. The battle between them has sometimes been open, sometimes concealed, but always continuous. A never-ceasing battle, which has invariably ended, either in a revolutionary alteration of the social system, or in the common destruction of the hostile classes.

In the earlier historical epochs we find almost everywhere a minute division of Society into classes or ranks, a variety of grades in social position. In ancient Rome we find Patricians, Knights, Plebeians, Slaves; in mediaeval Europe, Feudal Lords, Vassals, Burghers, Journeymen, Serfs; and in each of these classes there were again grades and distinctions. Modern Bourgeois Society, proceeded from the ruins of the feudal system, but the Bourgeois régime has not abolished the antagonism of classes.

New classes, new conditions of oppression, new forms and modes of carrying on the struggle, have been substituted for the old ones. The characteristic of our Epoch, the Era of the Middle-class, or Bourgeoisie, is that the struggle between the various Social Classes, has been reduced to its simplest form. Society incessantly tends to be divided into two great camps, into two great hostile armies, the Bourgeoisie and the Proletariat.

The burgesses of the early Communes sprang from the Serfs of the Middle Ages, and from this Municipal class were developed the primitive elements of the modern Bourgeoisie. The discovery of the New World, the circumnavigation of Africa, gave the Middleclass – then coming into being – new fields of action. The colonization of America, the opening up of the East Indian and Chinese Markets, the Colonial Trade, the increase of commodities generally and of the means of exchange, gave an impetus, hitherto unknown, to Commerce, Shipping, and Manufactures; and aided the rapid evolution of the revolutionary element in the old decaying, feudal form of Society. The old feudal way of managing the industrial interest by means of guilds and monopolies was not found sufficient for the increased demand caused by the opening up of these new markets. It was replaced by the manufacturing system. Guilds vanished before the industrial Middle-class, and the division of labour between the different corporations was succeeded by the division of labour between the workmen of one and the same great workshop.

But the demand always increased, new markets came into play. The manufacturing system, in its turn, was found to be inadequate. At this point industrial Production was revolutionised by machinery and steam. The modern industrial system was developed in all its gigantic proportions; instead of the industrial Middle-class we find industrial millionaires, chiefs of whole industrial armies, the modern Bourgeois, or Middle-class Capitalists. The discovery of America was the first step towards the formation of a colossal market, embracing the whole world; whereby an immense development was given to Commerce, and to the means of communication by sea and land. This again reacted upon the industrial system, and the developement of the Bourgeoisie, the increase of their Capital, the superseding of all classes handed down to modern times from the Middle Ages, kept pace with the developement of Production, Trade, and Steam communication.

We find, therefore, that the modern Bourgeoisie are themselves the result of a long process of developement, of a series of revolutions in the modes of Production and Exchange. Each of the degrees of industrial evolution, passed through by the modern Middle-class, was accompanied by a corresponding degree of political developement. This class was oppressed under the feudal régime, it then assumed the form of armed and self-regulating associations in the mediaeval Municipalities; in one country we find it existing as a commercial republic, or free town; in another, as the third taxable Estate of the Monarchy; then during the prevalence of the manufacturing system (before the introduction of steam power) the Middle-class was a counterpoise to the Nobility in absolute Monarchies, and the groundwork of the powerful monarchical States generally. Finally, since the establishment of the modern industrial system, with its world-wide market, this class has gained the exclusive possession of political power in modern representative States. Modern Governments are merely Committees for managing the common affairs of the whole Bourgeoisie.

This Bourgeoisie has occupied an extremely revolutionary position in History. As soon as the Bourgeois got the upper hand, they destroyed all feudal, patriarchal, idyllic relationships between men. They relentlessly tore asunder the many-sided links of that feudal chain which bound men to their "natural superiors," and they left no bond of union between man and man, save that of bare self-interest, of cash payments. They changed personal dignity into market value, and substituted the single unprincipled freedom of trade for the numerous, hardly earned, chartered liberties of the Middle Ages. Chivalrous enthusiasm, the emotions of piety, vanished before the icy breath of their selfish calculations. In a word, the Bourgeoisie substituted shameless, direct, open spoliation, for the previous system of spoliation concealed under religious and political illusions. They stripped off that halo of sanctity which had surrounded the various modes of human activity, and had made them venerable, and venerated. They changed the physician, the jurisprudent, the priest, the poet, the philosopher, into their hired servants. They tore the touching veil of sentiment from domestic ties, and reduced family-relations to a mere question of hard cash. The Middle-classes have shown how the brutal physical force of the Middle Ages, so much admired by Reactionists, found its befitting complement in the laziest ruffianism. They have also shown what human activity is capable of accomplishing. They have done quite other kinds of marvellous work than Egyptian pyramids, Roman aqueducts, or Gothic Cathedrals; and their expeditions have far surpassed all former Crusades, and Migrations of nations.

The Bourgeoisie can exist only under the condition of continuously revolutionising machinery, or the instruments of Production. That is, perpetually changing the system of production, which again amounts to changing the whole system of social arrangements. Persistance in the old modes of Production was, on the contrary, the first condition of existence for all the preceding industrial Classes. A continual change in the modes of Production, a never ceasing state of agitation and social insecurity, distinguish the Bourgeois–Epoch from all preceding ones. The ancient ties between men, their opinions and beliefs – hoar with antiquity – are fast disappearing, and the new ones become worn out ere they can become firmly rooted. Everything fixed and stable vanishes, everything holy and venerable is desecrated, and men are forced to look at their mutual relations, at the problem of Life, in the soberest, the most matter of fact way.

The need of an ever-increasing market for their produce, drives the Bourgeoisie over the whole globe – they are forced to make settlements, to form connections, to set up means of communication everywhere. Through their command of a universal market, they have given a cosmopolitan tendency to the production and consumption of all countries. To the great regret of the Reactionists, the Bourgeoisie have deprived the modern Industrial System of its national foundation. The old national manufactures have been, or are being, destroyed. They are superseded by new modes of industry, whose introduction is becoming a vital question for all civilized nations, whose raw materials are not indigenous, but are brought from the remotest countries, and whose products are not merely consumed in the home market, but throughout the whole world. Instead of the old national wants, supplied by indigenous products, we everywhere find new wants, which can be supplied only by the productions of the remotest lands and climes. Instead of the old local and national feeling of self-sufficingness and isolation, we find a universal intercourse, an interdependence, amongst nations. The same fact obtains in the intellectual world. The intellectual productions of individual nations tend to become common property. National one-sidedness and mental limitation are fast becoming impossible, and a universal literature is being formed from the numerous national and local literatures. Through the incessant improvements in machinery and the mean of locomotion, the Bourgeoisie draw the most barbarous savages into the magic circle of civilization. Cheap goods are their artillery for battering down all Chinese walls, and their means of overcoming the obstinate hatred, entertained towards strangers by semi-civilized nations. The Bourgeoisie, by their competition, compel, under penalty of inevitable ruin, the universal adoption of their system of production; they force all nations to accept what is called civilization – to become Bourgeois – and thus the middle class fashions the world anew after its own image.

The Bourgeoisie has subjected the *country* to the ascendancy of the *town*; it has created enormous cities, and, by causing an immense increase of population in the manufacturing, as compared with the agricultural districts, has saved a great part of every people from the idiotism of country life. Not only have the Bourgeoisie made the country subordinate to the town, they have made barbarous and half-civilized tribes dependent on civilized nations, the agricultural on the manufacturing nations, the East on the West. The division of property, of the means of production, and of population, vanish under the Bourgeois régime. It agglomerates population, it centralises the means of production, and concentrates property in the hands of a few individuals. Political centralization is the necessary consequence of this. Independent provinces, with different interests, each of them surrounded by a separate line of customs and under separate local governments, are brought together as one nation, under the same government, laws, line of customs, tariff, the same national class-interest. The Bourgeois regime has only prevailed for about a century, but during that time it has called into being more gigantic powers of production than all preceding generations put together. The subjection of the elements of nature, the developement of machinery, the application of chemistry to agriculture and manufactures, railways, electric telegraphs, steam ships, the clearing and cultivations of whole continents, canalizing of thousands of rivers; large populations, whole industrial armies, springing up, as if by magic! What preceding generation ever dreamed of these productive powers slumbering within society?

We have seen that these means of production and traffic which served as the foundation of middle-class development, originated in feudal times. At a certain point in the evolution of these means, the arrangements under which feudal society produced and exchanged the feudal organization of agriculture and industrial production, – in a word, the feudal conditions of property – no longer corresponded to the increased productive power. These conditions now became a hindrance to it, – they were turned into fetters which had to be broken, and they were broken. They were superseded by unlimited competition, with a suitable social and political constitution, with the economical and political supremacy of the middle class. At the present moment a similar movement is going on before our eyes. Modern middle-class society, which has revolutionised the conditions of property, and called forth such colossal means of production and traffic, resembles the wizard who evoked the powers of darkness, but could neither master them, nor yet get rid of them when they had come at his bidding. The history of manufactures and commerce has been for many years the history of the revolts of modern productive power against the modern industrial system – against the modern conditions of property – which are vital conditions, not only of the supremacy of the middle-class, but of its very existence. It suffices to mention the commercial crises which, in each of their periodical occurrences, more and more endanger the existence of middle-class society. In such a crisis, not only is a quantity of industrial products destroyed, but a large portion of the productive power itself. A social epidemic breaks out, the epidemic of over-production, which would have appeared a contradiction in terms to all previous generations. Society finds itself suddenly thrown back into momentary barbarism; a famine, a devastating war, seems to have deprived it of the means of subsistence; manufactures and commerce appear annihilated, – and why? Because society possesses too much civilization, too many of the necessaries of life, too much industry, too much commerce. The productive power possessed by society no longer serves as the instrument of middle-class civilization, of the middle-class conditions of property; on the contrary, this power has become too mighty for this system, it is forcibly confined by these conditions; and whenever it surpasses these artificial limitations, it deranges the system of Bourgeois society, it endangers the existence of Bourgeois property. The social system of the middle-class has become too small to contain the riches it has called into being. How does the middle-class try to withstand these commercial crises? On the one hand, by destroying masses of productive power; on the other, by opening up new markets, and using up the old ones more thoroughly. That is, they prepare the way for still more universal and dangerous crises, and reduce the means of withstanding them. The weapons with which the middle-class overcame feudalism are now turned against the middle-class itself. And the Bourgeoisie have not only prepared the weapons for their own destruction, they have also called into existence the men that are destined to wield these weapons, namely, the modern working men, the *Proletarians*.

The developement of the Proletariat has kept pace with the development of the middle-class – that is, with the development of capital; for the modern working men can live only as long as they find work, and they find it only as long as their labour increases capital. These workers, who must sell themselves by piecemeal to the highest bidder, are a commodity like other articles of commerce, and, therefore, are equally subject to all the variations of the market, and the effects of competition. Through the division of labour and the extension of machinery, work has lost its individual character, and therefore its interest for the operative. He has become merely an accessory to, or a part of the machine, and all that is required of him is a fatiguing, monotonous, and merely mechanical operation. The expense the wages-slave causes the capitalist is, therefore, equal to the cost of his keep and of the propagation of his race. The price of labour, like that of any other commodity, is equal to the cost of its production. Therefore wages decrease in proportion as the work to be performed becomes mechanical, monotonous, fatiguing, and repulsive. Further, in proportion as the application of machinery and the division of labour increase, the amount of work increases also, whether it be through an increase in the hours of work, or in the quantity of it demanded in a given time, or through an increased rate of velocity of the machinery employed.

The modern industrial system has changed the little shop of the primitive patriarchal master into the large factory of the Bourgeois–capitalist. Masses of operatives are brought together in one establishment, and organized like a regiment of soldiers; they are placed under the superintendence of a complete hierarchy of officers and sub-officers. They are not only the slaves of the whole middle-class (as a body,) of the Bourgeois political régime, – they are the daily and hourly slaves of the machinery, of the foreman, of each individual manufacturing Bourgeois. This despotism is the more hateful, contemptible, and aggravating, because *gain* is openly proclaimed to be its only object and aim. In proportion as labour requires less physical force and less dexterity – that is, in proportion to the development of the modern industrial system – is the substitution of the labour of women and children for that of men. The distinctions of sex and age have no *social* meaning for the Proletarian class. Proletarians are merely so many instruments which cost more or less, according to their sex and age. When the using-up of the operative has been so far accomplished by the mill-owner that the former has got his wages, the rest of the Bourgeoisie, house-holders, shop-keepers, pawnbrokers, &c., fall upon him like so many harpies.

The petty Bourgeoisie, the inferior ranks of the middle-class, the small manu-facturers, merchants, tradesmen, and farmers, tend to become Proletarians, partly because their small capital succumbs to the competition of the millionaire, and partly because the modes of production perpetually changing, their peculiar skill loses its value. Thus the Proletariat is recruited from various sections of the population.

This Proletarian class passes through many phases of development, but its struggle with the middle-class dates from its birth. At first the struggle is carried on by individual workmen, then by those belonging to a single establishment, then by those of an entire trade in the same locality, against the individuals of the middle-class who directly use them up. They attack not only the middle-class system of production, but even the instruments of production; they destroy machinery and the foreign commodities which compete with their products; they burn down factories, and try to re-attain the position occupied by the producers of the middle ages. At this moment of development, the Proletariat forms a disorganized mass, scattered throughout the country, and divided by competition. A more compact union is not the effect of their own development, but is the consequence of a middle-class union; for the Bourgeoisie requires, and for the moment are still enabled to set the whole Proletariat in motion, for the furtherance of their own political ends; developed in this degree, therefore, the Proletarians do not fight their own enemies, but the enemies of their enemies, the remains of absolute monarchy, the land-owners, the non-manufacturing part of the Bourgeoisie and the petty shopocracy. The whole historical movement is thus, as yet, concentrated in the hands of the Bourgeoisie, every victory is won for them. But the increase of the Proletariat keeps pace with the evolution of production; the working-class is brought together in masses, and learns its own strength. The interests and position of different trades become similar, because machinery tends to reduce wages to the same level, and to make less and less difference between the various kinds of labour. The increasing competition amongst the middle-class, and the commercial crises consequent thereupon, make wages always more variable, while the incessant improvements in machinery make the position of the Proletarians more and more uncertain, and the collisions between the individual workmen and the individual masters, assume more and more the character of collisions between two classes. The workmen commence to form trades-unions against the masters; they turn out, to prevent threatened reductions in their wages. They form associations to help each other in, and to provision themselves for these occasional revolts. Here and there the struggles takes the form of riots.

From time to time the Proletarians are, for a moment, victorious, yet the result of their struggle is not an immediate advantage, but the ever increasing union amongst their class. This union is favoured by the facility of communication under the modern industrial system, whereby the Proletarians belonging to the remotest localities are placed in connection with each other. But connection is all that is wanting to change innumerable local struggles, having all the same character, into one national struggle – into a battle of classes. Every battle between different classes is a political battle, and the union, which it took, the burghers of the middle ages centuries to bring about, by means of their few and awkward roads, can be accomplished in a few years by the modern Proletarians, by means of railways and steamships. This organisation of the Proletarians into a class, and therewith into a political party, is incessantly destroyed by the competitive principle. Yet it always reappears, and each time it is stronger and more extensive. It compels the legal acknowledgment of detached Proletarian rights, by profiting of the divisions in the *bourgeois* camp. For example, the Ten Hours' Bill in England. The struggles of the ruling classes amongst themselves are favourable to the development of the Proletariat. The middle-class has always been in a state of perpetual warfare – first, against the aristocracy; and then against that part of itself whose interests are opposed to the further evolution of the industrial system; and, thirdly, against the *bourgeoisie* of other countries. During all of these battles, the middle-class has ever been obliged to appeal for help to the Proletarians, and so to draw the latter into the political movement. This class, therefore, has armed the Proletarians against itself, by letting them share in its own means of cultivation. Further, as we have already seen, the evolution of the industrial system has thrown a large portion of the ruling class into the ranks of the Proletarians, or at least rendered the means of subsistence very precarious for this portion. A new element of progress for the Proletariat. Finally, as the settlement of the class-struggle draws near, the process of dissolution goes on so rapidly within the ruling-class – within the worn-out body politic – that a small fraction of this class separates from it, and joins the revolutionary class, in whose hands lies the future. In the earlier revolutions a part of the *noblesse* joined the *bourgeoisie*; in the present one, a part of the *bourgeoisie* is joining the Proletariat, and particularly a part of the Bourgeois-ideologists, or middle-class thinkers, who have attained a theoretical knowledge of the whole historical movement.

The Proletariat is the only truly revolutionary Class amongst the present enemies of the Bourgeoisie. All the other classes of Society are being destroyed by the modern Industrial system, the Proletariat is its peculiar product. The small manufacturers, shopkeepers, proprietors, peasants, &c., all fight against the Bourgeoisie, in order to defend their position as small Capitalists. They are, therefore, not revolutionary, but conservative. They are even reactionary, for they attempt to turn backwards the chariot wheels of History. When these subordinate classes are revolutionary, they are so with reference to their necessary absorption into the Proletariat; they defend their future, not their present, interests, – they leave their own Class-point of view to take up that of the Proletariat.

The Mob, – this product of the decomposition of the lowest substrata of the old Social system, – is partly forced into the revolutionary Proletarian movement. The social position of this portion of the people makes it, however, in general a ready and venal tool for Reactionist intrigues.

The vital conditions of Society, as at present constituted, no longer exist for the Proletariat. Its very existence, is a flagrant contradiction to those conditions.

The Proletarian has no property; the relation in which he stands to his family has nothing in common with Middle-class family relationships; the modern system of industrial labour, the modern slavery of Labour under Capital, which obtains in England as in France, in America as in Germany, has robbed him of his National Character. Law, Morality, Religion, are for him so many Middle-class prejudices, under which so many Middle-class interests are concealed. All the hitherto dominant Classes, have tried to preserve the position they had already attained, by imposing the conditions under which they possessed and increased their possessions, upon the rest of Society. But the Proletarians can gain possession of the Productive power of Society, – of the instruments of Labour, – only by annihilating their own, hitherto acknowledged mode of appropriation and, with this, all previous modes of appropriation. The Proletarians have nothing of their own to secure, their task is to destroy all previously existing private securities and possessions. All the historical movements hitherto recorded were the movements of minorities, or movements in the interest of minorities. The Proletarian movement is the independent movement of the immense majority in favour of the immense majority. The Proletariat, the lowest stratum of existing society, cannot arouse, cannot rise without causing the complete disruption and dislocation of all the superincumbent classes.

Though the struggle of the Proletariat against the Bourgeoisie is not a National struggle in its Content, – or Reality – it is so in its Form. The Proletarians of every country must settle accounts with the Bourgeoisie there.

While we have thus sketched the general aspect presented by the development of the Proletariat, we have followed the more or less concealed Civil War pervading existing Society, to the point where it must break forth in an open Revolution, and where the Proletarians arrive at the supremacy of their own class through the violent fall of the Bourgeoisie. We have seen, that all previous forms of Society have rested upon the antagonism of oppressing and oppressed Classes. But in order to oppress a Class, the conditions under which it can continue at least its enslaved existence must be secured. The Serf in the Middle Ages, even within his serfdom, could better his condition and become a member of the Commune; the burghers could become a Middle-class under the yoke of feudal Monarchy. But the modern Proletarian, instead of improving his condition with the development of modern Industry, is daily sinking deeper and deeper even below the conditions of existence of his own Class. The Proletarian tends to become a pauper; and Pauperism is more rapidly developed than population and Wealth. From this it appears, that the Middle-class is incapable of remaining any longer the ruling Class of Society, and of compelling Society to adopt the conditions of Middle-class existence as its own vital conditions. This Class is incapable of governing, because it is incapable of ensuring the bare existence of its Slaves, even within the limits of their slavery, because it is obliged to keep them, instead of being kept by them. Society can no longer exist under this Class, that is, its existence is no longer compatible with that of Society. The most indispensable condition for the existence and supremacy of the Bourgeoisie, is the accumulation of Wealth in the hands of private individuals, the formation and increase of Capital. The condition upon which Capital depends is the Wages-system, and this system again, is founded upon the Competition of the Proletarians with each other. But the progress of the modern industrial system, towards which the Bourgeoisie lend an unconscious and involuntary support, tends to supersede the isolated position of Proletarians by the revolutionary Union of their Class, and to replace Competition by Association. The progress of the modern industrial system, therefore, cuts away, from under the feet of the Middle-class, the very ground upon which they produce and appropriate to themselves the produce of Labour. Thus the Bourgeoisie produce before all the men who dig their very grave. Their destruction and the victory of the Proletarians are alike unavoidable.

CHAPTER II

Proletarians and Communists

What relationship subsists between the Communists and the Proletarians? – The Communists form no separate party in opposition to the other existing working-class parties. They have no interest different from that of the whole Proletariat. They lay down no particular principles according to which they wish to direct and to shape the Proletarian movement. The Communists are distinguishable among the various sections of the Proletarian party on two accounts – namely, that in the different *national* Proletarian struggles, the Communists understand, and direct attention to, the common interest of the collective Proletariat, an interest independent of all nationality; and that, throughout the various phases of development assumed by the struggle between the Bourgeoisie and the Proletariat, the Communists always represent the interest of the Whole Movement. In a word, the Communists are the most advanced, the most progressive section, among the Proletarian parties of all countries; and this section has a theoretical advantage, compared with the bulk of the Proletariat – it has obtained an insight into the historical conditions, the march, and the general results of the Proletarian Movement. The more immediate aim of the Communists is that of all other Proletarian sections. *The organisation of the Proletariat as a class, the destruction of Middle-class supremacy, and the conquest of political power by the Proletarians.*

The theoretical propositions of the Communists are not based upon Ideas, or Principles, discovered by this or that Universal Reformer. Their propositions are merely general expressions for the actual conditions, causes, &c., of an existing battle between certain classes, the conditions of an historical Movement which is going on before our very eyes.

The abolition of existing conditions of Property does not form a distinguishing characteristic of Communism. All such conditions have been subject to a continual change, to the operation of many historical Movements. The French

Revolution, for example, destroyed the feudal conditions of property, and replaced them by Bourgeois ones. It is not, therefore, the *abolition of property generally* which distinguishes Communism; it is the *abolition of Bourgeois property*. But Modern Middle-class private property is the last and most perfect expression for that mode of Production and Distribution which rests on the antagonism of classes, on the using up of the many by the few. In this sense, indeed, the Communists might resume their whole Theory in that single expression – *The abolition of private property.*

It has been reproached to us, the Communists, that we wish to destroy the property which is the product of a man's own labour; self-acquired property, the basis of all personal freedom, activity, and independence. Self-acquired property! Do you mean the property of the small shopkeeper, small tradesman, small peasant, which precedes the present system of Middle-class property? We do not need to abolish that, the progress of industrial development is daily destroying it. Or do you mean modern Middle-class property? Does labour under the Wages-system create property for the Wages-slave, for the Proletarian? No. It creates Capital, that is, a species of property which plunders Wages-labour; for Capital can only increase on condition of creating a new supply of Wages-labour; in order to use it up anew.

Property, in its present form, rests upon the antagonism of Capital and Wages-labour. Let us look at both sides of this antithesis. To be a Capitalist means to occupy not only a personal, but a social position in the system of production. Capital is a collective product, and can be used and set in motion only by the common activity of many, or, to speak exactly, only by the united exertions of all the members of society. Capital is thus not an individual, it is a social, power. Therefore, when Capital is changed into property belonging in common to all the members of society, personal property is not thereby changed into social property. It *was* social property before. The social character only of property, in such a case, is changed. Property loses its *class* character. – Let us now turn to Wages-labour. The minimum rate of wages is the average price of Proletarian labour. And what is the minimum rate of wages? It is that quantity of produce which is necessary to conserve the working capacities of the labourer. What the Wages-slave can gain by his activity is merely what is requisite for the bare reproduction of his existence. We by no means wish to abolish this personal appropriation of the products of labour; an appropriation leaving no net profit, no surplus, to be applied to command the labour of others. We only wish to change the miserably insufficient character of this appropriation, whereby the producer lives only to increase Capital; that is, whereby he is kept alive only so far as it may be the interest of the ruling class. In Middle-class society, actual living labour is nothing but a means of increasing accumulated labour. In Communistic society, accumulated labour is only a means of enlarging, increasing, and varifying the vital process of the producers. In Middle-class society, the Past reigns over the Present. In Communistic society, the Present reigns over the Past. In Middle-class society, Capital is independent and personal, while the active individual is dependent and deprived of personality. And the destruction of such a system is called by Middle-class advocates, the destruction of personality and freedom. They are so far right, that the question in hand is the destruction of *Middle-class* personality, independence, and freedom. Within the present Middle-class conditions of production, freedom means free trade, freedom of buying and selling. But if trade, altogether, is to fall, so will free trade fall with the rest. The declamations about free trade, as all the remaining Bourgeois declamations upon the subject of freedom generally, have a meaning only when opposed to fettered trade, and to the enslaved tradesman of the Middle Ages; they have no meaning whatever in reference to the Communistic destruction of profit-mongering, of the Middle-class conditions of production, and of the Middle-class itself. You are horrified that we aim at the abolition of private property. But under your present system of society, private property has no existence for nine-tenths of its members; its existence is based upon the very fact that it exists not at all for nine-tenths of the population. You reproach us, then, that we aim at the abolition of a species of property which involves, as a necessary condition, the absence of all property for the immense majority of society. In a word, you reproach us that we aim at the destruction of YOUR property. That is precisely what we aim at.

From the moment when Labour can no longer be changed into Capital, – into money, or rent, – into a social power capable of being *monopolised*; that is, from the moment when personal property can no longer constitute itself as Middle-class property, from that moment you declare, that human personality is abolished. You acknowledge, then, that for you personality generally means the personality of the Bourgeois, the Middle-class proprietor. It is precisely this kind of personality which is to be destroyed. Communism deprives no one of the right of appropriating social products; it only takes away from him the power of appropriating the command over the labour of others. It has been objected that activity will cease, and a universal laziness pervade society, were the abolition of private property once accomplished. According to this view of the matter, Middle-class society ought, long since, to have been ruined through idleness; for under the present system, those who do work acquire no property, and those who acquire property do no work. This objection rests upon the tautological proposition, that there will be no Wages-labour whenever there is no Capital.

All the objections made to the Communistic mode of producing and distributing physical products, have also been directed against the production and distribution of intellectual products. As, in the opinion of the Bourgeois, the destruction of class property involves the cessation of appropriation, in like manner the cessation of class-civilisation, in his opinion, is identical with the cessation of civilisation generally. The civilisation whose loss he deplores, is the system of civilising men into machines.

But do not dispute with us, while you measure the proposed abolition of Middle-class property, by your Middle-class ideas of freedom, civilisation, jurisprudence, and the like. Your ideas are the necessary consequences of the

Middle-class conditions of property and production, as your jurisprudence is the Will of your class raised to the dignity of Law, a Will whose subject is given in the economical conditions of your class. The selfish mode of viewing the question, whereby you confound your transitory conditions of production and property with the eternal laws of Reason and Nature, is common to all ruling classes. What you understand with regard to Antique and Feudal property, you cannot understand with regard to modern Middle-class property. – The destruction of domestic ties! Even the greatest Radicals are shocked at this scandalous intention of the Communists. Upon what rests the present system, the Bourgeois system, of family relationships? Upon Capital, upon private gains, on profit-mongering. In its most perfect form it exists only for the Bourgeoisie, and it finds a befitting compliment in the compulsory celibacy of the Proletarians, and in public prostitution. The Bourgeois family system naturally disappears with the disappearance of its complement, and the destruction of both is involved in the destruction of Capital. Do you reproach us that we intend abolishing the using up of children by their parents? We acknowledge this crime. Or that we will abolish the most endearing relationships, by substituting a public and social system of education for the existing private one? And is not your system of education also determined by society? By the social conditions, within the limits of which you educate? by the more or less direct influence of society, through the medium of your schools, and so forth? The Communists do not invent the influence of society upon education; they only seek to change its character, to rescue education from the influence of a ruling class. Middle-class talk about domestic ties and education, about the endearing connection of parent and child, becomes more and more disgusting in proportion as the family ties of the Proletarians are torn asunder, and their children changed into machines, into articles of commerce, by the extension of the modern industrial system. But you intend introducing a community of women, shrieks the whole Middle-class like a tragic chorus. The Bourgeois looks upon his wife as a mere instrument of production; he is told that the instruments of production are to be used up in common, and thus he naturally supposes that women will share the common fate of other machines. He does not even dream that it is intended, on the contrary, to abolish the position of woman as a mere instrument of production. For the rest, nothing can be more ludicrous than the highly moral and religious horror entertained by the Bourgeoisie towards the pretended official community of women among the Communists. We do not require to introduce community of women, it has always existed. Your Middle-class gentry are not satisfied with having the wives and daughters of their Wages-slaves at their disposal,– not to mention the innumerable public prostitutes,– but they take a particular interest in seducing each other's wives. Middle-class marriage is in reality a community of wives. At the most, then, we could only be reproached for wishing to substitute an open, above-board community of women, for the present mean, hypocritical, sneaking kind of community. But it is evident enough that with the disappearance of the present conditions of production, the community of women occasioned by them, – namely, official and non-official prostitution will also disappear.

The Communists are further reproached with desiring to destroy patriotism, the feeling of Nationality. The Proletarian has no Fatherland. You cannot deprive him of that which he has not got. When the Proletariat obtains political supremacy, becomes the National Class, and constitutes itself as the Nation, – it will, indeed, be national, though not in the middleclass sense of the word. The National divisions and antagonisms presented by the European Nations, already tend towards obliteration through the development of the Bourgeoisie, through the influence of free-trade, a world-wide market, the uniformity of the modern modes of Production and the conditions of modern life arising out of the present industrial system.

The supremacy of the Proletariat will hasten this obliteration of national peculiarities, for the united action of – at least – all civilized countries is one of the first conditions of Proletarian emancipation. In proportion to the cessation of the using up of one individual by another, will be the cessation of the using up of one nation by another. The hostile attitude assumed by nations towards each other, will cease with the antagonisms of the classes into which each nation is divided.

The accusations against communism, which have been made from the Theological, Philosophical, and Ideological, points of view, deserve no further notice. Does it require any great degree of intellect to perceive that changes occur in our ideas, conceptions, and opinions, in a word, that the *consciousness* of man alters with every change in the conditions of his physical existence, in his social relations and position? Does not the history of Ideas show, that intellectual production has always changed with the changes in material production? The ruling ideas of any age have always been the ideas of the then ruling class. You talk of ideas which have revolutionized society; but you merely express the fact, that within the old form of society, the elements of a new one were being formed, and that the dissolution of the old ideas was keeping pace with the dissolution of the old conditions of social life. When the antique world was in its last agony, Christianity triumphed over the antique religion. When the dogmas of Christianity were superseded by the enlightenment of the eighteenth century, feudal society was concentrating its last efforts against the then revolutionary Bourgeoisie. The ideas of religious liberty and freedom of thought were the expressions of unlimited competition in the affairs and free trade in the sphere of intellect and religion. But you say, theological, moral, philosophical, political and legal ideas are subject to be modified by the progress of historical developement. Religion, ethics, philosophy, politics and jurisprudence are, however, of all times. And we find, besides certain eternal ideas, for example, Freedom, Justice, and the like, – which are common to all the various social phases and states. But communism destroys these eternal truths; it pretends to abolish religion and Ethics, instead of merely giving them a new form; Communism, therefore, contradicts all preceding modes of historical development. To what does this accusation amount? The history of all preceding states of society is simply the history of class antagonisms, which were fought under different conditions, and assumed different forms during the different historical epochs. Whatever form these antagonisms may have assumed, the using up of one part of society by another part, is a fact, common to the whole past. No wonder then, that the social consciousness of past ages should have a common ground, in spite of the multiplicity and diversity of social arrangements: that it should move in certain common forms of thinking, which will completely disappear with the disappearance of class antagonism. The communistic revolution is the most thorough going rupture, with the traditionary conditions of property, no wonder then, that its progress will involve the completest rupture with traditionary ideas.

But we must have done with the middleclass accusations against communism. We have seen that the first step in the proletarian revolution, will be the conquest of Democracy, *the elevation of the Proletariat to the state of the ruling class.* The Proletarians will use their political supremacy in order to deprive the middle-class of the command of capital; to centralise all instruments of production in the hands of the State, that is, in those of the whole proletariat organized as the ruling class, and to increase the mass of productive power with the utmost possible rapidity. It is a matter of course that this can be done, at first, only by despotic interference with the rights of property, and middle-class conditions of production. By regulations, in fact, which – economically considered – appear insufficient and untenable; which, therefore, in the course of the revolution, necessitate ulterior and more radical measures, and are unavoidable as a means towards a thorough change in the modes of production. These regulations will, of course, be different in different countries. But for the most advanced countries, the following will be pretty generally applicable: –

1. The national appropriation of the land, and the application of rent to the public revenue.
2. A heavy progressive tax.
3. Abolition of the right of inheritance.
4. Confiscation of the property of all emigrants and rebels.
5. Centralization of credit in the hands of the State, by means of a national bank, with an exclusive monopoly and a state-capital.
6. Centralization of all the means of communication in the hands of the state.
7. Increase of the national manufactories; of the instruments of production; the cultivation of waste lands and the improvement of the land generally according to a common plan.
8. Labour made compulsory for all; and the organization of industrial armies, especially for agriculture.
9. The union of manufacturing and agricultural industry; with a view of gradually abolishing the antagonism between town and country.
10. The public and gratuitous education of all children; the abolition of the present system of factory labour for children; the conjunction of education and material production with other regulations of a similar nature.

When Class distinctions will have finally disappeared, and production will have been concentrated in the hands of this Association which comprises the whole nation, the public power will lose its political character. Political power in the exact sense of the word, being the organised power of one class, which enables it to oppress another. When the proletariat has been forced to unite as a class during its struggle with the Bourgeoisie, when it has become the ruling class by a revolution, and as such has destroyed, by force, the old conditions of production, it destroys necessarily, with these conditions of production, it destroys necessarily, with these conditions of production, the conditions of existence of all class antagonism, of classes generally, and thus it destroys, also, its own supremacy as a class. The old Bourgeois Society, with its classes, and class antagonisms, will be replaced by an association, *wherein the free development of EACH is the condition of the free development of ALL.*

CHAPTER III

Socialist and Communist Literature

I. *Reactionary Socialism*

a. – FEUDAL SOCIALISM. The historical position of the French and English Aristocracy devolved upon them, at a certain period, the task of writing pamphlets against the social system of the modern Bourgeoisie. These Aristocracies were again beaten by a set of detestable parvenus and nobodies in the July days of 1830, and in the English Reform Bill movement. There could be no longer any question about a serious political struggle. There remained only the possibility of conducting a literary combat. But even in the territory of Literature, the old modes of speech, current during the Restoration, had become impossible. In order to excite sympathy, the Aristocracy had to assume the semblance of disinterestedness, and to draw up their accusation of the Bourgeoisie, apparently as advocates for the used-up Proletarians. The Aristocracy thus revenged themselves on their new masters, – by lampoons and fearful prophecies of coming woe. In this way feudal socialism arose – half lamentation, half libel, half echo of the Past, half prophecy of a threatening Future; – sometimes striking the very heart of the Bourgeoisie by its sarcastic, bitter judgments, but always accompanied by a certain tinge of the ludicrous, from its complete inability to comprehend the march of modern history. The Feudal Socialists waved the Proletarian alms-bag aloft, to assemble the people around them. But as often as the people came, they perceived upon the hind parts of theses worthies, the old feudal arms and quarterings, and abandoned them with a noisy and irreverent hilarity. A part of the French Legitimists and the party of Young England played this farce.

When the Feudalists show that their mode of exploitation (*using up one class by another*) was different from the Bourgeois mode, they forget that their mode was practicable only under circumstances and conditions which have passed away – never to return. When they show that the modern Proletariat never existed under their supremacy, they simply forget, that the modern Bourgeoisie is the necessary offspring of their own social order. For the rest, they so little conceal the reactionary nature of their criticism, that their chief reproach against the Bourgeoisie-régime is, that of having crated a class which is destined to annihilate the old social forms and arrangements altogether. It is not so much that the Bourgeoisie having created a Proletariat, but that this Proletariat is revolutionary. Hence, in their political practice, they take part in all reactionary measures against the working classes; and in ordinary life, despite their grandiloquent phrases, they condescend to gather the golden apples, and to give up chivalry, true love, and honour for the traffic in wool, butcher's meat, and corn. As the parson has always gone hand-in-hand with the landlord, so has Priestly Socialism with Feudal Socialism. Nothing is easier than to give Christian asceticism a tinge of Socialism. Has not Christianity itself vociferated against private property, marriage, and the powers that be? Have not charity, and mendicity, celibacy and mortification of the flesh, monastic life, and the supremacy of the Church been held up in the place of these things? Sacred Socialism is merely the holy water, with which the priest besprinkles the impotent wrath of the Aristocracy.

b. – SHOPOCRAT[2] SOCIALISM. The Feudal Aristocracy are not the only class who are or will be, destroyed by the Bourgeoisie. Not the only class, the conditions of whose existence become exhausted and disappear, under the modern middle-class system. The mediaeval burgesses and yeoman were the precursors of the modern middle-class. In countries possessing a small degree of industrial and commercial development, this intermediate class still vegetates side by side with the flourishing Bourgeoisie. In countries where modern civilization has been developed, a new intermediate class has been formed; floating as it were, between the Bourgeoisie and the Proletariat; and always renewing itself as a component part of Bourgeois society. Yet, the persons belonging to this class are constantly forced by competition downwards into the Proletariat, and the development of the modern industrial system will bring about the time when this small capitalist class will entirely disappear, and be replaced by managers and stewards, in commerce, manufactures, and agriculture. In countries like France, where far more than one half of the population are small freeholders, it was natural, that writers who took part with the Proletariat against the Bourgeoisie, should measure the Bourgeois-régime by the small-capitalist standard; and should envisage the Proletarian question from the small-capitalist point of view. In this way arose the system of Shopocrat Socialism. Sismondi is the head of this school, in England as well as in France. This school of socialism has dissected with great acuteness the modern system of production, and exposed the fallacies contained therein. It unveiled the hypocritical evasions of the political economists. It irrefutably demonstrated the destructive effects of machinery, and the division of labour; the concentration of capital and land in a few hands; over production; commercial crisis; the necessary destruction of the small capitalist; the misery of the Proletariat; anarchy in production, and scandalous inequality in the distribution of wealth; the destructive industrial wars of one nation with another; and the disappearance of old manners and customs, of patriarchal family arrangements, and of old nationalities. But in its practical application, this Shopocrat, or Small-Capitalist Socialism, wish either to re-establish the old modes of production and traffic, and with these, the old conditions of property, and old society altogether – or forcibly to confine the modern means of production and traffic within the limits of these antique conditions of property, which were actually destroyed, necessarily so, by these very means. In both cases, Shopocrat Socialism is, at the same time reactionary and Utopian. Corporations and guilds in manufactures, patriarchal idyllic arrangements in agriculture, are its beau ideal. This kind of Socialism has run to seed, and exhausted itself in silly lamentations over the past.

C. – GERMAN OR "TRUE" SOCIALISM.[3] The Socialist and Communist literature of France originated under the Bourgeois-régime, and was the literary expression of the struggle against middle-class supremacy. It was introduced into Germany at a time when the Bourgeoisie there had began their battle against Feudal despotism. German philosophers – half-philosophers and would-be literati – eagerly seized on this literature, and forgot that with the immigration of these French writings into Germany, the advanced state of French society, and of French class-struggles, had not, as a matter of course, immigrated along with them. This French literature, when brought into contact with the German phasis of social development, lost all its immediate practical significance, and assumed a purely literary aspect. It could appear in no other way than as idle speculation upon the best possible state of society, upon the realization of the true nature of man. In a similar manner, the German philosophers of the 18th century, considered the demands of the first French Revolution as the demands of "Practical Reason" in its general sense, and the will of the revolutionary French bourgeoisie, was for them the law of the pure will, of volition as it ought to be; the law of man's inward nature. The all-engrossing problem for the German literati was to bring the new French ideas into accordance with their old philosophic conscience; or rather, to appropriate the French ideas without leaving the philosophic point of view. This appropriation took place in the same way as one masters a foreign language; namely, by translation. It is known how the Monks of the middle-ages treated the manuscripts of the Greek and Roman classics. They wrote silly Catholic legends over the original text. The German literati did the very reverse, with respect to the profane French literature. They wrote their philosophical nonsense behind the French original. For example, behind the French critique of the modern money-system, they wrote, "Estrangement of Human Nature;" behind the French critique of the bourgeois-régime, they wrote, "Destruction of the Supremacy of the Absolute," and so forth. They baptized this interpolation of their philosophic modes of speech, with the French ideas by various names; "Philosophy in Action," "True Socialism," "The German Philosophy of Socialism,"

"Philosophical Foundation of Socialism," and the like. The socialist and communist literature of France was completely emasculated. And when it had ceased, in German hands, to express the struggle of one class against another, the Germans imagined they had overcome French one-sidedness. They imagined they represented, not true interests and wants, but the interests and wants of abstract truth; not the proletarian interest, but the interest of human nature, as man as belonging to no class, a native of no merely terrestrial countries, – of man, belonging of the misty, remote region of philosophical imagination. This German socialism, which composed its clumsy school themes with such exemplary solemnity, and then cried them along the street, gradually lost its pedantic and primitive innocence. The battle of the German, particularly of the Prussian bourgeoisie, against feudalism and absolute monarchy, in a word, the liberal movement, became more serious. True socialism had now the desired opportunity of placing socialist demands in opposition to the actual political movement; of hurling the traditionary second-hand Anathemas against liberalism, constitutional governments, bourgeois competition and free trade, bourgeois freedom of the press, bourgeois juries, bourgeois freedom and equality; the opportunity of preaching to the masses that they had nothing to gain and everything to lose by this middle-class movement. German socialism forgot, very opportunely, that the French polemics, whose unmeaning echo it was, – presupposed the modern middle-class system of society, with the corresponding physical conditions of social existence, and a suitable political constitution presupposed, in fact, the very things which had no existence in Germany, and which were the very things to be obtained by the middle-class movement. German socialism was used by the German despots and their followers, – priests, schoolmasters, bureaucrats and bullfrog country squires, – as a scarecrow to frighten the revolutionary middle-class. It was the agreeable finish to the grape-shot, and cat o'nine tails, with which these Governments replied to the first proletarian insurrections of Germany. While "true socialism" was thus employed in assisting the Governments against the German bourgeoisie, it also directly represented a reactionary interest, that of the German small capitalists and shopocracy. In Germany the real social foundation of the existing state of things, was this class, remaining since the 16th century, and always renewing itself under slightly different forms. Its preservation was the preservation of the existing order of things in Germany. The industrial and political supremacy of the bourgeoisie involved the annihilation of this intermediate class; on the one hand, by the centralisation of capital; on the other, by the creation of a revolutionary proletariat. German, or "true" socialism, appeared to this shopocracy as a means of killing two birds with one stone. It spread like an epidemic. The robe of speculative cobwebs, adorned with rhetorical flourishes and sickly sentimentalism, – in which the German socialists wrapped the dry bones of their eternal, absolute truths, increased the demand for their commodity among this public. And the German socialists were not wanting in due appreciation of their mission, to be the grand-iloquent representatives of the German shopocrats. They proclaimed the German nation to be the archetypal nation; the German cockneys, to be archetypal men. They gave every piece of cockney rascality a hidden socialist sense, whereby it was interpreted to mean the reverse of rascality. They reached the limits of their system, when they directly opposed the destructive tendancy of communism, and proclaimed their own sublime indifference towards all class-antagonism. With very few exceptions, all the so-called socialist and communist publications which circulate in Germany emanate from this school, and are enervating filthy trash.

II.   *Conservative, or Bourgeois Socialism*
A part of the Bourgeoisie desires to alleviate social dissonances, with a view of securing the existence of middle-class society. To this section belong economists, philanthropists, humanitarians, improvers of the condition of the working classes, patrons of charitable institutions, cruelty-to-animals-bill supporters, temperance advocates, in a word, hole and corner reformers of the most varied and piebald aspect. This middle-class Socialism has even been developed into complete systems. As an example we may cite Proudhon's *Philosophy of Poverty.* The socialist bourgeois wish to have the vital conditions of modern society without the accompanying struggles and dangers. They desire the existing order of things, *minus* the revolutionary and destructive element contained therein. They wish to have a bourgeoisie without a proletariat. The bourgeoisie, of course, consider the world wherein they reign, to be the best possible world. Bourgeois socialism developes this comfortable hypothesis into a complete system. When these socialists urge the proletariat to realize their system, to march towards the New Jerusalem, they ask in reality, that the proletariat should remain within the limits of existing society, and yet lay aside all bitter and unfavourable opinions concerning it. A second, less systematic, and more practical school of middle-class socialists, try to hinder all revolutionary movements among the producers, by teaching them that their condition cannot be improved by this or that political change, – but only by a change in the material conditions of life, in the economical arrangements of society. Yet, by a change in the modern life-conditions, these socialists do not mean the abolition of the middle-class modes of production and distribution, attainable only in a revolutionary manner; they mean administrative reforms, to be made within the limits of the old system, which, therefore, will leave the relation of capital and wages-labour untouched, – and, at most, will merely simplify the details and diminish the cost of bourgeois government. This kind of socialism finds its most fitting expression in empty rhetorical flourishes. Free Trade! for the benefit of the working classes. A tariff! for the benefit of the working classes. Isolated imprisonment and the silent system! for the benefit of the working classes. This last phrase is the only sincere and earnest one, among the whole stock in trade of the middle-class socialists. Their socialism consists in affirming, that the bourgeois is a bourgeois ... for the benefit of the working classes!

III. Critical-Utopian Socialism & Communism

We do not speak here of the literature, which, in all the great revolutions of modern times, has expressed the demands of the proletariat: as leveller pamphleteers, the writings of Babeuf and others. The first attempts of the proletariat towards directly forwarding its own class-interest, made during the general movement which overthrew feudal society, necessarily failed, – by reason of the crude, undeveloped form of the proletariat itself; as well as by the want of those material conditions for its emancipation, which are but the product of the bourgeois-epoch. The revolutionary literature, which accompanied this first movement of the proletariat, had necessarily a reactionary content. It taught a universal asceticism and a rude sort of equality.

The Socialist and communist systems, properly so-called, the systems of St. Simon, Owen, Fourier and others, originated in the early period of the struggle between the proletariat and the bourgeoisie, which we described in Chapter I. The inventors of these systems perceived the fact of class-antagonism, and the activity of the dissolvent elements within the prevailing social system. But they did not see any spontaneous historical action, any characteristic political movement, on the part of the proletariat. And because the development of class-antagonism keeps pace with the development of the industrial system, they could not find the material conditions for the emancipation of the proletariat; they were obliged to seek for a social science, for social laws, in order to create those conditions. Their personal inventive activity took the place of social activity, imaginary conditions of proletarian emancipation were substituted for the historical ones, and a subjective, fantastic organisation of society, for the gradual and progressive organisation of the proletariat as a class. The approaching phasis of universal history resolved itself, for them, into the propagandism and practical realization of their peculiar social plans. They had, indeed, the consciousness of advocating the interest of the producers as the most suffering class of society. The proletariat existed for them, only under this point of view of the most oppressed class. The undeveloped state of the class-struggle, and their own social position, induced these socialists to believe they were removed far above class-antagonism. They desired to improve the position of all the members of society, even of the most favoured. Hence, their continual appeals to the whole of society, even to the dominant class. You have only to understand their system, in order to see it is the best possible plan for the best possible state of society. Hence too, they reject all political, and particularly all revolutionary action, they desire to attain their object in a peaceful manner, and try to prepare the way for the new social gospel, by the force of example, by small, isolated experiments, which, of course, cannot but turn out signal *failures*. This fantastic representation of future society expressed thee feeling of a time when the proletariat was quite undeveloped, and had quite an imaginary conception of its own position, – it was the expression of an instinctive want for a universal social revolution. There are, however, critical elements contained in all these socialist and communist writings. They attack the foundation of existing society. Hence they contain a treasure of materials for the enlightenment of the Producers. Their positive propositions regarding a future state of society; e.g. abolition of the antagonism of town and country, of family institutions, of individual accumulation, of wages-labour, the proclamation of social harmony, the change of political power into a mere superintendence of production; – all these propositions expressed the abolition of class-antagonism, when this last was only commencing its evolution; and, therefore, they have, with these authors a purely Utopian sense. The importance of critical-utopian Socialism and Communism, stands in an inverted proportion to the progress of the historical movement. In proportion as the class battle is evolved and assumes a definite form, so does this imaginary elevation over it, this fantastic resistance to it, lose all practical worth, all theoretical justification. Hence, it happens, that although the originators of these systems were revolutionary in various respects, yet their followers have invariably formed reactionary sects. They hold fast by their master's old dogmas and doctrines, in opposition to the progressive historical evolution of the Proletariat. They seek, therefore, logically enough, to deaden class opposition, to mediate between the extremes. They still dream of the experimental realization of their social Utopias through isolated efforts, – the founding of a few phalanteres, of a few home colonies, of a small Icaria, – a duodecimo edition of the New Jerusalem; and they appeal to the philanthropy of Bourgeois hearts and purses for the building expences of these air-castles and chimeras. They gradually fall back into the category of the above mentioned reactionary or conservative Socialists, and distinguish themselves from these only by their more systematic pedantry, by their fanatical faith in the miraculous powers of their Social panacea. Hence, they violently oppose all political movements in the Proletariat, which indeed, can only be occasioned by a blind and wilful disbelief in the new Gospel. In France, the Fourierists oppose the Reformists; in England, the Owenites react against the Chartists.[4]

The Communists invariably support every revolutionary movement against the existing order of things, social and political. But in all these movements, they endeavour to point out the property question, whatever degree of development, in every particular case, it may have obtained – as the leading question. The Communists labour for the union and association of the revolutionary parties of all countries. The Communists disdain to conceal their opinions and ends. They openly declare, that these ends can be attained only by the overthrow of all hitherto existing social arrangements. Let the ruling classes tremble at a Communist Revolution. The Proletarians have nothing to lose in it save their chains. They will gain a World. Let the Proletarians of all countries unite!

Notes

EDITORS' INTRODUCTION

1. www.youtube.com/watch?v=oKUl4yfABE4 (accessed September 9, 2014).
2. The term "specter" renders *ein Gespenst* quite accurately (though "apparition" or "poltergeist" might be alternatives, and surely better than the "hobgoblin" of the first translation, done by Helen Macfarlane in 1850 – see Chapter 9). But the verb "haunting" (something of a stretch for *geht ... um*) recalls a ghost, which represents a dead person or entity – quite the opposite of Marx and Engels's overt argument that communism is alive and on the move, just misrepresented by its enemies. Derrida's (2006) "hauntology," powerful as it is, works from an image, rather than from an argument.
3. Somewhat qualified by Engels's uninspiring and pedantic note of 1888, saying "That is, all *written* history" (CW 6: 482 n; emphasis in original).
4. The "executive" is over-specific for the German *Staatsgewalt*; CM 239 reads "The power of the modern state."
5. Sadly perhaps – given Marshall Berman's book of this title (1988, repr. 2010) – a straightforward mistranslation dating from 1888 in which *Ständische* (i.e., of the *Stände* or medieval estates or "status groups" of society) is misread as a derivative of *stehen* (to stand), so CM 239 below translates the phrase as "feudal and fixed." Sperber (2013) misquotes the German text and translates risibly; see also the comments by Jem Thomas appended to this online review: www.lrb.co.uk/v35/n10/richard-j-evans/marx-v-the-rest (accessed September 19, 2014).
6. While "to win the battle of democracy" is a rousing verbal phrase, the German substantive is more simply *die Erkämpfung der Demokratie*; CM 251 reads "victory for democracy."
7. Tendentiously rendered as "inevitable" in the "authorized" English version.

I   RHINELAND RADICALS AND THE '48ERS

1. See the discussion in Chapter 6.
2. See the discussion in Chapter 5.

3. See the discussion in Chapter 6.
4. See the discussion in Chapter 4.
5. "Generalversammlung der demokratischen Gesellschaft in Köln am 4 August 1848."
   In *Der Wächter am Rhein*. Köln, 2. Dutzend, Nr. 1, 23.8.1848; for Weitling's speech,
   see "General-Versammlung der demokratischen Gesellschaft am 21. Juli im
   Eiser'schen Saale." 1. Dutzend, Nr. 9. 1848.

3   THE RHETORIC OF THE MANIFESTO

1. See also the discussion in Chapter 2.
2. On the idea of consciousness "in deliberation" with material conditions, see Wilkie
   1976, 233.
3. For a comparison of the texts in the *Manifesto* with earlier writings by both authors,
   see Carver 1983, 78–95.
4. On the Gothic and "spectral" dimension to Marx's thought, see Policante 2012.
5. See the discussion in Chapter 5.
6. See Lyon 1999 for an expanded account of different artistic and radical political
   manifestos. One example of the former is F. T. Marinetti's "The Foundation and
   Manifesto of Futurism" of 1908, which was later followed by various others with
   lesser impact than the first; see Marinetti 2006.

4   THE MANIFESTO IN MARX'S AND ENGELS'S LIFETIMES

1. For Marx's preface, see CW 29: 261–265; for Engels's review, see CW 16: 465–477.
   For a discussion of canon-formation in relation to Marx, see Thomas 1991. Marx
   actually lists his notable works at that point in 1859 as: *Manifesto* (CW 6: 477–517),
   Discourse on Free Trade (now little read) (CW 6: 450–465), *Poverty of Philosophy*
   (CW 6: 105–212) and unpublished lectures on wage-labor (CW 6: 692–693, n. 219).
   Marx's preface and Engels's review reached hardly anyone until their re-circulation
   in German in the early twentieth century.
2. Marx self-cited the *Manifesto* very briefly only four times between 1850 and 1872,
   and only once thereafter; see Kuczynski 1995, 171–176; for details of other small-
   scale circulations of some or all of the text between 1850 and 1872, see Kuczynski
   1995, 152–171, 177–194. For further listings, see Andréas 1963; for textual
   comparisons, see Draper 1994.
3. See the discussion in Chapter 3.
4. See the translation of 1850 by Helen Macfarlane transcribed for the present
   volume.
5. See the discussion in Chapter 1.
6. See the discussion in Chapter 6.
7. See the discussion in Chapter 5.
8. On the *Manifesto* in relation to the "Feuerbach chapter," see Sperber 2012, 203–204;
   but see Carver 2010b on the "German ideology" manuscripts in relation to
   authorship and content.

5   MARXISM AND THE MANIFESTO AFTER ENGELS

1. See the discussion in Chapter 4.
2. See the discussion in Chapter 2.
3. The 1909 English translation of *The Social Revolution* oddly translates this as "the military themselves proving untrustworthy."
4. See the discussion in Chapter 6.

6   THE PERMANENT REVOLUTION IN AND AROUND THE MANIFESTO

1. For the remainder of this chapter, page references will be to this work unless otherwise stated.
2. The revised 1906 edition of the text muddles this conclusion, appending to it the phrase, "with the possible exception of Russia." This partial but significant retreat from the permanent revolution was bound up with the theoretical gesture of admitting exceptions to the general pattern of capitalist development, and represented a political concession in the context of the SPD's internal struggles (see Day and Gaido 2011, 44–47, 51–58, 169–171, 373–377).
3. Significantly, this sentence was also removed in the later 1906 edition of the text.

8   HUNTING FOR WOMEN, HAUNTED BY GENDER: THE RHETORICAL LIMITS OF THE MANIFESTO

1. See also Chapter 3.
2. See the transcribed text in the present volume, and p. 287 n. 1.

9   THE MANIFESTO IN POLITICAL THEORY: ANGLOPHONE TRANSLATIONS AND LIBERAL RECEPTIONS

1. See the discussions in Chapters 5 and 6.
2. See the discussion in Chapter 4.
3. See the discussion in Chapter 3.
4. See the discussion in Chapter 2.
5. The Macfarlane translation as it appeared in *The Red Republican* of 1850 is exactingly transcribed in the present volume, including curiosities and infelicities of spelling and grammar. See pp. 261–282. Also see reprint in Macfarlane (2014).
6. The Carver translation is reproduced in the present volume. See pp. 237–260.
7. For the remainder of this paragraph, page references are to this work unless otherwise stated.
8. For the remainder of this paragraph, page references are to this work unless otherwise stated.
9. For the next three paragraphs, page references are to this work unless otherwise stated.

10   THE SPECTER OF THE MANIFESTO STALKS NEOLIBERAL GLOBALIZATION: RECONFIGURING MARXIST DISCOURSE(S) IN THE 1990S

1. See, e.g., Amin 1996; Burbach et al. 1996; Sweezy 1997; Tabb 1997; Wood 1997; Greider 1997; Sutcliffe 1998; Löwy 1998; Singer 1999; Foster 2000; Hersh and Brun 2000; and Katz 2001.
2. It should be noted that some meanings of *mondialisation* are often quite different from the one that is now usually translated as "globalization."
3. See, e.g., Waters 1995, 9; Sutcliffe 1998, 215; Löwy 1998; Tomlinson 1999, 76; Hersh and Brun 2000, 107; and Beck 2000, 22.

11   DECOLONIZING THE MANIFESTO: COMMUNISM AND THE SLAVE ANALOGY

1. This chapter emerges out of recent work I have undertaken looking at the relationship between classical political economy and Atlantic slavery; see Shilliam 2012b.
2. My thanks to Terrell Carver for discussions on these issues.
3. For the German I have consulted www.mlwerke.de/me/meo2/meo2_225.htm
4. For a particular take on this trope, see Baucom 2005; see also Ford III 2010.
5. I use the German provided here: www.mlwerke.de/me/meo4/meo4_361.htm
6. But see the suggestive comments by Marx in 1846 that distinguish between the "'indirect' slavery of the proletariat and the 'direct' slavery of 'Blacks' in the Americas"; Marx to Pavel Vasilyevich Annenkov, December 28, 1846, CW 38: 101.

12   THE MANIFESTO IN A LATE-CAPITALIST ERA: MELANCHOLY AND MELODRAMA

1. Debates about what qualities properly constitute "melodrama" are prolific. For central scholarship on melodrama in its various iterations, see Brooks 1995; Elsaesser 1987; Gledhill 1987; Mulvey 2009; Neale 1993; Williams 1998, 2001.
2. See also the discussion in Chapter 3.
3. For the purpose of this chapter, I leave to one side ongoing and important debates about the different roles and attributions of Marx and Engels in crafting the *Manifesto*. For a compelling analysis of Marx's and Engels's various roles, see Carver 1999, 22–23.

MANIFESTO OF THE COMMUNIST PARTY

1. Translation by Terrell Carver from a facsimile of the first German edition (1848) published in *Marx: Later Political Writings* (Cambridge: Cambridge University Press, 1996), pp. 1–30. Note that this translation is without the later amendments, footnotes and prefaces, thus catching the "hot off the press" moment of initial publication. For a variorum treatment of early editions of the *Manifesto* see Thomas Kuczynski (ed.), *Das Kommunistische Manifest* (Trier: Karl-Marx-Haus, 1995).

MANIFESTO OF THE GERMAN COMMUNIST PARTY

1. Translation by Helen Macfarlane published in *The Red Republican* (November 1850). This transcription retains the original spelling and punctuation, as well as occasional grammatical and other oddities (except evident printer's errors). Unlike the anonymously published German edition of 1848, the authors are identified here by the editor as "Citizens Charles Marx and Frederic Engels." For further information see Hal Draper, *The Adventures of the Communist Manifesto* (Alameda, CA: Center for Socialist History, 2004), and David Black (ed.), *Helen Macfarlane: The Red Republican* (Unkant Press, www.ammarxists.org, 2014); see also Black's biography *Helen Macfarlane* (Lanham, MD: Lexington Books, 2004).

2. The term in the original is *Kleinburger*; meaning small burghers, or citizens. A class, comprising small capitalists generally, whether small farmers, small manufacturers, or retail shopkeepers. As these last form the predominant element of this class in England. I have chosen the word *Shopocrat* to express the German term. – Translator's Note.

3. It was the set of writers characterized in the following chapter, who themselves called their theory, "TRUE SOCIALISM;" if, therefore, after perusing this chapter, the reader should not agree with them as to the name, this is no fault of the authors of the Manifesto. – Note of the Translator.

4. It is not to be forgotten that these lines were written before the revolution of February, and that the examples have, accordingly, reference to the state of parties of that time. – Note of the Translator.

Index